Home Science

For UGC-NET/SLET/JRF

Paper I, II and III

Objective Type Questions

Previous Years' Solved Papers

Atlantic Research Division

PUBLISHERS & DISTRIBUTORS (P) LTD

Published by

ATLANTIC

PUBLISHERS & DISTRIBUTORS (P) LTD

7/22, Ansari Road, Darya Ganj,
New Delhi-110002
Phones : +91-11-40775252, 23273880, 23275880, 23280451
Fax : +91-11-23285873
Web : www.atlanticbooks.com
E-mail : orders@atlanticbooks.com

Branch Office
5, Nallathambi Street, Wallajah Road,
Chennai-600002
Phones : +91-44-64611085, 32413319
E-mail : chennai@atlanticbooks.com

ISBN 978-81-269-1945-1

Printed in India at Nice Printing Press, A-33/3A, Site-IV,
Industrial Area, Sahibabad, Ghaziabad, U.P.

Preface

The University Grants Commission (UGC) conducts National Eligibility Test (NET) on various subjects twice every year, once each in June and December, to determine eligibility for college and university level lectureship and for award of Junior Research Fellowship (JRF), for Indian nationals in order to ensure minimum standards for the entrants in the teaching profession and research.

The book contains previous years solved papers (objective type questions) on the subject of Home Science, from June 2005 to December 2013. It covers all three papers (Paper I, II and III). In Paper I (General Paper on Teaching and Research Aptitude), and Paper II (Elective), solved papers have been included from June 2005. In Paper III (Core and Elective), solved papers of objective type questions have been included from June 2012, conforming to the existing UGC-NET pattern. In addition, five sets of Mock Tests for Paper I, II and III have been included in the book under Practice Papers. Answers have been given at the end of each set for self-check.

It will be useful for those preparing for UGC-NET/SLET/JRF in the subject of Home Science. It will give them a feel of the type of questions asked in NET in this subject, i.e. Multiple-choice, Matching type, True/False, Assertion-Reasoning type, etc. The papers included in this book will enable the students to judge their own level of competence besides adding to their knowledge. It will also help them revise the important questions in the entire syllabus and enhance their self-confidence. Suggestions for further improvement of the book are, however, welcome.

Atlantic Research Division

Contents

DECEMBER–2013

Note: This paper contains Sixty (60) multiple choice questions, each question carrying two (2) marks. Candidate is expected to answer any Fifty (50) questions. In case more than Fifty (50) questions are attempted, only the first Fifty (50) questions will be evaluated.

PAPER–I

1. The post-industrial society is designated as
   (a) Information society
   (b) Technology society
   (c) Mediated society
   (d) Non-agricultural society

2. The initial efforts for internet based communication was for
   (a) Commercial communication
   (b) Military purposes
   (c) Personal interaction
   (d) Political campaigns

3. Internal communication within institutions is done through
   (a) LAN (b) WAN
   (c) EBB (d) MMS

4. Virtual reality provides
   (a) Sharp pictures
   (b) Individual audio
   (c) Participatory experience
   (d) Preview of new films

5. The first virtual university of India came up in
   (a) Andhra Pradesh
   (b) Maharashtra
   (c) Uttar Pradesh
   (d) Tamil Nadu

6. Arrange the following books in chronological order in which they appeared. Use the code given below:
   (i) Limits to Growth
   (ii) Silent Spring
   (iii) Our Common Future
   (iv) Resourceful Earth

   Codes:
   (a) (i), (iii), (iv), (ii)
   (b) (ii), (iii), (i), (iv)
   (c) (ii), (i), (iii), (iv)
   (d) (i), (ii), (iii), (iv)

7. Which one of the following continents is at a greater risk of desertification?
   (a) Africa (b) Asia
   (c) South America (d) North America

8. "Women are closer to nature than men." What kind of perspective is this?
   (a) Realist (b) Essentialist
   (c) Feminist (d) Deep ecology

9. Which one of the following is not a matter a global concern in the removal of tropical forests?
   (a) Their ability to absorb the chemicals that contribute to depletion of ozone layer.
   (b) Their role in maintaining the oxygen and carbon balance of the earth.
   (c) Their ability to regulate surface and air temperatures, moisture content and reflectivity.
   (d) Their contribution to the biological diversity of the planet.

10. The most comprehensive approach to address the problems of manenvironment interaction is one of the following:

(a) Natural Resource Conservation Approach
(b) Urban-industrial Growth Oriented Approach
(c) Rural-agricultural Growth Oriented Approach
(d) Watershed Development Approach

11. The major source of the pollutant gas, carbon mono-oxide (CO), in urban areas is
(a) Thermal power sector
(b) Transport sector
(c) Industrial sector
(d) Domestic sector

12. In a fuel cell driven vehicle, the energy is obtained from the combustion of
(a) Methane (b) Hydrogen
(c) LPG (d) CNG

13. Which one of the following Councils has been disbanded in 2013?
(a) Distance Education Council (DEC)
(b) National Council for Teacher Education (NCTE)
(c) National Council of Educational Research and Training (NCERT)
(d) National Assessment and Accreditation Council (NAAC)

14. Which of the following statements are correct about the National Assessment and Accreditation Council?
1. It is an autonomous institution.
2. It is tasked with the responsibility of assessing and accrediting institutions of higher education.
3. It is located in Delhi.
4. It has regional offices.

Select the correct answer from the codes given below:

Codes:
(a) 1 and 3 (b) 1 and 2
(c) 1, 2 and 4 (d) 2, 3 and 4

15. The power of the Supreme Court of India to decide disputes between two or more States falls under its
(a) Advisory Jurisdiction
(b) Appellate Jurisdiction
(c) Original Jurisdiction
(d) Writ Jurisdiction

16. Which of the following statements are correct?
1. There are seven Union Territories in India.
2. Two Union Territories have Legislative Assemblies.
3. One Union Territory has a High Court.
4. One Union Territory is the capital of two States.

Select the correct answer from the codes given below:
(a) 1 and 3
(b) 2 and 4
(c) 2, 3 and 4
(d) 1, 2, 3 and 4

17. Which of the following statements are correct about the Central Information Commission?
1. The Central Information Commission is a statutory body.
2. The Chief Information Commissioner and other Information Commissioners are appointed by the President of India.
3. The Commission can impose a penalty upto a maximum of ₹ 25,000.
4. It can punish an errant officer.

Select the correct answer from the codes given below:

Codes:
(a) 1 and 2 (b) 1, 2 and 4
(c) 1, 2 and 3 (d) 2, 3 and 4

18. Who among the following conducted the CNN-IBN-The Hindu 2013 Election Tracker Survey across 267 constituencies in 18 States?
    (a) The Centre for the Study of Developing Societies (CSDS)
    (b) The Association for Democratic Reforms (ADR)
    (c) CNN and IBN
    (d) CNN, IBN and The Hindu

19. In certain code TEACHER is written as VGCEJGT. The code of CHILDREN will be
    (a) EKNJFTGP (b) EJKNFTGP
    (c) KNJFGTP (d) None of these

20. A person has to buy both apples and mangoes. The cost of one apple is ₹ 7 whereas that of a mango is ₹ 5. If the person has ₹ 38, the number of apples he can buy is
    (a) 1 (b) 2
    (c) 3 (d) 4

21. A man pointing to a lady said, "The son of her only brother is the brother of my wife". The lady is related to the man as
    (a) Mother's sister
    (b) Grand mother
    (c) Mother-in-law
    (d) Sister of father-in-law

22. In this series
    6, 4, 1, 2, 2, 8, 7, 4, 2, 1, 5, 3, 8, 6, 2, 2, 7, 1, 4, 1, 3, 5, 8, 6, how many pairs of successive numbers have a difference of 2 each?
    (a) 4 (b) 5
    (c) 6 (d) 8

23. The mean marks obtained by a class of 40 students is 65. The mean marks of half of the students is found to be 45. The mean marks of the remaining students is
    (a) 85 (b) 60
    (c) 70 (d) 65

24. Anil is twice as old as Sunita. Three years ago, he was three times as old as Sunita. The present age of Anil is
    (a) 6 years (b) 8 years
    (c) 12 years (d) 16 years

25. Which of the following is a social network?
    (a) amazon.com (b) eBay
    (c) gmail.com (d) Twitter

26. The population information is called parameter while the corresponding sample information is known as
    (a) Universe
    (b) Inference
    (c) Sampling design
    (d) Statistics

Read the following passage carefully and answer questions 27 to 32:

Heritage conservation practices improved worldwide after the International Centre for the Study of the Preservation and Restoration of Cultural Property (ICCROM) was established with UNESCO's assistance in 1959. The inter-governmental organisation with 126 member states has done a commendable job by training more than 4,000 professionals, providing practice standards, and sharing technical expertise. In this golden jubilee year, as we acknowledge its key role in global conservation, an assessment of international practices would be meaningful to the Indian conservation movement. Consistent investment, rigorous attention, and dedicated research and dissemination are some of the positive lessons to imbibe. Countries such as Italy have demonstrated that prioritising heritage with significant budget provision pays. On the other hand, India, which is no less endowed in terms of cultural capital, has a long way to go. Surveys indicate that in addition to the 6,600 protected monuments, there are over 60,000 equally valuable heritage structures that await attention. Besides the small group in the service of Archaeological Survey of India, there are only about 150 trained conservation professionals. In order to overcome this severe shortage the emphasis has been on setting up dedicated labs and training institutions. It would make much better sense for conservation to be made part of mainstream research and engineering institutes, as has been done in Europe.

Increasing funding and building institutions are the relatively easy part. The real challenge is to redefine international approaches to address local contexts. Conservation cannot limit itself to enhancing the art-historical value of the heritage structures, which international charters perhaps overemphasise. The effort has to be broad-based: It must also serve as a means to improving the quality of life in the area where the heritage structures are located. The first task therefore is to integrate conservation efforts with sound development plans that take care of people living in the heritage vicinity. Unlike in western countries, many traditional building crafts survive in India, and conservation practices offer an avenue to support them. This has been acknowledged by the Indian National Trust for Art and Cultural Heritage charter for conservation but is yet to receive substantial state support. More strength for heritage conservation can be mobilised by aligning it with the green building movement. Heritage structures are essentially eco-friendly and conservation could become a vital part of the sustainable building practices campaign in future.

27. The outlook for conservation heritage changed
    (a) after the establishment of the International Centre for the Study of the Preservation and Restoration of Cultural Property.
    (b) after training the specialists in the field.
    (c) after extending UNESCO's assistance to the educational institutions.
    (d) after ASI's measures to protect the monuments.

28. The inter-government organization was appreciated because of
    (a) increasing number of members to 126.
    (b) imparting training to professionals and sharing technical expertise.
    (c) consistent investment in conservation.
    (d) its proactive role in renovation and restoration.

29. Indian conservation movement will be successful if there would be
    (a) Financial support from the Government of India.
    (b) Non-governmental organisations role and participation in the conservation movement.
    (c) consistent investment, rigorous attention, and dedicated research and dissemination of awareness for conservation.
    (d) Archaeological Survey of India's meaningful assistance.

30. As per the surveys of historical monuments in India, there is very small number of protected monuments. As per given the total number of monuments and enlisted number of protected monuments, percentage comes to
    (a) 10 percent (b) 11 percent
    (c) 12 percent (d) 13 percent

31. What should India learn from Europe to conserve our cultural heritage?

(i) There should be significant budget provision to conserve our cultural heritage.
(ii) Establish dedicated labs and training institutions.
(iii) Force the government to provide sufficient funds.
(iv) Conservation should be made part of mainstream research and engineering institutes.

Choose correct answer from the codes given below:
(a) (i), (ii), (iii), (iv) (b) (i), (ii), (iv)
(c) (i), (ii) (d) (i), (iii), (iv)

32. INTACH is known for its contribution for conservation of our cultural heritage. The full form of INTACH is
(a) International Trust for Art and Cultural Heritage
(b) Intra-national Trust for Art and Cultural Heritage
(c) Integrated Trust for Art and Cultural Heritage
(d) Indian National Trust for Art and Cultural Heritage

33. While delivering lecture if there is some disturbance in the class, a teacher should
(a) keep quiet for a while and then continue.
(b) punish those causing disturbance.
(c) motivate to teach those causing disturbance.
(d) not bother of what is happening in the class.

34. Effective teaching is a function of
(a) Teacher's satisfaction.
(b) Teacher's honesty and commitment.
(c) Teacher's making students learn and understand.
(d) Teacher's liking for professional excellence.

35. The most appropriate meaning of learning is
(a) Acquisition of skills
(b) Modification of behaviour
(c) Personal adjustment
(d) Inculcation of knowledge

36. Arrange the following teaching process in order:
(i) Relate the present knowledge with previous one
(ii) Evaluation
(iii) Reteaching
(iv) Formulating instructional objectives
(v) Presentation of instructional materials
(a) (i), (ii), (iii), (iv), (v)
(b) (ii), (i), (iii), (iv), (v)
(c) (v), (iv), (iii), (i), (ii)
(d) (iv), (i), (v), (ii), (iii)

37. CIET stands for
(a) Centre for Integrated Education and Technology
(b) Central Institute for Engineering and Technology
(c) Central Institute for Education Technology
(d) Centre for Integrated Evaluation Techniques

38. Teacher's role at higher education level is to
(a) provide information to students.
(b) promote self learning in students.
(c) encourage healthy competition among students.
(d) help students to solve their problems.

39. The Verstehen School of Understanding was popularised by
(a) German Social Scientists
(b) American Philosophers
(c) British Academicians
(d) Italian Political Analysts

40. The sequential operations in scientific research are
(a) Co-variation, Elimination of Spurious Relations, Generalisation, Theorisation

(b) Generalisation, Co-variation, Theorisation, Elimination of Spurious Relations
(c) Theorisation, Generalisation, Elimination of Spurious Relations, Co-variation
(d) Elimination of Spurious Relations, Theorisation, Generalisation, Co-variation

41. In sampling, the lottery method is used for
(a) Interpretation
(b) Theorisation
(c) Conceptualisation
(d) Randomisation

42. Which is the main objective of research?
(a) To review the literature
(b) To summarize what is already known
(c) To get an academic degree
(d) To discover new facts or to make fresh interpretation of known facts

43. Sampling error decreases with the
(a) decrease in sample size
(b) increase in sample size
(c) process of randomization
(d) process of analysis

44. The principles of fundamental research are used in
(a) action research
(b) applied research
(c) philosophical research
(d) historical research

45. Users who use media for their own ends are identified as
(a) Passive audience
(b) Active audience
(c) Positive audience
(d) Negative audience

46. Classroom communication can be described as
(a) Exploration
(b) Institutionalisation
(c) Unsignified narration
(d) Discourse

47. Ideological codes shape our collective
(a) Productions (b) Perceptions
(c) Consumptions (d) Creations

48. In communication, myths have power, but are
(a) uncultural. (b) insignificant.
(c) imprecise. (d) unpreferred.

49. The first multi-lingual news agency of India was
(a) Samachar
(b) API
(c) Hindustan Samachar
(d) Samachar Bharati

50. Organisational communication can also be equated with
(a) intra-personal communication.
(b) inter-personal communication.
(c) group communication.
(d) mass communication.

51. If two propositions having the same subject and predicate terms are such that one is the denial of the other, the relationship between them is called
(a) Contradictory (b) Contrary
(c) Sub-contrary (d) Sub-alternation

52. Ananya and Krishna can speak and follow English. Bulbul can write and speak Hindi as Archana does. Archana talks with Ananya also in Bengali. Krishna cannot follow Bengali. Bulbul talks with Ananya in Hindi. Who can speak and follow English, Hindi and Bengali?
(a) Archana (b) Bulbul
(c) Ananya (d) Krishna

53. A stipulative definition may be said to be
(a) Always true
(b) Always false
(c) Sometimes true, sometimes false
(d) Neither true nor false

54. When the conclusion of an argument follows from its premise/premises conclusively, the argument is called
(a) Circular argument
(b) Inductive argument
(c) Deductive argument
(d) Analogical argument

55. Saturn and Mars are planets like the earth. They borrow light from the Sun and moves around the Sun as the Earth does. So those planets are inhabited by various orders of creatures as the earth is. What type of argument is contained in the above passage?
(a) Deductive (b) Astrological
(c) Analogical (d) Mathematical

56. Given below are two premises. Four conclusions are drawn from those two premises in four codes. Select the code that states the conclusion validly drawn.
Premises:
(i) All saints are religious. (major)
(ii) Some honest persons are saints. (minor)
Codes:
(a) All saints are honest.
(b) Some saints are honest.
(c) Some honest persons are religious.
(d) All religious persons are honest

Following table provides details about the Foreign Tourist Arrivals (FTAs) in India from different regions of the world in different years. Study the table carefully and answer questions from 57 to 60 based on this table.

Region	Number of Foreign Tourist Arrivals		
	2007	2008	2009
Western Europe	1686083	1799525	1610086
North America	1007276	1027297	1024469
South Asia	982428	1051846	982633
South East Asia	303475	332925	348495
East Asia	352037	355230	318292
West Asia	171661	215542	201110
Total FTAs in India	5081504	5282603	5108579

57. Find out the region that contributed around 20 percent of the total foreign tourist arrivals in India in 2009.
(a) Western Europe
(b) North America
(c) South Asia
(d) South East Asia

58. Which of the following regions has recorded the highest negative growth rate of foreign tourist arrivals in India in 2009?
(a) Western Europe
(b) North America
(c) South Asia
(d) West Asia

59. Find out the region that has been showing declining trend in terms of share of foreign tourist arrivals in India in 2008 and 2009.
(a) Western Europe (b) South East Asia
(c) East Asia (d) West Asia

60. Identify the region that has shown hyper growth rate of foreign tourist arrivals than the growth rate of the total FTAs in India in 2008.
(a) Western Europe
(b) North America
(c) South Asia
(d) East Asia

ANSWERS

1. (a)	2. (b)	3. (a)	4. (c)	5. (d)
6. (c)	7. (a)	8. (b)	9. (a)	10. (d)
11. (b)	12. (b)	13. (a)	14. (b)	15. (c)
16. (d)	17. (c)	18. (a)	19. (b)	20. (d)
21. (d)	22. (c)	23. (a)	24. (c)	25. (d)
26. (d)	27. (a)	28. (b)	29. (c)	30. (b)
31. (b)	32. (d)	33. (c)	34. (c)	35. (b)
36. (d)	37. (c)	38. (b)	39. (a)	40. (a)
41. (d)	42. (d)	43. (b)	44. (b)	45. (b)
46. (d)	47. (b)	48. (c)	49. (c)	50. (c)
51. (a)	52. (c)	53. (d)	54. (c)	55. (c)
56. (c)	57. (b)	58. (d)	59. (a)	60. (c)

PAPER–II

Note: This paper contains fifty (50) objective type questions, each question carrying two (2) marks. All questions are compulsory.

1. Maillard reaction takes place in the following cooking procedure:
   (a) Prolonged cooking of milk with sugar
   (b) Prolonged cooking of milk with salt
   (c) Prolonged cooking of milk with vegetables
   (d) Prolonged cooking of milk with cereal

2. β-carotene in the body changes into Retinol in
   (a) Liver (b) Pancreas
   (c) Gall Bladder (d) Intestine

3. Total parenteral nutrition involves
   (a) use of the large central vein to deliver life sustaining nourishment
   (b) use of peripheral veins to deliver nourishment
   (c) ingestion of food through the oral route
   (d) use of a tube to deliver full fluid or commercial formulae

4. Which of the following is not a theory of clothing?
   (a) Modesty (b) Individuality
   (c) Protection (d) Adornment

5. Which of the following is not a plain weave fabric?
   (a) Percale (b) Calico
   (c) Drill (d) Chintz

6. The most durable, long lasting and low maintenance metal used commonly for construction of household equipment is
   (a) Aluminium (b) Iron
   (c) Stainless steel (d) Copper

7. "The Protection of Children from Sexual Offences Act" was enacted in
   (a) 1986 (b) 1956
   (c) 2013 (d) 2012

8. Marionettes are also called
   (a) String puppets
   (b) Rod puppets
   (c) Shadow puppets
   (d) Finger puppets

9. Advertising is based on the following function of communication:
   (a) Instruction (b) Information
   (c) Influence (d) Integration

10. An experimenter conducts an experiment using a control group containing 8 subject and an experimental group containing 8 subjects. How many degrees of freedom are there in this experimental design if the groups were matched?
    (a) 7 (b) 8
    (c) 14 (d) 15

11. Following properties of egg are used in food preparation:
    I. Emulsification II. Coagulation
    III. Tenderisation IV. Leavening

Codes:
(a) I, II & III (b) II, III & IV
(c) I, II & IV (d) All of these

12. Following nutrients play role in synthesis of haemoglobin:
I. Vitamin C II. Iron
III. Vitamin B_{12} IV. Protein
Codes:
(a) II and III are correct.
(b) I and IV are correct.
(c) I, II and III are correct.
(d) All of the above are correct.

13. Tools of management used at the top management level are
I. Staff duty lists
II. Menus
III. Plans for sales
IV. Expansion
V. Leadership
VI. Time and work schedules
Codes:
(a) I, III, VI (b) II, IV, V
(c) III, IV, V (d) I, V, VI

14. Which of the following are textile repeat units?
I. Shape II. Half drop
III. Balance IV. All over
V. Brick
Codes:
(a) I, IV and V are correct.
(b) II, IV and V are correct.
(c) III, IV and V are correct.
(d) II, III and V are correct.

15. Which of the following yarns are novelty yarns?
I. Retine II. Slub
III. Cable IV. Boncle
V. Cord
Codes:
(a) I, II and V are correct.
(b) II, IV and V are correct.
(c) I, II and IV are correct.
(d) II, III and IV are correct.

16. Which of the following cladding materials improve the efficiency of a base metal of a vessel with poor conductivity which is used for surface cooking?
I. Cooper II. Vanadium
III. Aluminium IV. Stainless steel
V. Brass
Codes:
(a) I, III, IV (b) I, III, V
(c) I, II, III (d) I, IV, V

17. Gardner's Multiple Intelligences include
(A) linguistic (B) musical
(C) dramatic (D) interpersonal
Codes:
(a) (B), (C), (D) (b) (A), (B), (D)
(c) (A), (B), (C) (d) (A), (C), (D)

18. Result Demonstration is undertaken when
I. The process is very long
II. The outputs are to be compared
III. The process is very short
IV. The relative advantage of a method is to be shown
Codes:
(a) I, II and III are correct.
(b) I, II and IV are correct.
(c) I and II are correct.
(d) I and III are correct.

19. Outdoor Publicity Media include
I. Posters II. Flip Charts
III. Banners IV. Flash cards
Codes:
(a) I and II are correct.
(b) II and III are correct.
(c) III and IV are correct.
(d) I and III are correct.

20. Following are non-parametric tests:
(A) Kruskal-Wallis Test
(B) ANOVA
(C) Pearson's r
(D) Sign Test
(E) Man-Whitney Test

Codes:
(a) (C), (D), (E) (b) (A), (C), (E)
(c) (A), (B), (C) (d) (A), (E), (D)

21. **Assertion (A):** Gums are used to replace fat partially in meat hamburger to reduce the fat calories.
Reason (R): Gums are not fat substitutes, but their hydrophyllic properties allow them to hold water and keep food moist and soft.
Codes:
(a) Both (A) and (R) are true & (R) is the correct explanation of (A).
(b) (A) is correct, but (R) is not correct.
(c) Both (A) and (R) are true, but (R) is not the correct explanation of (A).
(d) Both (A) & (R) are not correct.

22. **Assertion (A):** Excess of iodine ingestion can be harmful.
Reason (R): Excess iodine inhibits the synthesis of thyroid hormone.
Codes:
(a) Both (A) and (R) are true and (R) is the correct explanation.
(b) Both (A) and (R) are false.
(c) (A) is true, but (R) is false.
(d) (A) is false, but (R) is true.

23. **Assertion (A):** Hepatic encephalopathy is a condition characterized by degenerative changes in the brain and neurological symptoms.
Reason (R): The failing liver cannot inactivate, detoxify or metabolize certain substances.
Codes:
(a) Both (A) and (R) are true and (R) is the correct explanation.
(b) Both (A) and (R) are true, but (R) is not the correct explanation.
(c) Both (A) and (R) are false.
(d) (A) is false, but (R) is the correct explanation.

24. **Assertion (A):** A dart can be shifted from one place to another without changing the fit of the garment.
Reason (R): In shifting of darts, angles of the darts remain same.
Codes:
(a) Both (A) and (R) are correct.
(b) Both (A) and (R) are incorrect.
(c) (A) is correct, but (R) is incorrect.
(d) (A) is incorrect, but (R) is correct.

25. **Assertion (A):** Silk is as resilient as wool.
Reason (R): Silk fibre also contains cystine linkages.
Codes:
(a) Both (A) and (R) are correct.
(b) Both (A) and (R) are incorrect.
(c) (A) is correct, but (R) is incorrect.
(d) (A) is incorrect, but (R) is correct.

26. **Assertion (A):** Painting walls and ceiling with light colour, matt finish paint will reduce the size of the room.
Reason (R): The matt finish even though the colour is light will absorb the light by creating illusion of advancing effect.
Codes:
(a) Both (A) and (R) are true.
(b) Both (A) and (R) are false.
(c) (A) is true, but (R) is false.
(d) (A) is false, but (R) is true.

27. **Assertion (A):** Freud's Oedipus conflict for boys and Electra conflict for girls takes place during adolescence.
Reason (R): Id impulses transfer to the genitals and the child finds pleasure in genital stimulation during this stage.
Codes:
(a) Both (A) and (R) are correct.
(b) (R) is correct and (A) is wrong.
(c) (A) is correct and (R) is wrong.
(d) Both (A) and (R) are incorrect.

28. **Assertion (A):** Literacy is indispensable for National Development.

Reason (R): India cannot make rapid progress unless ignorance is wiped out.

Codes:

(a) Both (A) and (R) are false.
(b) (A) is true and (R) is false.
(c) Both (A) and (R) are true.
(d) (A) is false and (R) is true.

29. **Assertion (A):** Social scientists use indigenous channels of communication.

Reason (R): The indigenous channels of communication are formal in nature.

Codes:

(a) Both (A) and (R) are true.
(b) Both (A) and (R) are false.
(c) (A) is true, (R) is false.
(d) (A) is false, (R) is true.

30. **Assertion (A):** A random sample is a systematic form of sample selection that is representative of a population.

Reason (R): Hypothesis testing is always about a population and not about a sample in inferential statistics.

Codes:

(a) (A) is true, but (R) is false.
(b) Both (A) and (R) are false.
(c) Both (A) and (R) are true and (R) is the correct explanation of (A).
(d) (A) is false, but (R) is true.

31. Arrange the following steps in Jelly preparation in the correct sequence:

(A) Test the extract for pectin content.
(B) Pour hot into sterilized jar.
(C) Boil the fruit with citric acid and water until tender.
(D) Wash and slice the fruit.
(E) Add sugar to extract & boil vigorously without stirring.
(F) Strain the contents through muslin cloth to get clear extract.
(G) Perform sheet test for readiness.

Codes:

(a) (D), (C), (A), (G), (F), (E), (B)
(b) (C), (D), (F), (G), (A), (E), (B)
(c) (D), (E), (F), (C), (A), (G), (B)
(d) (D), (C), (F), (A), (E), (G), (B)

32. Arrange the following vegetables in decreasing order of β-carotene:

(i) Pumpkin
(ii) Carrot
(iii) Beet
(iv) Green leafy vegetables

Codes:

(a) (i), (ii), (iii), (iv)
(b) (ii), (iii), (iv), (i)
(c) (iii), (i), (ii), (iv)
(d) (iv), (ii), (i), (iii)

33. Give the correct sequence of steps in standardizing a recipe

I. Test the recipe
II. Evaluate yield, number and size of portions
III. Evaluate for acceptability
IV. Analyse proportion of ingredients
V. Determine problems with preparation

Codes:

(a) I, III, II, V, IV (b) IV, V, I, II, III
(c) I, IV, III, II, V (d) IV, I, II, V, III

34. Give the correct sequence in the merchandizing of apparels:

I. Fabric sourcing
II. Production execution and tracking
III. Costing and negotiations
IV. Preparing lab dippings, printing, etc.
V. Developing sample

Codes:

(a) III, I, IV, V, II (b) III, I, IV, II, V
(c) I, II, III, IV, V (d) I, IV, III, II, V

35. Give the correct sequence in the manufacturing of viscose rayon

I. Steeping process
II. Churning process
III. Conditioning of wood pulp
IV. Ageing process

Codes:

(a) II, III, IV, I (b) III, I, IV, II
(c) IV, III, II, I (d) I, III, II, IV

36. Arrange in correct sequence the stage of an interior design process:
   I. Bubble diagram
   II. Schematic diagram
   III. Detailed drawing
   IV. Construction administration
   V. Execution

   Codes:
   (a) II, III, I, V, IV (b) II, I, III, V, IV
   (c) I, V, III, II, IV (d) I, II, III, V, IV

37. Organize the stages in the correct sequence:
   (A) Generativity Vs. Stagnation
   (B) Intimacy Vs. Isolation
   (C) Industry Vs. Inferiority diffusions
   (D) Identity Vs. Identity confusion
   (E) Ego integrity Vs. Despair

   Codes:
   (a) (C), (A), (B), (D), (E)
   (b) (C), (D), (B), (A), (E)
   (c) (C), (B), (D), (A), (E)
   (d) (A), (D), (B), (E), (C)

38. The steps followed in training for development are in the following sequential order:
   (A) Evaluation
   (B) Implementation
   (C) Programme Development
   (D) Follow up
   (E) Need Assessment

   Codes:
   (a) (E), (C), (B), (D), (A)
   (b) (E), (C), (B), (A), (D)
   (c) (E), (C), (A), (B), (D)
   (d) (E), (B), (D), (A), (C)

39. Arrange the following models of communication in descending order of their inception:
   (A) Berl's Model of Communication
   (B) Schromm's Model of Communication
   (C) Lasswell's Model of Communication
   (D) Shannon-Weaver Model of Communication

   Codes:
   (a) (D), (A), (B), (C) (b) (A), (D), (B), (C)
   (c) (B), (A), (D), (C) (d) (B), (C), (D), (A)

40. Arrange the steps involved in construction of a frequency polygon in the correct sequence:
   (A) Place a dot above the mid-point of each class interval at a height equal to the frequency.
   (B) Connect the dots with the straight line.
   (C) Construct a frequency distribution in table form.
   (D) Decide a suitable scale for the axes.
   (E) Label the class interval mid-points along horizontal axis.

   Codes:
   (a) (D), (C), (E), (A), (B)
   (b) (C), (D), (E), (A), (B)
   (c) (D), (A), (C), (B), (E)
   (d) (C), (A), (D), (E), (B)

41. Match the foods given in List I with pigments given in List II:

List I	List II
A. Meat	i. Xanthophyll
B. Tomato	ii. Anthoxanthin
C. Brinjal	iii. Chlorophyll
D. Turnip	iv. Myoglobin
E. Corn	v. Anthocyanin
	vi. Lycopene

Codes:	A	B	C	D	E
(a)	iv	iii	v	vi	i
(b)	ii	i	v	vi	iii
(c)	iv	vi	v	ii	i
(d)	v	vi	iv	iii	i

42. Match the retinol requirement (μg/day) given in List II with age group given in List I:

List I	List II
A. School child	i. 600
B. Pregnant woman	ii. 950
C. Lactating woman	iii. 400
D. Adolescent boy	iv. 800
	v. 350

Codes:	A	B	C	D
(a)	i	ii	iii	iv
(b)	iii	iv	ii	i
(c)	ii	iii	iv	v
(d)	iv	v	ii	iii

43. Match the following processing methods in List I with foods involved in List II:

List I	List II
A. Germination	i. Oils, butter, flours
B. Fermentation	ii. Dehydrated foods
C. Fortification	iii. Pulses, grains
D. Preservation	iv. Doughs & batters

Codes:	A	B	C	D
(a)	iv	i	iii	ii
(b)	iii	ii	i	iv
(c)	ii	iii	i	iv
(d)	iii	iv	i	ii

44. Match the symbols given in List I with the care meanings given in List II:

List I	List II
A.	i. Drying
B.	ii. Wash
C.	iii. Iron
D.	iv. Professional cleaning
	v. Bleach

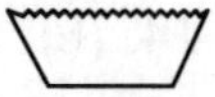

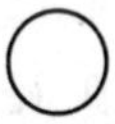

Codes:	A	B	C	D
(a)	i	ii	v	iii
(b)	iii	i	ii	iv
(c)	ii	v	iv	i
(d)	v	iii	i	ii

45. Match the instrument given in List I with the property tested given in List II:

List I

A. Pick glass
B. Beesley balance
C. Densimeter
D. Spectrophotometer

List II

i. Colour shade of fabric
ii. Thread count
iii. Direct yarn count
iv. Fabric construction
v. Tensile stiffness

Codes:	A	B	C	D
(a)	i	ii	iii	v
(b)	ii	iv	iii	i
(c)	ii	iii	iv	i
(d)	iii	v	i	iv

46. Match the following resources:

List I

A. Individual resource
B. Family resource
C. Community resource
D. Environmental resources

List II

i. House ii. Museum
iii. Forest iv. Energy
v. Money vi. Competency

Codes:	A	B	C	D
(a)	iv	ii	iii	vi
(b)	iv	i	ii	iii
(c)	iv	v	ii	iii
(d)	v	i	iii	iv

47. Match the list of methods of child study in List I with most appropriate groups in List II:

List I

A. Questionnaire
B. Observations
C. Interviews
D. Psychometric tests

List II

i. Infants
ii. Large samples of literate adults
iii. Adolescents with psychological problems
iv. In-depth data from rural women
v. Measurement of home environment

Codes:	A	B	C	D
(a)	iv	i	iii	ii
(b)	v	iii	i	ii
(c)	ii	i	iv	iii
(d)	ii	iv	i	v

48. Match the following PRA methods from List I with their salient features from List II:

List I

A. Transact walk
B. Seasonal diagramming
C. Ranking and scoring
D. Focussed group discussion

List II

i. Agriculture-related decisions
ii. Identifying geographic features
iii. Seeking opinions
iv. Promoting creativity
v. Expression of preferences

Codes:	A	B	C	D
(a)	ii	i	v	iii
(b)	iii	v	i	ii
(c)	iv	v	i	ii
(d)	ii	i	v	iv

49. Match the following methods of training form List I with their major objective mentioned in the List II:

List I

A. Role Play
B. Case Study
C. Discussion
D. Demonstration

List II

i. Stimulating creative ideas
ii. Problem solving
iii. Motivation
iv. Self-directed learning
v. Skill development

Codes:	A	B	C	D
(a)	v	i	ii	iv
(b)	iv	ii	i	v
(c)	iv	ii	i	iii
(d)	i	ii	iii	v

50. Match the items in List I with items in List II:

List I	List II
A. $\mu \pm 2\sigma$	i. 99.7%
B. $\mu \pm 3\sigma$	ii. 66%
C. $\mu \pm 1\sigma$	iii. $p = 0.045$
D. $\alpha < 0.05$	iv. 95%
E. $\alpha < 0.01$	v. $p = .002$
	vi. 99%
	vii. 68%
	viii. $p = 0.055$

Codes:	A	B	C	D	E
(a)	iv	i	vii	iii	v
(b)	iv	i	ii	viii	v
(c)	vi	i	ii	iii	viii
(d)	iv	vi	vii	viii	v

ANSWERS

1. (a)	2. (a)	3. (a)	4. (b)	5. (c)
6. (c)	7. (d)	8. (a)	9. (c)	10. (a)
11. (c)	12. (d)	13. (c)	14. (b)	15. (c)
16. (b)	17. (d)	18. (b)	19. (d)	20. (d)
21. (a)	22. (a)	23. (a)	24. (a)	25. (b)
26. (a)	27. (d)	28. (c)	29. (c)	30. (c)
31. (d)	32. (d)	33. (d)	34. (a)	35. (b)
36. (d)	37. (b)	38. (b)	39. (c)	40. (b)
41. (c)	42. (b)	43. (d)	44. (c)	45. (c)
46. (d)	47. (c)	48. (a)	49. (b)	50. (a)

PAPER–III

Note: This paper contains seventy-five (75) objective type questions of two (2) marks each. All questions are compulsory.

1. The frequency with which a job position falls vacant in a organization is referred to as

(a) Employee turnover
(b) Absenteeism
(c) Induction
(d) Reinforcement

2. The fortificant used in iodized salt is
(a) Sodium iodide
(b) Potassium iodate
(c) Sodium iodate
(d) Potassium iodide

3. Serum Vitamin D level ____ are indicative of sub-clinical Vitamin D deficiency.
(a) < 20 ng/dl (b) < 10 ng/dl
(c) < 30 ng/dl (d) < 5 ng/dl

4. Following is not a method of nutritional assessment using Biochemical Method:
(a) Urinary iodine
(b) Haemoglobin estimation
(c) Serum retinol
(d) Blood Pressure

5. In the study of language the terms surface structure and deep structure can be associated with
(a) Albert Bandura
(b) Noam Chomsky
(c) Jane Elliot
(d) B.F. Skinner

6. The overall female literacy according to Census 2011 is
(a) 54.6% (b) 10.8%
(c) 65.5% (d) 38.2%

7. Which of the following is not a hand printing technique?
(a) Duplex (b) Screen
(c) Block (d) Stencil

8. Which of the following garment finishers is used for finishing number of garments together?
(a) Form Press (b) Tunnel
(c) Buck Press (d) Die Press

9. Electromayography is a method used for measuring
(a) Muscle fatigue
(b) Electric phenomenon occurring in the muscle
(c) Electric phenomenon occurring in the bones
(d) Efficiency of tissues

10. The Act which governs Consumer Disputes Redressal Forum is
(a) The Bureau of Indian Standards Act
(b) The Consumer Protection Act
(c) The Trade Merchandise Mark Act
(d) Restrictive Trade Practices Act

11. 'Diffusion of Innovation' Theory was proposed by
(a) Evrett Rogers
(b) Aristotle
(c) Wilbur Schramm
(d) Shannon and Weaver

12. International Literacy Day is celebrated on
(a) 8th September (b) 8th October
(c) 8th November (d) 8th August

13. Operating expenses in any food service organization include
I. Labour
II. Depreciation
III. Replacement and maintenance
IV. Rent
V. Food
Codes:
(a) II, III, IV (b) I, II, IV
(c) II, IV, V (d) I, III, V

14. Following food components have antioxidant effects:
I. Sesame lignans II. Phenols
III. Carotenoid IV. Vitamin E
V. Vitamin D VI. Vitamin C
Codes:
(a) III, V, II, VI (b) V, I, II, III
(c) II, III, IV, VI (d) I, II, III, V

15. The following are the tests for measuring pectin concentration:

I. Alcohol Test
II. Boiling point Test
III. Jelmeter Test
IV. Sheet test

Codes:

(a) I & II (b) II & IV
(c) I & III (d) All of these

16. Important functions of calcium are
I. Formation of bone
II. Neuromuscular excitation
III. Blood coagulation
IV. Membrane permeability
V. Maintain osmotic equilibrium

Codes:

(a) I and IV (b) I, II, III and IV
(c) I, II, III and V (d) I, III, IV and V

17. Fruits such as mangoes, papaya, peaches and apricots are rich source of
I. Antioxidants II. Carbohydrates
III. Soluble fibre IV. Protein

Codes:

(a) I, II, IV (b) I, II, III
(c) II, III, IV (d) None of these

18. Mid Day Meal (MDM) Programme for school children between 6–11 years of age involves the following:
I. Monitors growth of the children
II. Provide 450 kCals and 8–12 g protein/day
III. Provide hot cooked meals
IV. Provide timely immunization
V. Improve school attendance

Codes:

(a) II, III and IV (b) II, III and V
(c) I, II and V (d) II, IV and V

19. Common symptoms of Alzheimer's disease are
(A) Disorientation
(B) Joint pain
(C) Anxiety and anger
(D) Upper respiratory infections
(E) Memory loss

Codes:

(a) (D), (A) and (E)
(b) (B), (D) and (A)
(c) (C), (B) and (E)
(d) (A), (C) and (E)

20. Egocentrism leads to a variety of illogical features of thought in preschoolers
(A) animistic thinking
(B) irreversibility
(C) perception bound
(D) metacognition

Codes:

(a) (A), (B), (C) (b) (B), (C), (D)
(c) (C), (D), (A) (d) (D), (A), (B)

21. Which are the statutory bodies required to be set up under the Juvenile Justice (Care and Protection) Act 2000?
(A) Councils for Rights
(B) Observation Homes
(C) Juvenile Welfare Boards
(D) Antenatal Clinics
(E) Child Welfare Committees

Codes:

(a) (A), (B) and (C)
(b) (B), (D) and (C)
(c) (A), (C) and (E)
(d) (B), (C) and (E)

22. Oxidizing bleaching agents include:
I. Sodium hypochlorite
II. Hydrogen peroxide
III. Ozone
IV. Sodium bisulphate

Codes:

(a) II, III and IV are correct.
(b) I, II and III are correct.
(c) I, II and IV are correct.
(d) I, III and IV are correct.

23. Specifications in a production unit affect the following:
I. Consistency in fit
II. Costs
III. Intrinsic quality
IV. Materials used

Codes:
(a) I & II are correct.
(b) II & III are correct.
(c) III & IV are correct.
(d) All the above are correct.

24. Persian carpets are divided into three groups:
I. Obee
II. Farsh/Qali
III. Qalichech
IV. Gelim/Zilu
V. Pagan
Codes:
(a) I, II and III are correct.
(b) II, IV and V are correct.
(c) III, IV and V are correct.
(d) II, III and IV are correct.

25. Which of the following methods are used for controlling the use of income?
I. Mental Check
II. Evaluation of Expenditure
III. Savings and Investment
IV. Mechanical Check
V. Record Keeping
VI. Budgeting
Codes:
(a) II, III, VI
(b) I, IV, V
(c) III, V, VI
(d) I, IV, V, VI

26. Types of traction (important in the development of goal character in activities) include
I. Operation traction
II. Object traction
III. Time traction
IV. Batch traction
V. Process traction
VI. Machine traction
VII. Line traction
Codes:
(a) II, IV, V, VI, VII
(b) II, III, IV, V, VII
(c) I, IV, V, VI, VII
(d) II, III, IV, V, VI

27. In the managerial subsystem of systems approach to management, the sources of demands and resources of inputs are:
I. Events in micro-habitat
II. Family goals
III. Feed back
IV. Goods and services of a family
V. Events in macro-habitat
VI. Decisions and standards
Codes:
(a) I, III, IV, V
(b) II, III, V, VI
(c) I, II, IV, V
(d) I, II, V, VI

28. The effects of magic Bullet Theory of Mass Media are
I. Promotion of innovation.
II. Popularization of radio and television.
III. Emergence of advertising industry.
IV. Hitler's monopolization of the mass media.
Codes:
(a) I, II, III and IV are correct.
(b) I, II and III are correct.
(c) II, III and IV are correct.
(d) Only I is correct.

29. The impact of Information, Communication, Technologies, ICTs in practice is evident in
I. Networks in society
II. Digital divide
III. E-commerce
IV. Grapevines
Codes:
(a) I, II, III and IV are correct.
(b) I, II and IV are correct.
(c) I, II and III are correct.
(d) II and III are correct.

30. The essential features of leaders training includes the following:
I. Participatory atmosphere
II. Group interaction
III. Realistic venues
IV. Create work opportunities

Codes:
(a) I, II, III and IV are correct.
(b) II, III, IV are correct.
(c) II, III, I are correct.
(d) Only IV is correct.

31. **Assertion (A):** Antioxidant rich diet can minimize toxicity and maximize potential health benefits.
Reason (R): Diet rich in fruits and vegetables provide Vitamin A, Vitamin C and Vitamin E, etc. at higher than RDA levels.
Codes:
(a) (A) is wrong and (R) is right.
(b) (A) is right, but (R) is wrong.
(c) (A) is right and (R) is the correct explanation.
(d) (A) is right, but (R) is incorrect explanation.

32. **Assertion (A):** Obesity and Heart Disease is a result of excessive energy intake and reduced physical activity.
Reason (R): Sedentary lifestyle and availability of high energy density foods leads to degenerative disease.
Codes:
(a) (A) and (R) are true, but (R) is not the correct explanation of (A).
(b) (A) is true and (R) is false.
(c) (A) and (R) are true and (R) is the correct explanation of (A).
(d) Both (A) and (R) are false.

33. **Assertion (A):** Bakery products are rich in hydrogenated fat containing transfats.
Reason (R): Excess consumption of foods rich in transfat increases the risk to develop noncommunicable diseases.
Codes:
(a) (A) and (R) are correct and (R) is partial explanation of (A).
(b) (A) and (R) are correct and (R) is complete explanation of (A).
(c) (A) is correct, but (R) is incorrect.
(d) (A) is incorrect, but (R) is correct.

34. **Assertion (A):** In nutrition assessment, biochemical tests are useful in early detection of nutritional deficiency.
Reason (R): Such laboratory tests confirm the sub-clinical form.
Codes:
(a) (A) is correct, but (R) is not correct explanation of (A).
(b) (A) is correct, but (R) is partially correct.
(c) (A) is incorrect and (R) is correct.
(d) (A) is correct and (R) is correct explanation.

35. **Assertion (A):** Indians are at increase risk to develop metabolic syndrome X.
Reason (R): Primary indicators of syndrome X are central obesity, abnormal glucose tolerance, low level of HDL.
Codes:
(a) Both (A) and (R) are false.
(b) Both (A) and (R) are true and (R) is partially true.
(c) Both (A) and (R) are true and (R) is completely true.
(d) (A) is false and (R) is true.

36. **Assertion (A):** Between 2 and 6 years the preschoolers improve in a wide variety of skills such as perception, attention and logical thinking.
Reason (R): Myelinization and synaptic pruning of neural fibres together with brain increasing from 70 to 90 percent adult weight leads to dramatic changes in skills.
Codes:
(a) Both (A) and (R) are correct.
(b) (R) is correct and (A) is wrong.
(c) (A) is correct and (R) is wrong.
(d) Both (A) and (R) are wrong.

37. **Assertion (A):** Authoritative parenting styles is a democratic, rational approach in which children's rights are respected.
Reason (R): A democratic and rational approach in parenting may lead to children not respecting their parents.
Codes:
(a) Both (A) and (R) are correct.
(b) (R) is correct and (A) is wrong.
(c) (A) is correct and (R) is wrong.
(d) Both (A) and (R) are wrong.

38. **Assertion (A):** To uncover cultural meanings of children and adults behaviour human development researchers have borrowed ethnographic methods from the field of anthropology.
Reason (R): It uses participant observation to understand the unique values and social processes of a culture.
Codes:
(a) Both (A) and (R) are wrong.
(b) (R) is correct and (A) is wrong.
(c) (A) is correct and (R) is wrong.
(d) Both (A) and (R) are correct.

39. **Assertion (A):** Fibres containing high proportion of amorphous regions are markedly prone to crease.
Reason (R): This is because of the absence of intermolecular binding forces.
Codes:
(a) Both (A) and (R) are true.
(b) Both (A) and (R) are false.
(c) (A) is true, but (R) is false.
(d) (A) is false, but (R) is true.

40. **Assertion (A):** Recent developments on finishing focus on reducing consumption of water, energy and chemicals.
Reason (R): They are non-renewable resources which are used for finishing textiles.
Codes:
(a) Both (A) and (R) are true.
(b) Both (A) and (R) are false.
(c) (A) is true, but (R) is false.
(d) (A) is false, but (R) is true.

41. **Assertion (A):** Traditional Kantha is a sustainable textile.
Reason (R): It is traditionally made from waste textile material.
Codes:
(a) Both (A) and (R) are true.
(b) Both (A) and (R) are false.
(c) (A) is true, but (R) is false.
(d) (A) is false, but (R) is true.

42. **Assertion (A):** A source or means, is considered if it is available and recognized only in present context.
Reason (R): A source or means which may not have any utility at present but has a potential for use in future could not be considered as a resource.
Codes:
(a) (A) is true, but (R) is false.
(b) (A) is wrong and (R) is true.
(c) Both (A) and (R) are true.
(d) Both (A) and (R) are false.

43. **Assertion (A):** Static work results due to static muscle contraction required to hold the body or any segment of it in a fixed position without contributing to work performance.
Reason (R): Occlusion of blood vessels during muscular activity could be a serious detriment to blood flow in the muscles resulting in pain and muscle weakness.
Codes:
(a) (A) is true, but (R) is false.
(b) (A) is wrong and (R) is true.
(c) Both (A) and (R) are true.
(d) Both (A) and (R) are false.

44. **Assertion (A):** Non-formal educational interventions are important for developing societies.
Reason (R): Non-formal education is more flexible in terms of time and age.

Codes:
(a) (A) is true, but (R) is false.
(b) (A) is true, but (R) is not the reason.
(c) (A) is true and (R) is the reason.
(d) (A) is false, but (R) is true.

45. **Assertion (A):** Diffusion of innovation is the adoption of technical and social innovations.
Reason (R): Rogers presented the communication strategy for development.
Codes:
(a) (A) is true and (R) is false.
(b) Both (A) and (R) are true, but (R) is not the reason for it.
(c) Both (A) and (R) are true and (R) is the right reason for it.
(d) (A) is false and (R) is true.

46. Arrange the steps used in planning of meals by using food exchange list:
(A) Use the food exchanges for planning menu.
(B) Distribute the above food exchanges between meals.
(C) Estimate the amount of different food exchanges that provide required energy and protein (Food Exchange Plan).
(D) Record personal data for determining RDA.
Codes:
(a) (A), (B), (C), (D)
(b) (C), (A), (B), (D)
(c) (D), (B), (C), (A)
(d) (D), (C), (B), (A)

47. Arrange fruits in decreasing order as per their fibre content:
(A) Water melon (B) Banana
(C) Papaya (D) Apple
(E) Sapota (F) Guava
Codes:
(a) (D), (F), (E), (A), (B), (C)
(b) (F), (E), (D), (C), (B), (A)
(c) (B), (D), (C), (E), (A), (F)
(d) (B), (D), (A), (F), (C), (E)

48. Arrange the following steps in the planning of a new unit in the proper sequence:
I. Organize a planning team
II. Prepare a prospectus
III. Design development
IV. Preliminary study
V. Architectural features
VI. Menu analysis
Codes:
(a) I, II, IV, VI, V, III
(b) IV, II, I, VI, V, III
(c) IV, I, VI, III, II, V
(d) III, II, I, IV, VI, V

49. Arrange in correct sequence the metabolic changes occurring in uncontrolled diabetic state:
I. Dehydration
II. Glycosuria
III. Peripheral circulatory failure
IV. Loss of water and electrolytes
V. Anuria
VI. Decrease Renal Blood Flow
VII. Coma and death
Codes:
(a) I, II, III, VI, V, IV, VII
(b) II, IV, I, III, VI, V, VII
(c) II, I, III, IV, VI, V, VII
(d) II, I, IV, III, V, VI, VII

50. Arrange the following needs according to Maslow's Need Hierarchy Theory:
I. Love
II. Self Actualisation
III. Safety
IV. Physiological
V. Esteem
Codes:
(a) IV, I, III, V, II
(b) IV, III, I, V, II
(c) III, IV, II, I, II
(d) II, III, IV, V, I

51. Arrange according to cognitive attainment:
(A) Object permanence
(B) Reflexive schemes
(C) Deferred imitation
(D) Centration
(E) Hierarchical classification
Codes:
(a) (C), (B), (A), (D), (E)
(b) (B), (A), (C), (D), (E)
(c) (A), (B), (D), (E), (C)
(d) (B), (A), (D), (C), (E)

52. Arrange in accordance with Kohlberg's stages of Moral Development:
(A) Good boy – Good girl orientation
(B) Punishment and obedience orientation
(C) Instrumental purpose orientation
(D) Social contract orientation
(E) Social order maintaining orientation
Codes:
(a) (A), (B), (C), (E), (D)
(b) (B), (C), (A), (E), (D)
(c) (B), (A), (E), (D), (C)
(d) (C), (B), (A), (E), (D)

53. Give the correct sequence of wet spinning:
(A) Stretching
(B) Washing and chemical treatment
(C) Solidifying filaments in a coagulating bath
(D) Drying
(E) Winding
Codes:
(a) (C), (B), (A), (D), (E)
(b) (B), (C), (A), (E), (D)
(c) (C), (A), (B), (D), (E)
(d) (A), (B), (C), (D), (E)

54. What is the sequence in the production of line assembly for trousers?
(A) Production of back of trousers
(B) Production of front of trousers
(C) Pre-preparation of pockets, fly and labels
(D) Assembling of garment parts
Codes:
(a) (C), (A), (B), (D)
(b) (D), (A), (C), (B)
(c) (A), (C), (D), (B)
(d) (B), (D), (C), (A)

55. Arrange the following steps of a pathway chart in a sequential order:
I. Draw the plan of the place.
II. Analyse the observation.
III. Insert nails and connect thread.
IV. Observe the movement and wind the thread.
V. Discuss the suggestions with the worker for repeated task.
VI. Draw suggestion for improvement.
Codes:
(a) I, III, II, IV, V, VI
(b) III, I, IV, II, V, VI
(c) I, IV, II, III, VI
(d) I, III, IV, II, VI, V

56. Write the correct sequence of the steps involved in controlling:
I. Establish standards.
II. Device suitable measures of performance.
III. Analyse the performance based on standards.
IV. Measure performance against standards.
V. Set right deviations if required.
Codes:
(a) II, I, III, V, IV (b) II, III, I, IV, V
(c) II, I, IV, V, III (d) II, IV, V, III, I

57. Give in the sequential order the steps to be followed while preparing a budget:
I. Estimating the total expected income.
II. Estimating the cost of desired items.
III. Listing the commodities and services needed.
IV. Checking the plan for realism.
V. Balancing expected income and expenditure.
VI. Writing out the plan.

Codes:
(a) I, III, II, V, IV, VI
(b) III, II, I, V, IV, VI
(c) III, I, II, IV, V, VI
(d) I, II, IV, III, VI, V

58. Arrange the following in the descending order of hierarchy:
I. Jilla Panchayat
II. Gram Panchayat
III. Block Panchayat
IV. Gram Sabha
Codes:
(a) IV, II, III and I (b) I, III, II and IV
(c) II, IV, III and I (d) III, IV, II and I

59. The steps followed in process of transfer of information by a person to another person are in the following sequential order:
I. Idealism II. Transmission
III. Encoding IV. Decoding
V. Receiving VI. Action
Codes:
(a) I, II, III, IV, VI and V
(b) I, III, II, V, IV and VI
(c) VI, V, IV, III, II and I
(d) I, III, II, V, VI and IV

60. The steps in executing the programme of training includes the following sequence:
I. Building a training group
II. Introduction of the participants
III. Reception of trainees
IV. Registration of participants
V. Monitoring of programmes
Codes:
(a) III, IV, II, I and V
(b) III, IV, II, V and I
(c) I, II, III, IV and V
(d) III, I, II, IV and V

61. Match the markers in List I with cut off values in List II:
List I
A. Normal Systolic B.P. (mmHg)
B. Normal Dystolic B.P. (mmHg)
C. Normal adult BMI (kg/m^2)
D. HbAIC (%)
E. Fasting blood sugar (mg/de)
F. Serum cholesterol level (mg/de)
List II
i. < 80 ii. < 120
iii. 200 iv. 240
v. < 7 vi. 18.5 to 24.9
vii. < 100 – 120

Codes:	A	B	C	D	E	F
(a)	i	ii	vi	v	vii	iii
(b)	iii	i	v	vii	ii	iv
(c)	ii	i	vi	v	vii	iii
(d)	ii	i	v	vi	iii	iv

62. Match the following marks of standardization in List I with the products in List II:
List I
A. BIS B. FPO
C. Agmark D. MMPO
E. MPO
List II
i. Milk products
ii. Coffee, tea, infant foods
iii. Meat products
iv. Oil, ghee, pulses, and spices
v. Fruit squashes

Codes:	A	B	C	D	E
(a)	iii	iv	ii	i	v
(b)	ii	v	iv	i	iii
(c)	iv	v	i	ii	iii
(d)	i	iii	ii	iv	v

63. Match the disease condition given in List I with the nutrient to be restricted given in List II:

List I	List II
A. Celiac	i. Fibre
B. Typhoid	ii. Sodium
C. Renal failure	iii. Gluten
D. Atherosclerosis	iv. Fat
E. Liver	v. Saturated fatty acids
F. Hypertension	vi. MCT
	vii. protein

Codes:	A	B	C	D	E	F
(a)	ii	vi	iv	i	v	iii
(b)	iv	vii	i	v	vi	ii
(c)	iii	i	vii	v	iv	ii
(d)	iii	vii	ii	iv	vi	i

64. Match Consumption Unit (CU) given in List II with Age Group given in List I:

List I Age Group

A. Adolescent (12 – 21 yrs.)
B. Adult female sedentary worker
C. Adult female heavy worker
D. Children 7 – 9 yrs.

List II Consumption Union

i. 0.8 ii. 1.2
iii. 1.0 iv. 0.7
v. 1.6

Codes:	A	B	C	D
(a)	iii	ii	v	iv
(b)	iii	ii	i	iv
(c)	iii	i	ii	iv
(d)	ii	iii	iv	v

65. Match the micro-organism given in List I with the food-borne disease condition in List II:

List I	List II
A. Salmonella	i. Dysentery
B. Shigella	ii. Amoebic dysentery
C. Clostridium	iii. Tuberculosis
D. Protozoa	iv. Hepatitis
E. Virus	v. Enteric fever
	vi. Botulism

Codes:	A	B	C	D	E
(a)	ii	v	i	vi	iii
(b)	v	iii	ii	vi	iv
(c)	v	i	vi	ii	iv
(d)	i	v	vi	ii	iii

66. Match the laws in List I with the group they are applicable to in List II:

List I

A. PWD Act B. CL (P&R) Act
C. JJ (C&P) Act D. PNDT Act
E. HAMA

List II

i. Destitute children
ii. Disabled persons
iii. Working children
iv. Hindu adoptive parents
v. Pregnant women
vi. Minority women

Codes:	A	B	C	D	E
(a)	v	vi	i	iii	ii
(b)	v	ii	i	iii	iv
(c)	ii	iii	i	v	iv
(d)	ii	i	vi	iii	iv

67. Match the theorists in List I with their theories in List II:

List I

A. Vygotsky B. Konrad Lorenz
C. Piaget D. Freud
E. Erikson

List II

i. Psychoanalytic
ii. Cognitive development
iii. Psychosocial
iv. Ethology
v. Socio-cultural
vi. Social learning

Codes:	A	B	C	D	E
(a)	v	iv	ii	i	iii
(b)	iv	v	ii	i	vi
(c)	iii	iv	ii	i	vi
(d)	i	ii	iii	vi	v

68. Match the dyes given in List I with their properties given in List II:

List I

A. Acid dyes
B. Azoic dyes
C. Sulphur dyes
D. Vat dyes

List II

i. Water insoluble dispersion
ii. Applied as reduced leuco compound
iii. Applied with a Mordant
iv. Dye developed within the textile from a chemical reaction

v. Water insoluble dye
vi. Water soluble anionic dye

Codes:	A	B	C	D
(a)	i	ii	iii	vi
(b)	vi	iv	v	ii
(c)	ii	iii	v	vi
(d)	vi	i	ii	iii

69. Match the colour problems given in List I with their descriptions given in List II:

List I

A. Frosting B. Tendering
C. Barre D. Metamerism

List II

i. Weak areas in a fabric resulting from chemical damage
ii. Horizontal off shade band across fabric
iii. Same colour appears different under different light sources
iv. Change of colour due to localized abrasive wear
v. Unintentional shade variation within a piece of fabric

Codes:	A	B	C	D
(a)	iv	ii	v	i
(b)	iv	i	ii	iii
(c)	ii	iii	iv	v
(d)	v	iv	iii	ii

70. Match the traditional textile fabrics given in List I with the descriptions given in List II:

List I

A. Chobe
B. Thirma
C. Ratan Chowk Bhat
D. Chhabri Bhat

List II

i. Patola with cross diagonal design
ii. Phulkari done on white khaddar
iii. Red Phulkari with triangular designs in yellow pat
iv. Patola with basket design
v. Patola with human figures

Codes:	A	B	C	D
(a)	i	v	iv	ii
(b)	iv	i	ii	v
(c)	ii	iv	iii	i
(d)	iii	ii	i	iv

71. Match the following family type with their stages of family life cycle:

List I Family Types

A. Normal nuclear family
B. Childless family
C. Single parent family with adopted child
D. Joint family
E. Extended family

List II Stages

i. Expanding stage continue
ii. Beginning, expanding and contracting family
iii. Expanding and contracting stage
iv. Beginning stage with expanding stage
v. Beginning stage continue
vi. Contracting stage

Codes:	A	B	C	D	E
(a)	ii	iii	i	v	iv
(b)	ii	v	iii	i	iv
(c)	ii	v	i	iii	iv
(d)	i	iii	ii	v	iv

72. Match the following movements with joints muscle or activity involved:

List I Movements

A. Ballistic movement
B. Fixed movement
C. Static contraction
D. Flexers and extensors
E. Co-contraction

List II Joints/Muscles/Activities

i. Contraction of flexion and contractors
ii. Shoulder joint
iii. Anti-gravity muscle
iv. Elbow joints
v. Lifting of an immovable object
vi. Antagonistic muscles

Codes:	A	B	C	D	E
(a)	iv	v	iii	i	ii
(b)	ii	v	i	iv	iii
(c)	ii	iv	v	iii	i
(d)	ii	v	iv	i	iii

73. Match the type of audio-visual aids given in List I with the aids given in List II:

List I	List II
A. 2D	i. Field visit
B. 3D	ii. Poster
C. Projected aid	iii. Model
D. Non-projected aid	iv. Films
	v. Bulletin Board

Codes:	A	B	C	D
(a)	ii	iii	iv	i
(b)	ii	iii	i	iv
(c)	ii	iii	v	iv
(d)	ii	iii	iv	v

74. Match the following:

List I

A. Budgeting B. Monitoring
C. Auditing D. Reporting

List II

i. Gathering and analysis of data
ii. Allocation of funds for implementation of project
iii. To improve the working of the system
iv. Formal record of programme

Codes:	A	B	C	D
(a)	i	ii	iii	iv
(b)	ii	i	iii	iv
(c)	iv	iii	ii	i
(d)	i	ii	iv	iii

75. Match the following basic functions of communication with their characteristic features:

List I

A. Information B. Instruction
C. Influence D. Integration

List II

i. Initiation of communication by superiors
ii. Adopting oneself to environment
iii. Changing behaviour in desirable direction
iv. Maintaining societal stability

Codes:	A	B	C	D
(a)	ii	i	iii	iv
(b)	ii	i	iv	iii
(c)	i	ii	iii	iv
(d)	iv	iii	ii	i

ANSWERS

1. (a)	2. (b)	3. (a)	4. (d)	5. (b)
6. (c)	7. (a)	8. (b)	9. (b)	10. (b)
11. (a)	12. (a)	13. (a)	14. (c)	15. (b)
16. (b)	17. (b)	18. (b)	19. (d)	20. (a)
21. (d)	22. (b)	23. (d)	24. (d)	25. (b)
26. (b)	27. (c)	28. (c)	29. (c)	30. (c)
31. (c)	32. (c)	33. (b)	34. (d)	35. (b)
36. (a)	37. (b)	38. (d)	39. (a)	40. (a)
41. (a)	42. (d)	43. (a)	44. (c)	45. (b)
46. (d)	47. (b)	48. (b)	49. (b)	50. (b)
51. (b)	52. (b)	53. (c)	54. (a)	55. (d)
56. (c)	57. (b)	58. (b)	59. (b)	60. (a)
61. (c)	62. (b)	63. (c)	64. (c)	65. (c)
66. (c)	67. (a)	68. (b)	69. (b)	70. (d)
71. (b)	72. (c)	73. (d)	74. (b)	75. (a)

JUNE–2013

Note: This paper contains Sixty (60) multiple choice questions, each question carrying two (2) marks. Candidate is expected to answer any Fifty (50) questions. In case more than Fifty (50) questions are attempted, only the first Fifty (50) questions will be evaluated.

PAPER–I

1. Which one of the following references is written as per Modern Language Association (MLA) format?
   (a) Hall, Donald. Fundamentals of Electronics,
   New Delhi: Prentice Hall of India, 2005
   (b) Hall, Donald, Fundamentals of Electronics,
   New Delhi: Prentice Hall of India, 2005
   (c) Hall, Donald, Fundamentals of Electronics,
   New Delhi: Prentice Hall of India, 2005
   (d) Hall, Donald. Fundamentals of Electronics.
   New Delhi: Prentice Hall of India, 2005

2. A workshop is
   (a) a conference for discussion on a topic.
   (b) a meeting for discussion on a topic.
   (c) a class at a college or a university in which a teacher and the students discuss a topic.
   (d) a brief intensive course for a small group emphasizing the development of a skill or technique for solving a specific problem.

3. A working hypothesis is
   (a) a proven hypothesis for an argument.
   (b) not required to be tested.
   (c) a provisionally accepted hypothesis for further research.
   (d) a scientific theory.

Read the following passage carefully and answer the questions (4 to 9):

The Taj Mahal has become one of the world's best known monuments. This domed white marble structure is situated on a high plinth at the southern end of a four-quartered garden, evoking the gardens of paradise, enclosed within walls measuring 305 by 549 metres. Outside the walls, in an area known as Mumtazabad, were living quarters for attendants, markets, serais and other structures built by local merchants and nobles. The tomb complex and the other imperial structures of Mumtazabad were maintained by the income of thirty villages given specifically for the tomb's support. The name Taj Mahal is unknown in Mughal chronicles, but it is used by contemporary Europeans in India, suggesting that this was the tomb's popular name. In contemporary texts, it is generally called simply the Illuminated Tomb (Rauza-i-Munavvara).

Mumtaz Mahal died shortly after delivering her fourteenth child in 1631. The Mughal court was then residing in Burhanpur. Her remains were temporarily buried by the grief-stricken emperor in a spacious garden known as Zainabad on the bank of the river Tapti. Six months later her body was transported to Agra, where it was interred in land chosen for the mausoleum. This land, situated south of the Mughal city on the bank of the Jamuna, had belonged to the Kachhwaha rajas since the time of Raja Man Singh and was purchased from the then current raja, Jai Singh. Although contemporary chronicles indicate Jai Singh's willing cooperation in this exchange, extant *farmans* (imperial commands) indicate that the final price was not settled until almost two years after the mausoleum's commencement. Jai Singh's further cooperation was insured by imperial orders issued between 1632 and 1637 demanding that he provide stone masons and carts to transport marble from the mines at Makrana, within his "ancestral domain", to Agra where both the Taj Mahal and Shah Jahan's additions to the Agra fort were constructed concurrently.

Work on the mausoleum was commenced early in 1632. Inscriptional evidence indicates much of the tomb was completed by 1636. By 1643, when Shah Jahan most lavishly celebrated the 'Urs ceremony for Mumtaz Mahal', the entire complex was virtually complete.

4. Marble stone used for the construction of the Taj Mahal was brought from the ancestral domain of Raja Jai Singh. The name of the place where mines of marble is
   (a) Burhanpur (b) Makrana
   (c) Amber (d) Jaipur
5. The popular name Taj Mahal was given by
   (a) Shah Jahan
   (b) Tourists
   (c) Public
   (d) European travellers
6. Point out the true statement from the following:
   (a) Marble was not used for the construction of the Taj Mahal.
   (b) Red sand stone is non-visible in the Taj Mahal complex.
   (c) The Taj Mahal is surrounded by a four-quartered garden known as Char Bagh.
   (d) The Taj Mahal was constructed to celebrate the 'Urs ceremony for Mumtaz Mahal'.
7. In the contemporary texts the Taj Mahal is known
   (a) Mumtazabad
   (b) Mumtaz Mahal
   (c) Zainabad
   (d) Rauza-i-Munavvara
8. The construction of the Taj Mahal was completed between the period
   (a) 1632 – 1636 A.D.
   (b) 1630 – 1643 A.D.
   (c) 1632 – 1643 A.D.
   (d) 1636 – 1643 A.D.
9. The documents indicating the ownership of land, where the Taj Mahal was built, known as
   (a) Farman
   (b) Sale Deed
   (c) Sale-Purchase Deed
   (d) None of the above
10. In the process of communication, which one of the following is in the chronological order?
    (a) Communicator, Medium, Receiver, Effect, Message
    (b) Medium, Communicator, Message, Receiver, Effect
    (c) Communicator, Message, Medium, Receiver, Effect
    (d) Message, Communicator, Medium, Receiver, Effect
11. *Bengal Gazette*, the first Newspaper in India was started in 1780 by
    (a) Dr. Annie Besant
    (b) James Augustus Hicky
    (c) Lord Cripson
    (d) A.O. Hume

12. Press censorship in India was imposed during the tenure of the Prime Minister
(a) Rajiv Gandhi
(b) Narasimha Rao
(c) Indira Gandhi
(d) Deve Gowda

13. Communication via New media such as computers, teleshopping, internet and mobile telephony is termed as
(a) Entertainment
(b) Interactive communication
(c) Developmental communication
(d) Communitarian

14. Classroom communication of a teacher rests on the principle of
(a) Infotainment
(b) Edutainment
(c) Entertainment
(d) Enlightenment

15. ________ is important when a teacher communicates with his/her student.
(a) Sympathy (b) Empathy
(c) Apathy (d) Antipathy

16. In a certain code GALIB is represented by HBMJC. TIGER will be represented by
(a) UJHFS (b) UHJSF
(c) JHUSF (d) HUJSF

17. In a certain cricket tournament 45 matches were played. Each team played once against each of the other teams. The number of teams participated in the tournament is
(a) 8 (b) 10
(c) 12 (d) 14

18. The missing number in the series 40, 120, 60, 180, 90, ?, 135 is
(a) 110 (b) 270
(c) 105 (d) 210

19. The odd numbers from 1 to 45 which are exactly divisible by 3 are arranged in an ascending order. The number at 6th position is
(a) 18 (b) 24
(c) 33 (d) 36

20. The mean of four numbers a, b, c, d is 100. If c = 70, then the mean of the remaining numbers is
(a) 30 (b) $\frac{85}{2}$
(c) $\frac{170}{3}$ (d) 110

21. If the radius of a circle is increased by 50%, the perimeter of the circle will increase by
(a) 20% (b) 30%
(c) 40% (d) 50%

22. If the statement 'some men are honest' is false, which among the following statements will be true. Choose the correct code given below:
(i) All men are honest.
(ii) No men are honest.
(iii) Some men are not honest.
(iv) All men are dishonest.

Codes:
(a) (i), (ii) and (iii)
(b) (ii), (iii) and (iv)
(c) (i), (iii) and (iv)
(d) (ii), (i) and (iv)

23. Choose the proper alternative given in the codes to replace the question mark.
Bee – Honey, Cow – Milk, Teacher –?
(a) Intelligence (b) Marks
(c) Lessons (d) Wisdom

24. P is the father of R and S is the son of Q and T is the brother of P. If R is the sister of S, how is Q related to T?
(a) Wife
(b) Sister-in-law
(c) Brother-in-law
(d) Daughter-in-law

25. A definition put forward to resolve a dispute by influencing attitudes or stirring emotions is called
(a) Lexical (b) Persuasive
(c) Stipulative (d) Precisions

26. Which of the codes given below contains only the correct statements?
Statements:
(i) Venn diagram is a clear method of notation.
(ii) Venn diagram is the most direct method of testing the validity of categorical syllogisms.
(iii) In Venn diagram method the premises and the conclusion of a categorical syllogism is diagrammed.
(iv) In Venn diagram method the three overlapping circles are drawn for testing a categorical syllogism.
Codes:
(a) (i), (ii) & (iii)
(b) (i), (ii) & (iv)
(c) (ii), (iii) & (iv)
(d) (i), (iii) & (iv)

27. Inductive reasoning presupposes
(a) unity in human nature
(b) integrity in human nature
(c) uniformity in human nature
(d) harmony in human nature

Read the table below and based on this table answer questions from 28 to 33:

Area under Major Horticulture Crops
(in lakh hectares)

Year	Fruits	Vegetables	Flowers	Total Horti-culture Area
2005-06	53	72	1	187
2006-07	56	75	1	194
2007-08	58	78	2	202
2008-09	61	79	2	207
2009-10	63	79	2	209

28. Which of the following two years have recorded the highest rate of increase in area under the total horticulture?
(a) 2005–06 & 2006–07
(b) 2006–07 & 2008–09
(c) 2007–08 & 2008–09
(d) 2006–07 & 2007–08

29. Shares of the area under flowers, vegetables and fruits in the area under total horticulture are respectively:
(a) 1, 38 and 30 percent
(b) 30, 38 and 1 percent
(c) 38, 30 and 1 percent
(d) 35, 36 and 2 percent

30. Which of the following has recorded the highest rate of increase in area during 2005-06 to 2009-10?
(a) Fruits
(b) Vegetables
(c) Flowers
(d) Total horticulture

31. Find out the horticultural crop that has recorded an increase of area by around 10 percent from 2005-06 to 2009-10.
(a) Fruits
(b) Vegetables
(c) Flowers
(d) Total horticulture

32. What has been the share of area under fruits, vegetables and flowers in the area under total horticulture in 2007-08?
(a) 53 percent (b) 68 percent
(c) 79 percent (d) 100 percent

33. In which year, area under fruits has recorded the highest rate of increase?
(a) 2006-07 (b) 2007-08
(c) 2008-09 (d) 2009-10

34. 'www' stands for
(a) work with web
(b) word wide web

(c) world wide web
(d) worth while web

35. A hard disk is divided into tracks which is further subdivided into
(a) Clusters (b) Sectors
(c) Vectors (d) Heads

36. A computer program that translates a program statement by statement into machine language is called a/an
(a) Compiler (b) Simulator
(c) Translator (d) Interpreter

37. A Gigabyte is equal to
(a) 1024 Megabytes
(b) 1024 Kilobytes
(c) 1024 Terabytes
(d) 1024 Bytes

38. A Compiler is a software which converts
(a) characters to bits
(b) high level language to machine language
(c) machine language to high level language
(d) words to bits

39. Virtual memory is
(a) an extremely large main memory.
(b) an extremely large secondary memory.
(c) an illusion of extremely large main memory.
(d) a type of memory used in super computers.

40. The phrase 'tragedy of commons' is in the context of
(a) tragic event related to damage caused by release of poisonous gases.
(b) tragic conditions of poor people.
(c) degradation of renewable free access resources.
(d) climate change.

41. Kyoto Protocol is related to
(a) Ozone depletion
(b) Hazardous waste
(c) Climate change
(d) Nuclear energy

42. Which of the following is a source of emissions leading to the eventual formation of surface ozone as a pollutant?
(a) Transport sector
(b) Refrigeration and Airconditioning
(c) Wetlands
(d) Fertilizers

43. The smog in cities in India mainly consists of
(a) Oxides of sulphur
(b) Oxides of nitrogen and unburnt hydrocarbons
(c) Carbon monoxide and SPM
(d) Oxides of sulphur and ozone

44. Which of the following types of natural hazards have the highest potential to cause damage to humans?
(a) Earthquakes
(b) Forest fires
(c) Volcanic eruptions
(d) Droughts and Floods

45. The percentage share of renewable energy sources in the power production in India is around
(a) 2-3% (b) 22-25%
(c) 10-12% (d) < 1%

46. In which of the following categories the enrolment of students in higher education in 2010-11 was beyond the percentage of seats reserved?
(a) OBC students
(b) SC students
(c) ST students
(d) Woman students

47. Which one of the following statements is not correct about the University Grants Commission (UGC)?
(a) It was established in 1956 by an Act of Parliament.
(b) It is tasked with promoting and coordinating higher education.
(c) It receives Plan and Non-Plan funds from the Central Government.

(d) It receives funds from State Governments in respect of State Universities.

48. Consider the statement which is followed by two arguments (I) and (II):
Statement: Should India switch over to a two party system?
Arguments: (I) Yes, it will lead to stability of Government.
(II) No, it will limit the choice of voters.
(a) Only argument (I) is strong.
(b) Only argument (II) is strong.
(c) Both the arguments are strong.
(d) Neither of the arguments is strong.

49. Consider the statement which is followed by two arguments (I) and (II):
Statement: Should persons with criminal background be banned from contesting elections?
Arguments: (I) Yes, it will decriminalise politics.
(II) No, it will encourage the ruling party to file frivolous cases against their political opponents.
(a) Only argument (I) is strong.
(b) Only argument (II) is strong.
(c) Both the arguments are strong.
(d) Neither of the arguments is strong.

50. Which of the following statement(s) is/are correct about a Judge of the Supreme Court of India?
1. A Judge of the Supreme Court is appointed by the President of India.
2. He holds office during the pleasure of the President.
3. He can be suspended, pending an inquiry.
4. He can be removed for proven misbehaviour or incapacity.

Select the correct answer from the codes given below:

Codes:
(a) 1, 2 and 3 (b) 1, 3 and 4
(c) 1 and 3 (d) 1 and 4

51. In the warrant of precedence, the Speaker of the Lok Sabha comes next only to
(a) The President
(b) The Vice-President
(c) The Prime Minister
(d) The Cabinet Ministers

52. The blackboard can be utilised best by a teacher for
(a) putting the matter of teaching in black and white
(b) making the students attentive
(c) writing the important and notable points
(d) highlighting the teacher himself

53. Nowadays the most effective mode of learning is
(a) self-study
(b) face-to-face learning
(c) e-learning
(d) blended learning

54. At the primary school stage, most of the teachers should be women because they
(a) can teach children better than men.
(b) know basic content better than men.
(c) are available on lower salaries.
(d) can deal with children with love and affection.

55. Which one is the highest order of learning?
(a) Chain learning
(b) Problem-solving learning
(c) Stimulus-response learning
(d) Conditioned-reflex learning

56. A person can enjoy teaching as a profession when he
(a) has control over students.
(b) commands respect from students.
(c) is more qualified than his colleagues.
(d) is very close to higher authorities.

57. "A diagram speaks more than 1000 words." The statement means that the teacher should
    (a) use diagrams in teaching.
    (b) speak more and more in the class.
    (c) use teaching aids in the class.
    (d) not speak too much in the class.
58. A research paper
    (a) is a compilation of information on a topic.
    (b) contains original research as deemed by the author.
    (c) contains peer-reviewed original research or evaluation of research conducted by others.
    (d) can be published in more than one journal.
59. Which one of the following belongs to the category of good 'research ethics'?
    (a) Publishing the same paper in two research journals without telling the editors.
    (b) Conducting a review of the literature that acknowledges the contributions of other people in the relevant field or relevant prior work.
    (c) Trimming outliers from a data set without discussing your reasons in a research paper.
    (d) Including a colleague as an author on a research paper in return for a favour even though the colleague did not make a serious contribution to the paper.
60. Which of the following sampling methods is not based on probability?
    (a) Simple Random Sampling
    (b) Stratified Sampling
    (c) Quota Sampling
    (d) Cluster Sampling

ANSWERS

1. (d)	2. (d)	3. (c)	4. (b)	5. (d)
6. (c)	7. (d)	8. (c)	9. (a)	10. (c)
11. (b)	12. (c)	13. (b)	14. (b)	15. (b)
16. (a)	17. (b)	18. (b)	19. (c)	20. (d)
21. (d)	22. (b)	23. (d)	24. (b)	25. (b)
26. (b)	27. (c)	28. (d)	29. (a)	30. (c)
31. (b)	32. (b)	33. (a)	34. (c)	35. (b)
36. (d)	37. (a)	38. (b)	39. (c)	40. (c)
41. (c)	42. (a)	43. (b)	44. (d)	45. (c)
46. (a)	47. (d)	48. (c)	49. (a)	50. (d)
51. (c)	52. (c)	53. (d)	54. (d)	55. (d)
56. (b)	57. (c)	58. (c)	59. (b)	60. (c)

PAPER–II

Note: This paper contains fifty (50) objective type questions, each question carrying two (2) marks. All questions are compulsory.

1. The primary reason for parboiling is
    (a) Whiten the rice
    (b) Enhance cooking time
    (c) Conserve nutrients
    (d) To favour geletinisation
2. Recommendations for visible dietary fat intake for an adult Indian woman (moderate worker) as suggested by ICMR is
    (a) 25 g per day (b) 20 g per day
    (c) 30 g per day (d) 40 g per day
3. Which of the following equipment is used for keeping cooked food warm in a cafeteria?

(a) Recaud (b) Bain Marie
(c) Food Trolley (d) Smorgashord

4. Which of the following is not a theory of the origin of clothing?
(a) Protection (b) Tattooing
(c) Adornment (d) Modesty

5. Which of the following is not a stretch fibre?
(a) Neoprene (b) Spandex
(c) Elastane (d) Viscose

6. The gas that is found in compressor of refrigerator is
(a) Freon 10 (b) Freon 11
(c) Freon 12 (d) Freon 13

7. Developmental period from birth to 8 to 12 months known as
(a) Toddler (b) Infancy
(c) Teen (d) Peer

8. The target group for National Literacy Mission is
(a) Below 15 years (b) 35-44 years
(c) 15-35 years (d) 15-65 years

9. ______ is an intense educational activity for motivating and mobilizing a community to action.
(a) Brainstorming (b) Colloquium
(c) Campaign (d) Symposium

10. Which distribution should be used in order to find out where certain scores rank relative to all others:
(a) Frequency Polygon
(b) Probability Distribution
(c) Grouped Frequency Distribution
(d) Cumulative Frequency Distribution

11. Which of the two nutrients are responsible for green ring formation in boiled egg?
I. Iron II. Protein
III. Calcium IV. Sulphur
V. Copper
Codes:
(a) II and III (b) III and V
(c) I and IV (d) II and V

12. Which of the following foods are rich in omega 3 fatty acids?
I. Lard II. Butter
III. Fatty fish IV. Olive oil
V. Mustard seeds VI. Walnuts
Codes:
(a) I, II, III (b) III, V, VI
(c) V, VI, II (d) VI, III, IV

13. Which of the following terms are associated with sanitation:
I. JIT II. MBO
III. HACCP IV. BARS
V. GHP
Codes:
(a) I and III (b) II and IV
(c) III and V (d) IV and I

14. Principles in textile design are:
I. Proportion II. Balance
III. Light IV. Harmony
V. Rhythm
Codes:
(a) I, II, III, IV are correct.
(b) I, II, IV, V are correct.
(c) II, III, IV, V are correct.
(d) III, I, II, IV are correct.

15. Electronic and microprocessor controlled alternatives in weaving have resulted in
I. Better and assured quality fabrics
II. High noise and vibration
III. Higher rate of production
IV. Consistency and reliable performance
Codes:
(a) I, II and III are correct.
(b) I, III and IV are correct.
(c) II, III and IV are correct.
(d) I, II and IV are correct.

16. Anthropometric is concerned with structural dimensions which are:
I. Weight
II. Body position
III. Height
IV. Waist circumference
V. Body posture

Codes:

(a) I, II, III (b) I, II, IV
(c) I, III, IV (d) I, II, V

17. To meet the individual differences the curriculum should be:
    I. Lengthy II. Formal
    III. Informal IV. Flexible

    Codes:
    (a) I and II are correct.
    (b) II and III are correct.
    (c) I, II and IV are correct.
    (d) II and IV are correct.

18. Which of the following aspects are closely related to Programme Planning?
    I. Plan of work
    II. Calender of work
    III. Supervision
    IV. Coordination

    Codes:
    (a) I and II are correct.
    (b) II and III are correct.
    (c) III and IV are correct.
    (d) I and IV are correct.

19. Credibility in communication means:
    I. Trustworthiness II. Competence
    III. Complete IV. Profitable

    Codes:
    (a) I and II are correct.
    (b) II and III are correct.
    (c) III and IV are correct.
    (d) I and III are correct.

20. Power of statistical test of a mean depends on:
    I. Particular H_A that is assumed true if H_0 is false.
    II. Value of α chosen
    III. Size of sample
    IV. Variability of the population under study.

    Codes:
    (a) I & II (b) I, III & IV
    (c) II & III (d) All of the above

21. **Assertion (A):** Gluten is formed when flour is mixed with water and kneaded to make a dough.
    Reason (R): It helps in the browning of chappati when cooked by dry heat.

    Codes:
    (a) (A) is true and (R) is false.
    (b) Both (A) and (R) are false.
    (c) (A) is false and (R) is true.
    (d) Both (A) and (R) are true.

22. **Assertion (A):** Breast milk is nutritionally 'tailor made' for infants.
    Reason (R): Breast milk contains the bifidus factor which promotes the growth of lactobacilli and inhibits the growth of *E. coli*.

    Codes:
    (a) Both (A) and (R) are true.
    (b) Both (A) and (R) are false.
    (c) (A) is true but (R) is false.
    (d) (A) is false but (R) is true.

23. **Assertion (A):** A purchase order is a list of items given to the supplier.
    Reason (R): It is based on the layout prospectus developed in the food service unit.

    Codes:
    (a) Both (A) and (R) are correct.
    (b) (A) is false but (R) is true.
    (c) (A) is true but (R) is false.
    (d) Both (A) and (R) are false.

24. **Assertion (A):** People choose to dress in the style that makes a statement about their personalities.
    Reason (R): As per their wish to be perceived by the outside society.

    Codes:
    (a) (A) is correct, but (R) is wrong.
    (b) (A) is wrong, but (R) is correct.
    (c) Both (A) and (R) are correct.
    (d) Both (A) and (R) are wrong.

25. **Assertion (A):** Velvet is delivered on specially constructed frames.
Reason (R): It prevents the pile from getting crushed.
Codes:
(a) Both (A) and (R) are correct.
(b) Both (A) and (R) are incorrect.
(c) (A) is correct but (R) is incorrect.
(d) (R) is correct but (A) is incorrect.

26. **Assertion (A):** Proper placement of cooking, preparation and washing areas (centres) minimize the cost of operation.
Reason (R): Existence of cooking, washing and preparation areas close to each other reduces excessive walk and time taken in operation.
Codes:
(a) (A) is false, but (R) is true.
(b) (A) is true, but (R) is false.
(c) Both (A) and (R) are true.
(d) Both (A) and (R) are false.

27. **Assertion (A):** Prematures tend to make good social adjustments throughout life than those born at full term.
Reason (R): The parental over protectiveness adversely affects their behavioural response.
Codes:
(a) Both (A) and (R) are correct.
(b) Both (A) and (R) are wrong.
(c) (A) is correct but (R) is wrong.
(d) (A) is wrong but (R) is correct.

28. **Assertion (A):** Senses are the gateways to learning.
Reason (R): Learning activities should engage a maximum number of senses by using audio-visual aids.
Codes:
(a) (A) is correct, (R) is wrong.
(b) (A) is correct, (R) is correct.
(c) (A) is not correct, (R) is correct.
(d) (A) and (R) are not correct.

29. **Assertion (A):** Newspaper is a print media. It is one of the mass media.
Reason (R): All mass media are print media.
Codes:
(a) Both (A) and (R) are true.
(b) (A) is true, but (R) is false.
(c) Both (A) and (R) are false.
(d) (A) is false, but (R) is true.

30. **Assertion (A):** Test retest is the method used to test the reliability of the measurement instrument.
Reason (R): The measurement instrument to collect data should have both reliability and validity.
Codes:
(a) (A) is true, but (R) is false.
(b) Both (A) and (R) are false.
(c) Both (A) and (R) are true, but (R) is not the correct explanation of (A).
(d) (A) is false but (R) is true.

31. Write the steps involved in cheese preparation in the correct sequence:
I. Addition of enzyme
II. Curd cutting and cooking
III. Acidification of milk
IV. Curd draining and cheddaring
V. Pasteurization of milk
VI. Salting and pressing
VII. Ripening
Codes:
(a) I, II, IV, VII, III, V, VI
(b) V, III, I, II, IV, VI, VII
(c) III, II, I, VI, V, VII, IV
(d) I, IV, II, V, VI, VII, III

32. Give the sequential order of the symptoms of vitamin A deficiency.
I. Night Blindness II. Keratinization
III. Xerophthalmia IV. Keratomalacia
Codes:
(a) I, III, II, IV (b) I, II, IV, III
(c) I, II, III, IV (d) II, III, IV, I

33. Give the procedure for hiring an employee in the right sequence:
    I. Advertisement
    II. Interview
    III. Medical examination
    IV. Screening of applications
    V. Verification of reference
    VI. Testing skills

    Codes:
    (a) I, III, V, II, IV, VI
    (b) I, IV, VI, II, V, III
    (c) IV, II, V, VI, III, I
    (d) VI, I, III, V, IV, II

34. Give the correct sequence of work that goes in the cutting room of the garment industry.
    I. Spreading the fabric to form a lay.
    II. Cutting the fabric.
    III. Planning and reproduction of marker.
    IV. Bundling of cutwork for the sewing room.

    Codes:
    (a) III, I, II, IV (b) I, II, III, IV
    (c) II, III, IV, I (d) IV, III, II, I

35. Give the correct sequence in the processing of textiles:
    (A) Singeing (B) Scouring
    (C) Bleaching (D) Designing
    (E) Mercerization

    Codes:
    (a) (B), (A), (E), (C), (D)
    (b) (A), (D), (B), (C), (E)
    (c) (A), (E), (B), (D), (C)
    (d) (D), (C), (A), (E), (B)

36. The sequential order of financial management is
    I. Analyse financial resources.
    II. Prioritize goals and set standards.
    III. Make a budget to control spending and saving.
    IV. Establish systematic financial management practices.

    Codes:
    (a) IV, III, II, I (b) II, I, IV, III
    (c) I, II, III, IV (d) II, III, IV, I

37. Give the correct sequence of stages of human development considering the chronological age:
    I. Toddler
    II. Early adolescence
    III. Infant
    IV. Youth
    V. Teenager

    Codes:
    (a) I, III, IV, V, II (b) III, I, II, V, IV
    (c) II, III, V, I, IV (d) V, I, II, III, IV

38. Arrange in sequence the year of recommendation for Non-formal education in different commission and policies.
    I. National Policy on Education
    II. Kothari Commission
    III. National Education Policy
    IV. New National Policy on Education

    Codes:
    (a) II, I, III, IV (b) I, II, III, IV
    (c) III, II, I, IV (d) I, III, II, IV

39. Give the correct sequence of the procedure to be adopted in organising audio-visual programme:
    I. Planning II. Presentation
    III. Follow-up IV. Preparation

    Codes:
    (a) I, II, IV, III (b) I, IV, II, III
    (c) IV, I, II, III (d) III, IV, II, I

40. Arrange the following steps of research in the correct sequence:
    I. Review of Literature
    II. Rationale
    III. Objectives
    IV. Methodology
    V. Interpretation
    VI. Results

Codes:
(a) II, III, I, IV, VI, V
(b) I, II, III, IV, VI, V
(c) III, II, I, IV, V, VI
(d) II, I, III, IV, V, VI

41. Match the foods in List I to the colour pigment in List II:

List I (Foods)	List II (Colour pigment)
A. Carrot	i. Anthocyanins
B. Beet root	ii. Anthoxanthins
C. Plums	iii. Carotenoids
D. Cauliflower	iv. Betalains
E. Broccoli	v. Chlorophylls

Codes:	A	B	C	D	E
(a)	ii	v	iii	iv	i
(b)	iv	i	ii	v	iii
(c)	i	iii	ii	v	iv
(d)	iii	iv	i	ii	v

42. Match the foods in List I with its rich nutrients in List II:

List I (Foods)	List II (Nutrients)
A. Papaya	i. Iron
B. Orange	ii. Calcium
C. Dates	iii. Vit. C
D. Ragi	iv. Vit. A
	v. Vit. B_{12}

Codes:	A	B	C	D
(a)	v	ii	iii	iv
(b)	ii	iii	iv	i
(c)	iv	iii	i	ii
(d)	iii	ii	v	i

43. Match the items given in List I with List II:

List I	List II
A. MBO	i. Sanitation
B. CCP	ii. Management
C. Perpetual Inventory	iii. Storage
D. Al a carte	iv. Menu
E. Specification	v. Purchase
	vi. Sales

Codes:	A	B	C	D	E
(a)	ii	i	iii	iv	v
(b)	i	ii	iv	v	vi
(c)	i	ii	iv	iii	v
(d)	vi	i	ii	iv	iii

44. Match the items given in List I with their descriptions given in List II.

List I
A. Godet B. Gusset
C. Peplum D. Gores

List II
i. Piece attached at sleeve
ii. Short flare attached to the waist of a garment
iii. Triangular piece attached at the hemline
iv. Panels in a garment

Codes:	A	B	C	D
(a)	i	ii	iii	iv
(b)	ii	iv	i	iii
(c)	iii	i	ii	iv
(d)	ii	iii	iv	i

45. Match the equipment given in List I with the end products for which they are used given in List II:

List I	List II
A. Pad steam range	i. Fibre and yarn
B. Crimp tester	ii. Dyeing
C. Air permeability	iii. Yarn
D. Hairiness meter	iv. Fabric

Codes:	A	B	C	D
(a)	i	ii	iii	iv
(b)	iii	iv	i	ii
(c)	ii	i	iv	iii
(d)	iv	iii	ii	i

46. Match List I with List II

List I
A. Physiological needs
B. Safety needs
C. Social needs
D. Esteem needs
E. Self-actualization

List II
i. Freedom from fear
ii. Food and Shelter

iii. Self-respect
iv. Social interaction
v. Self-discipline
vi. Self-conscious

Codes:	A	B	C	D	E
(a)	ii	iii	vi	iv	v
(b)	ii	i	iv	iii	v
(c)	i	iv	ii	iii	v
(d)	iv	iii	ii	i	v

47. Match List I correctly with List II:

List I
A. Over-protectiveness
B. Permissiveness
C. Rejection
D. Acceptance

List II
i. Aggressiveness
ii. Over-dependency
iii. Confident
iv. Irresponsible
v. Inferior

Codes:	A	B	C	D
(a)	iv	i	ii	iii
(b)	ii	iv	i	iii
(c)	iii	ii	iv	v
(d)	v	iii	iv	ii

48. Match the concepts related to extension in List I with their meaning given in List II:

List I
A. Motivation B. Learning
C. Need D. Interest

List II
i. A desire on the part of an individual to learn.
ii. An inner state that energizes, activates or moves and directs human behaviour towards goals.
iii. It is a process by which a person becomes changed in his behaviour through self-activity.
iv. A gap between 'what is' and 'what ought to be'.

Codes:	A	B	C	D
(a)	iii	iv	ii	i
(b)	iv	iii	i	ii
(c)	ii	iii	iv	i
(d)	i	iii	iv	ii

49. Match the items given in List I with List II:

List I
A. Overhead Projector
B. LCD Projector
C. Slide Projector
D. Motion Picture

List II
i. Slides
ii. Films
iii. Flannel
iv. Transparency Sheet Projector
v. Power Point

Codes:	A	B	C	D
(a)	iv	v	i	ii
(b)	iii	i	v	iv
(c)	ii	v	i	iii
(d)	i	iii	iv	v

50. Match the items in List I with List II:

List I
A. Median B. Wilcoxon Test
C. Symmetric D. Tukey's HSD
E. Type I Error

List II
i. Post hoecomparison
ii. Arithmetic average of distribution
iii. Non-paramatic test distribution
iv. Mean and median are of equal value
v. Mid-way point between top and bottom halves of distribution
vi. H_0 is falsely rejected

Codes:	A	B	C	D	E
(a)	v	i	ii	iii	vi
(b)	v	iii	iv	i	vi
(c)	ii	i	v	iii	vi
(d)	v	i	iv	iii	vi

ANSWERS

1. (c)	2. (a)	3. (b)	4. (b)	5. (d)
6. (c)	7. (b)	8. (c)	9. (c)	10. (d)
11. (c)	12. (b)	13. (c)	14. (b)	15. (b)
16. (c)	17. (d)	18. (a)	19. (a)	20. (d)
21. (a)	22. (a)	23. (c)	24. (c)	25. (a)
26. (c)	27. (d)	28. (b)	29. (b)	30. (c)
31. (b)	32. (a)	33. (b)	34. (a)	35. (b)
36. (b)	37. (b)	38. (a)	39. (b)	40. (a)
41. (d)	42. (c)	43. (a)	44. (c)	45. (c)
46. (b)	47. (b)	48. (c)	49. (a)	50. (b)

PAPER–III

Note: This paper contains seventy-five (75) objective type questions of two (2) marks each. All questions are compulsory.

1. The Emulsifier used in mayonnaise is
   (a) Myoglobin (b) Cellulose
   (c) Soya protein (d) Lecithin
2. Following food is a rich source of retinol:
   (a) Milk (b) Carrot
   (c) Spinach (d) Soyabean
3. Gluten Free Diet (GFD) is given to patients with
   (a) Crohn's Disease
   (b) Celiac Disease
   (c) Irritable Bowel Disease (IBD)
   (d) Liver Disease
4. Tube feeding is also known as
   (a) Parentral nutrition
   (b) Enteral nutrition
   (c) Total parentral nutrition
   (d) Supplemental nutrition
5. Zero budget is used in institutions where
   (a) the past three years financial report form the basis.
   (b) trend of sales is the indicator.
   (c) operations have to be evaluated afresh.
   (d) 10% escalation charges are added to previous year's expenditure.
6. The term Pre-basic Education is given by
   (a) Rabindranath Tagore
   (b) Tarabai Modak
   (c) Mahatma Gandhi
   (d) Maria Montessori
7. Psychosocial theory is given by
   (a) Piaget (b) Erickson
   (c) Hurlock (d) Kolberg
8. The function of Ego is based on
   (a) Pleasure principle
   (b) Reality principle
   (c) Reflex action
   (d) Practical experience
9. The process of cutting materials by means of a high velocity jet of high temperature ionized gas (argon) is called
   (a) Laser cutting (b) Plasma cutting
   (c) Water jet cutting (d) Die cutting
10. LEAF stands for
    (a) Lasting Ecologically Apparels and Fabrics
    (b) Labelling Ecologically Approved Fabrics
    (c) Latest Ecologically Approved Fashion
    (d) Lean Ecological Apparel and Fashion
11. A bedspread used for ceremonial occasions made with Kantha Embroidery
    (a) Sujani (b) Suber
    (c) Sainchi (d) Sangli
12. When black colour is added to any colour it is called
    (a) Chroma (b) Tint
    (c) Shade (d) Colour value

13. Market is a place where, there is
(a) exchange of services.
(b) shaping of goods and services.
(c) exchange of goods and services.
(d) finishing of goods.

14. Among the following symbols from pathway chart, indicate the one which is used for delay.
(a) □ (b) ○
(c) △ (d) ▭

15. ______ is a systematic arrangement and display of visual materials under a roof to create awareness and arouse interest in the minds of the learners about an idea.
(a) Demonstrations (b) Blackboard
(c) Posters (d) Exhibition

16. ______ Five-year Plan onwards there has been a marked shift in the approach to women's issues from 'Welfare', to 'Development'.
(a) Fourth (b) Fifth
(c) Sixth (d) Seventh

17. For assessing nutritional status, following methods can be used:
I. IQ Test
II. Dietary Survey
III. Anthropometry
IV. Psychological Tests
V. Clinical Examination
Codes:
(a) II, III, V (b) I, II, III
(c) III, IV, V (d) II, IV, V

18. Following are essential amino acids:
I. Isoleucine II. Alanine
III. Lysine IV. Leucine
V. Arginine
Codes:
(a) I, II, V (b) II, IV, V
(c) I, III, IV (d) V, II, I

19. Maillard Reaction occurs in the following food items:
(A) Toast (B) Lime juice
(C) Milk cake (D) Fried onions
(E) Crust of cake (F) Cut apples
Codes:
(a) (B), (D), (F) (b) (A), (C), (E)
(c) (C), (E), (B) (d) (E), (D), (C)

20. Which of the following are rich sources of cholesterol?
I. Egg II. Ice Cream
III. Soya oil IV. Cereals
V. Pulses VI. Barfi
Codes:
(a) IV, V, II (b) III, II, I
(c) II, III, VI (d) I, II, VI

21. Which of the following are the symptoms of diabetes Mellitus?
I. Polyuria II. Hypoglycemia
III. Glycosuria IV. Polyphagia
V. Edema VI. Taste acuity
Codes:
(a) I, III, IV (b) IV, II, III
(c) VI, IV, V (d) II, IV, V

22. The following records have to be maintained for calculating food cost:
I. Standardised recipes
II. Cash receipt
III. Invoice of perishables
IV. Census
V. Store room issues
VI. Purchase order
Codes:
(a) I, II, V & IV (b) II, III, I & V
(c) IV, II, III & I (d) II, III, IV & V

23. Sustainable development consists of constituent parts:
I. Environmental sustainability
II. Economic sustainability
III. Socio-political sustainability
IV. Cultural sustainability
V. Low-economic sustainability

Codes:
(a) II, III, IV & V (b) I, II, IV & V
(c) I, II, III & IV (d) I, III, IV & V

24. The appropriate way to stimulate sense of touch is
I. Massage
II. Expose to different texture
III. Gentle care and touch
IV. Playing with the child
Codes:
(a) I and II are correct.
(b) I, II and III are correct.
(c) II, III and IV are correct.
(d) All are correct.

25. Parental role in the family changes during
I. Child bearing stage
II. Child rearing stage
III. Establishing stage
IV. Reconstruction stage
Codes:
(a) I and III are correct.
(b) II, III and IV are correct.
(c) I and II are correct.
(d) All are correct.

26. Lock stitch is
I. Reversible
II. Stretchable
III. Non-reversible
IV. Used for precise stitching
Codes:
(a) II and III are correct.
(b) II and IV are correct.
(c) I and IV are correct.
(d) I and III are correct.

27. Japanese traditional costumes include
I. Kimono II. Yukata
III. Tatami IV. Zanshi
Codes:
(a) I, III and IV are correct.
(b) I, II and IV are correct.
(c) II, III and IV are correct.
(d) I, II and III are correct.

28. Digital printing leads to:
I. Economic short runs
II. Sampling in multiple colours
III. Increase in downtime
IV. Mass customization
Codes:
(a) I, II and III are correct.
(b) II, III and IV are correct.
(c) I, III and IV are correct.
(d) I, II and IV are correct.

29. The following climatic factors affect the human body:
I. Air Temperature II. Air Movement
III. Air Humidity IV. Surface Texture
V. Surrounding Background
Codes:
(a) II, III, V (b) V, I, IV
(c) I, II, III (d) II, IV, V

30. The top of range utensils include
I. Skillets II. Source pans
III. Pressure pans IV. Muffin pans
V. Pie pans
Codes:
(a) II, IV, V (b) V, I, III
(c) I, IV, V (d) I, II, III

31. Types of market are:
I. Free market product
II. Oligopoly market
III. Monopoly market
IV. Perfect competition
V. Mix market
Codes:
(a) V, I, II (b) IV, V, I
(c) II, III, IV (d) V, II, I

32. Three dimensional aids used for class room teaching are:
I. Specimen II. Flashcards
III. Models IV. Slides
Codes:
(a) I, II and III are correct.
(b) I and III are correct.
(c) II and III are correct.
(d) II and IV are correct.

33. Which of the following gives the meaning of monitoring?
    I. Finding out the weaknesses of programme implementation.
    II. Watching periodically the progress of a programme.
    III. Knowing the position in relation to the programme.
    IV. To achieve the subject matter.

    Codes:
    (a) I, II and IV are correct.
    (b) I, II and III are correct.
    (c) II, III and IV are correct.
    (d) I, III and IV are correct.

34. Which of the following comes under the three-tier system of Panchayati Raj?
    I. Village Panchayat
    II. Self-Help Groups
    III. Mahila Mandal
    IV. Zilla Parishad

    Codes:
    (a) I and IV are correct.
    (b) II and III are correct.
    (c) III and IV are correct.
    (d) IV and II are correct.

35. **Assertion (A):** 24 hours diet recall method is the most accurate method of diet survey.
    Reason (R): Food wastage can be measured by 24 hours diet recall method.

    Codes:
    (a) (A) is true but (R) is false.
    (b) Both (A) and (R) are false.
    (c) (A) is false but (R) is true.
    (d) Both (A) and (R) are true.

36. **Assertion (A):** Food irradiation is a process of food. Preservation in which food is exposed to ionizing energy.
    Reason (R): Usually isotopes of selenium and chromium are used.

    Codes:
    (a) (A) is true but (R) is false.
    (b) Both (A) and (R) are true.
    (c) (A) is false but (R) is true.
    (d) Both (A) and (R) are false.

37. **Assertion (A):** Regular monitoring of weight gain in infants is one of the commonest method of their health assessment.
    Reason (R): It is expected that a healthy baby should double its weight in a year.

    Codes:
    (a) Both (A) and (R) are true.
    (b) Both (A) and (R) are false.
    (c) (A) is true but (R) is false.
    (d) (A) is false but (R) is true.

38. **Assertion (A):** Gastric ulcers are localized erosions of the mucosal lining of the alimentary tract that comes in contact with the pancreatic juices.
    Reason (R): Highly nervous, emotional, ambitious and aggressive individuals are more prone to ulcers.

    Codes:
    (a) (A) is true and (R) is false.
    (b) (A) is wrong and (R) is true.
    (c) Both (A) and (R) are false.
    (d) Both (A) and (R) are true.

39. **Assertion (A):** In 'Theory Y', the attitude held by the manager is optimistic.
    Reason (R): He believes that employees under proper condition need to be guided and supervised.

    Codes:
    (a) (A) is true but (R) is false.
    (b) (A) is false but (R) is true.
    (c) Both (A) and (R) are true.
    (d) Both (A) and (R) are false.

40. The causes of increasing social evils are:
    I. Lack of creative parenting.
    II. The concept of education for job not for life.
    III. Unhealthy mass and multimedia communication.
    IV. No emphasis is given regarding human values, civic responsibilities and learning life skills.

Codes:
(a) I and III are correct.
(b) II and IV are correct.
(c) I, II and IV are correct.
(d) All are correct.

41. **Assertion (A):** Disabled children should be educated with only disabled ones.
Reason (R): Only disabled can understand the problems and possibilities of disabled.
Codes:
(a) Both (A) and (R) are correct.
(b) (A) is correct but (R) is wrong.
(c) (A) is wrong but (R) is correct.
(d) Both (A) and (R) are wrong.

42. **Assertion (A):** Helping the needy, homeless, abused and street children should be made compulsory to all the government employees and business holders for the nation's progress.
Reason (R): It is very difficult to change the attitude of the people.
Codes:
(a) Both (A) and (R) are correct.
(b) Both (A) and (R) are wrong.
(c) (A) is wrong but (R) is correct.
(d) (A) is correct but (R) is wrong.

43. **Assertion (A):** Dominance of the unpleasant emotions during childhood distort their outlook on life and relationship with others.
Reason (R): As they do not try to establish warm and friendly contacts with others because of their disagreeable behaviour.
Codes:
(a) Both (A) and (R) are correct.
(b) Both (A) and (R) are wrong.
(c) (A) is correct but (R) is wrong.
(d) (A) is wrong but (R) is correct.

44. **Assertion (A):** Denim fabric is generally made of open end rotor yarns in both warp and weft.
Reason (R): This method is less labour intensive and faster than conventional spinning methods however it is limited to coarser yarns.
Codes:
(a) (A) is correct but (R) is wrong.
(b) (A) is wrong but (R) is correct.
(c) Both (A) and (R) are correct.
(d) Both (A) and (R) are wrong.

45. **Assertion (A):** It is possible to dye textiles containing fibres having different dye affinity, with one solid colour using a single dye bath.
Reason (R): Dyes having affinity for different fibre types can be used to produce one solid colour.
Codes:
(a) (A) is correct but (R) is wrong.
(b) (A) is wrong and (R) is correct.
(c) Both (A) and (R) are correct.
(d) Both (A) and (R) are wrong.

46. **Assertion (A):** General fatigue results from the stress of performing tedious and boring activities and this lacks personal satisfaction.
Reason (R): Straneous and disliked activities when performed by workers, this may lead to fatigue and stress and hence the worker is not satisfied.
Codes:
(a) (A) is false, but (R) is true.
(b) (A) is true, but (R) is only partly true.
(c) (A) is true, but (R) is false.
(d) Both (A) and (R) are true.

47. **Assertion (A):** Human Engineering is one of the Ergonomics is also referred to as human factors.
Reason (R): The focus of the study is on worker fatigue.
Codes:
(a) (A) is correct but (R) is wrong.
(b) (A) is wrong and (R) is correct.

(c) Both (A) and (R) are correct.
(d) Both (A) and (R) are wrong.

48. **Assertion (A):** Extension and transfer of technology are also used interchangeably, but the two are same.
Reason (R): Extension is an educational process, transfer of technology includes additional functions of input supply and agricultural services.
Codes:
(a) (A) and (R) are not correct.
(b) (A) is not correct but (R) is correct.
(c) (A) and (R) are correct.
(d) (A) is correct but (R) is not correct.

49. **Assertion (A):** Entrepreneurs are born and not made.
Reason (R): Entrepreneurs are also made by the financial and promotional support given by the government.
Codes:
(a) (A) is correct, (R) is wrong.
(b) Both (A) and (R) are wrong.
(c) (A) is not correct, (R) is correct.
(d) Both (A) and (R) are correct.

50. Arrange the following foods in descending order according to Vitamin C content of foods:
I. Egg II. Dates
III. Amla IV. Spinach
V. Apple
Codes:
(a) I, II, III, IV, V (b) V, III, I, II, IV
(c) II, IV, V, III, I (d) III, IV, V, II, I

51. Give the sequential order of the stage of development of Atherosclerotic lesions:
I. Fatty streaks
II. Formation of connective tissue cells with fat and cholesterol
III. Thickening of intimal layers
IV. Plague formation
V. Atheroma formation
VI. Ulceration
VII. Thrombosis
Codes:
(a) III, IV, II, V, I, VI, VII
(b) II, I, IV, III, VII, VI, V
(c) I, II, III, VII, IV, V, VI
(d) II, III, I, IV, V, VI, VII

52. Give the correct sequence of a purchasing procedure used in a food service unit.
I. Selection of source
II. Writing specification
III. Requiring the Market price
IV. Checking Invoice
V. Placing order
VI. Maintaining record
VII. Recognition of needs
Codes:
(a) VII, II, I, III, V, IV, VI
(b) II, VII, I, III, IV, V, VI
(c) IV, V, III, II, I, VII, VI
(d) IV, V, III, VII, I, II, VI

53. Write the correct sequence of mentally challenged children considering their IQ level:
I. Moron II. Gifted
III. TMR IV. EMR
V. Genius
Codes:
(a) V, II, III, IV, I (b) II, IV, V, III, I
(c) I, III, IV, II, V (d) IV, I, III, V, II

54. Write the sequential order of the development of play among children.
I. Parallel play II. Associative play
III. Solitary play IV. Group play
V. Co-operative play
Codes:
(a) V, I, IV, II, III (b) III, IV, I, II, V
(c) II, III, V, I, IV (d) III, I, II, IV, V

55. What is the sequence in Fashion Merchandising?
I. Awareness of market trends and fashion forecast.
II. Sampling
III. Knowledge and sourcing of fabrics and trims

IV. Selling
V. Negotiation with Vendors
Codes:
(a) I, III, V, II, IV (b) II, I, III, V, IV
(c) V, I, II, III, IV (d) I, III, V, IV, II

56. Give the correct sequence for preparation of woollen fabric
I. Crabbing II. Bleaching
III. Carbonizing IV. Fulling
Codes:
(a) III, II, I, IV (b) I, III, IV, II
(c) II, IV, III, I (d) IV, I, II, III

57. Write in correct sequence:
I. Planning II. Feedback
III. Organization IV. Implementation
Codes:
(a) I, II, III, IV (b) IV, III, II, I
(c) III, IV, II, I (d) I, IV, III, II

58. Arrange guides of storage in sequence:
I. Place frequently used items first
II. Provide sufficient clearance
III. Store unlike items
IV. Sort items according to functions
V. Stack items having same dimensions
Codes:
(a) I, IV, III, II, V (b) V, III, I, IV, II
(c) IV, III, V, II, I (d) II, III, IV, I, V

59. Arrange in correct sequence the steps to be adopted in the evaluation of extension programme:
I. Objective
II. Sampling
III. Collection of information
IV. Analysis of data
V. Look for significant changes
VI. Report writing
Codes:
(a) VI, I, III, II, V, IV
(b) II, III, IV, V, I, VI
(c) III, II, I, IV, VI, V
(d) I, II, III, IV, V, VI

60. Arrange in correct sequence the year-wise imitation of important systems of extension in India.
I. Community Development Block
II. Democratic Decentralization
III. Community Development Programme
IV. National Extension Service
Codes:
(a) I, IV, III, II (b) II, III, I, IV
(c) III, IV, I, II (d) IV, I, III, II

61. Arrange in correct sequence the steps to be followed for self-employment:
I. Draft a business plan
II. Analyse the business
III. Personal evaluation
IV. Make it legal
V. Set up shop
VI. Get financed
VII. Trial and Error
Codes:
(a) I, II, III, V, VI, IV, VII
(b) III, II, IV, I, VI, V, VII
(c) II, I, V, IV, VI, III, VII
(d) III, VI, IV, I, II, V, VII

62. Match the properties of egg given in List I with the food items given in List II:
List I (Properies of egg)
A. Interfering B. Coating
C. Clarifying D. Emulsifying
E. Thickening F. Leavening
List II (Food items)
i. Custard ii. Mayonnaise
iii. Cake iv. Cutlet
v. Clear soup vi. Ice cream
vii. Short crust pastry

Codes:	**A**	**B**	**C**	**D**	**E**	**F**
(a)	vi	iv	v	ii	i	iii
(b)	i	ii	v	iv	vi	vii
(c)	iii	ii	i	v	vi	iv
(d)	vii	v	iv	ii	iii	i

63. Match the spices in List I with its sources in List II:

List I

A. Asafoetida B. Saffron
C. Clove D. Mace
E. Turmeric F. Fenugreek

List II

i. Flower bud ii. Lentil
iii. Gum resin iv. Fragrant stigma
v. Aromatic root vi. Orange fleshy cover
vii. Bark

Codes:	A	B	C	D	E	F
(a)	i	ii	iii	vi	v	iv
(b)	iii	iv	i	vi	v	ii
(c)	i	vi	ii	v	iv	iii
(d)	ii	v	vi	vii	i	iii

64. Match the hormones in List I with diseases in List II:

List I (Hormones)

A. Insulin B. TSH
C. Renin Angiotensin D. Cortisol

List II (Diseases)

i. Goitre
ii. Hypertension
iii. Cushing Syndrome
iv. Diabetes
v. Gout

Codes:	A	B	C	D
(a)	i	ii	iii	iv
(b)	iii	iv	i	v
(c)	iv	i	ii	iii
(d)	v	iv	ii	iii

65. Match the following equipments in List I with areas in food service units in List II

List I (Equipments)	List II (Food service units)
A. Weighing balance	i. Cold store
B. Food trolley	ii. Preparation
C. Food processor	iii. Store room (dry)
D. Salamander	iv. Pantry
E. Steam cooker	v. Production
	vi. Service counter

Codes:	A	B	C	D	E
(a)	i	iii	iv	ii	v
(b)	ii	i	iii	vi	v
(c)	iv	ii	i	iii	vi
(d)	iii	vi	ii	iv	v

66. Match the foods in List I with additives in List II:

List I	List II
A. Butter	i. BHA
B. Cake	ii. Sodium Benzoate
C. Oil	iii. Baking powder
D. Rose syrup	iv. Annatto
E. Orange squash	v. MSG
	vi. Cochineal

Codes:	A	B	C	D	E
(a)	i	ii	iv	iii	v
(b)	ii	i	iii	v	iv
(c)	iv	iii	v	vi	i
(d)	iv	iii	i	vi	ii

67. Match List I correctly with List II:

List I

A. Anorexia nervosa B. Dementia
C. Addiction D. Pragmatism

List II

i. Learning by doing
ii. Eating disorder
iii. Psychological dependence
iv. Neurological disorder
v. Emotional imbalance

Codes:	A	B	C	D
(a)	v	ii	iii	iv
(b)	iv	ii	i	iii
(c)	iii	iv	ii	v
(d)	ii	v	i	iii

68. Match the List I correctly with List II:

List I

A. Froebel
B. McMillan sisters
C. Science experience
D. Story telling

List II

i. Germination
ii. Puppet show
iii. Nursery school
iv. Father of Kindergarten
v. Field visit

Codes:	A	B	C	D
(a)	v	iii	iv	ii
(b)	iv	iii	i	ii
(c)	ii	iii	i	iv
(d)	iii	ii	iv	v

69. Match the fabrics given in List I with their weaves given in List II:

List I	List II
A. Huckaback	i. Surface figure weave
B. Dotted Swiss	ii. Basket weave
C. Hopsacking	iii. Twill weave
D. Gaberdine	vi. Leno weave
E. Gauze	v. Dobby weave

Codes:	A	B	C	D	E
(a)	v	i	ii	iii	iv
(b)	i	ii	iii	iv	v
(c)	iv	iii	i	v	ii
(d)	ii	iv	v	i	iii

70. Match the dyes in List I with characteristics given in List II:

List I

A. Vat dyes B. Reactive dyes
C. Direct dyes D. Disperse dyes

List II

i. Forms a co-valent bond with fibres
ii. Non-ionic in nature used for synthetic fibres
iii. Carboxylic group
iv. Anionic in nature with poor wash fastness

Codes:	A	B	C	D
(a)	ii	iii	i	iv
(b)	iii	i	iv	ii
(c)	i	iv	iii	ii
(d)	iv	iii	ii	i

71. Match the equipments from List I to their principles of work from List II:

List I (Equipments)

A. Microwave B. Refrigerator
C. Washing D. Vacuum cleaner

List II (Principles of work)

i. Agitation & Centrifugation
ii. Suction
iii. Radiation machine
iv. Condensation
v. Convection

Codes:	A	B	C	D
(a)	vi	i	ii	iii
(b)	i	iii	ii	iv
(c)	iii	iv	i	ii
(d)	ii	iii	iv	v

72. Match the details of list of items in List I with List II:

List I

A. One wall kitchen
B. Parallel wall kitchen
C. "L" shaped kitchen
D. "V" shaped kitchen

List II

i. Two major appliance one and third on adjacent wall
ii. Two major kitchen appliances one and third on opposite wall
iii. Sink, refrigerator, range on one wall
iv. One major appliance on each of three adjacent walls

Codes:	A	B	C	D
(a)	i	ii	iv	iii
(b)	iii	ii	i	iv
(c)	iv	i	ii	iii
(d)	iii	iv	i	ii

73. Match the items given in List I with List II:

List I

A. Indira Awaas Yojana
B. Pradhan Mantri Gram Sadak Yojana
C. Integrated Women Sanitary Complex
D. Integrated Child Development Services

List II

i. Sanitation
ii. Women and child welfare

iii. Road connectivity
iv. Shelter

Codes:	A	B	C	D
(a)	iii	i	ii	iv
(b)	iv	iii	i	ii
(c)	iv	iii	ii	i
(d)	ii	i	iv	iii

74. Match the nature of projection given in List I with its projections List II:

List I

A. Direct projection
B. Indirect projection
C. Reflective projection
D. Non-projected

List II

i. Opaque projector
ii. Television
iii. Cinema projector
iv. Over head projector

Codes:	A	B	C	D
(a)	iii	iv	i	ii
(b)	iv	i	ii	iii
(c)	iii	i	iv	ii
(d)	ii	iii	i	iv

75. Match the organizations given in List I with their roles given in List II:

List I	List II
A. Mobile cretches	i. Regulation
B. IWS	ii. Research
C. ICAR	iii. Culture
D. UNESCO	iv. Exports
	v. Child's health

Codes:	A	B	C	D
(a)	i	ii	iii	iv
(b)	iv	v	iii	ii
(c)	v	iv	ii	iii
(d)	ii	iii	iv	i

ANSWERS

1. (d)	2. (a)	3. (b)	4. (b)	5. (c)
6. (c)	7. (b)	8. (b)	9. (b)	10. (b)
11. (a)	12. (c)	13. (c)	14. (c)	15. (d)
16. (b)	17. (a)	18. (c)	19. (b)	20. (d)
21. (a)	22. (b)	23. (c)	24. (b)	25. (c)
26. (c)	27. (b)	28. (d)	29. (c)	30. (d)
31. (c)	32. (b)	33. (b)	34. (a)	35. (b)
36. (a)	37. (c)	38. (b)	39. (a)	40. (d)
41. (d)	42. (d)	43. (a)	44. (c)	45. (c)
46. (d)	47. (a)	48. (b	49. (c)	50. (d)
51. (d)	52. (a)	53. (c)	54. (d)	55. (a)
56. (a)	57. (d)	58. (c)	59. (d)	60. (c)
61. (b)	62. (a)	63. (b)	64. (c)	65. (d)
66. (d)	67. (d)	68. (b)	69. (a)	70. (b)
71. (c)	72. (c)	73. (b)	74. (a)	75. (c)

DECEMBER–2012

Note: This paper contains Sixty (60) multiple choice questions, each question carrying two (2) marks. Candidate is expected to answer any Fifty (50) questions. In case more than Fifty (50) questions are attempted, only the first Fifty (50) questions will be evaluated.

PAPER–I

1. The English word 'Communication' is derived from the words
   (a) Communis and Communicare
   (b) Communist and Commune
   (c) Communism and Communalism
   (d) Communion and Common sense
2. Chinese Cultural Revolution leader Mao Zedong used a type of communication to talk to the masses is known as
   (a) Mass line communication
   (b) Group communication
   (c) Participatory communication
   (d) Dialogue communication
3. Conversing with the spirits and ancestors is termed as
   (a) Transpersonal communication
   (b) Intrapersonal communication
   (c) Interpersonal communication
   (d) Face-to-face communication
4. The largest circulated daily newspaper among the following is
   (a) The Times of India
   (b) The Indian Express
   (c) The Hindu
   (d) The Deccan Herald
5. The pioneer of the silent feature film in India was
   (a) K.A. Abbas
   (b) Satyajit Ray
   (c) B.R. Chopra
   (d) Dada Sahib Phalke
6. Classroom communication of a teacher rests on the principle of
   (a) Infotainment (b) Edutainment
   (c) Entertainment (d) Power equation
7. The missing number in the series:
   0, 6, 24, 60, 120, ?, 336, is
   (a) 240 (b) 220
   (c) 280 (d) 210
8. A group of 7 members having a majority of boys is to be formed out of 6 boys and 4 girls. The number of ways the group can be formed is
   (a) 80 (b) 100
   (c) 90 (d) 110
9. The number of observations in a group is 40. The average of the first 10 members is 4.5 and the average of the remaining 30 members is 3.5. The average of the whole group is
   (a) 4 (b) 15/2
   (c) 15/4 (d) 6
10. If MOHAN is represented by the code KMFYL, then COUNT will be represented by
    (a) AMSLR (b) MSLAR
    (c) MASRL (d) SAMLR
11. The sum of the ages of two persons A and B is 50. 5 years ago, the ratio of their

ages was 5/3. The present age of A and B are

(a) 30, 20 (b) 35, 15
(c) 38, 12 (d) 40, 10

12. Let *a* means minus (–), *b* means multiplied by (×), C means divided by (÷) and D means plus (+). The value of 90 D 9 *a* 29 C 10 *b* 2 is

(a) 8 (b) 10
(c) 12 (d) 14

13. Consider the Assertion I and Assertion II and select the right code given below:

Assertion I : Even Bank-lockers are not safe. Thieves can break them and take away your wealth. But thieves cannot go to heaven. So you should keep your wealth in heaven.

Assertion II: The difference of skin-colour of beings is because of the distance from the sun and not because of some permanent traits. Skin-colour is the result of body's reaction to the sun and its rays.

Codes:

(a) Both the assertions I and II are forms of argument.
(b) The assertion I is an argument but the assertion II is not.
(c) The assertion II is an argument but the assertion I is not.
(d) Both the assertions are explanations of facts.

14. By which of the following proposition, the proposition 'some men are not honest' is contradicted?

(a) All men are honest.
(b) Some men are honest.
(c) No men are honest.
(d) All of the above.

15. A stipulative definition is

(a) always true
(b) always false
(c) sometimes true sometimes false
(d) neither true nor false

16. Choose the appropriate alternative given in the codes to replace the question mark.

Examiner – Examinee, Pleader – Client, Preceptor – ?

(a) Customer (b) Path-finder
(c) Perceiver (d) Disciple

17. If the statement 'most of the students are obedient' is taken to be true, which one of the following pair of statements can be claimed to be true?

I. All obedient persons are students.
II. All students are obedient.
III. Some students are obedient.
IV. Some students are not disobedient.

Codes:

(a) I & II (b) II & III
(c) III & IV (d) II & IV

18. Choose the right code:

A deductive argument claims that:

I. The conclusion does not claim something more than that which is contained in the premises.
II. The conclusion is supported by the premise/premises conclusively.
III. If the conclusion is false, then premise/premises may be either true or false.
IV. If premise/combination of premises is true, then conclusion must be true.

Codes:

(a) I and II (b) I and III
(c) II and III (d) All the above

On the basis of the data given in the following table, give answers to questions from 19 to 24:

Government Expenditures on Social Services
(As percent of total expenditure)

Sl.No.	Items	2007-08	2008-09	2009-10	2010-11
	Social Services	11.06	12.94	13.06	14.02
(a)	Education, sports & youth affairs	4.02	4.04	3.96	4.46
(b)	Health & family welfare	2.05	1.91	1.90	2.03
(c)	Water supply, housing, etc.	2.02	2.31	2.20	2.27
(d)	Information & broadcasting	0.22	0.22	0.20	0.22
(e)	Welfare to SC/ST & OBC	0.36	0.35	0.41	0.63
(f)	Labour and employment	0.27	0.27	0.22	0.25
(g)	Social welfare & nutrition	0.82	0.72	0.79	1.06
(h)	North-eastern areas	0.00	1.56	1.50	1.75
(i)	Other social services	1.29	1.55	1.87	1.34
	Total Government expenditure	100.00	100.00	100.00	100.00

19. How many activities in the social services are there where the expenditure has been less than 5 percent of the total expenditures incurred on the social services in 2008-09?
(a) One (b) Three
(c) Five (d) All the above

20. In which year, the expenditures on the social services have increased at the highest rate?
(a) 2007-08 (b) 2008-09
(c) 2009-10 (d) 2010-11

21. Which of the following activities remains almost stagnant in terms of share of expenditures?
(a) North-eastern areas
(b) Welfare to SC/ST & OBC
(c) Information & broadcasting
(d) Social welfare and nutrition

22. Which of the following item's expenditure share is almost equal to the remaining three items in the given years?
(a) Information & broadcasting
(b) Welfare to SC/ST and OBC
(c) Labour and employment
(d) Social welfare & nutrition

23. Which of the following items of social services has registered the highest rate of increase in expenditures during 2007-08 to 2010-11?
(a) Education, sports & youth affairs
(b) Welfare to SC/ST & OBC
(c) Social welfare & nutrition
(d) Overall social services

24. Which of the following items has registered the highest rate of decline in terms of expenditure during 2007-08 to 2009-10?
(a) Labour and employment
(b) Health & family welfare
(c) Social welfare & nutrition
(d) Education, sports & youth affairs

25. ALU stands for
(a) American Logic Unit
(b) Alternate Local Unit
(c) Alternating Logic Unit
(d) Arithmetic Logic Unit

26. A Personal Computer uses a number of chips mounted on a circuit board called
(a) Microprocessor (b) System Board
(c) Daughter Board (d) Mother Board

27. Computer Virus is a
(a) Hardware (b) Bacteria
(c) Software (d) None of these

28. Which one of the following is correct?

(a) $(17)_{10} = (17)_{16}$
(b) $(17)_{10} = (17)_{8}$
(c) $(17)_{10} = (10111)_{2}$
(d) $(17)_{10} = (10001)_{2}$

29. The file extension of MS-Word document in Office 2007 is ______.
(a) .pdf (b) .doc
(c) .docx (d) .txt

30. ______ is a protocol used by e-mail clients to download e-mails to your computer.
(a) TCP (b) FTP
(c) SMTP (d) POP

31. Which of the following is a source of methane?
(a) Wetlands
(b) Foam Industry
(c) Thermal Power Plants
(d) Cement Industry

32. 'Minamata disaster' in Japan was caused by pollution due to
(a) Lead (b) Mercury
(c) Cadmium (d) Zinc

33. Biomagnification means increase in the
(a) concentration of pollutants in living organisms
(b) number of species
(c) size of living organisms
(d) biomass

34. Nagoya Protocol is related to
(a) Climate change
(b) Ozone depletion
(c) Hazardous waste
(d) Biodiversity

35. The second most important source after fossil fuels contributing to India's energy needs is
(a) Solar energy (b) Nuclear energy
(c) Hydropower (d) Wind energy

36. In case of earthquakes, an increase of magnitude 1 on Richter Scale implies
(a) a ten-fold increase in the amplitude of seismic waves.
(b) a ten-fold increase in the energy of the seismic waves.
(c) two-fold increase in the amplitude of seismic waves.
(d) two-fold increase in the energy of seismic waves.

37. Which of the following is not a measure of Human Development Index?
(a) Literacy Rate
(b) Gross Enrolment
(c) Sex Ratio
(d) Life Expectancy

38. India has the highest number of students in colleges after
(a) the U.K. (b) the U.S.A.
(c) Australia (d) Canada

39. Which of the following statement(s) is/are not correct about the Attorney General of India?
1. The President appoints a person, who is qualified to be a Judge of a High Court, to be the Attorney General of India.
2. He has the right of audience in all the Courts of the country.
3. He has the right to take part in the proceedings of the Lok Sabha and the Rajya Sabha.
4. He has a fixed tenure.
Select the correct answer from the codes given below:

Codes:
(a) 1 and 4 (b) 2, 3 and 4
(c) 3 and 4 (d) 3 only

40. Which of the following prefix President Pranab Mukherjee desires to be discontinued while interacting with Indian dignitaries as well as in official notings?
1. His Excellency 2. Mahamahim
3. Hon'ble 4. Shri/Smt.

Select the correct answer from the codes given below:

Codes:

(a) 1 and 3 (b) 2 and 3
(c) 1 and 2 (d) 1, 2 and 3

41. Which of the following can be done under conditions of financial emergency?
   1. State Legislative Assemblies can be abolished.
   2. Central Government can acquire control over the budget and expenditure of States.
   3. Salaries of the Judges of the High Courts and the Supreme Court can be reduced.
   4. Right to Constitutional Remedies can be suspended.

   Select the correct answer from the codes given below:

   Codes:

   (a) 1, 2 and 3 (b) 2, 3 and 4
   (c) 1 and 2 (d) 2 and 3

42. Match List I with List II and select the correct answer from the codes given below:

   List I
   (A) Poverty Reduction Programme
   (B) Human Development Scheme
   (C) Social Assistance Scheme
   (D) Minimum Need Scheme

   List II
   (i) Mid-day Meals
   (ii) Indira Awas Yojana (IAY)
   (iii) National Old Age Pension (NOAP)
   (iv) MNREGA

Codes:	**A**	**B**	**C**	**D**
(a)	(iv)	(i)	(iii)	(ii)
(b)	(ii)	(iii)	(iv)	(i)
(c)	(iii)	(iv)	(i)	(ii)
(d)	(iv)	(iii)	(ii)	(i)

43. For an efficient and durable learning, learner should have
   (a) ability to learn only
   (b) requisite level of motivation only
   (c) opportunities to learn only
   (d) desired level of ability and motivation

44. Classroom communication must be
   (a) Teacher centric
   (b) Student centric
   (c) General centric
   (d) Textbook centric

45. The best method of teaching is to
   (a) impart information
   (b) ask students to read books
   (c) suggest good reference material
   (d) initiate a discussion and participate in it

46. Interaction inside the classroom should generate
   (a) Argument (b) Information
   (c) Ideas (d) Controversy

47. "Spare the rod and spoil the child", gives the message that
   (a) punishment in the class should be banned.
   (b) corporal punishment is not acceptable.
   (c) undesirable behaviour must be punished.
   (d) children should be beaten with rods.

48. The type of communication that the teacher has in the classroom, is termed as
   (a) Interpersonal
   (b) Mass communication
   (c) Group communication
   (d) Face-to-face communication

49. Which one of the following is an indication of the quality of a research journal?
   (a) Impact factor (b) h-index
   (c) g-index (d) i10-index

50. Good 'research ethics' means
   (a) Not disclosing the holdings of shares/stocks in a company that sponsors your research.

(b) Assigning a particular research problem to one Ph.D./research student only.
(c) Discussing with your colleagues confidential data from a research paper that you are reviewing for an academic journal.
(d) Submitting the same research manuscript for publishing in more than one journal.

51. Which of the following sampling methods is based on probability?
(a) Convenience sampling
(b) Quota sampling
(c) Judgement sampling
(d) Stratified sampling

52. Which one of the following references is written according to American Psychological Association (APA) format?
(a) Sharma, V. (2010). Fundamentals of Computer Science.
New Delhi: Tata McGraw Hill
(b) Sharma, V. 2010. Fundamentals of Computer Science.
New Delhi: Tata McGraw Hill
(c) Sharma.V. 2010. Fundamentals of Computer Science,
New Delhi: Tata McGraw Hill
(d) Sharma, V. (2010), Fundamentals of Computer Science,
New Delhi: Tata McGraw Hill

53. Arrange the following steps of research in correct sequence:
1. Identification of research problem
2. Listing of research objectives
3. Collection of data
4. Methodology
5. Data analysis
6. Results and discussion
(a) 1, 2, 3, 4, 5, 6 (b) 1, 2, 4, 3, 5, 6
(c) 2, 1, 3, 4, 5, 6 (d) 2, 1, 4, 3, 5, 6

54. Identify the incorrect statement:
(a) A hypothesis is made on the basis of limited evidence as a starting point for further investigations.
(b) A hypothesis is a basis for reasoning without any assumption of its truth.
(c) Hypothesis is a proposed explanation for a phenomenon.
(d) Scientific hypothesis is a scientific theory.

Read the following passage carefully and answer the questions (55 to 60):

The popular view of towns and cities in developing countries and of urbanization process is that despite the benefits and comforts it brings, the emergence of such cities connotes environmental degradation, generation of slums and squatters, urban poverty, unemployment, crimes, lawlessness, traffic chaos etc. But what is the reality? Given the unprecedental increase in urban population over the last 50 years from 300 million in 1950 to 2 billion in 2000 in developing countries, the wonder really is how well the world has coped, and not how badly.

In general, the urban quality of life has improved in terms of availability of water and sanitation, power, health and education, communication and transport. By way of illustration, a large number of urban residents have been provided with improved water in urban areas in Asia's largest countries such as China, India, Indonesia and Philippines. Despite that, the access to improved water in terms of percentage of total urban population seems to have declined during the last decade of 20th century, though in absolute numbers, millions of additional urbanites, have been provided improved services. These countries have made significant progress in the provision of sanitation services too, together, providing for an additional population of more than 293 million citizens within a decade (1990-2000). These improvements must be viewed against the backdrop of rapidly increasing urban population, fiscal crunch and strained human resources and efficient and quality-oriented public management.

55. The popular view about the process of urbanization in developing countries is
    (a) Positive (b) Negative
    (c) Neutral (d) Unspecified
56. The average annual increase in the number of urbanites in developing countries, from 1950 to 2000 A.D. was close to
    (a) 30 million (b) 40 million
    (c) 50 million (d) 60 million
57. The reality of urbanization is reflected in
    (a) How well the situation has been managed.
    (b) How badly the situation has gone out of control.
    (c) How fast has been the tempo of urbanization.
    (d) How fast the environment has degraded.
58. Which one of the following is not considered as an indicator of urban quality of life?
    (a) Tempo of urbanization
    (b) Provision of basic services
    (c) Access to social amenities
    (d) All of the above
59. The author in this passage has tried to focus on
    (a) Extension of Knowledge
    (b) Generation of Environmental Consciousness
    (c) Analytical Reasoning
    (d) Descriptive Statement
60. In the above passage, the author intends to state
    (a) The hazards of the urban life
    (b) The sufferings of the urban life
    (c) The awareness of human progress
    (d) The limits to growth

ANSWERS

1. (a)	2. (d)	3. (a)	4. (a)	5. (d)
6. (b)	7. (d)	8. (b)	9. (c)	10. (a)
11. (a)	12. (d)	13. (a)	14. (a)	15. (d)
16. (c)	17. (c)	18. (d)	19. (d)	20. (d)
21. (c)	22. (d)	23. (d)	24. (b)	25. (d)
26. (d)	27. (c)	28. (d)	29. (b)	30. (d)
31. (a)	32. (b)	33. (a)	34. (d)	35. (c)
36. (a)	37. (c)	38. (b)	39. (d)	40. (c)
41. (c)	42. (a)	43. (d)	44. (b)	45. (d)
46. (c)	47. (c)	48. (c)	49. (a)	50. (a)
51. (d)	52. (a)	53. (b)	54. (d)	55. (b)
56. (a)	57. (a)	58. (a)	59. (d)	60. (d)

PAPER–II

Note: This paper contains fifty (50) objective type questions, each question carrying two (2) marks. All questions are compulsory.

1. What is the primary reason for blanching food?
    (a) Cleans the food
    (b) Prevents pest infestation
    (c) Inactivates enzymes in food
    (d) Prevents food from drying
2. RDA's for Indian women are based on reference woman who has
    (a) Body weight 50 kg and height 1.40 m
    (b) Body weight 55 kg and height 1.61 m

(c) Body weight 48 kg and height 1.56 m
(d) Body weight 52 kg and height 1.37 m

3. Which of the following is not a management approach?
(a) Classic
(b) System Approach
(c) Human Relation
(d) Double Entry System

4. Which of the following holds the bobbin in the sewing machine?
(a) Feed dog
(b) Pressure foot
(c) Oscillating hook
(d) Thread take up lever

5. Which of the following does not represent Kasuti Embroidery?
(a) Menthi (b) Aari
(c) Gavanti (d) Murgi

6. Principle of operation of an electric water heater is by
(a) Convection (b) Radiation
(c) Conduction (d) Induction

7. Sociometry is a tool to measure child's
(a) Intelligence level
(b) Behaviour problems
(c) Relationship with peers
(d) Relationship with parents

8. DRDA is functioning at
(a) District level (b) Block level
(c) Village level (d) State level

9. ABC of Poster
(a) Attractive, Brief, Clear
(b) Attention, Brief, Clarity
(c) Attractive, Bold, Clear
(d) Attractive, Bold, Colourful

10. Type I error is made when
(a) True null hypothesis is rejected
(b) True null hypothesis is accepted
(c) False null hypothesis is rejected
(d) False null hypothesis is accepted

11. Which of the following foods are rich in omega 3 fatty acids?
(A) Lard (B) Butter
(C) Fatty fish (D) Olive oil
(E) Mustard seeds (F) Walnut
Codes:
(a) (A), (B), (C) (b) (C), (E), (F)
(c) (E), (F), (B) (d) (F), (C), (D)

12. Which of the following micro-organisms cause food borne intoxication?
(A) *Staphylococcus aureus*
(B) *E. coli*
(C) *Clostridium botulinum*
(D) *Listeria monocytogenes*
(E) *Salmonella*
Codes:
(a) (A) and (B) (b) (A) and (C)
(c) (C) and (D) (d) (D) and (E)

13. Which of the following equipments are not used in the kitchen?
(A) Oven (B) Cooking range
(C) Tally machine (D) Baine marie
(E) Blender (F) Potato peeler
Codes:
(a) (A) and (D) (b) (A) and (C)
(c) (C) and (D) (d) (E) and (F)

14. Correct layouts of unidirectional fabrics for garment cutting are
(i) Crosswise fold (ii) Lengthwise fold
(iii) Double fold (iv) Open
Codes:
(a) (i), (ii) and (iii) are correct.
(b) (ii), (iii) and (iv) are correct.
(c) (i), (iii) and (iv) are correct.
(d) (i), (ii) and (iv) are correct.

15. Following are novelty yarns.
(i) Crepe yarn (ii) Bouclé yarn
(iii) Slub yarn (iv) Flock yarn
Codes:
(a) (i), (ii) and (iv) are correct.
(b) (i), (iii) and (iv) are correct.

(c) (i), (ii) and (iii) are correct.
(d) (ii), (iii) and (iv) are correct.

16. Components of immplementing are
(i) Adjusting (ii) Facilitating
(iii) Controlling (iv) Checking
Codes:
(a) (i) and (iii) are correct.
(b) (ii) and (iii) are correct.
(c) (ii) and (iv) are correct.
(d) (iii) and (iv) are correct.

17. Language development in children is promoted through:
(i) Story telling
(ii) Conversation
(iii) Social participation
(iv) Solitary play
Codes:
(a) (i) and (iii) are correct.
(b) (ii) and (iii) are correct.
(c) (i), (ii) and (iii) are correct.
(d) (ii), (iii) and (iv) are correct.

18. Aspects of a Good Lesson Plan
(i) Objectives
(ii) Teacher's Activities
(iii) Learning Experiences
(iv) Teaching Aids
(v) Appraisal
Codes:
(a) (i), (iii), (iv) and (v) are correct.
(b) (ii), (iii), (iv) and (v) are correct.
(c) (i), (iv) and (v) are correct.
(d) All of the above.

19. Which among the following are the community services offered in the interest of the public?
(i) Protection (ii) Transport
(iii) Social (iv) Communication
Codes:
(a) (i), (ii) and (iii) are correct.
(b) (ii), (iii) and (iv) are correct.
(c) (i), (ii) and (iv) are correct.
(d) (i), (iii) and (iv) are correct.

20. The variance is
(i) directly proportional to the average squared difference between all pairs of observations.
(ii) smallest when calculated from the mean.
(iii) denoted by symbol σ
(iv) described as the dispersion of the distribution
Codes:
(a) (i), (ii) and (iv) are correct.
(b) (i), (ii) and (iii) are correct.
(c) (ii), (iii) and (iv) are correct.
(d) All are correct.

21. **Assertion (A):** Pasteurization in milk is done to destroy the microbes.
Reason (R): It is tested for the presence of lactic acid in milk.
Codes:
(a) Both (A) and (R) are false.
(b) Both (A) and (R) are true.
(c) (A) is true but (R) is false.
(d) (A) is false but (R) is true.

22. **Assertion (A):** Acute Renal Failure means the kidneys have failed suddenly.
Reason (R): Various toxins or severe blood loss or trauma affect kidney functioning.
Codes:
(a) (A) is false and (R) is true.
(b) Both (A) and (R) are true.
(c) Both (A) and (R) are false.
(d) (A) is true and (R) is false.

23. **Assertion (A):** Invoice is a document that comes with supplies.
Reason (R): Cash payment has to be made on the basis of it.
Codes:
(a) (A) and (R) are true.
(b) (A) and (R) are false.
(c) (R) is true, (A) is false.
(d) (A) is true, (R) is false.

24. **Assertion (A):** Both garment bias and true bias can be used for finishing necklines.
    Reason (R): Both have same amount of stretch.
    Codes:
    (a) Both (A) and (R) are false.
    (b) (A) is true and (R) is false.
    (c) Both (A) and (R) are true.
    (d) (A) is false and (R) is true.
25. **Assertion (A):** Cross dyeing and union dyeing are same.
    Reason (R): Both may produce multicoloured effects.
    Codes:
    (a) Both (A) and (R) are false.
    (b) (A) is true and (R) is false.
    (c) Both (A) and (R) are true.
    (d) (A) is false and (R) is true.
26. **Assertion (A):** Standing in a static posture is fatiguing.
    Reason (R): Blood circulation is affected in the extremities while standing for work.
    Codes:
    (a) (A) is false but (R) is true.
    (b) (A) is true and (R) is false.
    (c) Both (A) and (R) are true, but (R) is not the complete explanation.
    (d) Both (A) and (R) are false.
27. **Assertion (A):** Self-concept is an image of a person. It is the way one perceives oneself; one's abilities and limitations.
    Reason (R): Self-concept is the understanding of the self, in comparison to the past self, without social comparison.
    Codes:
    (a) Both (A) and (R) are correct.
    (b) (R) is correct and (A) is wrong.
    (c) (A) is correct and (R) is wrong.
    (d) Both (A) and (R) are wrong.
28. **Assertion (A):** Home is a place for development of both sexes through equal opportunities.
    Reason (R): The personal and professional development of both sexes is not possible within home.
    Codes:
    (a) Both (A) and (R) are true.
    (b) (A) is false and (R) is true.
    (c) (A) is true, but (R) is false.
    (d) Both (A) and (R) are false.
29. **Assertion (A):** Electronic media is a mass media.
    Reason (R): All mass media are not electronic media.
    Codes:
    (a) (A) is correct, but (R) is wrong.
    (b) Both (A) and (R) are wrong.
    (c) Both (A) and (R) are correct.
    (d) (A) is wrong, but (R) is correct.
30. **Assertion (A):** The existence of a correlation between two variables can be shown to exist only when there is variability.
    Reason (R): If one of the variables is a constant, with no variability, then the correlation coefficient is not even defined.
    Codes:
    (a) Both (A) and (R) are true and (R) is the correct explanation.
    (b) Both (A) and (R) are not true.
    (c) (A) is true and (R) is false.
    (d) (A) is false and (R) is true.
31. Give the sequence of stages of sugar cookery in making brittle.
    (A) Soft ball (B) Soft crack
    (C) Hard crack (D) Two thread
    (E) Firm ball
    Codes:
    (a) (A), (B), (C), (E), (D)
    (b) (D), (A), (E), (B), (C)
    (c) (E), (D), (C), (B), (A)
    (d) (B), (D), (E), (A), (C)

32. For a successful outcome of the nutrition programme for the community, state the sequential order of steps to be taken.
(A) Implementation
(B) Mobilising resources
(C) Monitoring and evaluation
(D) Prioritise problem
(E) Identify target
(F) Setting objectives
Codes:
(a) (E), (D), (F), (B), (A), (C)
(b) (A), (D), (E), (F), (B), (C)
(c) (D), (E), (F), (A), (B), (C)
(d) (D), (F), (E), (B), (C), (A)

33. Give the correct sequence of managerial functions listed below:
(A) Reporting (B) Staffing
(C) Planning (D) Organising
(E) Co-ordinating (F) Budgeting
(G) Directing
Codes:
(a) (C), (D), (B), (F), (G), (A), (E)
(b) (C), (D), (B), (G), (E), (A), (F)
(c) (B), (D), (F), (C), (A), (G), (E)
(d) (E), (G), (D), (F), (B), (A), (C)

34. Give the correct sequence for applying the following in a garment:
(A) Interlining (B) Interfacing
(C) Underlining (D) Lining
Codes:
(a) (A), (B), (C), (D) (b) (B), (C), (A), (D)
(c) (C), (D), (B), (A) (d) (D), (A), (C), (B)

35. Give the correct sequence of removing lipstick stain from fabric.
(A) Wash in hot soapy water.
(B) Sponge with a grease solvent.
(C) Bleach the stain.
(D) Rinse in hot water and dry in sun.
Codes:
(a) (A), (B), (C), (D)
(b) (D), (C), (B), (A)
(c) (C), (D), (A), (B)
(d) (B), (A), (C), (D)

36. How are colours classified? Indicate the correct sequence.
(a) Secondary, primary, intermediate, tertiary, quaternary
(b) Binary, primary, intermediate, quaternary, tertiary
(c) Primary, secondary, intermediate, tertiary, quarternary
(d) Binary, secondary, intermediate, tertiary, quaternary

37. Arrange constituent processes of observational learning in correct sequence:
(i) Production (ii) Motivation
(iii) Retention (iv) Attention
Codes:
(a) (iii), (iv), (i) and (ii)
(b) (iv), (iii), (i) and (ii)
(c) (ii), (i), (iii) and (iv)
(d) (i), (ii), (iii) and (iv)

38. The sequential order of Extension Educational Process is
(i) Objectives (ii) Teaching
(iii) Situation (iv) Reconsideration
(v) Evaluation
Codes:
(a) (ii), (i), (iii), (iv), (v)
(b) (iii), (ii), (i), (v), (iv)
(c) (iii), (i), (ii), (v), (iv)
(d) (i), (iii), (ii), (iv), (v)

39. Panchayati Raj Institution in the hierarchy of governance from grassroots upwards is
(A) Gram Sabha
(B) Block Panchayat
(C) District Panchayat
(D) Gram Panchayat
Codes:
(a) (C), (B), (D), (A)
(b) (D), (A), (B), (C)
(c) (A), (B), (D), (C)
(d) (A), (D), (B), (C)

40. Arrange the correct sequence of steps in Research.
    (i) Review of Literature
    (ii) Objectives
    (iii) Rationale
    (iv) Methodology
    (v) Interpretation
    (vi) Results
    Codes:
    (a) (ii), (iii), (iv), (i), (vi), (v)
    (b) (iii), (ii), (i), (iv), (vi), (v)
    (c) (i), (iii), (ii), (iv), (v), (vi)
    (d) (ii), (i), (iv), (iii), (v), (vi)

41. Match the foods in List I with its rich nutrients in List II:

List I (Food)	**List II (Nutrients)**
(A) Papaya	(i) Iron
(B) Orange	(ii) Calcium
(C) Dates	(iii) Vitamin C
(D) Ragi	(iv) Vitamin A

Codes:	**A**	**B**	**C**	**D**
(a)	(i)	(ii)	(iii)	(iv)
(b)	(ii)	(iii)	(iv)	(i)
(c)	(iv)	(iii)	(i)	(ii)
(d)	(iii)	(ii)	(iv)	(i)

42. Match the following biochemical tests in List I to the diseases in List II:

List I (Biochemical Tests)	**List II (Disease)**
(A) Creatinine	(i) Hepatic
(B) Bilirubin	(ii) Coronary
(C) T_3T_4	(iii) Kidney
(D) LDL	(iv) Thyriod

Codes:	**A**	**B**	**C**	**D**
(a)	(ii)	(iii)	(iv)	(i)
(b)	(iii)	(i)	(iv)	(ii)
(c)	(iv)	(iii)	(ii)	(i)
(d)	(ii)	(iii)	(i)	(iv)

43. Match the records in List I with the Department in List II where they are used:

List I (Records)	**List II (Department)**
(A) Stock book	(i) Purchase
(B) KOT	(ii) Personnel
(C) Payroll	(iii) Store record
(D) Specifications	(iv) Dining room

Codes:	**A**	**B**	**C**	**D**
(a)	(i)	(ii)	(iii)	(iv)
(b)	(iii)	(iv)	(ii)	(i)
(c)	(ii)	(iii)	(i)	(iv)
(d)	(iv)	(iii)	(ii)	(i)

44. Match List I with List II:
    List I
    (A) Diagonal basting
    (B) Hemming
    (C) Herring bone stitch
    (D) Buttonhole stitch
    List II
    (i) Permanent stitch
    (ii) Functional as well as decorative
    (iii) Temporary stitch
    (iv) Decorative stitch

Codes:	**A**	**B**	**C**	**D**
(a)	(i)	(iv)	(iii)	(ii)
(b)	(ii)	(iii)	(i)	(iv)
(c)	(iii)	(i)	(iv)	(ii)
(d)	(iv)	(iii)	(ii)	(i)

45. Match List I with List II:
    List I
    (A) Wale (B) Weft
    (C) Warp (D) Courses
    List II
    (i) Series of loops extending crosswise
    (ii) Longitudinal yarns
    (iii) Crosswise yarns
    (iv) Column of loops parallel to length

Codes:	**A**	**B**	**C**	**D**
(a)	(i)	(iv)	(iii)	(ii)
(b)	(ii)	(i)	(iv)	(iii)
(c)	(iv)	(iii)	(ii)	(i)
(d)	(iii)	(ii)	(i)	(iv)

46. Match List I with List II:

List I

(A) Orientation of the building
(B) Disposition of rooms
(C) Personal protection
(D) Spaciousness

List II

(i) Grouping (ii) Roominess
(iii) Aspect (iv) Privacy

Codes:	A	B	C	D
(a)	(i)	(ii)	(iii)	(iv)
(b)	(iv)	(ii)	(iii)	(i)
(c)	(iii)	(i)	(iv)	(ii)
(d)	(iv)	(ii)	(i)	(iii)

47. Match the items of List I with List II:

List I

(A) First menstruation
(B) Authoritative parenting
(C) Observational learning
(D) ICCW

List II

(i) Albert Bandura
(ii) Balwadis and day care centres
(iii) Spermache
(iv) Democratic parenting
(v) Menarche
(vi) Permissive parenting

Codes:	A	B	C	D
(a)	(v)	(iv)	(i)	(ii)
(b)	(iii)	(i)	(ii)	(iv)
(c)	(iv)	(ii)	(i)	(iii)
(d)	(v)	(iv)	(ii)	(i)

48. Match List I with List II:

List I

(A) Personal letter
(B) Method demonstration
(C) Television
(D) Campaign

List II

(i) Audio-visual aid
(ii) Mass contact method
(iii) Individual contact method
(iv) Group contact method

Codes:	A	B	C	D
(a)	(iii)	(ii)	(i)	(iv)
(b)	(iv)	(i)	(iii)	(ii)
(c)	(ii)	(iii)	(iv)	(i)
(d)	(iii)	(iv)	(i)	(ii)

49. Match the following in List I with List II:

List I

(A) Use of goods and services
(B) Handling money
(C) Income generation
(D) Values

List II

(i) Parker
(ii) Entrepreneurship
(iii) Standard of living
(iv) Budget

Codes:	A	B	C	D
(a)	(iii)	(iv)	(ii)	(i)
(b)	(i)	(ii)	(iii)	(iv)
(c)	(ii)	(i)	(iv)	(iii)
(d)	(iv)	(iii)	(ii)	(i)

50. Match the method of research tools from List I to List II:

List I

(a) A planned methodical watching the subject or situation.
(b) The opinion of subjects in group are observed and noted by researcher.
(c) A document that contains a set of questions.
(d) A set of structured questions in which responses are recorded by researcher.

List II

(i) Focus Group Discussion
(ii) Interview
(iii) Observation
(iv) Questionnaire

Codes:	A	B	C	D
(a)	(i)	(iv)	(ii)	(iii)
(b)	(i)	(iii)	(iv)	(ii)
(c)	(iii)	(i)	(iv)	(ii)
(d)	(ii)	(i)	(iv)	(iii)

ANSWERS

1. (c)	2. (b)	3. (d)	4. (c)	5. (b)
6. (d)	7. (c)	8. (a)	9. (a)	10. (a)
11. (b)	12. (b)	13. (c)	14. (b)	15. (d)
16. (b)	17. (c)	18. (d)	19. (c)	20. (a)
21. (c)	22. (b)	23. (d)	24. (a)	25. (d)
26. (c)	27. (c)	28. (c)	29. (c)	30. (a)
31. (b)	32. (a)	33. (b)	34. (b)	35. (d)
36. (c)	37. (b)	38. (c)	39. (d)	40. (b)
41. (c)	42. (b)	43. (b)	44. (c)	45. (c)
46. (c)	47. (a)	48. (d)	49. (a)	50. (c)

PAPER–III

Note: This paper contains seventy-five (75) objective type questions of two (2) marks each. All questions are compulsory.

1. The S.N.F. of standard milk should be as follows:
   (a) 8.5% (b) 7.2%
   (c) 6.5% (d) 5.2%
2. The period of human embryo is
   (a) 2 – 4 weeks (b) 1 – 8 weeks
   (c) 2 – 8 weeks (d) 2 – 6 weeks
3. Level of Intelligent Quotient of educable mentally challenged child is
   (a) 0 – 25 (b) 50 – 75
   (c) 25 – 50 (d) 75 – 100
4. Conversation is a
   (a) Listening skill (b) Intellectual skill
   (c) Expressive skill (d) Receptive skill
5. Degree of polymerization for polyester ranges between
   (a) 50 – 70 (b) 90 – 115
   (c) 115 – 140 (d) 140 – 165
6. Which of the following can finish hundreds of garments at one time by a single operator?
   (a) Carousel jeans finisher
   (b) Steam dolly
   (c) Tunnel finisher
   (d) Suction counter table
7. Indicate the region, separating one system from another, in the systems approaches to management
   (a) Boundary (b Interface
   (c) Exchanger (d) Divider
8. Bending and carrying respectively belong to which kind of effort?
   (a) Pedal and Mental
   (b) Torsal and Manual
   (c) Manual and Pedal
   (d) Pedal and Torsal
9. Vanaspati is an adulterant in
   (a) Malt (b) Haldi
   (c) Ghee and butter (d) Saffron
10. The process of assessing the progress of a project based on predetermined indicators and objectives of the programme is known as
    (a) Planning (b) Implementation
    (c) Monitoring (d) Evaluation
11. Performance appraisals and review committees in an organization are examples of
    (a) Outline evaluation
    (b) Internal evaluation
    (c) External evaluation
    (d) Summative evaluation
12. Organization chart is also known as
    (a) Tree chart (b) Flow chart
    (c) Flip chart (d) Striptease chart
13. Which are the chemicals used for artificial ripening of fruits?
    (A) Ethephon (B) Benzene
    (C) Methanol (D) Calcium carbide
    (a) (A) & (B) (b) (B) & (C)
    (c) (C) & (D) (d) (D) & (A)

14. Components of the National vitamin A Prophylaxis Programme are:
    (A) Providing supplementary nutrition
    (B) Distributing mega doses of vitamin A
    (C) Feeding colostrum
    (D) Encouraging consumption of fruits & veg.
    (E) All of the above
    (a) (A), (B), (C) (b) (E)
    (c) (B) & (D) (d) (B), (C), (D)

15. Which of the following are not used for financial management?
    (A) Variable cost
    (B) Trial balance
    (C) Performance appraisal
    (D) Fixed cost
    (E) Break even analysis
    (F) SWOT
    Codes:
    (a) (A) and (F) (b) (C) and (F)
    (c) (A), (B) and (F) (d) (E), (F) and (B)

16. The symptoms in kidney failure patients are
    (A) GFR 90 ml/min
    (B) GFR 20 ml or less/min
    (C) Oliguria
    (D) Polyuria
    (E) Oedema
    Codes:
    (a) (A), (B) & (C) (b) (A), (C) & (E)
    (c) (D), (E) & (A) (d) (B), (C) & (E)

17. To avoid diaper rash:
    I. Change wet diapers immediately.
    II. Use soft pants on diapers.
    III. Avoid using diapers till rashes disappear.
    IV. Clean and dry the area before putting a fresh diaper.
    Codes:
    (a) I and II are correct.
    (b) I and IV are correct.
    (c) I, III and IV are correct.
    (d) II and IV are correct.

18. Immunization is necessary for children:
    I. To develop defense mechanism in the body.
    II. To increase nutritional status.
    III. To reduce discomfort.
    IV. To reduce incidence of viral and infectious diseases.
    Codes:
    (a) I and II are correct.
    (b) II and IV are correct.
    (c) I and IV are correct.
    (d) III and IV are correct.

19. Dominant emotions are always:
    I. Pleasant II. Unpleasant
    III. Strong IV. Rare
    Codes:
    (a) I and II are correct.
    (b) I, II and III are correct.
    (c) II and IV are correct.
    (d) All are correct.

20. Following tests are mandatory for exports of children's clothing.
    I. Zipper strength II. Snap strength
    III. Needle detection IV. Seam strength
    Codes:
    (a) I, III and IV are correct.
    (b) I, II and III are correct.
    (c) II, III and IV are correct.
    (d) I, II and IV are correct.

21. Which of the following blends have best flame retardancy?
    I. Cotton – Wool
    II. Cotton – Spandex
    III. Modacrylic – Spandex
    IV. Modacrylic – Wool
    V. Aramid – PVC
    Codes:
    (a) I and II are correct.
    (b) IV and V are correct.
    (c) II and III are correct.
    (d) III and IV are correct.

22. Which of the following thread packages are not suitable for use on industrial machines?

I. Spools II. Cops
III. Vicones IV. Cones

Codes:
(a) I and IV are correct.
(b) III and IV are correct.
(c) I and II are correct.
(d) II and III are correct.

23. Which among the following are advertised under 'classified category'?
I. Job vacancy II. Matrimonial
III. Coffee powder IV. Bicycles

Codes:
(a) I and II are correct.
(b) II and III are correct.
(c) III and IV are correct.
(d) I, II and IV are correct.

24. The affective components of workers are
I. Attitudes II. Skills
III. Feelings IV. Interests

Codes:
(a) I, II and III are correct.
(b) I, III and IV are correct.
(c) II, III and IV are correct.
(d) I, II and IV are correct.

25. Goals of the elderly include:
I. Family relations
II. Good health
III. Education
IV. Vocational pursuits

Codes:
(a) II and III are correct.
(b) III and IV are correct.
(c) I and III are correct.
(d) I and II are correct.

26. Voluntary organisations are involved in the following activities:
(A) Welfare
(B) Policy decision making
(C) Advocacy
(D) Networking

Codes:
(a) (B), (C) and (D) are correct.
(b) (A) and (D) are correct.
(c) (A) and (C) are correct.
(d) (A), (C) and (D) are correct.

27. Channels for participatory communication are
(A) Community Radio
(B) Participatory Video
(C) Street theatre
(D) Films

Codes:
(a) (A), (B) and (C) are correct.
(b) (B), (C) and (D) are correct.
(c) (B) and (D) are correct.
(d) (D) and (A) are correct.

28. Local leaders in development programme planning are also considered to be
(A) Key communicators
(B) Opinion leaders
(C) Information leaders
(D) Change agents

Codes:
(a) (A), (B) and (D) are correct.
(b) (B), (C) and (D) are correct.
(c) All are correct.
(d) (A), (B) and (C) are correct.

29. **Assertion (A):** Bulimia nervosa is defined by little eating or reduced intake of food over a long period of time.
Reason (R): Little eating is used to describe the consumption of food that is much smaller than most people would eat during a similar period of time.

Codes:
(a) (A) is true (R) is false.
(b) (A) is false (R) is true.
(c) Both (A) & (R) are true.
(d) Both (A) & (R) are false.

30. **Assertion (A):** The menu is the heart of the entire establishment on which all activities are centered.
Reason (R): The menu determines the materials to be purchased, equipments to be used, current food trends and even the

style of leadership and workman's compensation.

Codes:

(a) Both (A) and (R) are correct.
(b) (A) is correct but (R) is partially correct.
(c) (A) is correct but (R) is false.
(d) Both (A) and (R) are false.

31. **Assertion (A):** Consumption of plenty of fruits and vegetables protects individuals from certain cancers.

Reason (R): The antioxidants present in fruits and vegetables help in removal of free radicals.

Codes:

(a) Both (A) and (R) are false.
(b) Both (A) and (R) are true.
(c) (A) is true, (R) is false.
(d) (A) is false (R) is true.

32. **Assertion (A):** Mentally challenged people have no right for marriage.

Reason (R): They are unable to bear and rear children.

Codes:

(a) Both (A) and (R) are correct.
(b) Both (A) and (R) are wrong.
(c) (A) is correct (R) is wrong explanation.
(d) (A) is wrong (R) is correct explanation.

33. **Assertion (A):** Consistent sleep routines are advisable for all children right from birth.

Reason (R): It increases separation anxiety and deprives stimulation.

Codes:

(a) Both (A) and (R) are correct.
(b) Both (A) and (R) are wrong.
(c) (A) is correct (R) is wrong explanation.
(d) (A) is wrong (R) is correct explanation.

34. **Assertion (A):** Post mature babies are generally long and thin as they receive insufficient blood supply towards the end of gestation.

Reason (R): The aged placenta is less efficient to supply oxygen.

Codes:

(a) Both (A) and (R) are correct.
(b) (A) is correct (R) is wrong explanation.
(c) (A) is wrong (R) is correct explanation.
(d) Both (A) and (R) are wrong.

35. **Assertion (A):** Marker efficiency can be enhanced by pattern engineering.

Reason (R): It divides the awkwardly shaped patterns in two pieces.

Codes:

(a) Both (A) and (R) are correct.
(b) Both (A) and (R) are incorrect.
(c) (A) is correct but (R) is incorrect.
(d) (A) is incorrect but (R) is correct.

36. **Assertion (A):** A dart can be relocated without changing the fit.

Reason (R): Shifting of dart to various places does not change the angle of dart.

Codes:

(a) Both (A) and (R) are correct.
(b) Both (A) and (R) are wrong.
(c) (A) is correct but (R) is wrong.
(d) (A) is wrong but (R) is correct.

37. **Assertion (A):** To identify the polyester fibre it is important to negate the presence of nylon and acrylic by dissolving in hot phenol and concentrated nitric acid.

Reason (R): Polyester is insoluble in both hot phenol and concentrated nitric acid.

Codes:

(a) (A) is right but (R) is wrong.
(b) (A) is wrong but (R) is correct.
(c) Both (A) and (R) are correct.
(d) Both (A) and (R) are wrong.

38. **Assertion (A):** Motion against gravity are slower than those with gravity.

Reason (R): A good example is pushing chopped vegetable into a bowl kept at a lower level.

Codes:
(a) (A) is correct and (R) is wrong.
(b) (A) is wrong and (R) is correct.
(c) Both (A) and (R) are wrong.
(d) Both (A) and (R) are correct.

39. **Assertion (A):** Ergonomics is also referred to as 'Human Factors'.
Reason (R): The focus of the study is on worker fatigue.
Codes:
(a) (A) is correct but (R) is wrong.
(b) (A) is wrong and (R) is correct.
(c) Both (A) and (R) are correct.
(d) Both (A) and (R) are wrong.

40. **Assertion (A):** Communication whether interpersonal or between social systems involves interface, the common boundary of two systems.
Reason (R): The interface between families and other systems remain the same irrespective of their income.
Codes:
(a) (A) is correct but (R) is wrong.
(b) Both (A) and (R) are correct.
(c) (A) is wrong, but (R) is correct.
(d) Both (A) and (R) are wrong.

41. **Assertion (A):** Mass Communication is not appropriate for participatory communication.
Reason (R): Mass Communication is largely monologue.
Codes:
(a) (A) is correct but (R) is wrong.
(b) (A) is wrong but (R) is correct.
(c) Both (A) and (R) are correct.
(d) Both (A) and (R) are wrong.

42. **Assertion (A):** A good communicator is a good listener.
Reason (R): Communication is a cyclic process.
Codes:
(a) Both (A) and (R) are correct.
(b) (A) is correct but (R) is not correct.
(c) (A) is not correct but (R) is correct.
(d) Both (A) and (R) are not correct.

43. **Assertion (A):** Need assessment is carried out to identify the gap between the present and the desired situation.
Reason (R): Objectives of programme planning are based on need assessment.
Codes:
(a) (A) is correct, (R) is wrong.
(b) (A) is not correct, but (R) is correct.
(c) Both (A) and (R) are correct.
(d) Both (A) and (R) are not correct.

44. Arrange in the right sequence the steps taken in planning a physical facility for food service unit.
(A) Planning Team
(B) Menu Analysis
(C) Architectural Features
(D) Prospectus
(E) Budget
(F) Feasibility Study
Codes:
(a) (A), (B), (D), (C), (F), (E)
(b) (A), (F), (C), (D), (E), (B)
(c) (D), (A), (F), (B), (C), (E)
(d) (F), (E), (D), (C), (B), (A)

45. Arrange in the correct sequence, the symptoms of diabetes as they appear with advancement of disease:
(A) Dehydration (B) Glycosuria
(C) Polyurea (D) Ketosis
(E) Hyperglycemia (F) Diabetic coma
Codes:
(a) (E), (C), (B), (D), (A), (F)
(b) (E), (B), (C), (A), (D), (F)
(c) (B), (A), (C), (E), (F), (D)
(d) (C), (B), (A), (D), (E), (F)

46. Arrange the following fatty acids in the sequence with increasing degree of unsaturation:
(A) Linoleic acid
(B) γ linolenic acid
(C) Eicosapentaenic acid

(D) Oleic acid
(E) Arachdonic acid
Codes:
(a) (C), (B), (E), (D), (A)
(b) (D), (A), (B), (E), (C)
(c) (A), (C), (E), (B), (D)
(d) (A), (B), (D), (E), (C)

47. Arrange the following in order of establishment in correct sequence:
I. Integrated Child Development Scheme (ICDS)
II. Central Social Welfare Board (CSWB)
III. Convention on the rights of child (CRC)
IV. National Council of Education, Research and Training (NCERT)
Codes:
(a) II, I, III, IV (b) II, IV, I, III
(c) III, II, IV, I (d) I, III, IV, II

48. Write the correct sequence of early language development stages:
I. Cooing II. Babbling
III. Crying IV. Gestures
V. Utterance
Codes:
(a) I, III, II, V, IV (b) III, IV, II, I, V
(c) I, II, III, IV, V (d) III, I, II, IV, V

49. Arrange Abraham Maslow's Hierarchy of needs in correct sequence:
I. Security needs
II. Self-esteem
III. Physiological needs
IV. Self-actualization
Codes:
(a) III, IV, I, II (b) III, I, II, IV
(c) I, III, IV, II (d) II, I, III, IV

50. Give the sequence of wool manufacturing and processing:
I. Lap formation
II. Separation of tops and nails
III. Grading of fibres
IV. Carbonizing
V. Scouring
VI. Washing and oiling
Codes:
(a) II, I, III, V, VI, IV
(b) III, I, II, IV, V, VI
(c) V, IV, III, I, II, VI
(d) III, V, IV, VI, I, II

51. Give the sequence of weaving operations
I. Drawing
II. Looming and weaving
III. Warp and Weft winding
IV. Denting
V. Warping and Sizing
Codes:
(a) V, IV, I, III, II (b) III, V, I, IV, II
(c) I, IV, V, II, III (d) I, IV, II, III, V

52. What is the sequence followed in the merchandising department of a garment industry?
I. Costing
II. Booking order
III. Raw material procurements
IV. Designing and sampling
V. Selling the concept
VI. Production follow up
Codes:
(a) V, II, IV, I, III, VI
(b) II, IV, VI, V, I, III
(c) I, II, V, III, VI, IV
(d) IV, I, II, V, III, VI

53. Sequence the general objectives of Ergonomics according to their order of importance:
I. Efficiency II. Comfort
III. Health and Safety IV. Productivity
Codes:
(a) I, II, III, IV (b) II, III, I, IV
(c) II, IV, III, I (d) IV, III, II, I

54. According to Mundel, each higher level brings about changes in motion in the level below it. Arrange the changes in the proper sequence:

I. Body portions and motions
II. Working arrangements and equipment
III. Finished product
IV. Raw materials
V. Production sequence

Codes:
(a) I, II, III, IV, V (b) I, III, V, II, IV
(c) I, II, V, III, IV (d) V, III, II, I, IV

55. Given are four acts pertaining to consumerism in India. Identify the correct order in which they were enacted:
I. Prevention of Food Adulteration Act
II. Standards of Weight and Measures Act
III. Essential Commodities Act
IV. Consumer Protection Act

Codes:
(a) I, III, II, IV (b) I, II, III, IV
(c) III, II, I, IV (d) II, IV, III, I

56. Organise the following steps in the sequential order of Programme Management:
(A) Situation Analysis
(B) Evaluation
(C) Identifying objectives
(D) Executing plan

Codes:
(a) (C), (A), (D), (B)
(b) (A), (C), (D), (B)
(c) (A), (D), (B), (C)
(d) (B), (D), (C), (A)

57. Arrange sequentially the following steps of planning incentives in an enterprise:
(A) Developing achievement reward relationship
(B) Measuring achievement
(C) Selecting the objectives
(D) Designing a system

Codes:
(a) (D), (A), (B), (C)
(b) (A), (B), (C), (D)
(c) (B), (C), (D), (A)
(d) (C), (B), (A), (D)

58. The correct sequence for curriculum
(A) Tentative curriculum
(B) Consideration of curriculum needs
(C) Evaluation of tentative curriculum
(D) Pilot testing of tentative curriculum

Codes:
(a) (A), (B), (C), (D)
(b) (B), (A), (D), (C)
(c) (C), (A), (B), (D)
(d) (D), (C), (B), (A)

59. Match the active components from List I with species in List II:

List I (Active component)
A. Allyl isothiocynate B. Allin
C. Curcumin D. Eugeniol

List II (Spice)
i. Turmeric ii. Clove
iii. Mustard iv. Garlic
v. Pepper

Codes:	**A**	**B**	**C**	**D**
(a)	v	iv	i	ii
(b)	iii	v	i	iv
(c)	iii	iv	i	ii
(d)	ii	iii	iv	v

60. Match deficiency diseases from List I with their symptoms in List II.

List I	**List II**
A. Rickets	i. Delirium
B. Fluorosis	ii. Parasthesia
C. Beri beri	iii. Mottled teeth
D. Pallegra	iv. Kyphosis
	v. Polyurea

Codes:	**A**	**B**	**C**	**D**
(a)	v	iii	i	ii
(b)	iii	iv	v	i
(c)	iv	iii	v	i
(d)	iv	iii	ii	i

61. Match the following List I with items in List II:

List I
A. Expectancy theory
B. Scientific management

C. Perpetual inventory
D. Table de hote menu
E. Record
F. Sales mix

List II

i. Menu of the day
ii. Set menu
iii. Taylor
iv. Small heater placed on side table
v. Exact amount of products in store
vi. Frequency of menu items selected by customers
vii. V room

Codes:	A	B	C	D	E	F
(a)	i	iii	ii	vi	iv	v
(b)	ii	iv	vii	i	v	iii
(c)	vii	iii	v	ii	iv	vi
(d)	ii	iv	vi	v	i	iii

62. Match the disease in List I to symptoms in List II:

List I (Disease)

A. CHF
B. Dyslipidemia
C. Diabetes
D. Vitamin D deficiency

List II (Symptoms)

i. Increased LDL
ii. Parasthesia
iii. Peripheral oedema
iv. Polydypsia
v. Fat malabsorption

Codes:	A	B	C	D
(a)	ii	v	i	iii
(b)	v	iii	ii	v
(c)	iv	v	ii	i
(d)	iii	i	iv	v

63. Match the items in List I with List II:

List I

A. D.P.T. B. Jealousy
C. Maria Montessori D. Havighurst

List II

i. Sensorial training
ii. Whooping cough
iii. Baumrind's parenting styles
iv. Negative emotion
v. Developmental tasks

Codes:	A	B	C	D
(a)	ii	iv	i	v
(b)	iv	ii	i	iii
(c)	ii	iii	v	i
(d)	v	i	iii	iv

64. Match the items in List I with List II:

List I

A. Howard Gardener
B. Cephalocaudal
C. Dr. Virginia
D. Head start

List II

i. Apgar scale
ii. 1965
iii. Developmental tasks
iv. Head to toe
v. Multiple intelligence

Codes:	A	B	C	D
(a)	iii	i	ii	v
(b)	ii	iv	iii	i
(c)	v	iv	iii	ii
(d)	i	iv	v	iii

65. Match the items in List I with List II:

List I

A. Active learning
B. Heightened emotionality
C. Electra complex
D. Visit to post office

List II

i. Freud
ii. Adolescence
iii. Outdoor play
iv. First hand experiences
v. Emotional disturbance
vi. Field Trip

Codes:	A	B	C	D
(a)	iii	v	ii	iv
(b)	iv	ii	i	vi
(c)	i	v	ii	iii
(d)	iii	i	iv	ii

66. Match the denim washes given in List I with their effect given in List II:

List I

A. Acid wash B. Atari
C. Enzyme wash D. Sand blasting
E. Sulphur bottom

List II

i. Selective fading of edges
ii. Faded and softer look
iii. Contrasts in colour
iv. Grey or yellow effects on removal of indigo
v. Abraded look

Codes:	A	B	C	D	E
(a)	i	ii	iii	iv	v
(b)	iii	i	ii	v	iv
(c)	v	iv	i	ii	iii
(d)	iv	iii	v	i	ii

67. Match the items in List I with the items in List II:

List I

A. Throat plate B. Feed dog
C. Pressure foot D. Stop motion

List II

i. Holds the fabric in place
ii. Provides smooth surface for stitching
iii. Stops the sewing mechanisms
iv. Moves the fabric ahead

Codes:	A	B	C	D
(a)	i	iii	ii	iv
(b)	ii	iv	i	iii
(c)	iii	ii	iv	i
(d)	iv	i	iii	ii

68. Match the garments given in List I with the type of case given in List II:

List I	List II
A. Saree blouse	i. Style ease
B. Jackets	ii. Negative
C. Kurta	iii. Layered ease
D. Swim suit	iv. Comfort ease

Codes:	A	B	C	D
(a)	i	iv	ii	iii
(b)	ii	i	iii	iv
(c)	iii	ii	iv	i
(d)	iv	iii	i	ii

69. Match the traditional Indian textiles of List I with the centre of productions given in List II:

List I	List II
A. Baluchari	i. Patan
B. Paithani	ii. Murshidabad
C. Mushroo	iii. Dhacca
D. Jamdhani	iv. Yeola

Codes:	A	B	C	D
(a)	iv	iii	ii	i
(b)	iii	i	iv	ii
(c)	ii	iv	i	iii
(d)	i	ii	iii	iv

70. Match the items in List I with List II:

List I

A. Overlapping
B. Ordering
C. Ability to process information
D. Dovetailing

List II

i. Elaboration
ii. Intermittent attention to 2 or more tasks
iii. Creating meaningful sequence
iv. Fixed interaction pattern
v. Concurrent attention to 2 or more tasks

Codes:	A	B	C	D
(a)	v	iv	iii	i
(b)	i	iii	iv	v
(c)	iv	ii	v	i
(d)	v	iii	i	ii

71. Match the items in List I with List II:

List I

A. Work performance
B. Muscular fatigue
C. Assisted living
D. Gravity

List II

i. EMG ii. Pedometer
iii. Calories iv. Elederly
v. Posture

Codes:	A	B	C	D
(a)	v	iv	i	ii
(b)	iv	i	iii	ii

(c)	iii	i	iv	v
(d)	v	iii	iv	ii

72. Match the following items in List I with List II:

List I
A. Study of elderly
B. Study of man machine systems
C. Study of angles of body bend
D. Study of body dimensions

List II
i. Goniometer ii. Anthropometer
iii. Geriatrics iv. Ergonomics
v. Flexi curve

Codes:	A	B	C	D
(a)	iii	iv	i	ii
(b)	i	ii	iv	iii
(c)	iii	iv	ii	i
(d)	iv	iii	i	ii

73. Match the following items in List I with List II:

List I
A. Specimen B. Model
C. Diorama D. Mockups

List II
i. Enlarged version of original
ii. Miniature replica of an object in working condition
iii. Miniature replica of an object
iv. Scenic representation of the original
v. Sample which represents the whole

Codes:	A	B	C	D
(a)	v	ii	iv	i
(b)	iv	v	i	ii
(c)	iii	iv	ii	i
(d)	v	iii	iv	ii

74. Match the communication function in List I with its most appropriate description in List II:

List I
A. Affinity B. Information
C. Persuasion D. Entertainment

List II
i. Change behaviour of others
ii. To play and have fun
iii. Obtain facts
iv. Seek to establish relationships
v. To command respect

Codes:	A	B	C	D
(a)	iv	iii	i	ii
(b)	ii	i	iii	iv
(c)	v	iii	i	ii
(d)	ii	iv	v	iii

75. Match the following items in List I with List II:

List I	List II
A. NREGA	i. Sanitation
B. NRHM	ii. Child health and nutrition
C. TSC	iii. Health
D. ICDS	iv. Employment
	v. Environment

Codes:	A	B	C	D
(a)	ii	i	iii	iv
(b)	iv	iii	i	ii
(c)	v	iii	i	ii
(d)	iii	i	v	iv

ANSWERS

1. (a)	2. (c)	3. (d)	4. (c)	5. (c)
6. (c)	7. (a)	8. (b)	9. (c)	10. (c)
11. (b)	12. (b)	13. (d)	14. (c)	15. (b)
16. (d)	17. (b)	18. (c)	19. (b)	20. (b)
21. (b)	22. (c)	23. (a)	24. (b)	25. (d)
26. (d)	27. (a)	28. (c)	29. (b)	30. (b)
31. (b)	32. (b)	33. (c)	34. (a)	35. (a)
36. (a)	37. (c)	38. (d)	39. (a)	40. (a)
41. (c)	42. (a)	43. (c)	44. (c)	45. (b)
46. (b)	47. (b)	48. (d)	49. (b)	50. (d)
51. (b)	52. (a)	53. (b)	54. (c)	55. (a)
56. (b)	57. (d)	58. (b)	59. (c)	60. (d)
61. (c)	62. (d)	63. (a)	64. (c)	65. (b)
66. (b)	67. (b)	68. (d)	69. (c)	70. (d)
71. (c)	72. (a)	73. (d)	74. (a)	75. (b)

JUNE–2012

Note: This paper contains Sixty (60) multiple choice questions, each question carrying two (2) marks. Candidate is expected to answer any Fifty (50) questions. In case more than Fifty (50) questions are attempted, only the first Fifty (50) questions will be evaluated.

PAPER–I

1. Video-Conferencing can be classified as one of the following types of communication:
   (a) Visual one way
   (b) Audio-Visual one way
   (c) Audio-Visual two way
   (d) Visual two way

2. MC National University of Journalism and Communication is located at
   (a) Lucknow (b) Bhopal
   (c) Chennai (d) Mumbai

3. All India Radio (A.I.R.) for broadcasting was named in the year
   (a) 1926 (b) 1936
   (c) 1946 (d) 1956

4. In India for broadcasting TV programmes which system is followed?
   (a) NTCS (b) PAL
   (c) NTSE (d) SECAM

5. The term 'DAVP' stands for
   (a) Directorate of Advertising & Vocal Publicity
   (b) Division of Audio-Visual Publicity
   (c) Department of Audio-Visual Publicity
   (d) Directorate of Advertising & Visual Publicity

6. The term "TRP" is associated with TV shows stands for
   (a) Total Rating Points
   (b) Time Rating Points
   (c) Thematic Rating Points
   (d) Television Rating Points

7. Which is the number that comes next in the following sequence?
   2, 6, 12, 20, 30, 42, 56, ______
   (a) 60 (b) 64
   (c) 72 (d) 70

8. Find the next letter for the series YVSP ………
   (a) N (b) M
   (c) O (d) L

9. Given that in a code language, '645' means 'day is warm'; '42' means 'warm spring' and '634' means 'spring is sunny'; which digit represents 'sunny'?
   (a) 3 (b) 2
   (c) 4 (d) 5

10. The basis of the following classification is:
    'first President of India' 'author of Godan' 'books in my library', 'blue things' and 'students who work hard'
    (a) Common names
    (b) Proper names
    (c) Descriptive phrases
    (d) Indefinite description

11. In the expression 'Nothing is larger than itself' the relation 'is larger than' is
    (a) Antisymmetric (b) Asymmetrical
    (c) Intransitive (d) Irreflexive

12. **Assertion (A):** There are more laws on the books today than ever before, and

more crimes being committed than ever before.

Reason (R): Because to reduce crime we must eliminate the laws.

Choose the correct answer from below:

(a) (A) is true, (R) is doubtful and (R) is not the correct explanation of (A).

(b) (A) is false, (R) is true and (R) is the correct explanation of (A).

(c) (A) is doubtful, (R) is doubtful and (R) is not the correct explanation of (A).

(d) (A) is doubtful, (R) is true and (R) is not the correct explanation of (A).

13. If the proposition "All men are not mortal" is true then which of the following inferences is correct? Choose from the code given below:

1. "All men are mortal" is true.
2. "Some men are mortal" is false.
3. "No men are mortal" is doubtful.
4. "All men are mortal" is false.

Codes:

(a) 1, 2 and 3 (b) 2, 3 and 4
(c) 1, 3 and 4 (d) 1 and 3

14. Determine the nature of the following definition: "Abortion" means the ruthless murdering of innocent beings.

(a) Lexical (b) Persuasive
(c) Stipulative (d) Theoretical

15. Which one of the following is not an argument?

(a) Devadutt does not eat in the day so he must be eating at night.

(b) If Devadutt is growing fat and if he does not eat during the day, he will be eating at night.

(c) Devadutt eats in the night so he does not eat during the day.

(d) Since Devadutt does not eat in the day, he must be eating in the night.

16. Venn diagram is a kind of diagram to

(a) represent and assess the validity of elementary inferences of syllogistic form.

(b) represent but not assess the validity of elementary inferences of syllogistic form.

(c) represent and assess the truth of elementary inferences of syllogistic form.

(d) assess but not represent the truth of elementary inferences of syllogistic form.

17. Reasoning by analogy leads to

(a) certainty
(b) definite conclusion
(c) predictive conjecture
(d) surety

18. Which of the following statements are false? Choose from the code given below:

1. Inductive arguments always proceed from the particular to the general.
2. A cogent argument must be inductively strong.
3. A valid argument may have a false premise and a false conclusion.
4. An argument may legitimately be spoken of as 'true' or 'false'.

Codes:

(a) 2, 3 and 4 (b) 1 and 3
(c) 2 and 4 (d) 1 and 2

19. Six persons A, B, C, D, E and F are standing in a circle. B is between F and C, A is between E and D, F is to the left of D. Who is between A and F?

(a) B (b) C
(c) D (d) E

20. The price of petrol increases by 25%. By what percentage must a customer reduce the consumption so that the earlier bill on the petrol does not alter?

(a) 20% (b) 25%
(c) 30% (d) 33.33%

21. If Ram knows that y is an integer greater than 2 and less than 7 and Hari knows that y is an integer greater than 5 and less than 10, then they may correctly conclude that
(a) y can be exactly determined
(b) y may be either of two values
(c) y may be any of three values
(d) there is no value of y satisfying these conditions

22. Four pipes can fill a reservoir in 15, 20, 30 and 60 hours respectively. The first one was opened at 6 AM, second at 7 AM, third at 8 AM and the fourth at 9 AM. When will the reservoir be filled?
(a) 11 AM (b) 12 Noon
(c) 1 PM (d) 1:30 PM

The total electricity generation in a country is 97 GW. The contribution of various energy sources is indicated in percentage terms in the Pie Chart given below:

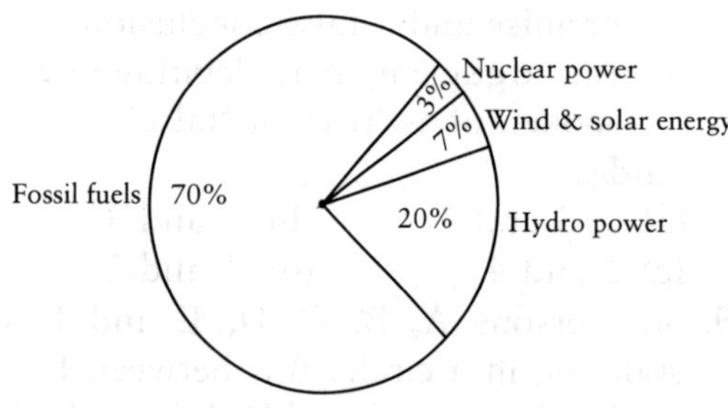

23. What is the contribution of wind and solar power in absolute terms in the electricity generation?
(a) 6.79 GW (b) 19.4 GW
(c) 9.7 GW (d) 29.1 GW

24. What is the contribution of renewable energy sources in absolute terms in the electricity generation?
(a) 29.1 GW (b) 26.19 GW
(c) 67.9 GW (d) 97 GW

25. TCP/IP is necessary if one is to connect to the
(a) Phone lines (b) LAN
(c) Internet (d) a Server

26. Each character on the keyboard of computer has an ASCII value which stands for
(a) American Stock Code for Information Interchange
(b) American Standard Code for Information Interchange
(c) African Standard Code for Information Interchange
(d) Adaptable Standard Code for Information Change

27. Which of the following is not a programming language?
(a) Pascal (b) Microsoft Office
(c) Java (d) C++

28. Minimum number of bits required to store any 3 digit decimal number is equal to
(a) 3 (b) 5
(c) 8 (d) 10

29. Internet explorer is a type of
(a) Operating System
(b) Compiler
(c) Browser
(d) IP address

30. POP3 and IMAP are e-mail accounts in which
(a) One automatically gets one's mail everyday
(b) One has to be connected to the server to read or write one's mail
(c) One only has to be connected to the server to send and receive e-mail
(d) One does not need any telephone lines

31. Irritation in eyes is caused by the pollutant
(a) Sulphur dioxide (b) Ozone
(c) PAN (d) Nitrous oxide

32. Which is the source of chlorofluorocarbons?
(a) Thermal power plants
(b) Automobiles
(c) Refrigeration and Airconditioning
(d) Fertilizers

33. Which of the following is not a renewable natural resource?
(a) Clean air (b) Fertile soil
(c) Fresh water (d) Salt

34. Which of the following parameters is not used as a pollution indicator in water?
(a) Total dissolved solids
(b) Coliform count
(c) Dissolved oxygen
(d) Density

35. S and P waves are associated with
(a) floods (b) wind energy
(c) earthquakes (d) tidal energy

36. Match List I and List II and select the correct answer from the codes given below:

List I
(A) Ozone hole
(B) Greenhouse effect
(C) Natural hazards
(D) Sustainable development

List II
(i) Tsunami (ii) UV radiations
(iii) Methane (iv) Eco-centrism

Codes:	A	B	C	D
(a)	(ii)	(iii)	(i)	(iv)
(b)	(iii)	(ii)	(i)	(iv)
(c)	(iv)	(iii)	(i)	(ii)
(d)	(iv)	(ii)	(iii)	(i)

37. Indian Institute of Advanced Study is located at
(a) Dharmshala (b) Shimla
(c) Solan (d) Chandigarh

38. Indicate the number of Regional Offices of National Council of Teacher Education.
(a) 04 (b) 05
(c) 06 (d) 08

39. Which of the following rights was considered the "Heart and Soul" of the Indian Constitution by Dr. B.R. Ambedkar?
(a) Freedom of Speech
(b) Right to Equality
(c) Right to Freedom of Religion
(d) Right to Constitutional Remedies

40. Who among the following created the office of the District Collector in India?
(a) Lord Cornwallis
(b) Warren Hastings
(c) The Royal Commission on Decentralisation
(d) Sir Charles Metcalfe

41. The Fundamental Duties of a citizen include
1. Respect for the Constitution, the National Flag and the National Anthem.
2. To develop the scientific temper.
3. Respect for the Government.
4. To protect Wildlife.

Choose the correct answer from the codes given below:
Codes:
(a) 1, 2 and 3 (b) 1, 2 and 4
(c) 2, 3 and 4 (d) 1, 3, 4 and 2

42. The President of India takes oath
(a) to uphold the sovereignty and integrity of India.
(b) to bear true faith and allegiance to the Constitution of India.
(c) to uphold the Constitution and laws of the country.
(d) to preserve, protect and defend the Constitution and the law of the country.

43. If you get an opportunity to teach a visually challenged student along with normal students, what type of treatment would you like to give him in the class?
 (a) Not giving extra attention because majority may suffer.
 (b) Take care of him sympathetically in the classroom.
 (c) You will think that blindness is his destiny and hence you cannot do anything.
 (d) Arrange a seat in the front row and try to teach at a pace convenient to him.

44. Which of the following is not a characteristic of a good achievement test?
 (a) Reliability (b) Objectivity
 (c) Ambiguity (d) Validity

45. Which of the following does not belong to a projected aid?
 (a) Overhead projector
 (b) Blackboard
 (c) Epidiascope
 (d) Slide projector

46. For a teacher, which of the following methods would be correct for writing on the blackboard?
 (a) Writing fast and as clearly as possible.
 (b) Writing the matter first and then asking students to read it.
 (c) Asking a question to students and then writing the answer as stated by them.
 (d) Writing the important points as clearly as possible.

47. A teacher can be successful if he/she
 (a) helps students in becoming better citizens
 (b) imparts subject knowledge to students
 (c) prepares students to pass the examination
 (d) presents the subject matter in a well-organized manner

48. Dynamic approach to teaching means
 (a) Teaching should be forceful and effective
 (b) Teachers should be energetic and dynamic
 (c) The topics of teaching should not be static, but dynamic
 (d) The students should be required to learn through activities

49. The research that aims at immediate application is
 (a) Action Research
 (b) Empirical Research
 (c) Conceptual Research
 (d) Fundamental Research

50. When two or more successive footnotes refer to the same work which one of the following expressions is used?
 (a) ibid. (b) et. al
 (c) op. cit. (d) loc. cit.

51. Nine year olds are taller than seven year olds. This is an example of a reference drawn from
 (a) Vertical study
 (b) Cross-sectional study
 (c) Time-series study
 (d) Experimental study

52. Conferences are meant for
 (a) Multiple target groups
 (b) Group discussions
 (c) Show-casing new research
 (d) All of the above

53. Ex Post Facto research means
 (a) The research is carried out after the incident
 (b) The research is carried out prior to the incident
 (c) The research is carriesd out along with the happening of an incident
 (d) The research is carried out keeping in mind the possibilities of an incident

54. Research ethics do not include
(a) Honesty (b) Subjectivity
(c) Integrity (d) Objectivity

Read the following passage carefully and answer the questions 55 to 60:

James Madison said, "A people who mean to be their own governors must arm themselves with power that knowledge gives." In India, the Official Secrets Act, 1923 was a convenient smokescreen to deny members of the public access to information. Public functioning has traditionally been shrouded in secrecy. But in a democracy in which people govern themselves, it is necessary to have more openness. In the maturing of our democracy, right to information is a major step forward; it enables citizens to participate fully in the decision-making process that affects their lives so profoundly. It is in this context that the address of the Prime Minister in the Lok Sabha is significant. He said, "I would only like to see that everyone, particularly our civil servants, should see the Bill in a positive spirit; not as a draconian law for paralyzing Government, but as an instrument for improving Government-Citizen interface resulting in a friendly, caring and effective Government functioning for the good of our People." He further said, "This is an innovative Bill, where there will be scope to review its functioning as we gain experience. Therefore, this is a piece of legislation, whose working will be kept under constant reviews."

The Commission, in its Report, has dealt with the application of the Right to Information in Executive, Legislature and Judiciary. The judiciary could be a pioneer in implementing the Act in letter and spirit because much of the work that the Judiciary does is open to public scrutiny, Government of India has sanctioned an e-governance project in the Judiciary for about ₹700 crores which would bring about systematic classification, standardization and categorization of records. This would help the judiciary to fulfil its mandate under the Act. Similar capacity building would be required in all other public authorities. The transformation from non-transparency to transparency and public accountability is the responsibility of all three organs of State.

55. A person gets power
(a) by acquiring knowledge
(b) from the Official Secrets Act, 1923
(c) through openings
(d) by denying public information

56. Right to Information is a major step forward to
(a) enable citizens to participate fully in the decision-making process
(b) to make the people aware of the Act
(c) to gain knowledge of administration
(d) to make the people Government friendly

57. The Prime Minister considered the Bill
(a) to provide power to the civil servants
(b) as an instrument for improving Government-citizen interface resulting in a friendly, caring and effective Government
(c) a draconian law against the officials
(d) to check the harassment of the people

58. The Commission made the Bill effective by
(a) extending power to the executive authorities
(b) combining the executive and legislative power
(c) recognizing Judiciary a pioneer in implementing the act in letter and spirit
(d) educating the people before its implementation

59. The Prime Minister considered the Bill innovative and hoped that

(a) It could be reviewed based on the experience gained on its functioning.
(b) The civil servants would see the Bill in a positive spirit.
(c) It would not be considered as a draconian law for paralyzing Government.
(d) All of the above.

60. The transparency and public accountability is the responsibility of three organs of the State. These three organs are
(a) Lok Sabha, Rajya Sabha and Judiciary
(b) Lok Sabha, Rajya Sabha and Executive
(c) Judiciary, Legislature and the Commission
(d) Legislature, Executive and Judiciary

ANSWERS

1. (c)	2. (b)	3. (b)	4. (b)	5. (d)
6. (a)	7. (c)	8. (b)	9. (a)	10. (c)
11. (d)	12. (a)	13. (b)	14. (b)	15. (b)
16. (a)	17. (c)	18. (c)	19. (c)	20. (a)
21. (a)	22. (c)	23. (a)	24. (b)	25. (c)
26. (b)	27. (b)	28. (d)	29. (c)	30. (c)
31. (c)	32. (c)	33. (d)	34. (d)	35. (c)
36. (a)	37. (b)	38. (a)	39. (d)	40. (b)
41. (b)	42. (d)	43. (d)	44. (c)	45. (b)
46. (d)	47. (a)	48. (d)	49. (a)	50. (a)
51. (b)	52. (d)	53. (a)	54. (b)	55. (a)
56. (a)	57. (b)	58. (c)	59. (d)	60. (d)

PAPER–II

Note: This paper contains fifty (50) objective type questions, each question carrying two (2) marks. All questions are compulsory.

1. From which plant source gluten is derived?
(a) Soya (b) Rice
(c) Corn (d) Wheat

2. HDL is synthesized and secreted from
(a) Pancreas (b) Liver
(c) Kidneys (d) Muscles

3. Which food service system produces food at a central unit and distributes processed food to other smaller units.
(a) Conventional (b) Assembly line
(c) Commissary (d) Cook and Chill

4. Which of the following governs the selection of needle?
(a) Type of thread
(b) Type of fabric
(c) Stitch length
(d) Tension of thread

5. Which of the following is not a design repeat?
(a) Drop (b) Mirror
(c) Rotary (d) Satin

6. The term 'Therbligs' was given by
(a) Prang
(b) Gilbreth
(c) Denmann W. Ross
(d) Mundell

7. Releasing pent up emotional energy is
(a) Body Control
(b) Emotional Catharsis

(c) Mental Balance
(d) Emotional Security

8. Deliberate manipulation of people's beliefs, values and behaviour through words, gestures, images is known as
(a) Publicity (b) Propaganda
(c) Persuasion (d) Perception

9. Triggering the mind of participants to finding out solutions for a problem is called as
(a) Colloquism (b) Symposium
(c) Debate (d) Brain Storming

10. Chi-square test is used
(a) When there are only two groups for comparison
(b) When the data is in frequencies
(c) To check accuracy of data
(d) When there are three or more groups for comparison

11. Which of the following foods are produced by involving lactic acid fermentation?
(A) Beer (B) Yogurt
(C) Cheese (D) Vinegar
Codes:
(a) (A) and (B) (b) (B) and (C)
(c) (C) and (D) (d) (D) and (A)

12. Which of the following foods do not contain gluten and is acceptable for patients with celiac disease to consume?
(A) Wheat flour (B) Rice flour
(C) Gram flour (D) Corn flour
Codes:
(a) (B), (C), (D) are correct
(b) (A), (B), (C) are correct
(c) (C), (D), (A) are correct
(d) (D), (A), (B) are correct

13. The tool of Management that does not deal with personnel
(A) Organization chart
(B) Production schedule
(C) Job description
(D) Job specification
(E) Budget
(F) Communication
Codes:
(a) (A) and (B) (b) (B) and (E)
(c) (E) and (C) (d) (F) and (B)

14. In a pattern, darts can be replaced by
(i) tucks (ii) gather
(iii) style line (iv) control seam
Codes:
(a) (i) and (ii) are correct
(b) (ii) and (iii) are correct
(c) (ii) and (iv) are correct
(d) (iii) and (iv) are correct

15. Which of the following methods of printing are currently practised largely in the Indian textile industry?
(i) Screen Printing (ii) Digital
(iii) Roller Printing (iv) Block Printing
Codes:
(a) (ii), (iii) and (iv) are correct
(b) (i), (ii) and (iii) are correct
(c) (i), (iii) and (iv) are correct
(d) (i), (ii) and (iv) are correct

16. Which among the following are neutral colours?
I. Black II. Red
III. Green IV. White
Codes:
(a) I, II and III are correct
(b) I and II are correct
(c) I and III are correct
(d) I and IV are correct

17. Development is a product of
(i) Heredity and Environment
(ii) Learning and Maturation
(iii) Learning and Training
(iv) Learning through observation
Codes:
(a) (i), (ii) and (iii) are correct
(b) (i) and (ii) are correct

(c) (ii), (iii) and (iv) are correct
(d) (i) and (iv) are correct

18. Non-formal education is
(i) an organised
(ii) systematic
(iii) highly institutionalised
(iv) an educational activity
Codes:
(a) (i), (ii) and (iv) are correct
(b) (i) and (ii) are correct
(c) (i), (ii) and (iii) are correct
(d) (ii), (iii) and (iv) are correct

19. Which of the following are visual aids?
(i) Blackboard
(ii) Posters
(iii) Public address system
(iv) Flash cards
Codes:
(a) (i), (iii) and (iv) are correct
(b) (i), (ii) and (iv) are correct
(c) (ii) and (iv) are correct
(d) (i), (ii) and (iii) are correct

20. The most appropriate statistical test for analysing qualitative data is
(i) Pearson's r (ii) Sign test
(iii) Kruskal-Wallis test (iv) F-test
Codes:
(a) (i) & (ii) are correct
(b) (iii) & (iv) are correct
(c) (i) & (iii) are correct
(d) (ii) & (iii) are correct

21. **Assertion (A):** Browning in condensed milk occurs due to Millard reaction.
Reason (R): It is due to reaction between reducing sugar and fat.
Codes:
(a) Both (A) and (R) are true.
(b) Both (A) and (R) are false.
(c) (A) is true, but (R) is false.
(d) (A) is false, but (R) is true.

22. **Assertion (A):** Energy requirements during lactation is higher than during pregnancy.
Reason (R): As the turn over of iron is greater during lactation because of milk secretion.
Codes:
(a) Both (A) and (R) are true.
(b) Both (A) and (R) are false.
(c) (A) is true, but (R) is false.
(d) (A) is false, but (R) is true.

23. **Assertion (A):** Large food service institutions use formal competitive bid buying.
Reason (R): Here the purchaser goes to the wholesale market and bids the price.
Codes:
(a) Both (A) and (R) are true.
(b) Both (A) and (R) are false.
(c) (A) is true, but (R) is false.
(d) (A) is false, but (R) is true.

24. **Assertion (A):** Break point of the collar is marked on the placket extension.
Reason (R): Roll line turns back from the centre front line.
Codes:
(a) Both (A) and (R) are false.
(b) Both (A) and (R) are true.
(c) (A) is correct, but (R) is false.
(d) (A) is false, but (R) is correct.

25. **Assertion (A):** Brocade, Huckaback, Jacquard and tapestry can be classified under same category.
Reason (R): All can be made on the Jacquard loom.
Codes:
(a) Both (A) and (R) are false.
(b) Both (A) and (R) are correct.
(c) (A) is correct, but (R) is false.
(d) (A) is false, but (R) is correct.

26. **Assertion (A):** Home Management is not an all encompassing concept compared to decision making or problem solving.
Reason (R): Home Management does not consider the totality of managerial functioning.

Codes:
(a) (A) is false, but (R) is true
(b) (A) is true and (R) is false
(c) Both (A) and (R) are true, but (R) is not the complete explanation.
(d) Both (A) and (R) are false.

27. **Assertion (A):** Ego deals with the real world. It is based on reality principle.
Reason (R): Ego searches for real objects to satisfy the need. The hungry person must get real food to satisfy the hunger.
Codes:
(a) Both (A) and (R) are true, (R) is the correct explanation.
(b) Both (A) and (R) are true, (R) is not correct explanation.
(c) (A) is true, but (R) is false.
(d) (A) is false, but (R) is true.

28. **Assertion (A):** Confidentiality is an essential quality of the counsellor.
Reason (R): Counselling relationship will be effective only if the counsellor maintains confidentiality.
Codes:
(a) Both (A) and (R) are true.
(b) Both (A) and (R) are false.
(c) (A) is true, but (R) is false.
(d) (A) is false, but (R) is true.

29. **Assertion (A):** All individuals in a social system do not adopt an innovation at the same time.
Reason (R): But they adopt innovation in an ordered time sequence.
Codes:
(a) Both (A) and (R) are true.
(b) Both (A) and (R) are false.
(c) (A) is true, but (R) is false.
(d) (A) is false, but (R) is true.

30. **Assertion (A):** A non-symmetric distribution is also described as skewed distribution.
Reason (R): In a skewed distribution the length of one of the tails, relative to the central section is disproportionate to the other.
Codes:
(a) Both (A) and (R) are true and (R) is the correct explanation.
(b) Both (A) and (R) are true.
(c) (A) is false, but (R) is true.
(d) (A) is true, but (R) is false.

31. Arrange the right sequence in decreasing order of protein content in food.

i. Bread	ii. Cheese
iii. Butter	iv. Boiled egg

Codes:

(a) i, ii, iii, iv	(b) ii, iii, iv, i
(c) iii, i, ii, iv	(d) iv, ii, i, iii

32. Give the sequential involvement of enzymes for the digestion of food in the GIT.

(A) Iso maltase	(B) Pepsin
(C) Ptylin	(D) Amylase

Codes:

(a) (A), (B), (D), (C)	(b) (C), (B), (D), (A)
(c) (D), (A), (B), (C)	(d) (B), (A), (C), (D)

33. Give the sequence in which a purchase officer places a purchase order?
(A) Develops order form
(B) Identifies the vendor
(C) Writes specification
(D) Identifies need
(E) Selects method of purchase
Codes:
(a) (A), (B), (C), (E), (D)
(b) (D), (C), (A), (E), (B)
(c) (B), (C), (E), (A), (D)
(d) (C), (A), (E), (B), (D)

34. Give the correct sequence in the production of garments:

(A) labelling	(B) assembling
(C) cutting	(D) bundling

Codes:
(a) (D), (B), (A), (C)
(b) (A), (C), (B), (D)

(c) (D), (C), (B), (A)
(d) (D), (A), (B), (C)

35. Give the correct sequence of producing synthetic fibres.
(A) Treatment with finishing chemicals
(B) Extrusion
(C) Polymerization
(D) Dissolving in solution
Codes:
(a) (B), (A), (D), (C)
(b) (D), (C), (A), (B)
(c) (A), (B), (C), (D)
(d) (C), (D), (B), (A)

36. Indicate the correct sequence of activities in the Home Management process.
(a) Planning, organisation, feedback, implementation.
(b) Planning, organisation, implementation, feedback.
(c) Planning, implementation, organisation, feedback.
(d) Planning, feedback, organisation, implementation.

37. Arrange the stages of Psycho-Social development in correct sequence
(i) Generativity Vs. Stagnation
(ii) Identity Vs. Role confusion
(iii) Ego Integrity Vs. Despair
(iv) Initiative Vs. Guilt
Codes:
(a) (i), (ii), (iii) and (iv)
(b) (iv), (ii), (i) and (iii)
(c) (iii), (ii), (iv) and (i)
(d) (ii), (iv), (i) and (iii)

38. Steps to be followed in applying Participatory Rural Appraisal (PRA) techniques
(i) Build up personal rapport with villagers.
(ii) Identify villagers who are willing to share their experiences.
(iii) Setting the climate for discussion.
(iv) Meet the villagers.
(v) Select suitable place for interview.
(vi) Show full interest and enthusiasm.
Codes:
(a) (i), (iv), (ii), (v), (iii), (vi)
(b) (iv), (v), (iii), (i), (vi), (ii)
(c) (iv), (i), (ii), (vi), (iii), (v)
(d) (v), (vi), (i), (iv), (iii), (ii)

39. Arrange the stages of the adoption process in correct sequence.
(i) Interest (ii) Awareness
(iii) Evaluation (iv) Adoption
(v) Trial
Codes:
(a) (i), (ii), (iii), (v), (iv)
(b) (v), (i), (ii), (iv), (iii)
(c) (ii), (i), (iii), (v), (iv)
(d) (iii), (v), (ii), (i), (iv)

40. Sequence the following scales of measurement from the lowest to the highest:
(i) Interval scale (ii) Ordinal scale
(iii) Nominal scale (iv) Ratio scale
Codes:
(a) (ii), (iii), (i), (iv) (b) (iv), (i), (ii), (iii)
(c) (iii), (ii), (i), (iv) (d) (iii), (ii), (iv), (i)

41. Match the foods in List I to it's pigments in List II:

List I (Food)	**List II (Pigments)**
(A) Beet root	i. Flavones
(B) Carrot	ii. Betalin
(C) Onions	iii. Chlorophyll
(D) Spinach	iv. Carotenoids

Codes:	**A**	**B**	**C**	**D**
(a)	i	ii	iii	iv
(b)	ii	iv	i	iii
(c)	iii	ii	iv	i
(d)	iv	iii	i	ii

42. Match the glands with their respective hormones.
(A) α cells pancreas i. Adrenal corticoid steroid
(B) Adrenal cortex ii. Insulin

(C) β cells pancreas iii. Prolactin
(D) Pituitary iv. Glucagon

Codes:	A	B	C	D
(a)	iv	i	ii	iii
(b)	i	ii	iii	iv
(c)	iv	iii	i	ii
(d)	ii	i	iii	iv

43. Match the catering unit with the right type of method of service.

Catering Unit	Method of Service
(A) Cafeteria	i. Centralized
(B) Hospital	ii. Scramble
(C) Railways	iii. Buffet
(D) Conference hall	iv. Plated service

Codes:	A	B	C	D
(a)	i	ii	iii	iv
(b)	ii	i	iv	iii
(c)	iii	iv	i	ii
(d)	iv	iii	ii	i

44. Match the fashion terms given in List I with their meanings given in List II.

List I	List II
(A) Classic	i. exclusive custom fitted clothing
(B) Fad	ii. ready to wear
(C) Haute-couture	iii. last through ages
(D) Pret-a-porter	iv. short lived craze

Codes:	A	B	C	D
(a)	i	ii	iii	iv
(b)	iii	iv	i	ii
(c)	ii	iii	iv	i
(d)	iv	i	ii	iii

45. Match List I with List II.

List I	List II
(A) Cotton	i. Plant stem
(B) Pineapple	ii. Seed hair
(C) Flax	iii. Plant leaf
(D) Coir	iv. Fruit husk

Codes:	A	B	C	D
(a)	ii	iii	i	iv
(b)	i	ii	iv	iii
(c)	iii	iv	ii	i
(d)	iv	i	iii	ii

46. Match the following in List I with List II.

List I

I. Human II. Resources
III. Routine decisions IV. Proportion

List II

1. Interrelated Resources
2. Recurring
3. Golden oblong decisions
4. Intangible

Codes:	I	II	III	IV
(a)	4	1	2	3
(b)	4	1	3	2
(c)	1	2	3	4
(d)	2	4	1	3

47. Match the items in List I with List II.

List I

I. Clay Modelling
II. Pre-basic education
III. International Women's day
IV. Beneficiaries of Supplementary nutrition in ICDS

List II

1. M.K. Gandhi
2. 6 months–72 months children
3. Imagination & creativity
4. 8th March
5. 8th July

Codes:	I	II	III	IV
(a)	3	2	5	1
(b)	2	5	4	2
(c)	3	1	4	2
(d)	1	3	2	4

48. Match the following in List I with List II.

List I

(A) Change in knowledge
(B) Change in attitude
(C) Change in confidence
(D) Change in skill

List II

i. Self-reliance
ii. Doing things

iii. What people know
iv. Reaction towards certain things

Codes:	A	B	C	D
(a)	ii	iv	iii	i
(b)	iii	i	ii	iv
(c)	iii	iv	i	ii
(d)	iv	i	ii	iii

49. Match the traditional methods of communication with the State in India.

List I	List II
(A) Odissi	i. Kerala
(B) Oyil Attam	ii. Karnataka
(C) Kathakali	iii. Tamil Nadu
(D) Yakshgana	iv. Orissa

Codes:	A	B	C	D
(a)	iv	iii	i	ii
(b)	ii	i	iv	iii
(c)	iv	ii	i	iii
(d)	iii	iv	ii	i

50. Match the symbols in List I with words in List II.

List I	List II
(A) md	i. Chi-square
(B) Σ	ii. mean
(C) χ^2	iii. Sum of confidence
(D) $\overline{X}$	iv. Median

Codes:	A	B	C	D
(a)	ii	i	iii	iv
(b)	iv	iii	i	ii
(c)	i	ii	iv	iii
(d)	iv	iii	ii	i

ANSWERS

1. (d)	2. (b)	3. (c)	4. (b)	5. (c)
6. (b)	7. (b)	8. (b)	9. (d)	10. (b)
11. (b)	12. (a)	13. (b)	14. (c)	15. (c)
16. (d)	17. (b)	18. (a)	19. (b)	20. (d)
21. (c)	22. (c)	23. (c)	24. (c)	25. (a)
26. (d)	27. (a)	28. (a)	29. (a)	30. (a)
31. (d)	32. (b)	33. (b)	34. (c)	35. (d)
36. (b)	37. (b)	38. (c)	39. (c)	40. (c)
41. (b)	42. (a)	43. (b)	44. (b)	45. (a)
46. (a)	47. (c)	48. (c)	49. (a)	50. (b)

PAPER–III

Note: This paper contains seventy-five (75) objective type questions of two (2) marks each. All questions are compulsory.

1. Normal BMI for adult Asians as suggested by WHO is
   (a) 18 – 23 kg/m^2 (b) 19 – 24 kg/m^2
   (c) 20 – 25 kg/m^2 (d) 21 – 26 kg/m^2
2. Generally visually impaired persons have visual acuity of
   (a) 2/200 (b) 20/100
   (c) 20/70 (d) 20/200
3. The female sex hormone is
   (a) Androgen (b) Prolactin
   (c) Estrogen (d) Oxytocin
4. Colostrum is very good as it is rich in proteins and ____.
   (a) Carbohydrates (b) Minerals
   (c) Vitamins (d) Antibodies
5. Which of the following is sheared from a living sheep?
   (a) Flannel (b) Fleece
   (c) Felt (d) Moire
6. Which of the following is a stationary knife?
   (a) Band (b) Round
   (c) Straight (d) Die
7. Which of the following is a double pointed dart?
   (a) Flange (b) French
   (c) Fish (d) Dressmakers

8. A portion of output re-entered as input to affect succeeding output is
(a) Feedback
(b) Deferred resource
(c) Throughput
(d) Black box

9. Eliminating or combining parts of jobs is suggested by incorporating changes in
(a) tools
(b) posture
(c) production sequence
(d) raw materials

10. The recommended height of the work surface in the kitchen for efficient operation is
(a) 4 inches below the elbow
(b) 5 inches below elbow level
(c) 3 inches below elbow level
(d) 6 inches below the elbow

11. A group of persons whom an individual consults before taking an important decision is known as
(a) Formal groups
(b) Informal groups
(c) Reference groups
(d) Interest groups

12. Approaches to understand women's participation in development have gone through the following phases:
(a) Welfare, Women in Development, Gender and Development
(b) Welfare, Gender and Development, Women in Development
(c) Women in Development, Welfare, Gender and Development
(d) Gender and Development, Women in Development, Welfare

13. Putting the last as first, means
(a) Reversals in learning
(b) Destination of man
(c) Blue print approach
(d) Content centric teaching

14. Following are the symptoms of Diabetes Mellitus:
(A) Polyuria (B) Hypoglycaemia
(C) Glycosuria (D) Polyphagia
(E) Edema (F) Taste acuity
(a) (A), (C) and (D) (b) (D), (B) and (C)
(c) (F), (D) and (C) (d) (B), (D) and (E)

15. Which of the following are not deficiency diseases?
(A) Xerophthalmia (B) Dyslipidemia
(C) Osteomalacia (D) Keratomalacia
(E) Anorexia Nervosa
(a) (A) & (C) (b) (A) & (B)
(c) (B) & (E) (d) (D) & (E)

16. Which of the following packages are examples of aseptic packaging?
(A) Tetra pack boxes (B) Paper bag
(C) Milk bottle (D) Plastic bag
(E) Aluminium foil
(a) (C) & (E) (b) (A) & (E)
(c) (C) & (D) (d) (A) & (C)

17. Which of the following are not new trends of Management?
(A) JIT (B) TQM
(C) MBO (D) BARS
(E) PERT (F) ERG
(a) (E) and (B) are correct.
(b) (D) and (F) are correct.
(c) (E) and (C) are correct.
(d) (A) and (C) are correct.

18. Family directly influences personality of the child by
I. Communication II. Moulding
III. Directing IV. Controlling
(a) I, II, III are correct.
(b) I and II are correct.
(c) II and IV are correct.
(d) Only I is correct.

19. Disciplining is a way of improving:
I. Mannerisms
II. Aesthetic sense
III. Moral values
IV. Educational values

(a) I and II are correct.
(b) II, III and IV are correct.
(c) I, III and IV are correct.
(d) III and IV are correct.

20. Right to survival of children includes
I. Right to Birth and Registration
II. Right to Express
III. Right to Health and Nutrition
IV. Right to Participation
(a) I, II and III are correct.
(b) I and III are correct.
(c) I, III and IV are correct.
(d) III and IV are correct.

21. Following chemicals used in the textile industry are hazardous:
(i) azo compounds
(ii) enzymes
(iii) chlorine compounds
(iv) hydrogen peroxide
(a) (iii) and (iv) are correct.
(b) (i) and (iv) are correct.
(c) (i) and (ii) are correct.
(d) (i) and (iii) are correct.

22. Which of the following stitches are used in chikankari embroidery?
(i) Kamal kadai (ii) Negi
(iii) Fanda (iv) Bijli
(v) Pechni
(a) (i), (iii) and (iv) are correct.
(b) (ii), (iv) and (v) are correct.
(c) (iii), (iv) and (v) are correct.
(d) (i), (iv) and (v) are correct.

23. Name the components included in the 'Macro-habitat' concept of systems approach to management.
I. Man-made and natural space
II. Biological contents of the physical environment of the family system.
III. Biological contents of the physical environment of the personal system.
IV. Economic actions of the family.
(a) I and III are correct.
(b) II and III are correct.
(c) I and II are correct.
(d) II and IV are correct.

24. The effects of mental fatigue are
I. decreased attention
II. decreased motivation
III. increased mental performance
IV. impaired perception and thinking
Codes:
(a) I, II, III and IV are correct.
(b) I, II and IV are correct.
(c) I, II and III are correct.
(d) I and II are correct.

25. Packaging serves the purpose of
I. Protection of merchandise
II. Enhancement of product value
III. Value addition of product
IV. Advertising the product
Codes:
(a) I, II and IV are correct.
(b) I, II and III are correct.
(c) II, III and IV are correct.
(d) I, III and IV are correct.

26. As per the Human Development Report, the dimensions for measuring 'human development' in any country are
(A) Longevity
(B) Happiness
(C) Knowledge
(D) Decent Standard of living
Codes:
(a) (A), (B) and (D) are correct.
(b) (A), (C) and (D) are correct.
(c) (B), (C) and (D) are correct.
(d) (A), (B) and (C) are correct.

27. Feedback covers the following functions in communication:
(A) Facilitates action
(B) Improves learning
(C) Removes barriers
(D) Informs audience
Codes:
(a) (A), (B) and (D) are correct.
(b) (B), (C) and (D) are correct.

(c) (A), (B) and (C) are correct.
(d) (B), (D) and (A) are correct.

28. The objectives of non-formal education are
(A) to raise the extent of functional literacy
(B) to provide lifelong education
(C) to compliment formal education in schools
(D) to prepare individuals for self-employment

Codes:
(a) (A), (B) and (C) are correct.
(b) (B), (C) and (D) are correct.
(c) (A), (B) and (D) are correct.
(d) (A), (B), (C) and (D) are correct.

29. **Assertion (A):** Microkjeldahl method is used for analysis of proteins.
Reason (R): Percentage of sulphur is measured to calculate protein content.
Codes:
(a) Both (A) and (R) are true.
(b) Both (A) and (R) are false.
(c) (A) is true, (R) is false.
(d) (A) is false, (R) is true.

30. **Assertion (A):** Marketing is a business strategy designed to attract customers and influence their purchasing power.
Reason (R): Process charts, work sampling and Pareto charts help in achieving it.
Codes:
(a) Both (A) and (R) are correct.
(b) (A) is correct, but (R) is false.
(c) Both (A) and (R) are false.
(d) (A) is false, but (R) is correct.

31. **Assertion (A):** Atherosclerosis is the pathological process that underlines majority of vascular diseases.
Reason (R): The formation of plaques due to the collection of lipids narrows the lumen of blood vessels.
Codes:
(a) Both (A) & (R) are true.
(b) Both (A) & (R) are false.
(c) (A) is true (R) is partially true.
(d) Both (A) & (R) are partially true.

32. **Assertion (A):** Adopting a child carries special challenges as the adoptive parents need to deal with integrating the child into the family.
Reason (R): Adopted children are always problematic.
Codes:
(a) Both (A) and (R) are correct.
(b) Both (A) and (R) are wrong.
(c) (A) is correct (R) is wrong explanation.
(d) (A) is wrong (R) is correct explanation.

33. **Assertion (A):** Physical and psychological readiness of children to enter school affects the personality.
Reason (R): Children who are physically and psychologically ready will make satisfactory adjustment and develop favourable attitude towards education.
Codes:
(a) Both (A) and (R) are wrong.
(b) Both (A) and (R) are correct.
(c) (A) is correct (R) is wrong explanation.
(d) (A) is wrong (R) is correct explanation.

34. **Assertion (A):** Couples need genetic counselling before conceiving.
Reason (R): Genetic defects lead to multiple births.
Codes:
(a) Both (A) and (R) are correct.
(b) (A) is correct, but (R) is wrong explanation.
(c) (A) is wrong, (R) is correct explanation.
(d) Both (A) and (R) are wrong.

35. **Assertion (A):** Plisse has a permanently puckered surface.

Reason (R): Caustic soda printed on the fabric shrinks the fabric.

Codes:

(a) Both (A) and (R) are false.
(b) Both (A) and (R) are correct.
(c) (A) is correct, but (R) is false.
(d) (A) is false, but (R) is correct.

36. **Assertion (A):** Plasma and nano technologies are the latest finishing technologies used in the textile industry.

Reason (R): They produce aesthetic effects but are not eco-friendly.

Codes:

(a) (A) is correct, but (R) is false.
(b) Both (A) and (R) are false.
(c) Both (A) and (R) are correct.
(d) (A) is false, but (R) is correct.

37. **Assertion (A):** Lock stitch is appropriate for stitching stretch fabrics.

Reason (R): Lock stitch stretches with fabric stretch.

Codes:

(a) (A) is right, but (R) is wrong.
(b) (A) is wrong, but (R) is right.
(c) Both (A) and (R) are right.
(d) Both (A) and (R) are wrong.

38. **Assertion (A):** Throughput is the activity outside the system boundary.

Reason (R): 'Blackbox' describes the unknown throughput.

Codes:

(a) (A) is correct, but (R) is wrong.
(b) (A) is wrong, but (R) is correct.
(c) Both (A) and (R) are correct.
(d) Both (A) and (R) are wrong.

39. **Assertion (A):** Physiological fatigue can occur in situations other than those in a relatively high work-load period.

Reason (R): Performing disliked tasks is the major cause for physiological fatigue.

Codes:

(a) (A) is correct, but (R) is wrong.
(b) (A) is wrong, but (R) is correct.
(c) Both (A) and (R) are correct, but (R) is not the correct explanation.
(d) Both (A) and (R) are wrong.

40. **Assertion (A):** Ergonomics is defined as 'fitting the task to the man'.

Reason (R): Poor relationship between work, worker and work environment reduces the stress of workers.

Codes:

(a) (A) is correct, but (R) is wrong.
(b) (A) is wrong, but (R) is correct.
(c) Both (A) and (R) are correct.
(d) Both (A) and (R) are wrong.

41. **Assertion (A):** Summative evaluation tries to measure end results of a programme.

Reason (R): This will help to decide whether to continue or discontinue the programme.

Codes:

(a) Both (A) and (R) are correct, (R) is the correct explanation.
(b) Both (A) and (R) are correct, (R) is not the correct explanation.
(c) (A) is true, but (R) is false.
(d) (A) is false, but (R) is true.

42. **Assertion (A):** Intrapersonal communication is important for self-reflection.

Reason (R): Self-reflection is important for communicating with others.

Codes:

(a) (A) is true, but (R) is false.
(b) Both (A) and (R) are true.
(c) (A) is false, but (R) is true.
(d) Both (A) and (R) are true, but (R) is not the correct explanation.

43. **Assertion (A):** Poverty is essentially a social phenomenon and only secondarily a material or physical phenomenon.

Reason (R): Poverty is the socio-economic phenomenon whereby the resources available to a society are used to satisfy the wants of the few while many do not have even their basic needs met.

Codes:

(a) (A) is false, but (R) is true.
(b) Both (A) and (R) are correct.
(c) Both (A) and (R) are not correct.
(d) (A) is true, but (R) is false.

44. Arrange in the right sequence, the changes that take place in cereals during moist cooking and cooling:
(A) Retrogradation
(B) Synerisis
(C) Water absorption
(D) Change in viscosity
(E) Recrystallization
(a) (C), (D), (B), (A), (E)
(b) (A), (B), (C), (D), (E)
(c) (D), (C), (E), (B), (A)
(d) (C), (D), (A), (E), (B)

45. Give the sequential progression of symptoms from hepatitis to cirrhosis:
(A) increased bilirubin
(B) abdominal tenderness and jaundice
(C) nausea, anorexia, vomiting
(D) oesophageal varicose
(E) oedema and ascitis
(F) portal hypertension
(a) (B), (C), (D), (A), (E), (F)
(b) (B), (A), (D), (F), (C), (E)
(c) (A), (C), (F), (D), (B), (E)
(d) (C), (B), (A), (F), (D), (E)

46. Arrange in right sequence the procedure used in selecting a food service employee:
(A) Appointment letter
(B) Internal source
(C) Determining need
(D) Establishment of wage
(E) Advertisement
(F) Interview
(G) Orientation
(a) (B), (A), (E), (F), (G), (C), (D)
(b) (C), (E), (F), (G), (A), (B), (D)
(c) (D), (B), (A), (C), (G), (F), (E)
(d) (C), (B), (E), (F), (D), (A), (G)

47. Arrange the stages of psycho-sexual development in correct sequence:
I. Phallic stage II. Genital stage
III. Oral stage IV. Latency stage
V. Anal stage
(a) II, IV, I, V, III (b) I, II, III, V, IV
(c) III, V, I, IV, II (d) V, IV, III, II, I

48. Arrange the stages of child development in correct sequence:
I. Antenatal II. Prenatal
III. Neonatal IV. Infancy
V. Toddlerhood
(a) II, III, I, IV, V (b) II, I, III, IV, V
(c) I, II, IV, III, V (d) I, II, III, IV, V

49. Identify the correct sequencing order in the process of listening:
I. Understanding II. Remembering
III. Receiving IV. Evaluating
V. Responding
(a) III, I, II, V, IV (b) II, I, III, V, IV
(c) I, II, IV, III, V (d) V, III, IV, I, II

50. Give the sequence for denim washing:
(i) Bleaching
(ii) Clean up to adjust desired effect
(iii) Tinting/Dyeing
(iv) Softening
(v) Desizing, Scouring
(vi) Enzyme wash or stone wash

Codes:

(a) (ii), (i), (v), (vi), (iii), (iv)
(b) (v), (vi), (ii), (i), (iii), (iv)
(c) (iii), (i), (ii), (vi), (v), (iv)
(d) (v), (iv), (vi), (i), (iii), (ii)

51. Give the correct sequence for cotton processing:
(i) Singeing
(ii) Printing
(iii) Bleaching
(iv) Scouring
(v) Curing and heat setting
(vi) Desizing

Codes:
(a) (i), (iii), (iv), (v), (ii), (vi)
(b) (ii), (iv), (i), (iii), (vi), (v)
(c) (i), (vi), (iv), (iii), (ii), (v)
(d) (iv), (i), (vi), (iii), (ii), (v)

52. Give the sequence for design development process of garments for fashion industry:
(i) Designing by maintaining identity of brand
(ii) Presentation
(iii) Study of forecast
(iv) Identifying target market
(v) Study of current trends
(vi) Making design brief
Codes:
(a) (vi), (iv), (v), (iii), (i), (ii)
(b) (iii), (iv), (ii), (i), (v), (vi)
(c) (v), (ii), (iv), (vi), (i), (iii)
(d) (i), (v), (iii), (iv), (vi), (ii)

53. Arrange the following in the proper sequence of communication:
I. Message II. Source
III. Decoder IV. Encoder
V. Destination
Codes:
(a) (I), (II), (III), (IV), (V)
(b) (II), (I), (IV), (III), (V)
(c) (II), (I), (III), (IV), (V)
(d) (II), (I), (III), (V), (IV)

54. Arrange in sequence the channels of distribution:
I. Wholesaler II. Manufacturer
III. Consumer IV. Retailer
Codes:
(a) I, II, III, IV (b) II, III, I, IV
(c) II, I, IV, III (d) III, IV, II, I

55. Arrange Maslow's 'Hierarchy of needs' in the proper sequence:
I. Physiological II. Social
III. Safety IV. Self-esteem
V. Self-actualisation
Codes:
(a) I, III, II, IV, V (b) I, II, III, IV, V
(c) V, IV, III, II, I (d) I, IV, III, II, V

56. Arrange the following programmes of adult education in India in chronological order of their inception:
(A) National Adult Education Programme (NAEP)
(B) National Literacy Mission (NLM)
(C) Total Literacy Campaign (TLC)
(D) Continuing Education
Codes:
(a) (B), (D), (C), (A)
(b) (D), (C), (B), (A)
(c) (C), (B), (A), (D)
(d) (A), (B), (C), (D)

57. The correct sequence of steps involved in behaviour change communication are
(i) Action (ii) Interest
(iii) Attention (iv) Satisfaction
(v) Conviction (vi) Desire
Codes:
(a) (ii), (vi), (iv), (iii), (i), (v)
(b) (iii), (ii), (vi), (v), (i), (iv)
(c) (i), (ii), (iii), (iv), (v), (vi)
(d) (vi), (v), (iv), (iii), (ii), (i)

58. Arrange the following phrases used by Laswell in his model of communication:
(A) To whom (B) In which channel
(C) Says what (D) Who
(E) With what effect
Codes:
(a) (B), (D), (C), (A), (E)
(b) (E), (A), (B), (C), (D)
(c) (D), (C), (B), (A), (E)
(d) (C), (A), (E), (D), (A)

59. Match the nutrient fortified in List I with foods in List II:

List I (Nutrient)	List II (Foods)
(A) Iron	(i) Hydrogenated fat
(B) Iodine	(ii) Milk

(C) Vitamin D (iii) Biscuits
(D) Vitamins A and D (iv) Salt
(v) Sugar

Codes:	A	B	C	D
(a)	(v)	(iv)	(i)	(ii)
(b)	(iii)	(iv)	(ii)	(i)
(c)	(v)	(ii)	(iii)	(i)
(d)	(iv)	(v)	(ii)	(iii)

60. Match the Nutritional Assessment Methods in List I with Tools used for measurement in List II:

List I (Nutrient)
(A) Dietary Survey (B) Anthropometry
(C) Biochemical (D) Clinical

List II (Foods)
(i) Hb
(ii) Bitot spot
(iii) FFQ
(iv) Bomb Calorimeter
(v) MUAC
(vi) HPLC

Codes:	A	B	C	D
(a)	(iii)	(vi)	(iv)	(i)
(b)	(iv)	(iii)	(i)	(vi)
(c)	(vi)	(iv)	(v)	(ii)
(d)	(iii)	(v)	(i)	(ii)

61. Match the symptoms in List I with the disease in List II:

List I (Symptoms)
(A) Steatorrhea
(B) Neuropsychiatric
(C) Increased loss
(D) Platelet

List II (Disease)
(i) Hepatic encephalopathy
(ii) CVD
(iii) Gout of proteins in urine
(iv) Malabsorption aggregation
(v) Nephrotic syndrome

Codes:	A	B	C	D
(a)	(iii)	(iv)	(i)	(ii)
(b)	(iv)	(i)	(v)	(iii)
(c)	(v)	(iii)	(i)	(ii)
(d)	(ii)	(i)	(iv)	(iii)

62. Match List I with List II:

List I
(A) Grapevine (B) Benchmark
(C) Fish Diagram (D) Variable Cost
(E) Market Mix

List II
(i) Consists of 4 'P'
(ii) Cost that increase with sales
(iii) Informal method of communication
(iv) Focus on different causes of problem
(v) Set of goals based on what is achievable
(vi) Frequency with which customer select menu items

Codes:	A	B	C	D	E
(a)	(iii)	(v)	(iv)	(ii)	(i)
(b)	(i)	(iv)	(vi)	(ii)	(v)
(c)	(ii)	(vi)	(i)	(iii)	(v)
(d)	(iii)	(v)	(ii)	(i)	(iv)

63. Match the items in List I with List II:

List I
I. Sucking and eye blinking
II. Less than 2.5 kg of birth weight
III. Empty nest
IV. Pairing of stimuli

List II
1. Classical conditioning
2. Loneliness
3. Operant conditioning
4. Permanent Reflex
5. Small for date
6. Broken Homes

Codes:	I	II	III	IV
(a)	5	2	6	3
(b)	6	5	2	3
(c)	2	4	6	1
(d)	4	5	2	1

64. Match the items in List I with List II:

List I
I. Germination
II. Equilibration

III. Sudden Infant Death Syndrome
IV. Kindergarten

List II

1. Sleeping on stomach and soft surfaces
2. Balance
3. Viral infection
4. Piaget
5. Science experience
6. Froebel

Codes:	I	II	III	IV
(a)	1	2	3	4
(b)	5	4	1	6
(c)	2	1	6	4
(d)	3	4	2	5

65. Match the items in List I with List II:

List I

I. T.A.T.
II. Cooperative and Helpful behaviour
III. BCG
IV. Development

List II

1. Immediately after birth
2. Quantitative
3. Projective technique
4. Prosocial behaviour
5. Intelligence test
6. Qualitative

Codes:	I	II	III	IV
(a)	3	4	1	6
(b)	2	3	5	4
(c)	3	2	4	1
(d)	2	3	1	5

66. Match List I with List II:

List I

(A) Velvet (B) Velveteen
(C) Velcro (D) Velour

List II

(i) Short thick pile of cotton
(ii) Woven nylon strip of hooks eyes
(iii) Filling pile surface
(iv) Warp pile surface of silk

Codes:	A	B	C	D
(a)	(i)	(ii)	(iii)	(iv)
(b)	(iv)	(iii)	(ii)	(i)
(c)	(iii)	(i)	(iv)	(ii)
(d)	(ii)	(iv)	(i)	(iii)

67. Match the terms used in dyeing given in List I with their description given in List II:

List I

(A) Migration (B) Prosting
(C) Fading (D) Crocking

List II

(i) Loss of colour due to sunlight
(ii) Transference of colour to another fabric by rubbing
(iii) Change in colour due to localized abrasion
(iv) Transference of colour from one area of fabric to another

Codes:	A	B	C	D
(a)	(i)	(ii)	(iii)	(iv)
(b)	(ii)	(i)	(iv)	(iii)
(c)	(iv)	(iii)	(i)	(ii)
(d)	(iii)	(iv)	(ii)	(i)

68. Match the garment production systems given in List I with their descriptions given in List II:

List I

(A) Unit Production System
(B) Modular Production System
(C) Progressive Bundle System
(D) Section or Process

List II

(i) Empowered work team
(ii) Assembly of a complete panel by a single operator
(iii) automatic transfer from workstation to workstation
(iv) Gradually assembled as production system bundles more through

Codes:	A	B	C	D
(a)	(i)	(iv)	(ii)	(iii)
(b)	(iii)	(i)	(iv)	(ii)

(c)	(ii)	(iii)	(i)	(iv)
(d)	(iv)	(ii)	(iii)	(i)

69. Match List I with List II:

List I

(A)  [symbol] (B) 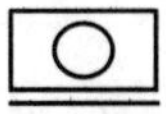 [symbol]

(C) 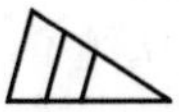 [symbol] (D)  [symbol]

List II

(i) Only non-chlorine bleach
(ii) Tumble dry, permanent press
(iii) Professionally dry clean
(iv) Delicate/gentle wash

Codes:	**A**	**B**	**C**	**D**
(a)	(iii)	(ii)	(iv)	(i)
(b)	(iv)	(i)	(ii)	(iii)
(c)	(i)	(iv)	(iii)	(ii)
(d)	(ii)	(iii)	(i)	(iv)

70. Match the following in List I with List II:

List I

I. Transferring II. Producing
III. Investing IV. Exchanging

List II

1. Adjusting availability of resources
2. Inventory of resources
3. Reduce available resources
4. Create added resources

Codes:	**I**	**II**	**III**	**IV**
(a)	3	4	1	2
(b)	3	4	2	1
(c)	1	2	3	4
(d)	4	3	2	1

71. Match the following in List I with List II:

List I

I. Met demands II. Used resources
III. Goals IV. Adjusting

List II

1. Change in action
2. Demands requiring action
3. Shift in stock
4. Value-based objectives
5. Component of output

Codes:	**I**	**II**	**III**	**IV**
(a)	5	4	2	3
(b)	4	3	2	1
(c)	5	2	1	4
(d)	5	3	2	1

72. Match the following in List I with List II:

List I	**List II**
I. Brands	1. BIS
II. Process Chart	2. Word
III. Trademarks	3. Symbol
IV. Standards	4. Pen and Pencil
	5. Pin and thread

Codes:	**I**	**II**	**III**	**IV**
(a)	2	3	4	1
(b)	3	4	2	1
(c)	1	3	4	2
(d)	4	2	1	3

73. Match the items in List I with List II:

List I (Early Extension Efforts)

(A) Gurgaon Experiment
(B) Sriniketan Experiment
(C) Marthandum Experiment
(D) Etawah Pilot Project

List II (Name of the Proponent)

(i) Mahatma Gandhi
(ii) Spencer Hatch
(iii) Rabindranath Tagore
(iv) Albert T. Mayor
(v) F.L. Brayne

Codes:	**A**	**B**	**C**	**D**
(a)	(iv)	(i)	(ii)	(v)
(b)	(i)	(iii)	(iv)	(ii)
(c)	(iii)	(i)	(v)	(iv)
(d)	(v)	(iii)	(ii)	(iv)

74. Match the items in List I with List II:

List I

(A) David K. Berto
(B) Edgar Dale
(C) Rogers, E.M.
(D) Robert Chambers

List II

(i) Diffusion of innovations
(ii) Communication Model

(iii) Rapid Rural Appraisal
(iv) Cone of Experience
(v) Panchayati Raj

Codes:	A	B	C	D
(a)	(iv)	(iii)	(ii)	(i)
(b)	(iii)	(iv)	(ii)	(i)
(c)	(ii)	(i)	(iii)	(iv)
(d)	(ii)	(iv)	(i)	(iii)

75. Match the eminent social activist in List I with movement they spearheaded in List II:

List I
(A) Medha Patkar
(B) Sundarlal Bahuguna
(C) Mahatma Gandhi
(D) Vinoba Bhave

List II
(i) Narmada Bachao
(ii) Bhoodan
(iii) Corruption
(iv) Freedom
(v) Chipko Project

Codes:	A	B	C	D
(a)	(iii)	(iv)	(ii)	(i)
(b)	(ii)	(i)	(iii)	(iv)
(c)	(i)	(v)	(iv)	(ii)
(d)	(i)	(v)	(ii)	(iv)

ANSWERS

1. (a)	2. (d)	3. (c)	4. (d)	5. (b)
6. (a)	7. (c)	8. (a)	9. (c)	10. (c)
11. (c)	12. (a)	13. (a)	14. (a)	15. (c)
16. (d)	17. (b)	18. (b)	19. (c)	20. (b)
21. (d)	22. (c)	23. (c)	24. (b)	25. (a)
26. (b)	27. (c)	28. (c)	29. (c)	30. (b)
31. (c)	32. (c)	33. (b)	34. (b)	35. (b)
36. (a)	37. (d)	38. (b)	39. (a)	40. (a)
41. (a)	42. (d)	43. (b)	44. (d)	45. (d)
46. (d)	47. (c)	48. (b)	49. (a)	50. (b)
51. (c)	52. (a)	53. (b)	54. (c)	55. (a)
56. (d)	57. (b)	58. (c)	59. (b)	60. (d)
61. (b)	62. (a)	63. (d)	64. (b)	65. (a)
66. (b)	67. (c)	68. (b)	69. (b)	70. (a)
71. (d)	72. (b)	73. (d)	74. (d)	75. (c)

DECEMBER–2011

Note: This paper contains Sixty (60) multiple choice questions, each question carrying two (2) marks. Candidate is expected to answer any Fifty (50) questions. In case more than Fifty (50) questions are attempted, only the first Fifty (50) questions will be evaluated.

PAPER–I

1. Photo bleeding means
   (a) Photo cropping
   (b) Photo placement
   (c) Photo cutting
   (d) Photo colour adjustment

2. While designing communication strategy feed-forward studies are conducted by
   (a) Audience (b) Communicator
   (c) Satellite (d) Media

3. In which language the newspapers have highest circulation?
   (a) English (b) Hindi
   (c) Bengali (d) Tamil

4. Aspect ratio of TV Screen is
   (a) 4 : 3 (b) 3 : 4
   (c) 2 : 3 (d) 2 : 4

5. Communication with oneself is known as
   (a) Organisational Communication
   (b) Grapevine Communication
   (c) Interpersonal Communication
   (d) Intrapersonal Communication

6. The term 'SITE' stands for
   (a) Satellite Indian Television Experiment
   (b) Satellite International Television Experiment
   (c) Satellite Instructional Television Experiment
   (d) Satellite Instructional Teachers Education

7. What is the number that comes next in the sequence?
   2, 5, 9, 19, 37, __
   (a) 76 (b) 74
   (c) 75 (d) 50

8. Find the next letter for the series MPSV.....
   (a) X (b) Y
   (c) Z (d) A

9. If '367' means 'I am happy'; '748' means 'you are sad' and '469' means 'happy and sad' in a given code, then which of the following represents 'and' in that code?
   (a) 3 (b) 6
   (c) 9 (d) 4

10. The basis of the following classification is 'animal', 'man', 'house', 'book', and 'student':
    (a) Definite descriptions
    (b) Proper names
    (c) Descriptive phrases
    (d) Common names

11. **Assertion (A):** The coin when flipped next time will come up tails.
    Reason (R): Because the coin was flipped five times in a row, and each time it came up heads.
    Choose the correct answer from below:
    (a) Both (A) and (R) are true, and (R) is the correct explanation of (A).
    (b) Both (A) and (R) are false, and (R) is the correct explanation of (A).

(c) (A) is doubtful, (R) is true, and (R) is not the correct explanation of (A).
(d) (A) is doubtful, (R) is false, and (R) is the correct explanation of (A).

12. The relation 'is a sister of' is
(a) non-symmetrical (b) symmetrical
(c) asymmetrical (d) transitive

13. If the proposition "Vegetarians are not meat eaters" is false, then which of the following inferences is correct? Choose from the codes given below:
1. "Some vegetarians are meat eaters" is true.
2. "All vegetarians are meat eaters" is doubtful.
3. "Some vegetarians are not meat eaters" is true.
4. "Some vegetarians are not meat eaters" is doubtful.

Codes:
(a) 1, 2 and 3 (b) 2, 3 and 4
(c) 1, 3 and 4 (d) 1, 2 and 4

14. Determine the nature of the following definition:
'Poor' means having an annual income of ₹ 10,000.
(a) persuasive (b) precising
(c) lexical (d) stipulative

15. Which one of the following is not an argument?
(a) If today is Tuesday, tomorrow will be Wednesday.
(b) Since today is Tuesday, tomorrow will be Wednesday.
(c) Ram insulted me so I punched him in the nose.
(d) Ram is not at home, so he must have gone to town.

16. Venn diagram is a kind of diagram to
(a) represent and assess the truth of elementary inferences with the help of Boolean Algebra of classes.
(b) represent and assess the validity of elementary inferences with the help of Boolean Algebra of classes.
(c) represent but not assess the validity of elementary inferences with the help of Boolean Algebra of classes.
(d) assess but not represent the validity of elementary inferences with the help of Boolean Algebra of classes.

17. Inductive logic studies the way in which a premise may
(a) support and entail a conclusion
(b) not support but entail a conclusion
(c) neither support nor entail a conclusion
(d) support a conclusion without entailing it

18. Which of the following statements are true? Choose from the codes given below.
1. Some arguments, while not completely valid, are almost valid.
2. A sound argument may be invalid.
3. A cogent argument may have a probably false conclusion.
4. A statement may be true or false.

Codes:
(a) 1 and 2 (b) 1, 3 and 4
(c) Only 4 (d) 3 and 4

19. If the side of the square increases by 40%, then the area of the square increases by
(a) 60% (b) 40%
(c) 196% (d) 96%

20. There are 10 lamps in a hall. Each one of them can be switched on independently. The number of ways in which hall can be illuminated is
(a) 10^2 (b) 1023
(c) 2^{10} (d) 10!

21. How many numbers between 100 and 300 begin or end with 2?
(a) 100 (b) 110
(c) 120 (d) 180

22. In a college having 300 students, every student reads 5 newspapers and every newspaper is read by 60 students. The number of newspapers required is
(a) at least 30 (b) at most 20
(c) exactly 25 (d) exactly 5

The total CO_2 emissions from various sectors are 5 mmt. In the Pie Chart given below, the percentage contribution to CO_2 emissions from various sectors is indicated.

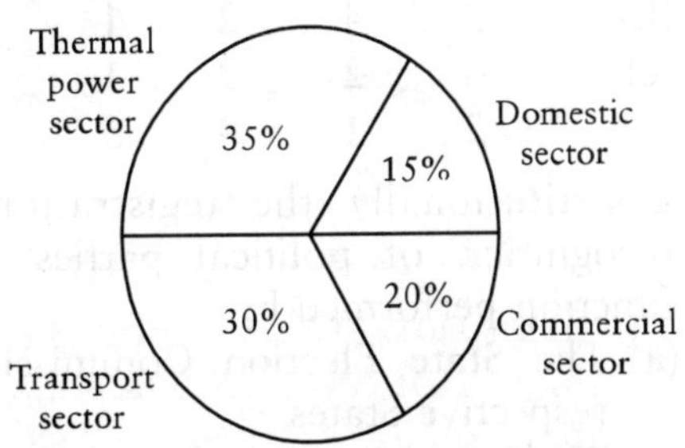

23. What is the absolute CO_2 emission from domestic sector?
(a) 1.5 mmt (b) 2.5 mmt
(c) 1.75 mmt (d) 0.75 mmt

24. What is the absolute CO_2 emission for combined thermal power and transport sectors?
(a) 3.25 mmt (b) 1.5 mmt
(c) 2.5 mmt (d) 4 mmt

25. Which of the following operating system is used on mobile phones?
(a) Windows Vista
(b) Android
(c) Windows XP
(d) All of the above

26. If $(y)_x$ represents a number y in base x, then which of the following numbers is smallest of all?
(a) $(1111)_2$ (b) $(1111)_8$
(c) $(1111)_{10}$ (d) $(1111)_{16}$

27. High level programming language can be converted to machine language using which of the following?
(a) Oracle (b) Compiler
(c) Mat lab (d) Assembler

28. HTML is used to create
(a) machine language program
(b) high level program
(c) web page
(d) web server

29. The term DNS stands for
(a) Domain Name System
(b) Defense Nuclear System
(c) Downloadable New Software
(d) Dependent Name Server

30. IPv4 and IPv6 are addresses used to identify computers on the internet. Find the correct statement out of the following:
(a) Number of bits required for IPv4 address is more than number of bits required for IPv6 address.
(b) Number of bits required for IPv4 address is same as number of bits required for IPv6 address.
(c) Number of bits required for IPv4 address is less than number of bits required for IPv6 address.
(d) Number of bits required for IPv4 address is 64.

31. Which of the following pollutants affects the respiratory tract in humans?
(a) Carbon monoxide
(b) Nitric oxide
(c) Sulphur di-oxide
(d) Aerosols

32. Which of the following pollutants is not emitted from the transport sector?
(a) Oxides of nitrogen
(b) Chlorofluorocarbons
(c) Carbon monoxide
(d) Poly aromatic hydrocarbons

33. Which of the following sources of energy has the maximum potential in India?
 (a) Solar energy
 (b) Wind energy
 (c) Ocean thermal energy
 (d) Tidal energy

34. Which of the following is not a source of pollution in soil?
 (a) Transport sector
 (b) Agriculture sector
 (c) Thermal power plants
 (d) Hydropower plants

35. Which of the following is not a natural hazard?
 (a) Earthquake (b) Tsunami
 (c) Flash floods (d) Nuclear accident

36. Ecological footprint represents
 (a) area of productive land and water to meet the resources requirement
 (b) energy consumption
 (c) CO_2 emissions per person
 (d) forest cover

37. The aim of value education to inculcate in students is
 (a) the moral values
 (b) the social values
 (c) the political values
 (d) the economic values

38. Indicate the number of Regional Offices of University Grants Commission of India.
 (a) 10 (b) 07
 (c) 08 (d) 09

39. One-rupee currency note in India bears the signature of
 (a) The President of India
 (b) Finance Minister of India
 (c) Governor, Reserve Bank of India
 (d) Finance Secretary of Government of India

40. Match the List I with the List II and select the correct answer from the codes given below:

List I (Commissions and Committees)
A. First Administrative Reforms Commission
B. Paul H. Appleby Committee I
C. K. Santhanam Committee
D. Second Administrative Reforms Commission

List II (Year)
1. 2005 2. 1962
3. 1966 4. 1953

Codes:	A	B	C	D
(a)	1	3	2	4
(b)	3	4	2	1
(c)	4	2	3	1
(d)	2	1	4	3

41. Constitutionally the registration and recognition of political parties is the function performed by
 (a) The State Election Commission of respective States
 (b) The Law Ministry of Government of India
 (c) The Election Commission of India
 (d) Election Department of the State Governments

42. The members of Gram Sabha are
 (a) Sarpanch, Upsarpanch and all elected Panchas
 (b) Sarpanch, Upsarpanch and village-level worker
 (c) Sarpanch, Gram Sevak and elected Panchas
 (d) Registered voters of Village Panchayat

43. By which of the following methods the true evaluation of the students is possible?
 (a) Evaluation at the end of the course
 (b) Evaluation twice in a year
 (c) Continuous evaluation
 (d) Formative evaluation

44. Suppose a student wants to share his problems with his teacher and he visits the teacher's house for the purpose, the teacher should

(a) contact the student's parents and solve his problem
(b) suggest him that he should never visit his house
(c) suggest him to meet the principal and solve the problem
(d) extend reasonable help and boost his morale

45. When some students are deliberately attempting to disturb the discipline of the class by making mischief, what will be your role as a teacher?
(a) Expelling those students
(b) Isolate those students
(c) Reform the group with your authority
(d) Giving them an opportunity for introspection and improve their behaviour

46. Which of the following belongs to a projected aid?
(a) Blackboard (b) Diorama
(c) Epidiascope (d) Globe

47. A teacher is said to be fluent in asking questions, if he can ask
(a) meaningful questions
(b) as many questions as possible
(c) maximum number of questions in a fixed time
(d) many meaningful questions in a fixed time

48. Which of the following qualities is most essential for a teacher?
(a) He should be a learned person
(b) He should be a well-dressed person
(c) He should have patience
(d) He should be an expert in his subject

49. A hypothesis is a
(a) law (b) canon
(c) postulate (d) supposition

50. Suppose you want to investigate the working efficiency of nationalised bank in India, which one of the following would you follow?
(a) Area Sampling
(b) Multi-stage Sampling
(c) Sequential Sampling
(d) Quota Sampling

51. Controlled group condition is applied in
(a) Survey Research
(b) Historical Research
(c) Experimental Research
(d) Descriptive Research

52. Workshops are meant for
(a) giving lectures
(b) multiple target groups
(c) showcase new theories
(d) hands on training/experience

53. Which one of the following is a research tool?
(a) Graph (b) Illustration
(c) Questionnaire (d) Diagram

54. Research is not considered ethical if it
(a) tries to prove a particular point.
(b) does not ensure privacy and anonymity of the respondent.
(c) does not investigate the data scientifically.
(d) is not of a very high standard.

Read the following passage carefully and answer the questions (55 to 60):

The catalytic fact of the twentieth century is uncontrollable development, consumerist society, political materialism, and spiritual devaluation. This inordinate development has led to the transcendental 'second reality' of sacred perception that biologically transcendence is a part of human life. As the century closes, it dawns with imperative vigour that the 'first reality' of enlightened rationalism and the 'second reality' of the Beyond have to be harmonised in a worthy state of man. The *de facto* values describe what we are, they portray the 'is' of our ethic, they are *est* values

(Latin *est* means is). The ideal values tell us what we ought to be, they are *esto* values (Latin *esto* 'ought to be'). Both have to be in the ebb and flow of consciousness. The ever new science and technology and the ever-perennial faith are two modes of one certainty, that is the wholeness of man, his courage to be, his share in Being.

The materialistic foundations of science have crumbled down. Science itself has proved that matter is energy, processes are as valid as facts, and affirmed the non-materiality of the universe. The encounter of the 'two cultures', the scientific and the humane, will restore the normal vision, and will be the bedrock of a 'science of understanding' in the new century. It will give new meaning to the ancient perception that quantity (measure) and quality (value) coexist at the root of nature. Human endeavours cannot afford to be humanistically irresponsible.

55. The problem raised in the passage reflects overall on
(a) Consumerism
(b) Materialism
(c) Spiritual devaluation
(d) Inordinate development

56. The *de facto* values in the passage means
(a) What is
(b) What ought to be
(c) What can be
(d) Where it is

57. According to the passage, the 'first reality' constitutes
(a) Economic prosperity
(b) Political development
(c) Sacred perception of life
(d) Enlightened rationalism

58. Encounter of the 'two cultures', the scientific and the human implies
(a) Restoration of normal vision
(b) Universe is both material and non-material
(c) Man is superior to nature
(d) Co-existence of quantity and quality in nature

59. The contents of the passage are
(a) Descriptive (b) Prescriptive
(c) Axiomatic (d) Optional

60. The passage indicates that science has proved that
(a) universe is material
(b) matter is energy
(c) nature has abundance
(d) humans are irresponsible

ANSWERS

1. (a)	2. (b)	3. (b)	4. (a)	5. (d)
6. (c)	7. (c)	8. (b)	9. (c)	10. (d)
11. (c)	12. (b)	13. (a)	14. (b)	15. (a)
16. (b)	17. (d)	18. (d)	19. (d)	20. (b)
21. (b)	22. (c)	23. (d)	24. (a)	25. (b)
26. (a)	27. (b)	28. (c)	29. (a)	30. (c)
31. (a)	32. (b)	33. (b)	34. (d)	35. (d)
36. (a)	37. (a)	38. (b)	39. (d)	40. (b)
41. (c)	42. (d)	43. (d)	44. (d)	45. (d)
46. (c)	47. (d)	48. (c)	49. (d)	50. (b)
51. (c)	52. (d)	53. (c)	54. (b)	55. (c)
56. (a)	57. (d)	58. (a)	59. (a)	60. (b)

PAPER–II

Note: This paper contains fifty (50) objective type questions, each question carrying two (2) marks. All questions are compulsory.

1. Moisture content of dehydrated potatoes, spinach, cauliflower, ragi should be
(a) 2 – 8% (b) 10 – 16%
(c) 18 – 24% (d) None of these

2. Major source of energy for the body is
   (a) Protein (b) Glucose
   (c) Fat (d) All of the above

3. The most sophisticated style and extremely formal service is
   (a) Waiter service (b) Self-service
   (c) Room service (d) Banquet service

4. A layout that is inappropriate for unidirectional fabric is
   (a) Lengthwise fold (b) Crosswise fold
   (c) Open fold (d) Double fold

5. Which of the following properties is not a primary property?
   (a) Strength (b) Tenacity
   (c) Flexibility (d) Density

6. Long-term and short-term goals are based on
   (a) Continuity (b) Duration
   (c) Interdependence (d) All the above

7. Rh incompatibility occurs, when blood of
   (a) Mother is Rh +ve and fetus is Rh –ve
   (b) Mother is Rh –ve and fetus is Rh +ve
   (c) Mother is Rh –ve and fetus is Rh –ve
   (d) Mother is Rh +ve and fetus is Rh +ve

8. Extension Education as a discipline of teaching programme started in early
   (a) 40s (b) 50s
   (c) 60s (d) 70s

9. The term Extension Education was first used in 1873 by the
   (a) Cambridge University
   (b) Oxford University
   (c) Banaras Hindu University
   (d) Delhi University

10. The researcher lives with the cultural community for a period of months or years is known as
    (a) Case study (b) Clinical study
    (c) Ethnography (d) Specimen record

11. Tocopherol is
    (i) Anticaking (ii) Antioxidant
    (iii) Antibiotic (iv) Vitamin
    Codes:
    (a) (ii) and (iv) are correct.
    (b) (i) and (iii) are correct.
    (c) (iv) and (i) are correct.
    (d) (iii) and (iv) are correct.

12. Three forms of Vitamin D are
    (i) Ergocalciferol
    (ii) Cholecalciferol
    (iii) 7-dehydrocholesterol
    (iv) Phytoergosterol
    Find out the correct combination according to code.
    (a) (ii), (iii), (iv) are correct.
    (b) (i), (iii), (iv) are correct.
    (c) (i), (ii), (iii) are correct.
    (d) (iv), (ii), (i) are correct.

13. Meal planning is important for:
    (i) Planning of food budget
    (ii) Nutritional adequacy
    (iii) Variety in diet
    (iv) Efficient utilization of resources
    Find out the correct combination according to code.
    (a) (i), (ii), (iii) and (iv) are correct.
    (b) (i) and (ii) are correct, but (i) and (iv) are incorrect.
    (c) (ii) and (iii) are correct, but (i) and (iv) are incorrect.
    (d) (i) and (iii) are correct, but (ii) and (iv) are incorrect.

14. While washing fabrics of protein fibres bleeding can be prevented by
    (i) Vinegar (ii) Common salt
    (iii) Washing soda (iv) Acetic acid
    Codes:
    (a) (i) and (ii) are correct.
    (b) (ii) and (iii) are correct.
    (c) (iii) and (iv) are correct.
    (d) (i) and (iv) are correct.

15. In a pattern darts can be replaced by
(i) Gathers (ii) Pin tucks
(iii) Style line (iv) Control seam
Codes:
(a) (i) and (ii) are correct.
(b) (ii) and (iii) are correct.
(c) (iii) and (iv) are correct.
(d) (i) and (iv) are correct.

16. The motivating factors to make decisions and choices are
(i) Resources (ii) Values
(iii) Goals (iv) Standards
Codes:
(a) (i), (ii) and (iv) are correct.
(b) (i), (ii) and (iii) are correct.
(c) (ii), (iii) and (iv) are correct.
(d) (i), (iii) and (iv) are correct.

17. Authoritarian child-rearing style
(i) Harsh control
(ii) Highly demanding
(iii) Lax control
(iv) Undemanding
(v) Firm control
(vi) Non-responsive
Codes:
(a) (i), (iii) and (iv) are correct.
(b) (iii), (ii) and (vi) are correct.
(c) (v), (ii) and (vi) are correct.
(d) (i), (ii) and (vi) are correct.

18. Extension learner learn the ideas and practices by
(i) Doing (ii) Reading
(iii) Watching (iv) Neighbour
Codes:
(a) (i), (ii) and (iii) are correct.
(b) (i), (iii) and (iv) are correct.
(c) (i) and (ii) are correct.
(d) (i) and (iii) are correct.

19. Innovative learner prefers specific teaching style;
(i) Discussion
(ii) Question and Answer
(iii) Independent Project
(iv) Audio Listening
Codes:
(a) (i), (ii) and (iii) are correct.
(b) (ii), (iii) and (iv) are correct.
(c) (i) and (ii) are correct.
(d) (ii) and (iii) are correct.

20. Which one of the following pairs is not correctly matched?
(a) The observational method is the most commonly used method to study – behaviour of individuals.
(b) Questionnaire can either be – structured or unstructured.
(c) Thematic apperception test is used to draw inferences about – respondent's, personality structure.
(d) Sociometry is a technique to study – emotional intelligence of children.

21. **Assertion (A):** Certain amino acids which are termed essential are to be obtained from protein in the diet.
Reason (R): Since they are not synthesized in human body.
Codes:
(a) (A) is true, but (R) is false.
(b) (A) and (R) are false.
(c) (A) is false, but (R) is true.
(d) (A) and (R) are true.

22. **Assertion (A):** People lose weight rapidly in the beginning when they start following weight reducing diet.
Reason (R): Glycogen stores are mobilized which is accompanied by loss of water.
Codes:
(a) (A) is true, but (R) is false.
(b) (A) and (R) are false.
(c) (A) and (R) are true.
(d) (A) is false, but (R) is true.

23. **Assertion (A):** Obesity and heart disease is a result of excessive energy intake and reduced physical activity.
Reason (R): Sedentary lifestyle and availability of high energy density foods leads to degenerative disease.
Codes:
(a) (A) is false and (R) is true.
(b) (A) is true and (R) is false.
(c) Both (A) and (R) are true.
(d) Both (A) and (R) are false.

24. **Assertion (A):** In a seam slits are given in onward curve.
Reason (R): Smaller area falls over bigger area.
Codes:
(a) Both (A) and (R) are true.
(b) (A) is correct but (R) is false.
(c) Both (A) and (R) are false.
(d) (A) is false, but (R) is true.

25. **Assertion (A):** Basket, ribbed, twill and satin are all basic weaves.
Reason (R): In all these weaves third set of yarn is used.
Codes:
(a) Both (A) and (R) are true.
(b) (A) is correct but (R) is false.
(c) Both (A) and (R) are false.
(d) (A) is false but (R) is true.

26. **Assertion (A):** Work simplification is the simplest, easiest and quickest method of doing a task.
Reason (R): Work simplification is a technique for accomplishing a task with least amount of energy.
Codes:
(a) (A) is true, but (R) is false.
(b) (A) is false, but (R) is true.
(c) Both (A) and (R) are true.
(d) Both (A) and (R) are false.

27. **Assertion (A):** 'Time out' is a form of punishment in which children are removed from the immediate setting until they are ready to act appropriately.
Reason (R): It is not a useful technique, because it does not provide enough time for children to change their behaviour.
Codes:
(a) Both (A) and (R) are true.
(b) (A) is true, but (R) is false.
(c) (A) is false, but (R) is true.
(d) Both (A) and (R) are false.

28. **Assertion (A):** NREGA recently named as (MGNREGA) Mahatma Gandhi National Rural Employment Guarantee Act on 2nd October 2009 was launched on 2nd Feb. 2006.
Reason (R): This is largest public employment guarantee programme of rural area which ultimately aims at better livelihood security of villagers.
Codes:
(a) Both (A) & (R) are true and (R) is the correct explanation.
(b) Both (A) & (R) are true but (R) is not the correct explanation.
(c) (A) is true, but (R) is false.
(d) (A) is false, but (R) is true.

29. **Assertion (A):** 73rd Constitutional Amendment 1992 gave Constitutional Status to Panchayat Raj Institutions. The amendment also made provision of 33 percent reservation for women.
Reason (R): This amendment has empowered women politically and has brought a sense of political responsibility by giving functional and financial autonomy to Panchayats.
Codes:
(a) Both (A) and (R) are true and (R) is the right explanation.
(b) Both (A) and (R) are true and (R) is not the correct explanation.
(c) (A) is true, but (R) is false.
(d) (A) is false, but (R) is true.

30. **Assertion (A):** Pretesting at the beginning of an experiment can produce a change in subjects.
    Reason (R): Pretesting may produce a practice effect making subjects more proficient in subsequent test performance.
    Codes:
    (a) Both (A) and (R) are false.
    (b) Both (A) and (R) are true.
    (c) (A) is true, but (R) is false.
    (d) (A) is false, but (R) is true.

31. Arrange the following foods in decreasing order of carotene content.
    (i) Jaggery (ii) Maize
    (iii) Curry leaves (iv) Pumpkin
    Codes:
    (a) (iv), (iii), (ii), (i) (b) (iii), (iv), (ii), (i)
    (c) (iii), (ii), (i), (iv) (d) (iv), (i), (ii), (iii)

32. Identify the correct order of food supplementation programme launched by Government of India:
    (a) ICDS, SNP, ANP, MDMP
    (b) SNP, MDMP, ANP, ICDS
    (c) ANP, MDMP, SNP, ICDS
    (d) ANP, SNP, ICDS, MDMP

33. Arrange the correct order of catering personnel according to seniority.
    (a) Manager, utility worker, cook, supervisor
    (b) Manager, cook, supervisor, utility worker
    (c) Manager, supervisor, cook, utility worker
    (d) Manager, utility worker, supervisor, cook

34. Give the correct sequence of steps followed while dyeing:
    (i) After treatment
    (ii) Preparation of fabric
    (iii) Preparation of dye bath
    (iv) Addition of exhaustion agents
    Codes:
    (a) (i), (ii), (iii), (iv) (b) (ii), (iii), (iv), (i)
    (c) (iii), (iv), (i), (ii) (d) (iv), (i), (ii), (iii)

35. Give the correct threading sequence pattern of a sewing machine.
    (i) Needle
    (ii) Spool
    (iii) Thread take up lever
    (iv) Tension discs
    Codes:
    (a) (i), (ii), (iv), (iii) (b) (ii), (iv), (iii), (i)
    (c) (iii), (i), (ii), (iv) (d) (iv), (iii), (i), (ii)

36. Arrange the following household activities on the basis of energy cost from light to very heavy:
    (i) Mopping floor
    (ii) Dusting furniture
    (iii) Grinding masala manually
    (iv) Ironing clothes
    Codes:
    (a) (ii), (iv), (iii), (i) (b) (iv), (i), (iii), (ii)
    (c) (ii), (iv), (i), (iii) (d) (iv), (ii), (i), (iii)

37. Arrange in a correct sequence.
    (i) Genital stage (ii) Anal stage
    (iii) Latency stage (iv) Phallic stage
    Codes:
    (a) (ii), (iv), (iii), (i) (b) (iv), (ii), (i), (iii)
    (c) (iii), (ii), (iv), (i) (d) (i), (iii), (ii), (iv)

38. Write the correct sequence of indigenous model.
    (i) Community
    (ii) Local problems
    (iii) Indigenous knowledge system
    (iv) Solution by experts using local material
    Codes:
    (a) (i), (ii), (iv) and (iii)
    (b) (i), (iii), (ii) and (iv)
    (c) (iv), (ii), (iii) and (i)
    (d) (i), (ii), (iii) and (iv)

39. Write the correct sequence of following media as per their appearance in India.

(i) Print (ii) Television
(iii) Radio (iv) Cinema

Codes:
(a) (i), (iv), (iii), (ii) (b) (ii), (iii), (iv), (i)
(c) (iii), (i), (iv), (ii) (d) (i), (ii), (iii), (iv)

40. Write the correct sequence of the steps in data analysis:
(i) Data entry
(ii) Statistical treatment
(iii) Coding
(iv) Tabulation

Codes:
(a) (iii), (i), (iv), (ii) (b) (iv), (iii), (i), (ii)
(c) (i), (iii), (iv), (ii) (d) (ii), (i), (iii), (iv)

41. Which one of the following pairs is correctly matched?
(a) Loss of liquid from solid food – *Syneresis*
(b) Mixing of one solid particle into another is an – *emulsion*
(c) Colloidal System in which the solid particles are dispersed in a liquid is a – *sol*
(d) Dispersion of one liquid into another is a – *gel*

42. Match an item in one list with an item in the other.

List I	List II
I. Turmeric	1. Argemone
II. Bengal gram flour	2. Starch
III. Mustard	3. Lathyrus sativus
IV. Milk	4. Metalin Yellow
	5. Amarnth

Codes:	I	II	III	IV
(a)	4	3	1	2
(b)	5	3	2	1
(c)	2	1	3	4
(d)	4	5	2	1

43. Match an item in List I with an item in other.

List I
I. Child care
II. Geriatric care
III. Care of sick
IV. Abandoned children

List II
1. Oldage Homes 2. Nursing Homes
3. Creche 4. Hostel
5. Orphanage

Codes:	I	II	III	IV
(a)	3	1	2	5
(b)	5	3	4	1
(c)	3	2	4	1
(d)	1	2	3	4

44. Match the machine parts given in List I with their functions given in List II.

List I
A. Pressure feet B. Feet dog
C. Throat plate D. Face plate

List II
1. Pushes fabric ahead after stitching
2. Provides smooth surface while stitching
3. Holds the fabric in place during stitching
4. Indicates the threading chart

Codes:	A	B	C	D
(a)	1	4	3	2
(b)	2	3	4	1
(c)	3	1	2	4
(d)	4	2	1	3

45. Match the fabrics given in List I with the characteristics given in List II.

List I	List II
A. Knits	1. Open work
B. Wovens	2. Web structure
C. Felt	3. Warps and wefts
D. Lace	4. Wales and courses

Codes:	A	B	C	D
(a)	1	4	3	2
(b)	2	1	4	3
(c)	3	2	1	4
(d)	4	3	2	1

46. Match the types of line in List I with their emotional effects in List II.

List I

I. Horizontal lines
II. Vertical lines
III. Diagonal lines
IV. Abandoned children

List II

1. Activity and dignity
2. Grace and flexibility
3. Rest and Repose
4. Movement and force

Codes:	I	II	III	IV
(a)	4	2	1	3
(b)	2	1	3	4
(c)	1	3	2	4
(d)	3	2	4	2

47. Match List I with List II.

List I

I. Behaviourism began with the work of
II. Viewed the child as tabula rasa
III. Founder of child study movement
IV. Viewed the child as developing within a complex system of relationships

List II

1. G. Stanley Hall
2. U. Bronfenbrenner
3. John Locke
4. John Watson

Codes:	I	II	III	IV
(a)	1	2	3	4
(b)	2	1	4	3
(c)	4	3	1	2
(d)	3	2	4	1

48. Match the following items in List I with List II.

List I	List II
I. Hindu Marriage Act	1. 1955
II. Medical Termination of Pregnancy	2. 2005
III. Dowry Prohibition Act	3. 1971
IV. Protection of Women from Domestic Violence Act	4. 1961

Codes:	I	II	III	IV
(a)	1	3	4	2
(b)	3	4	2	1
(c)	1	4	3	2
(d)	3	4	1	2

49. Match the following items in List I with List II.

List I

I. *Textbook of Mass Communication and Media*
II. *Extension Education and Communication*
III. *Participatory Rural Appraisal*
IV. *Education and Communication for Development*

List II

1. Neela Mukherjee
2. O.P. Dhama and O.P. Bhatnagar
3. Uma Joshi
4. V.K. Dubey and Indira Bishnoi

Codes:	I	II	III	IV
(a)	3	4	1	2
(b)	4	3	2	1
(c)	1	3	2	4
(d)	4	2	3	1

50. Match the statistical test in List I with the description in List II.

List I

I. Correlation II. Chi square
III. Paired *t*-test IV. Duncan test

List II

1. Comparison of means of more than two groups
2. Comparison of pre and post testing mean scores of a sample
3. Strength and direction of relationship between two variables
4. Data is in frequencies

Codes:	I	II	III	IV
(a)	3	4	2	1
(b)	1	2	3	4
(c)	4	3	1	2
(d)	2	1	4	3

ANSWERS

1. (a)	2. (a)	3. (d)	4. (a)	5. (a)
6. (d)	7. (b)	8. (c)	9. (a)	10. (c)
11. (a)	12. (c)	13. (d)	14. (d)	15. (c)
16. (d)	17. (a)	18. (d)	19. (b)	20. (c)
21. (a)	22. (c)	23. (d)	24. (b)	25. (b)
26. (c)	27. (a)	28. (d)	29. (a)	30. (b)
31. (b)	32. (a)	33. (c)	34. (b)	35. (c)
36. (c)	37. (b)	38. (d)	39. (a)	40. (c)
41. (b)	42. (a)	43. (a)	44. (c)	45. (c)
46. (b)	47. (c)	48. (a)	49. (a)	50. (a)

JUNE–2011

Note: This paper contains Sixty (60) multiple choice questions, each question carrying two (2) marks. Candidate is expected to answer any Fifty (50) questions. In case more than Fifty (50) questions are attempted, only the first Fifty (50) questions will be evaluated.

PAPER–I

1. A research paper is a brief report of research work based on
   (a) Primary Data only
   (b) Secondary Data only
   (c) Both Primary and Secondary Data
   (d) None of the above

2. Newton gave three basic laws of motion. This research is categorised as
   (a) Descriptive Research
   (b) Sample Survey
   (c) Fundamental Research
   (d) Applied Research

3. A group of experts in a specific area of knowledge assembled at a place and prepared a syllabus for a new course. The process may be termed as
   (a) Seminar (b) Workshop
   (c) Conference (d) Symposium

4. In the process of conducting research "Formulation of Hypothesis" is followed by
   (a) Statement of Objectives
   (b) Analysis of Data
   (c) Selection of Research Tools
   (d) Collection of Data

Read the following passage carefully and answer questions 5 to 10:

All historians are interpreters of text if they be private letters, Government records or parish birthlists or whatever. For most kinds of historians, these are only the necessary means to understanding something other than the texts themselves, such as a political action or a historical trend, whereas for the intellectual historian, a full understanding of his chosen texts is itself the aim of his enquiries. Of course, the intellectual history is particularly prone to draw on the focus of other disciplines that are habitually interpreting texts for purposes of their own, probing the reasoning that ostensibly connects premises and conclusions. Furthermore, the boundaries with adjacent subdisciplines are shifting and indistinct: the history of art and the history of science both claim a certain autonomy, partly just because they require specialised technical skills, but both can also be seen as part of a wider intellectual history, as is evident when one considers, for example, the common stock of knowledge about cosmological beliefs or moral ideals of a period.

Like all historians, the intellectual historian is a consumer rather than a producer of 'methods'. His distinctiveness lies in which aspect of the past he is trying to illuminate, not in having exclusive possession of either a corpus of evidence or a body of techniques. That being said, it does seem that the label 'intellectual history' attracts a disproportionate share of misunderstanding.

It is alleged that intellectual history is the history of something that never really mattered. The long dominance of the historical profession by political historians bred a kind of philistinism, an unspoken belief that power and its exercise was 'what mattered'. The prejudice was reinforced by the assertion that political action was never really the outcome of principles or ideas that were 'more flapdoodle'. The legacy of this precept is still discernible in the tendency to require ideas to have 'licensed' the political class before they can be deemed worthy of intellectual attention, as if there were some reasons why the history of art or science, of philosophy or literature, were somehow of interest and significance than the history of Parties or Parliaments. Perhaps in recent years the mirror-image of this philistinism has been more common in the claim that ideas of any one is of systematic expression or sophistication do not matter, as if they were only held by a minority.

Answer the following questions:

5. An intellectual historian aims to fully understand
   (a) the chosen texts of his own
   (b) political actions
   (c) historical trends
   (d) his enquiries
6. Intellectual historians do not claim exclusive possession of
   (a) conclusions
   (b) any corpus of evidence
   (c) distinctiveness
   (d) habitual interpretation
7. The misconceptions about intellectual history stem from
   (a) a body of techniques
   (b) the common stock of knowledge
   (c) the dominance of political historians
   (d) cosmological beliefs
8. What is philistinism?
   (a) Reinforcement of prejudice
   (b) Fabrication of reasons
   (c) The hold of land-owning classes
   (d) Belief that power and its exercise matter
9. Knowledge of cosmological beliefs or moral ideas of a period can be drawn as part of
   (a) literary criticism
   (b) history of science
   (c) history of philosophy
   (d) intellectual history
10. The claim that ideas of any one is of systematic expression do not matter, as if they were held by a minority, is
    (a) to have a licensed political class
    (b) a political action
    (c) a philosophy of literature
    (d) the mirror-image of philistinism
11. Public communication tends to occur within a more
    (a) complex structure
    (b) political structure
    (c) convenient structure
    (d) formal structure
12. Transforming thoughts, ideas and messages into verbal and non-verbal signs is referred to as
    (a) channelisation (b) mediation
    (c) encoding (d) decoding
13. Effective communication needs a supportive
    (a) economic environment
    (b) political environment
    (c) social environment
    (d) multi-cultural environment
14. A major barrier in the transmission of cognitive data in the process of communication is an individual's
    (a) personality (b) expectation
    (c) social status (d) coding ability
15. When communicated, institutionalised stereotypes become
    (a) myths (b) reasons
    (c) experiences (d) convictions
16. In mass communication, selective perception is dependent on the receiver's

(a) competence (b) pre-disposition
(c) receptivity (d) ethnicity

17. Determine the relationship between the pair of words NUMERATOR : DENOMINATOR and then select the pair of words from the following which have a similar relationship:
(a) fraction : decimal
(b) divisor : quotient
(c) top : bottom
(d) dividend : divisor

18. Find the wrong number in the sequence
125, 127, 130, 135, 142, 153, 165
(a) 130 (b) 142
(c) 153 (d) 165

19. If HOBBY is coded as IOBY and LOBBY is coded as MOBY; then BOBBY is coded as
(a) BOBY (b) COBY
(c) DOBY (d) OOBY

20. The letters in the first set have certain relationship. On the basis of this relationship, make the right choice for the second set
K/T : 11/20 :: J/R : ?
(a) 10/8 (b) 10/18
(c) 11/19 (d) 10/19

21. If A = 5, B = 6, C = 7, D = 8 and so on, what do the following numbers stand for?
17, 19, 20, 9, 8
(a) Plane (b) Moped
(c) Motor (d) Tonga

22. The price of oil is increased by 25%. If the expenditure is not allowed to increase, the ratio between the reduction in consumption and the original consumption is
(a) 1:3 (b) 1:4
(c) 1:5 (d) 1:6

23. How many 8s are there in the following sequence which are preceded by 5 but not immediately followed by 3?
5 8 3 7 5 8 6 3 8 5 4 5 8 4 7 6
5 5 8 3 5 8 7 5 8 2 8 5
(a) 4 (b) 5
(c) 7 (d) 3

24. If a rectangle were called a circle, a circle a point, a point a triangle and a triangle a square, the shape of a wheel is
(a) Rectangle (b) Circle
(c) Point (d) Triangle

25. Which one of the following methods is best suited for mapping the distribution of different crops as provided in the standard classification of crops in India?
(a) Pie diagram
(b) Chorochromatic technique
(c) Isopleth technique
(d) Dot method

26. Which one of the following does not come under the methods of data classification?
(a) Qualitative (b) Normative
(c) Spatial (d) Quantitative

27. Which one of the following is not a source of data?
(a) Administrative records
(b) Population census
(c) GIS
(d) Sample survey

28. If the statement 'some men are cruel' is false, which of the following statements/statement are/is true?
(i) All men are cruel.
(ii) No men are cruel.
(iii) Some men are not cruel.
(a) (i) and (iii) (b) (i) and (ii)
(c) (ii) and (iii) (d) Only (iii)

29. The octal number system consists of the following symbols

(a) 0 – 7 (b) 0 – 9
(c) 0 – 9, A – F (d) None of these

30. The binary equivalent of $(-19)_{10}$ in signed magnitude system is
(a) 11101100 (b) 11101101
(c) 10010011 (d) None of these

31. DNS in internet technology stands for
(a) Dynamic Name System
(b) Domain Name System
(c) Distributed Name System
(d) None of these

32. HTML stands for
(a) Hyper Text Markup Language
(b) Hyper Text Manipulation Language
(c) Hyper Text Managing Links
(d) Hyper Text Manipulating Links

33. Which of the following is type of LAN?
(a) Ethernet (b) Token Ring
(c) FDDI (d) All of the above

34. Which of the following statements is true?
(a) Smart cards do not require an operating system.
(b) Smart cards and PCs use some operating system.
(c) COS is smart card operating system.
(d) The communication between reader and card is in full duplex mode.

35. The Ganga Action Plan was initiated during the year
(a) 1986 (b) 1988
(c) 1990 (d) 1992

36. Identify the correct sequence of energy sources in order of their share in the power sector in India.
(a) Thermal > nuclear > hydro > wind
(b) Thermal > hydro > nuclear > wind
(c) Hydro > nuclear > thermal > wind
(d) Nuclear > hydro > wind > thermal

37. Chromium as a contaminant in drinking water in excess of permissible levels, causes
(a) Skeletal damage
(b) Gastrointestinal problem
(c) Dermal and nervous problems
(d) Liver/Kidney problems

38. The main precursors of winter smog are
(a) N_2O and hydrocarbons
(b) NO_x and hydrocarbons
(c) SO_2 and hydrocarbons
(d) SO_2 and ozone

39. Flash floods are caused when
(a) the atmosphere is convectively unstable and there is considerable vertical wind shear
(b) the atmosphere is stable
(c) the atmosphere is convectively unstable with no vertical windshear
(d) winds are catabatic

40. In mega cities of India, the dominant source of air pollution is
(a) transport sector
(b) thermal power
(c) municipal waste
(d) commercial sector

41. The first Open University in India was set up in the State of
(a) Andhra Pradesh
(b) Delhi
(c) Himachal Pradesh
(d) Tamil Nadu

42. Most of the Universities in India are funded by
(a) the Central Government
(b) the State Governments
(c) the University Grants Commission
(d) Private bodies and individuals

43. Which of the following organisations looks after the quality of Technical and Management education in India?
(a) NCTE (b) MCI
(c) AICTE (d) CSIR

44. Consider the following statements: Identify the statement which implies natural justice.

(a) The principle of natural justice is followed by the Courts.
(b) Justice delayed is justice denied.
(c) Natural justice is an inalienable right of a citizen.
(d) A reasonable opportunity of being heard must be given.

45. The President of India is
(a) the Head of State
(b) the Head of Government
(c) both Head of the State and the Head of the Government
(d) None of the above

46. Who among the following holds office during the pleasure of the President of India?
(a) Chief Election Commissioner
(b) Comptroller and Auditor General of India
(c) Chairman of the Union Public Service Commission
(d) Governor of a State

Questions 47 to 49 are based upon the following diagram in which there are three interlocking circles A, P and S where A stands for Artists, circle P for Professors and circle S for Sportspersons. Different regions in the figure are lettered from a to f:

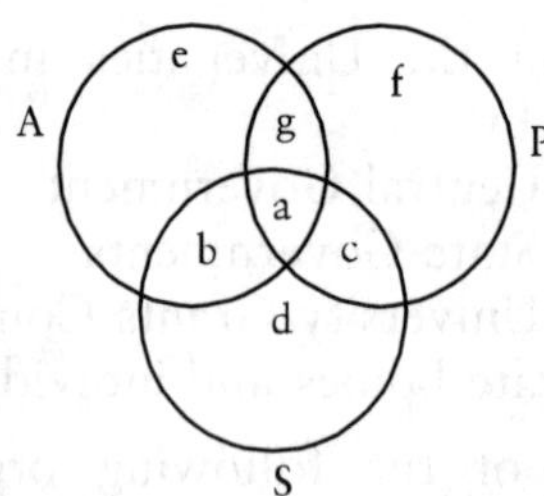

47. The region which represents artists who are neither sportsmen nor professors.
(a) d (b) e
(c) b (d) g

48. The region which represents professors, who are both artists and sportspersons.
(a) a (b) c
(c) d (d) g

49. The region which represents professors, who are also sportspersons, but not artists.
(a) e (b) f
(c) c (d) g

Questions 50 to 52 are based on the following data:

Measurements of some variable X were made at an interval of 1 minute from 10 A.M. to 10:20 A.M. The data, thus, obtained is as follows:

X: 60, 62, 65, 64, 63, 61, 66, 65, 70, 68
63, 62, 64, 69, 65, 64, 66, 67, 66, 64

50. The value of X, which is exceeded 10% of the time in the duration of measurement, is
(a) 69 (b) 68
(c) 67 (d) 66

51. The value of X, which is exceeded 90% of the time in the duration of measurement, is
(a) 63 (b) 62
(c) 61 (d) 60

52. The value of X, which is exceeded 50% of the time in the duration of measurement, is
(a) 66 (b) 65
(c) 64 (d) 63

53. For maintaining an effective discipline in the class, the teacher should
(a) Allow students to do what they like.
(b) Deal with the students strictly.
(c) Give the students some problem to solve.
(d) Deal with them politely and firmly.

54. An effective teaching aid is one which
(a) is colourful and good looking
(b) activates all faculties
(c) is visible to all students
(d) easy to prepare and use

55. Those teachers are popular among students who
(a) develop intimacy with them
(b) help them solve their problems
(c) award good grades
(d) take classes on extra tuition fee

56. The essence of an effective classroom environment is
(a) a variety of teaching aids
(b) lively student-teacher interaction
(c) pin-drop silence
(d) strict discipline

57. On the first day of his class, if a teacher is asked by the students to introduce himself, he should
(a) ask them to meet after the class
(b) tell them about himself in brief
(c) ignore the demand and start teaching
(d) scold the student for this unwanted demand

58. Moral values can be effectively inculcated among the students when the teacher
(a) frequently talks about values
(b) himself practises them
(c) tells stories of great persons
(d) talks of Gods and Goddesses

59. The essential qualities of a researcher are
(a) spirit of free enquiry
(b) reliance on observation and evidence
(c) systematisation or theorising of knowledge
(d) All of the above

60. Research is conducted to
1. Generate new knowledge
2. Not to develop a theory
3. Obtain research degree
4. Reinterpret existing knowledge

Which of the above are correct?
(a) 1, 3 & 2 (b) 3, 2 & 4
(c) 2, 1 & 3 (d) 1, 3 & 4

ANSWERS

1. (c)	2. (c)	3. (b)	4. (c)	5. (a)
6. (b)	7. (c)	8. (d)	9. (d)	10. (d)
11. (d)	12. (c)	13. (d)	14. (c)	15. (d)
16. (b)	17. (d)	18. (d)	19. (b)	20. (b)
21. (b)	22. (c)	23. (a)	24. (c)	25. (a)
26. (b)	27. (a)	28. (b)	29. (a)	30. (d)
31. (b)	32. (a)	33. (d)	34. (c)	35. (a)
36. (b)	37. (d)	38. (c)	39. (a)	40. (a)
41. (a)	42. (c)	43. (c)	44. (d)	45. (b)
46. (d)	47. (b)	48. (a)	49. (c)	50. (c)
51. (b)	52. (d)	53. (d)	54. (b)	55. (b)
56. (b)	57. (b)	58. (b)	59. (d)	60. (d)

PAPER–II

Note: This paper contains fifty (50) objective type questions, each question carrying two (2) marks. All questions are compulsory.

1. Mould inhibitor used in the preparation of bread is
(a) Sodium and calcium propionate
(b) Sodium chloride
(c) Calcium Carbonate
(d) None of the above

2. Recommended Allowance of Folic Acid for pregnant woman is
(a) 300 mcg (b) 100 mcg
(c) 500 mcg (d) 400 mcg

3. The record of food store inventory is kept in
(a) Stock Register (b) Cash Book
(c) Note Book (d) Diary

4. Which of the following darts is a double pointed dart?
   (a) Fish dart (b) Flange dart
   (c) French dart (d) Designers dart

5. Diagonal ridges are characteristic feature of which weave?
   (a) Twill (b) Dobby
   (c) Swivel (d) Jacquard

6. The component of controlling in which actions and outputs are examined in compliance with standard is
   (a) Adjusting (b) Changing
   (c) Checking (d) Assessing

7. Germ cells are formed by a process called
   (a) Meiosis (b) Mitosis
   (c) Ovulation (d) Crossing over

8. Extension work originated in various countries in different ways depending on local conditions as reported by
   (a) F.A.O.
   (b) W.H.O.
   (c) Planning Commission
   (d) I.C.A.R.

9. Problem-solving cycle in extension is given by
   (a) Dewey
   (b) Russel
   (c) Ensminger
   (d) Swanson and Claar

10. A predictive statement that relates an independent variable to a dependent variable
    (a) Objective
    (b) Hypothesis
    (c) Extraneous variable
    (d) Psychological variable

11. Cereals provide:
    I. Energy II. Iodine
    III. Vitamin A IV. Protein
    Find out the correct combination according to code.
    (a) I, II, III are correct
    (b) I and IV are correct
    (c) II and III are correct
    (d) I and III are correct

12. The best known enhancers of iron absorption in the body are
    I. Ascorbic acid II. Folic acid
    III. Lactoferrin IV. Polyphenols
    Find out the correct combination:
    (a) I and III are correct
    (b) III and II are correct
    (c) IV and II are correct
    (d) IV and I are correct

13. A cycle menu contains:
    I. Menu rotated at definite interval.
    II. A seven days' menu
    III. Set menu
    IV. Menu of the day
    Find out the correct combination
    (a) I, II, III are correct.
    (b) I and II are correct.
    (c) II and III are correct.
    (d) I and III are correct.

14. Sleeves most appropriate for infants garment are
    I. Leg of Mutton II. Saddler
    III. Kimono IV. Raglan
    Find the correct combination according to code.
    (a) I and II are correct
    (b) I and III are correct
    (c) II and III are correct
    (d) III and IV are correct

15. Chemical finishes exclusively given to cotton to increase lustre, strength and dyeability are
    I. Fulling II. Crabbing
    III. Bleaching IV. Mercerisation
    Find the correct combination according to Code.
    (a) I and II are correct.
    (b) II and III are correct.

(c) III and IV are correct.
(d) I and IV are correct.

16. Spaciousness in interiors can be achieved by
I. Using cool colour scheme
II. Using low furniture
III. Placing mirrors and glasses
IV. More numbers of windows and doors.
Codes:
(a) II, III and IV are correct.
(b) I, III and IV are correct.
(c) I, II, III are correct.
(d) I, II, IV are correct.

17. Planning a thematic unit in ECCE centre.
I. Assign each activity to one of the different developmental domains.
II. Brainstorm activities for selected theme.
III. Parent-teacher meetings.
IV. Select a theme.
Codes:
(a) I and III are correct.
(b) II and III are correct.
(c) IV, II and I are correct.
(d) III and IV are correct.

18. Which two approaches are good in communicating messages to the community?
I. Participatory Approach
II. Training and Visit Approach
III. Commodity Specialized Approach
IV. Direct approach by the community
Codes:
(a) I, II and III (b) I, II and IV
(c) I and IV (d) II, III and IV

19. Which are used for mass contact methods?
I. Personal calls
II. Circular letter
III. Radio and Television
IV. Tours
Codes:
(a) I, II and III (b) II, III and IV
(c) II and III (d) I and IV

20. Which one of the following pairs is not correctly matched?
(a) An in-depth study of a person is referred to as analytical study.
(b) In questionnaire, questions should proceed in a logical sequence from easy to move difficult questions.
(c) Rorschach test consists of ten cards having prints of ink blots.
(d) Quizzes and tests are used to assess the memorising and analytical ability of respondents.

21. **Assertion (A):** In an Indian diet 70-80% of calories are derived from cereals.
Reason (R): As they are fibre rich foods.
Codes:
(a) (A) is correct but (R) is incorrect.
(b) (A) is incorrect but (R) is correct.
(c) (A) and (R) are correct.
(d) (A) and (R) are incorrect.

22. **Assertion (A):** Celiac disease is an autoimmune inflammatory disease of small intestine.
Reason (R): It is precipitated by the ingestion of gluten.
Codes:
(a) (R) is correct but (A) is incorrect.
(b) (A) and (R) are correct.
(c) (A) is incorrect but (R) is correct.
(d) (A) and (R) are incorrect.

23. **Assertion (A):** A process chart is a simple technique for recording and analysing a job.
Reason (R): It uses illustration to describe the process so that the job can be condensed into a compact form.
Codes:
(a) Both (A) and (R) are true.
(b) (A) is true and (R) is false.
(c) (R) is false but (A) is true.
(d) (A) and (R) are false.

24. **Assertion (A):** Use of mordants is essential while using any type of dye.

Reason (R): Mordant increases the colour fastness of the dye.

Codes:

(a) (A) is false but (R) is true.
(b) (A) is true but (R) is false.
(c) Both (A) and (R) are false.
(d) Both (A) and (R) are true.

25. **Assertion (A):** Decorative Yoke can be cut on any grain of the fabric.

Reason (R): It supports the weight of the garment.

Codes:

(a) Both (A) and (R) are correct.
(b) Both (A) and (R) are false.
(c) (A) is correct but (R) is false.
(d) (A) is false but (R) is correct.

26. **Assertion (A):** The housing needs of family are based on demographic profits of family.

Reason (R): When the family passes through different stages of life cycle, i.e. from beginning till contracting stage, the space requirement increases.

Codes:

(a) Both (A) and (R) are true.
(b) Both (A) and (R) are false.
(c) (A) is true, but (R) is false.
(d) (A) is false, but (R) is true.

27. **Assertion (A):** Males are more likely to be affected by X-linked disorders.

Reason (R): Because their sex chromosomes are autosomes.

Codes:

(a) (A) is false but (R) is true.
(b) Both (A) and (R) are true.
(c) Both (A) and (R) are false.
(d) (A) is true but (R) is false.

28. **Assertion (A):** The Swarnjayanti Gram Swarojgar Yojna was launched in April 1999 and is the only self-employment programme currently being implemented.

Reason (R): It aims at promoting micro-enterprises and to bring the poor families above the poverty line.

Codes:

(a) Both (A) and (R) are true but (R) is not the correct explanation of (A).
(b) Both (A) and (R) are true and (R) is the correct explanation of (A).
(c) (A) is true but (R) is false.
(d) (A) is false but (R) is true.

29. **Assertion (A):** Right to Education Act which was implemented on 1st April, 2010 by Govt. of India.

Reason (R): It ensures education to all children of the country between the age of 6 yrs to 14 years.

Codes:

(a) Both (A) and (R) are true and (R) is correct explanation of (A).
(b) Both (A) and (R) are true but (R) is not the correct explanation of (A).
(c) (A) is true, but (R) is false.
(d) (A) is false, but (R) is true.

30. **Assertion (A):** Critical analysis of a research report is valuable for researcher.

Reason (R): Through a critical analysis the researcher gains some insight into the nature of a research problem, methods used and conclusions drawn.

Codes:

(a) (A) is true but (R) is false.
(b) Both (A) and (R) are true.
(c) (A) is false but (R) is true.
(d) Both (A) and (R) are false.

31. The proper sequence for estimation of crude fibre in food is

I. Drying and weighing of food.
II. Weighing of ground sample and defaulting.
III. Digestion with 1.25% H_2SO_4 and filtration.
IV. Digestion with 1.25% NaOH and filtration.

Codes:
(a) II, IV, I, III (b) II, III, IV, I
(c) IV, I, III, II (d) I, IV, II, III

32. Identify the correct order of ocular signs of vitamin A:
(a) Night blindness, Bitot's spot, Keratomalacia, Corneal Xerosis.
(b) Bitot's spot, Keratomalacia, Corneal Xerosis, Night blindness.
(c) Night blindness, Bitot's spot, Corneal Xerosis, Keratomalacia.
(d) Keratomalacia, Bitot's spot, Night blindness, Corneal Xerosis.

33. Arrange the correct sequence in the preparation of sandwich.
I. Preparing the filling
II. Collecting ingredients together
III. Applying butter on the slices
IV. Spreading the filling between the slices and cutting
Codes:
(a) III, IV, II, I (b) II, I, III, IV
(c) I, II, III, IV (d) II, I, IV, III

34. Give the correct sequence in weaving a fabric.
I. Shedding II. Picking
III. Let-off IV. Beat up
Codes:
(a) I, IV, III, II (b) II, III, IV, I
(c) III, I, II, IV (d) IV, II, I, III

35. Give the correct sequence of cutting a sleeve pattern.
I. Marking the stitching line.
II. Tracing the stitching line.
III. Cutting the sleeve pattern.
IV. Marking the cutting line.
Codes:
(a) II, I, IV, III (b) I, IV, III, II
(c) III, II, I, IV (d) IV, III, II, I

36. Arrange the following methods of resolving conflict in sequence from highest level to lowest level.
I. Voluntary submission
II. Conversion
III. Dominance
IV. Integration
Codes:
(a) II, I, III, IV (b) IV, II, I, III
(c) IV, I, II, III (d) I, II, IV, III

37. Arrange in a correct sequence:
I. Identity vs. Role confusion
II. Autonomy vs. Shame and doubt
III. Industry vs. Inferiority
IV. Initiative vs. Guilt
Codes:
(a) I, II, III, IV (b) II, IV, III, I
(c) IV, III, II, I (d) III, II, I, IV

38. Write the framework of Panchayat Raj system from lowest to highest.
I. Panchayat Samiti
II. Gram Panchayat
III. Zilla Parishad
Codes:
(a) I, II, III (b) II, I, III
(c) III, II, I (d) II, III, I

39. Write the steps of Adoption Process in an order.
I. Interest II. Evaluation
III. Awareness IV. Trial
Codes:
(a) III, I, IV, II (b) III, I, II, IV
(c) I, II, III, IV (d) IV, II, I, III

40. Write the correct sequence of the steps in the process of research designing.
I. Review of literature.
II. Organize and draft the research design.
III. Select area and subjects.
IV. Formulate problem.
Codes:
(a) I, II, III, IV (b) II, III, IV, I
(c) III, I, II, IV (d) IV, I, III, II

41. Match an item in List I with an item in List II.

List I	List II
I. Boiling	1. Chapati
II. Blanching	2. Rice
III. Baking	3. Pastry
IV. Roasting	4. Tomatoes
	5. Ice cream

Codes:	I	II	III	IV
(a)	1	4	3	2
(b)	2	4	3	1
(c)	2	1	3	5
(d)	1	5	2	4

42. Match an item in List I with an item in List II.

List I
I. Clostridium Perfringens
II. Entamoeba histolytica
III. Shigella bacterium
IV. Campylobacter Jejuni

List II
1. Bacillary dysentery
2. Diarrhoea
3. Amoebic dysentery
4. Gastroenteritis
5. Hepatitis A

Codes:	I	II	III	IV
(a)	4	3	1	2
(b)	1	2	3	4
(c)	3	4	2	1
(d)	1	3	4	2

43. Match an item in List I with an item in List II.

List I
I. Personal Management
II. Financial Management
III. Plant Management
IV. Market Management

List II
1. Cash book
2. Job specification
3. Production schedule
4. Discount
5. Insulation

Codes:	I	II	III	IV
(a)	2	1	3	4
(b)	4	3	2	1
(c)	1	2	4	3
(d)	3	1	2	4

44. Match the fabrics given in List I with the characteristics given in List II.

List I
I. Seer Sucker II. Satin
III. Terry towelling IV. Velvet

List II
1. Loops on the surface
2. Puckered effect
3. Smooth lustrous face and dull back
4. Short soft thick cut pile

Codes:	I	II	III	IV
(a)	1	4	2	3
(b)	3	2	4	1
(c)	2	3	1	4
(d)	4	1	3	2

45. Match the garments given in List I with the type of ease required given in List II.

List I (Garments)	List II (Types of ease)
I. Saree blouse	1. Style ease
II. Jackets	2. Negative ease
III. Kurta	3. Comfort ease
IV. Swim suit	4. Layered ease

Codes:	I	II	III	IV
(a)	2	1	3	4
(b)	3	4	1	2
(c)	1	2	4	3
(d)	4	3	2	1

46. Match the types of decisions in List I with the decision situations in List II.

List I
I. Technical Decisions
II. Economic Decisions
III. Social Decisions
IV. Legal Decisions

List II
1. To resolve value conflicts
2. For application of norms

3. To achieve single goal
4. To achieve multiple goals with limited resources

Codes:	I	II	III	IV
(a)	4	2	1	3
(b)	2	1	4	3
(c)	3	4	1	2
(d)	1	2	3	4

47. Match List I with List II.

List I

I. Concept of absorbent mind is important in the philosophy of
II. The author of *A Guide for Nursery School Teachers*
III. Literature is true vehicle of education
IV. Was actively associated with Balwadi type of preschool programme

List II

1. Tarabai Modak
2. Rabindranath Tagore
3. Rajalakshmi Murlidharan
4. Maria Montessori

Codes:	I	II	III	IV
(a)	4	3	2	1
(b)	3	2	4	1
(c)	1	2	3	4
(d)	2	4	1	3

48. Match the following items in List I with List II.

List I

I. Council for Advancement of people's Action and Rural Technology
II. Annapurna Yojana
III. Jawahar Rozgar Yojana
IV. Integrated Rural Development Programme

List II

1. 1980 2. 1989
3. 1986 4. 1999

Codes:	I	II	III	IV
(a)	3	4	2	1
(b)	4	2	1	3
(c)	2	1	3	4
(d)	1	2	4	3

49. Match the following items in List I with List II.

List I

I. Participatory Approach
II. Adoption
III. Culture
IV. Twelve Five Year Plan

List II

1. Following practices
2. 2007-2012
3. Direct participation of people
4. A learnt behaviour

Codes:	I	II	III	IV
(a)	3	4	1	2
(b)	4	2	1	3
(c)	3	2	4	1
(d)	1	2	4	3

50. Match the symbols in List I with words in List II.

List I	List II
I. X	1. Correlation coefficient
II. γ	2. Chi-square
III. ε	3. Mean
VI. χ^2	4. Sum of

Codes:	I	II	III	IV
(a)	1	2	3	4
(b)	2	3	4	1
(c)	3	1	4	2
(d)	4	3	1	2

ANSWERS

1. (a)	2. (d)	3. (a)	4. (a)	5. (a)
6. (a)	7. (a)	8. (c)	9. (a)	10. (b)
11. (b)	12. (d)	13. (b)	14. (d)	15. (c)
16. (c)	17. (c)	18. (a)	19. (c)	20. (a)
21. (a)	22. (b)	23. (a)	24. (d)	25. (a)
26. (a)	27. (c)	28. (a)	29. (a)	30. (b)
31. (b)	32. (c)	33. (c)	34. (c)	35. (d)
36. (c)	37. (c)	38. (b)	39. (c)	40. (b)
41. (b)	42. (d)	43. (a)	44. (c)	45. (d)
46. (c)	47. (a)	48. (a)	49. (b)	50. (c)

DECEMBER–2010

Note: This paper contains Sixty (60) multiple choice questions, each question carrying two (2) marks. Candidate is expected to answer any Fifty (50) questions. In case more than Fifty (50) questions are attempted, only the first Fifty (50) questions will be evaluated.

PAPER–I

1. Which of the following variables cannot be expressed in quantitative terms?
   (a) Socio-economic Status
   (b) Marital Status
   (c) Numerical Aptitude
   (d) Professional Attitude

2. A doctor studies the relative effectiveness of two drugs of dengue fever. His research would be classified as
   (a) Descriptive Survey
   (b) Experimental Research
   (c) Case Study
   (d) Ethnography

3. The term 'phenomenology' is associated with the process of
   (a) Qualitative Research
   (b) Analysis of Variance
   (c) Correlational Study
   (d) Probability Sampling

4. The 'Sociogram' technique is used to study
   (a) Vocational Interest
   (b) Professional Competence
   (c) Human Relations
   (d) Achievement Motivation

Read the following passage carefully and answer questions from 5 to 10.

It should be remembered that the nationalist movement in India, like all nationalist movements, was essentially a bourgeois movement. It represented the natural historical stage of development, and to consider it or to criticise it as a working-class movement is wrong. Gandhi represented that movement and the Indian masses in relation to that movement to a supreme degree, and he became the voice of Indian people to that extent. The main contribution of Gandhi to India and the Indian masses has been through the powerful movements which he launched through the National Congress. Through nation-wide action he sought to mould the millions, and largely succeeded in doing so, and changing them from a demoralised, timid and hopeless mass, bullied and crushed by every dominant interest, and incapable of resistance, into a people with self-respect and self-reliance, resisting tyranny, and capable of united action and sacrifice for a larger cause.

Gandhi made people think of political and economic issues and every village and every bazaar hummed with argument and debate on the new ideas and hopes that filled the people. That was an amazing psychological change. The time was ripe for it, of course, and circumstances and world conditions worked for this change. But a great leader is necessary to take advantage of circumstances and conditions. Gandhi was that leader, and he released many of the bonds that imprisoned and disabled our minds, and none of us who experienced it can ever forget that great feeling of release and exhilaration that came over the Indian people.

Gandhi has played a revolutionary role in India of the greatest importance because he knew how to make the most of the objective conditions and could reach the heart of the masses, while groups with a more advanced ideology functioned largely in the air because they did not fit in with those conditions and could therefore not evoke any substantial response from the masses.

It is perfectly true that Gandhi, functioning in the nationalist plane, does not think in terms of the conflict of classes, and tries to compose their differences. But the action he has indulged and taught the people has inevitably raised mass consciousness tremendously and made social issues vital. Gandhi and the Congress must be judged by the policies they pursue and the action they indulge in. But behind this, personality counts and colours those policies and activities. In the case of very exceptional person like Gandhi the question of personality becomes especially important in order to understand and appraise him. To us he has represented the spirit and honour of India, the yearning of her sorrowing millions to be rid of their innumerable burdens, and an insult to him by the British Government or others has been an insult to India and her people.

5. Which one of the following is true of the given passage?
   (a) The passage is a critique of Gandhi's role in Indian movement for independence
   (b) The passage hails the role of Gandhi in India's freedom movement
   (c) The author is neutral on Gandhi's role in India's freedom movement
   (d) It is an account of Indian National Congress's support to the working-class movement

6. The change that the Gandhian movement brought among the Indian masses was
   (a) Physical (b) Cultural
   (c) Technological (d) Psychological

7. To consider the nationalist movement or to criticise it as a working-class movement was wrong because it was a
   (a) historical movement
   (b) voice of the Indian people
   (c) bourgeois movement
   (d) movement represented by Gandhi

8. Gandhi played a revolutionary role in India because he could
   (a) preach morality
   (b) reach the heart of Indians
   (c) see the conflict of classes
   (d) lead the Indian National Congress

9. Groups with advanced ideology functioned in the air as they did not fit in with
   (a) objective conditions of masses
   (b) the Gandhian ideology
   (c) the class consciousness of the people
   (d) the differences among masses

10. The author concludes the passage by
   (a) criticising the Indian masses
   (b) the Gandhian movement
   (c) pointing out the importance of the personality of Gandhi
   (d) identifying the sorrows of millions of Indians

11. Media that exist in an interconnected series of communication—points are referred to as
   (a) Networked media
   (b) Connective media
   (c) Nodal media
   (d) Multimedia

12. The information function of mass communication is described as
   (a) diffusion (b) publicity
   (c) surveillance (d) diversion

13. An example of asynchronous medium is

(a) Radio (b) Television
(c) Film (d) Newspaper

14. In communication, connotative words are
(a) explicit (b) simple
(c) abstract (d) cultural

15. A message beneath a message is labelled as
(a) embedded text (b) internal text
(c) inter-text (d) sub-text

16. In analogue mass communication, stories are
(a) static (b) dynamic
(c) interactive (d) exploratory

17. Determine the relationship between the pair of words ALWAYS : NEVER and then select from the following pair of words which have a similar relationship
(a) often : rarely
(b) frequently : occasionally
(c) constantly : frequently
(d) intermittently : casually

18. Find the wrong number in the sequence 52, 51, 48, 43, 34, 27, 16
(a) 27 (b) 34
(c) 43 (d) 48

19. In a certain code, PAN is written as 31 and PAR as 35, then PAT is written in the same code as
(a) 30 (b) 37
(c) 39 (d) 41

20. The letters in the first set have certain relationship. On the basis of this relationship, make the right choice for the second set:
AF : IK : : LQ : ?
(a) MO (b) NP
(c) OR (d) TV

21. If 5472 = 9, 6342 = 6, 7584 = 6, what is 9236?
(a) 2 (b) 3
(c) 4 (d) 5

22. In an examination, 35% of the total students failed in Hindi, 45% failed in English and 20% in both. The percentage of those who passed in both subjects is
(a) 10 (b) 20
(c) 30 (d) 40

23. Two statements I and II given below are followed by two conclusions (a) and (b). Supposing the statements are true, which of the following conclusions can logically follow?
Statements:
I. Some flowers are red.
II. Some flowers are blue.
Conclusions:
(A) Some flowers are neither red nor blue.
(B) Some flowers are both red and blue.
(a) Only (A) follows
(b) Only (B) follows
(c) Both (A) and (B) follows
(d) Neither (A) nor (B) follows

24. If the statement 'all students are intelligent' is true, which of the following statements are false?
(i) No students are intelligent.
(ii) Some students are intelligent.
(iii) Some students are not intelligent.
(a) (i) and (ii) (b) (i) and (iii)
(c) (ii) and (iii) (d) Only (i)

25. A reasoning where we start with certain particular statements and conclude with a universal statement is called
(a) Deductive Reasoning
(b) Inductive Reasoning
(c) Abnormal Reasoning
(d) Transcendental Reasoning

26. What is the smallest number of ducks that could swim in this formation—two ducks in front of a duck, two ducks behind a duck and a duck between two ducks?

(a) 5 (b) 7
(c) 4 (d) 3

27. Mr. A, Miss B, Mr. C and Miss D are sitting around a table and discussing their trades.
(i) Mr. A sits opposite to the cook.
(ii) Miss B sits right to the barber.
(iii) The washerman sits right to the barber.
(iv) Miss D sits opposite to Mr. C.
What are the trades of A and B?
(a) Tailor and barber
(b) Barber and cook
(c) Tailor and cook
(d) Tailor and washerman

28. Which one of the following methods serve to measure correlation between two variables?
(a) Scatter Diagram
(b) Frequency Distribution
(c) Two-way Table
(d) Coefficient of Rank Correlation

29. Which one of the following is not an Internet Service Provider (ISP)?
(a) MTNL
(b) BSNL
(c) ERNET India
(d) Infotech India Ltd.

30. The hexadecimal number system consists of the symbols
(a) 0 - 7 (b) 0 - 9, A - F
(c) 0 - 7, A - F (d) None of these

31. The binary equivalent of $(-15)_{10}$ is (2's complement system is used)
(a) 11110001 (b) 11110000
(c) 10001111 (d) None of these

32. 1 GB is equal to
(a) 2^{30} bits (b) 2^{30} bytes
(c) 2^{20} bits (d) 2^{20} bytes

33. The set of computer programs that manage the hardware/software of a computer is called
(a) Compiler system
(b) Operation system
(c) Operating system
(d) None of these

34. SMIME in Internet technology stands for
(a) Secure Multipurpose Internet Mail Extension
(b) Secure Multimedia Internet Mail Extension
(c) Simple Multipurpose Internet Mail Extension
(d) Simple Multimedia Internet Mail Extension

35. Which of the following is not covered in 8 missions under the Climate Action Plan of Government of India?
(a) Solar power
(b) Waste to energy conversion
(c) Afforestation
(d) Nuclear energy

36. The concentration of Total Dissolved Solids (TDS) in drinking water should not exceed
(a) 500 mg/L (b) 400 mg/L
(c) 300 mg/L (d) 200 mg/L

37. 'Chipko' movement was first started by
(a) Arundhati Roy
(b) Medha Patkar
(c) Ila Bhatt
(d) Sunderlal Bahuguna

38. The constituents of photochemical smog responsible for eye irritation are
(a) SO_2 and O_3
(b) SO_2 and NO_2
(c) HCHO and PAN
(d) SO_2 and SPM

39. **Assertion (A):** Some carbonaceous aerosols may be carcinogenic.
Reason (R): They may contain polycyclic aromatic hydrocarbons (PAHs).
(a) Both (A) and (R) are correct and (R) is the correct explanation of (A).

(b) Both (A) and (R) are correct but (R) is not the correct explanation of (A).
(c) (A) is correct, but (R) is false.
(d) (A) is false, but (R) is correct.

40. Volcanic eruptions affect
(a) atmosphere and hydrosphere
(b) hydrosphere and biosphere
(c) lithosphere, biosphere and atmosphere
(d) lithosphere, hydrosphere and atmosphere

41. India's first Defence University is in the State of
(a) Haryana
(b) Andhra Pradesh
(c) Uttar Pradesh
(d) Punjab

42. Most of the Universities in India
(a) conduct teaching and research only
(b) affiliate colleges and conduct examinations
(c) conduct teaching/research and examinations
(d) promote research only

43. Which one of the following is not a Constitutional Body?
(a) Election Commission
(b) Finance Commission
(c) Union Public Service Commission
(d) Planning Commission

44. Which one of the following statements is not correct?
(a) Indian Parliament is supreme.
(b) The Supreme Court of India has the power of judicial review.
(c) There is a division of powers between the Centre and the States.
(d) There is a Council of Ministers to aid and advise the President.

45. Which one of the following statements reflects the republic character of Indian democracy?
(a) Written constitution
(b) No State religion
(c) Devolution of power to local Government institutions
(d) Elected President and directly or indirectly elected Parliament

46. Who among the following appointed by the Governor can be removed by only the President of India?
(a) Chief Minister of a State
(b) A member of the State Public Service Commission
(c) Advocate-General
(d) Vice Chancellor of a State University

47. If two small circles represent the class of the 'men' and the class of the 'plants' and the big circle represents 'mortality', which one of the following figures represent the proposition 'All men are mortal?.'

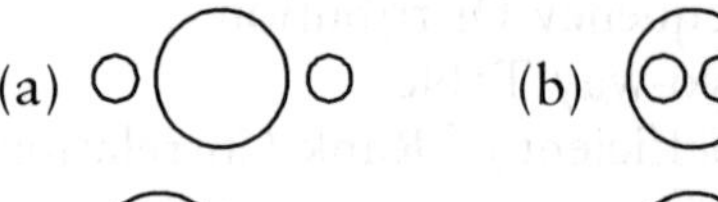

The following table presents the production of electronic items (TVs and LCDs) in a factory during the period from 2006 to 2010. Study the table carefully and answer the questions from 48 to 52:

Year	2006	2007	2008	2009	2010
TVs	6000	9000	13000	11000	8000
LCDs	7000	9400	9000	10000	12000

48. In which year, the total production of electronic items is maximum?
(a) 2006 (b) 2007
(c) 2008 (d) 2010

49. What is the difference between averages of production of LCDs and TVs from 2006 to 2008?

(a) 3000 (b) 2867
(c) 3015 (d) None of these

50. What is the year in which production of TVs is half the production of LCDs in the year 2010?
(a) 2007 (b) 2006
(c) 2009 (d) 2008

51. What is the ratio of production of LCDs in the years 2008 and 2010?
(a) 4:3 (b) 3:4
(c) 1:3 (d) 2:3

52. What is the ratio of production of TVs in the years 2006 and 2007?
(a) 6:7 (b) 7:6
(c) 2:3 (d) 3:2

53. Some students in a class exhibit great curiosity for learning. It may be because such children
(a) Are gifted
(b) Come from rich families
(c) Show artificial behaviour
(d) Create indiscipline in the class

54. The most important quality of a good teacher is
(a) Sound knowledge of subject matter
(b) Good communication skills
(c) Concern for students' welfare
(d) Effective leadership qualities

55. Which one of the following is appropriate in respect of teacher-student relationship?
(a) Very informal and intimate
(b) Limited to classroom only
(c) Cordial and respectful
(d) Indifferent

56. The academic performance of students can be improved if parents are encouraged to
(a) supervise the work of their wards
(b) arrange for extra tuition
(c) remain unconcerned about it
(d) interact with teachers frequently

57. In a lively classroom situation, there is likely to be
(a) occasional roars of laughter
(b) complete silence
(c) frequent teacher-student dialogue
(d) loud discussion among students

58. If a parent approaches the teacher to do some favour to his/her ward in the examination, the teacher should
(a) try to help him
(b) ask him not to talk in those terms
(c) refuse politely and firmly
(d) ask him rudely to go away

59. Which of the following phrases is not relevant to describe the meaning of research as a process?
(a) Systematic Activity
(b) Objective Observation
(c) Trial and Error
(d) Problem Solving

60. Which of the following is not an example of a continuous variable?
(a) Family size (b) Intelligence
(c) Height (d) Altitude

ANSWERS

1. (d)	2. (b)	3. (a)	4. (c)	5. (b)
6. (d)	7. (c)	8. (b)	9. (a)	10. (c)
11. (a)	12. (c)	13. (d)	14. (d)	15. (d)
16. (a)	17. (a)	18. (b)	19. (b)	20. (d)
21. (a)	22. (b)	23. (c)	24. (d)	25. (b)
26. (a)	27. (c)	28. (d)	29. (d)	30. (b)
31. (d)	32. (b)	33. (c)	34. (a)	35. (d)
36. (a)	37. (d)	38. (b)	39. (a)	40. (d)
41. (a)	42. (c)	43. (d)	44. (b)	45. (d)
46. (b)	47. (c)	48. (c)	49. (d)	50. (b)
51. (b)	52. (c)	53. (a)	54. (b)	55. (c)
56. (d)	57. (c)	58. (c)	59. (c)	60. (c)

PAPER–II

Note: This paper contains fifty (50) objective type questions, each question carrying two (2) marks. All questions are compulsory.

1. Absorption of Iron requires the following nutrients in the diet:
   (a) Vitamin C (b) Zinc
   (c) Iodine (d) Fat
2. Mental Retardation is an indicator of deficiency of
   (a) Vitamin A (b) Iodine
   (c) Calcium (d) Iron
3. Which of the following is an ω-3 (omega 3) fatty acid?
   (a) Linoleic acid
   (b) ∝-Linolenic acid
   (c) Arachadonic acid
   (d) Oleic acid
4. Which is the major protein found in milk?
   (a) Albumin (b) Casein
   (c) Myoglobin (d) Gliadin
5. The supplementary nutrition provided to preschooler at ICDS should provide
   (a) 350 calories and 10 g protein
   (b) 300 calories and 10 g protein
   (c) 600 calories and 16 g protein
   (d) 300 calories and 8 g protein
6. Following is not a direct system of yarn numbering:
   (a) Cotton count (b) Denier
   (c) Metric count (d) Tex
7. Series of loops that intersect horizontally in a fabric are called as
   (a) Courses (b) Wales
   (c) Warp (d) Weft
8. Preparation of the fabric for application of natural dyes is done by
   (a) Alizarine (b) Alum
   (c) Myrobalum (d) Turmeric
9. Job analysis is carried out by
   (a) Organisation of tasks.
   (b) Identification of skills required.
   (c) Collection of information related to nature of job.
   (d) Breaking down of job into parts and further evaluation.
10. Effective Management recognises the validity of
    (a) Resources
    (b) Decision Making
    (c) Management Process
    (d) Values and Standards
11. Bandura's social-cognitive learning asserts
    (a) Cognitive thinking and problem solving.
    (b) Learning behaviour, cognitive response pattern's social roles.
    (c) Cognitive problem-solving skills and capacities.
    (d) Learning specific observable responses.
12. Who is the Father of Kindergarten?
    (a) Pestalozzi (b) Rousseau
    (c) Locke (d) Froebel
13. Current developmental extension programmes adopt
    (a) Integrated approach
    (b) Multinational approach
    (c) Area development approach
    (d) Participatory approach
14. An effective extension programme
    (a) takes care of the needs of the target group.
    (b) works as per the Government.
    (c) works as per the extension workers' plans.
    (d) works within limited funds.
15. Good communication happens only when
    (a) More messages are given to more people.

(b) Right message is given in the right form and to right people.
(c) Various media are used to give messages.
(d) Messages are detailed and with illustrations.

16. Randomization model in research design is
(a) selecting random sample from population.
(b) randomly dividing the sample in two or more groups.
(c) selecting available sample.
(d) selecting cluster as a sample.

17. A variable that can be manipulated is
(a) Dependent variable
(b) Independent variable
(c) Continuous variable
(d) Discreet variable

18. An open-ended question elicits
(a) Leading answers (b) True data
(c) Objective results (d) Varied responses

19. **Assertion (A):** High salt and low potassium intakes are a risk factor for developing hypertension.
Reason (R): Consuming plenty of fruits & vegetables are recommended for hypertension.
(a) Both (A) and (R) are false.
(b) Both (A) and (R) are true.
(c) (A) is true and (R) is partially correct.
(d) (A) is false and (R) is correct.

20. **Assertion (A):** Egg yolk is used for making mayonnaise.
Reason (R): Egg yolk serves as an emulsifying agent in preparation of mayonnaise.
(a) (A) is false & (R) is true.
(b) Both (A) & (R) are false.
(c) (A) is true & (R) is false.
(d) Both (A) & (R) are true.

21. **Assertion (A):** Both vitamin A and fat are required for vision in the dark.
Reason (R): Fat helps in absorption of vitamin A in the gut.
(a) (A) is false & (R) is true.
(b) Both (A) & (R) are true.
(c) (R) is true & (A) is false.
(d) Both (A) & (R) are false.

22. **Assertion (A):** Rayon garments undergo progressive shrinkage.
Reason (R): Hence care has to be taken while drying and ironing.
(a) Both (A) & (R) are true.
(b) (A) is true, but (R) is false.
(c) (A) is false, but (R) is correct.
(d) (A) & (R) are false.

23. **Assertion (A):** Gores are vertical divisions within a garment.
Reason (R): They incorporate the dart shape in seams.
(a) Both (A) & (R) are false.
(b) Both (A) & (R) are correct.
(c) (A) is false, but (R) is true.
(d) (A) is true, but (R) is false.

24. **Assertion (A):** An experienced homemaker works with great care and there is an element of natural rhythm in her normal domestic activities.
Reason (R): In rhythmic work each muscle alternatively gets its chance to rest for an instant.
(a) (A) is true, but (R) is false.
(b) (A) is false, but (R) is true.
(c) Both (A) and (R) are false.
(d) Both (A) and (R) are true.

25. **Assertion (A):** Adolescent development takes place in social context.
Reason (R): This is because adolescent spends and interested in spending more time in social circle.
(a) (A) is true and (R) is false.
(b) (A) is false and (R) is true.

(c) Both (A) and (R) are true.
(d) Both (A) and (R) are false.

26. **Assertion (A):** Effective communication is a combination of seeing, learning and doing.
Reason (R): Exclusive use of AV aids makes, learning experiences complete.
(a) (A) is true, but (R) is false.
(b) (A) is false, but (R) is true.
(c) Both (A) and (R) are true.
(d) Both (A) and (R) are false.

27. **Assertion (A):** Posters used as audio-visual aids compel attention and motivate action.
Reason (R): Posters help in communicating as they present abstract information in a graphic way.
(a) Both (A) and (R) are false.
(b) (A) is true, but (R) is false.
(c) (A) is false, but (R) is true.
(d) Both (A) and (R) are true.

28. Give the correct sequence of steps involved in sugar cookery.
(A) Soft ball (B) Hard crack
(C) Carmel (D) 2 thread
(E) Hard ball
(a) (A) (B) (C) (D) (E)
(b) (B) (C) (D) (A) (E)
(c) (D) (A) (E) (B) (C)
(d) (C) (D) (A) (E) (B)

29. Give the correct sequence of foods in decreasing order of iron content.
(A) Liver (B) Apple
(C) Dates (D) Wheat flour
(E) Lotus stem
(a) (A) (C) (E) (D) (B)
(b) (A) (E) (D) (C) (A)
(c) (A) (B) (C) (D) (E)
(d) (B) (A) (E) (D) (C)

30. Give the correct sequence of appearance of symptoms of vitamin A deficiency.
(A) Bitot spots
(B) Conjunctival xerosis
(C) Night blindness
(D) Keratomalacia
(a) (C) (A) (B) (D) (b) (A) (C) (D) (B)
(c) (B) (A) (C) (D) (d) (D) (C) (B) (A)

31. Give the correct order of applying the four support materials in the garment.
(a) Interfacing, interlining, underlining, lining
(b) Interlining, interfacing, underlining, lining
(c) Interfacing, underlining, interlining, lining
(d) Underlining, interfacing, interlining, lining

32. Give the correct sequencing for processing a cotton fabric.
(a) Designing, bleaching, tentering, calendering
(b) Tentering, bleaching, designing, calendering
(c) Calendering, bleaching, designing, tentering
(d) Bleaching, designing, tentering, calendering

33. Arrange the following teaching learning methods in order of learner's ability:
(i) A video show
(ii) Laboratory method
(iii) Demonstration
(iv) Radio talk
Codes:
(a) (iv), (iii), (i), (ii) (b) (iv), (i), (iii), (ii)
(c) (iii), (iv), (i), (ii) (d) (i), (iii), (iv), (ii)

34. Arrange the steps of counselling process in right sequence.
1. Synthesis 2. Diagnosis
3. Analysis 4. Treatment and counselling
5. Follow up 6. Prognosis
(a) 1, 3, 4, 6, 2 and 5
(b) 3, 2, 6, 4, 5 and 1
(c) 4, 1, 2, 3, 5 and 6
(d) 3, 1, 2, 6, 4 and 5

35. Decision making is a process involving following steps in sequence
 i. Evaluate the alternatives
 ii. Identify the alternatives
 iii. Identify the problem
 iv. Make a decision
 v. Evaluate the decision

Codes:
(a) (iv), (iii), (v), (ii), (i)
(b) (iii), (i), (ii), (v), (iv)
(c) (iii), (ii), (i), (iv), (v)
(d) (ii), (iv), (ii), (i), (v)

36. Steps of curriculum planning are given below. Write them in correct order:
(i) Environment for learning.
(ii) Problems/needs of the learner.
(iii) Sequencing of contents.
(iv) Philosophical frame.

Codes:
(a) (iv), (ii), (i), (iii) (b) (i), (ii), (iii), (iv)
(c) (iv), (i), (ii), (iii) (d) (ii), (i), (iv), (iii)

37. Arrange the following steps in
(A) Sample Selection
(B) Research Question
(C) Data Collection
(D) Research Design
(E) Objectives

Codes:
(a) (B) (A) (D) (E) (C)
(b) (A) (B) (C) (D) (E)
(c) (A) (B) (E) (D) (C)
(d) (B) (E) (A) (D) (C)

38. Match the cooking method in List I with the temperature in List II:

List I (Cooking method)
(A) Pressure cooking (B) Frying
(C) Baking (D) Grilling

List II (Temperature)
(i) 180° – 220°C (ii) 250°C
(iii) > 100°C (iv) 110° – 240°C

Codes:	**A**	**B**	**C**	**D**
(a)	(iii)	(i)	(iv)	(ii)
(b)	(iii)	(ii)	(i)	(iv)
(c)	(ii)	(iii)	(iv)	(i)
(d)	(iv)	(i)	(ii)	(iii)

39. Match the colour of fruit and vegetable in List I with the pigment in List II:

List I (Colour of fruits and vegetables)	**List II (Pigment)**
(A) Green	(i) Carotenoids
(B) Deep yellow	(ii) Chlorophyll
(C) White	(iii) Anthocyanin
(D) Purple	(iv) Flavones

Codes:	**A**	**B**	**C**	**D**
(a)	(ii)	(iii)	(i)	(iv)
(b)	(iii)	(i)	(iv)	(ii)
(c)	(ii)	(i)	(iv)	(iii)
(d)	(iv)	(i)	(iii)	(ii)

40. Match the diseases given in List I with affected organ in List II:

List I	**List II**
(A) Neprosis	(i) Pancreas
(B) Diabetes	(ii) Kidney
(C) Arteriosclerosis	(iii) Intestine
(D) Celiac disease	(iv) Blood vessel
	(v) Heart

Codes:	**A**	**B**	**C**	**D**
(a)	(iii)	(v)	(ii)	(iv)
(b)	(i)	(ii)	(iii)	(iv)
(c)	(ii)	(i)	(v)	(iii)
(d)	(ii)	(i)	(iv)	(iii)

41. Match the fibre given in column I to the appearance given in column II:

Column I	**Column II**
(A) Wool	(i) Glass rod structure
(B) Linen	(ii) Scales
(C) Silk	(iii) Convolutions
(D) Cotton	(iv) Nodes

Codes:	**A**	**B**	**C**	**D**
(a)	(ii)	(iv)	(i)	(iii)
(b)	(i)	(ii)	(iii)	(iv)
(c)	(iii)	(i)	(iv)	(ii)
(d)	(iv)	(iii)	(ii)	(i)

42. Match the description given in column II with the terms given in column I:

Column I	Column II
(A) Avant Garde	(i) high fashion
(B) Houte couture	(ii) copied garment
(C) Knock off	(iii) ready to wear
(D) Pret-a-Porter	(iv) design ahead of its time

Codes:	A	B	C	D
(a)	(i)	(ii)	(iii)	(iv)
(b)	(ii)	(iii)	(iv)	(i)
(c)	(iii)	(iv)	(i)	(ii)
(d)	(iv)	(i)	(ii)	(iii)

43. Match the following list of standardization marks from List I with products in List II:

List I	List II
(A) Agmark	(i) Squash
(B) FPO	(ii) Shawl
(C) ISI	(iii) Honey
(D) Wool mark	(iv) Biscuits

Codes:	A	B	C	D
(a)	(i)	(iv)	(iii)	(ii)
(b)	(iv)	(iii)	(i)	(ii)
(c)	(iii)	(iv)	(i)	(ii)
(d)	(iii)	(i)	(iv)	(ii)

44. Match the following List I with List II:

List I

(A) Cross-sectional study
(B) Longitudinal study
(C) Naturalistic study
(D) Experimental study

List II

(i) observes children in natrually occurring situations.
(ii) observes same group(s) of children at different points of time.
(iii) observes children where circumstances are carefully controlled.
(iv) observes children of different ages at one point of time.

Codes:	A	B	C	D
(a)	(i)	(ii)	(iii)	(iv)
(b)	(ii)	(iii)	(iv)	(i)
(c)	(iv)	(ii)	(i)	(iii)
(d)	(iii)	(iv)	(ii)	(i)

45. Match the items in List I with List II:

List I	List II
(A) $\overline{X}$	(i) Sum of
(B) χ^2	(ii) Standard deviation
(C) σ	(iii) Chi square
(D) Σ	(iv) Mean

Codes:	A	B	C	D
(a)	(i)	(ii)	(iii)	(iv)
(b)	(ii)	(iii)	(i)	(iv)
(c)	(iii)	(i)	(vi)	(ii)
(d)	(iv)	(iii)	(ii)	(i)

46. Match the following items in List I with List II:

List I

(A) Acting skits (B) Discussion
(C) Evaluation (D) Resources

List II

(i) Books and reading material
(ii) Experience and activities through examination
(iii) Individual activity
(iv) Group activity

Codes:	A	B	C	D
(a)	(iii)	(iv)	(ii)	(i)
(b)	(iii)	(ii)	(i)	(iv)
(c)	(i)	(iii)	(ii)	(iv)
(d)	(i)	(ii)	(iii)	(iv)

47. Match the following item in List I with List II:

List I

(A) Readymade and Homemade
(B) Direct experience
(C) Dramatized experience
(D) Visual symbols

List II

(i) Role of a host
(ii) Diagrams
(iii) Exhibits
(iv) Preparing a meal

Codes:	A	B	C	D
(a)	(i)	(iv)	(iii)	(ii)
(b)	(iii)	(iv)	(i)	(ii)
(c)	(iii)	(i)	(ii)	(iv)
(d)	(iv)	(iii)	(ii)	(i)

Read the passage below and answer the questions that follow based on your understanding of the passage: (Q. No. 48 to 50)

More than 1 billion people in the world today, almost half of them women, live in unacceptable conditions of poverty, mostly in the developing countries. Poverty is a complex, multidimensional problem, with origins in both the national and international domains. In the early 1950s, nearly half of India's population was living in poverty. Since then, poverty has been declining, though slowly, and today vast disparities between and within India's states persist. It is estimated that women and children account for 73 percent of those below the poverty line. At the same time, the ratio of females to males in India is 933:1,000. Increased female labour force participation, particularly among the lowest-income households, is the single most important coping strategy of poor households. This trend makes female-headed households and poor women in general a distinct poverty group (Barrett and Beardmore, 2000).

Gender is central to how societies assign roles, responsibilities, resources, and rights between women and men. Allocation, distribution, utilization, and control of resources are thus incumbent upon gender relations embedded in both ideology and practice. Gender analyses do not merely focus on women, but also look at the ways in which men and women interact with each other and the gendered nature of their roles, relations and control over resources. Unfortunately, even today in most parts of the world there exist gender biases that disadvantage women. Therefore, it is sometimes inevitable that gender justice become synonymous with the rights of women and any discussion on gender and poverty in essence becomes a discussion on women and poverty. This is because, as with all other issues, women and men experience poverty in different ways.

The wide range of biases in society—among them unequal opportunities in education, employment and asset ownership—mean that women have fewer opportunities. Poverty accentuates gender gaps and when adversity strikes, it is women who often are most vulnerable (UNDP, 1997: 64). This increased vulnerability is most visible in cases of disaster, conflict or involuntary resettlement. Starting with discrimination against the girl-child, even before she is born, the life of the average Indian woman is one of deprivation in every sphere. The overall status of women in an Indian family is lower than that of men. The girl-child gets less nutrition, health care and education: a lesser childhood than the boy-child. She becomes a woman while still young, often missing out on adolescence and moving into early motherhood—quickly, and often at a young age. She has no say in any of these crucial events of her life, although they adversely affect her growth and development. The root of gender inequality, reflected in the higher incidence of poverty among women in India, is social and economic, not constitutional. The Constitution is firmly grounded in principles of liberty, fraternity, equality and justice. Women's rights to equality and freedom from discrimination are defined as justifiable fundamental rights.

48. The growth and development of girl child is not adversely affected by
    (a) Malnutrition
    (b) Early motherhood
    (c) Caste
    (d) Healthcare

49. Give the correct combination of causes of gender inequality in India.
    (A) Social (B) Economic
    (C) Malnutrition (D) Constitutional
    (a) (A) & (B) are correct.
    (b) (A), (B) & (D) are correct.
    (c) (C) & (D) are correct.
    (d) All the above are correct.
50. **Assertion (A):** Gender bias exists in India.
    Reason (R): Poverty is one of the factors for gender biases.
    (a) (A) is true & (R) is false.
    (b) (A) is false & (R) is true.
    (c) (A) is true & (R) is partially true.
    (d) Both (A) & (R) are false.

ANSWERS

1. (a)	2. (b)	3. (a)	4. (a)	5. (a)
6. (a)	7. (c)	8. (d)	9. (c)	10. (c)
11. (d)	12. (d)	13. (b)	14. (a)	15. (d)
16. (c)	17. (b)	18. (c)	19. (d)	20. (a)
21. (a)	22. (a)	23. (b)	24. (c)	25. (b)
26. (b)	27. (b)	28. (b)	29. (c)	30. (d)
31. (c)	32. (c)	33. (d)	34. (b)	35. (a)
36. (a)	37. (a)	38. (b)	39. (b)	40. (c)
41. (c)	42. (b)	43. (a)	44. (a)	45. (d)
46. (d)	47. (d)	48. (c)	49. (b)	50. (a)

JUNE–2010

Note: This paper contains Sixty (60) multiple choice questions, each question carrying two (2) marks. Candidate is expected to answer any Fifty (50) questions. In case more than Fifty (50) questions are attempted, only the first Fifty (50) questions will be evaluated.

PAPER–I

1. Which one of the following is the most important quality of a good teacher?
   (a) Punctuality and sincerity
   (b) Content mastery
   (c) Content mastery and reactive
   (d) Content mastery and sociable
2. The primary responsibility for the teacher's adjustment lies with
   (a) The children
   (b) The principal
   (c) The teacher himself
   (d) The community
3. As per the NCTE norms, what should be the staff strength for a unit of 100 students at B.Ed. level?
   (a) 1 + 7 (b) 1 + 9
   (c) 1 + 10 (d) 1 + 5
4. Research has shown that the most frequent symptom of nervous instability among teachers is
   (a) Digestive upsets
   (b) Explosive behaviour
   (c) Fatigue
   (d) Worry
5. Which one of the following statements is correct?
   (a) Syllabus is an annexure to the curriculum.
   (b) Curriculum is the same in all educational institutions.
   (c) Curriculum includes both formal and informal education.
   (d) Curriculum does not include methods of evaluation.
6. A successful teacher is one who is
   (a) Compassionate and disciplinarian
   (b) Quite and reactive
   (c) Tolerant and dominating
   (d) Passive and active

Read the following passage carefully and answer the questions 7 to 12.

The phrase "What is it like?" stands for a fundamental thought process. How does one go about observing and reporting on things and events that occupy segments of earth space? Of all the infinite variety of phenomena on the face of the earth, how does one decide what phenomena to observe? There is no such thing as a complete description of the earth or any part of it, for every microscopic point on the earth's surface differs from every other such point. Experience shows that the things observed are already familiar, because they are like phenomena that occur at home or because they resemble the abstract images and models developed in the human mind.

How are abstract images formed? Humans alone among the animals possess language; their words symbolise not only specific things but also mental images of classes of things. People can remember what they have seen or experienced because they attach a word symbol to them.

During the long record of our efforts to gain more and more knowledge about the face of the earth as the human habitat, there has been a continuing interplay between things and events. The direct observation through the senses is described as a percept; the mental image is described as a concept. Percepts are what some people describe as reality, in contrast to mental images, which are theoretical, implying that they are not real.

The relation of Percept to Concept is not as simple as the definition implies. It is now quite clear that people of different cultures or even individuals in the same culture develop different mental images of reality and what they perceive is a reflection of these preconceptions. The direct observation of things and events on the face of the earth is so clearly a function of the mental images of the mind of the observer that the whole idea of reality must be reconsidered.

Concepts determine what the observer perceives, yet concepts are derived from the generalisations of previous percepts. What happens is that the educated observer is taught to accept a set of concepts and then sharpens or changes these concepts during a professional career. In any one field of scholarship, professional opinion at one time determines what concepts and procedures are acceptable, and these form a kind of model of scholarly behaviour.

7. The problem raised in the passage reflects on
   (a) thought process
   (b) human behaviour
   (c) cultural perceptions
   (d) professional opinion
8. According to the passage, human beings have mostly in mind
   (a) Observation of things
   (b) Preparation of mental images
   (c) Expression through language
   (d) To gain knowledge
9. Concept means
   (a) A mental image
   (b) A reality
   (c) An idea expressed in language form
   (d) All the above
10. The relation of Percept to Concept is
    (a) Positive (b) Negative
    (c) Reflective (d) Absolute
11. In the passage, the earth is taken as
    (a) The Globe
    (b) The Human Habitat
    (c) A Celestial Body
    (d) A Planet
12. Percept means
    (a) Direct observation through the senses
    (b) A conceived idea
    (c) Ends of a spectrum
    (d) An abstract image
13. Action research means
    (a) A longitudinal research
    (b) An applied research
    (c) A research initiated to solve an immediate problem
    (d) A research with socio-economic objective
14. Research is
    (a) Searching again and again
    (b) Finding solution to any problem
    (c) Working in a scientific way to search for truth of any problem
    (d) None of the above
15. A common test in research demands much priority on
    (a) Reliability (b) Usability
    (c) Objectivity (d) All of the above
16. Which of the following is the first step in starting the research process?
    (a) Searching sources of information to locate problem
    (b) Survey of related literature
    (c) Identification of problem
    (d) Searching for solutions to the problem
17. If a researcher conducts a research on finding out which administrative style

contributes more to institutional effectiveness? This will be an example of
(a) Basic Research
(b) Action Research
(c) Applied Research
(d) None of the above

18. Normal Probability Curve should be
(a) Positively skewed
(b) Negatively skewed
(c) Leptokurtic skewed
(d) Zero skewed

19. In communication, a major barrier to reception of messages is
(a) audience attitude
(b) audience knowledge
(c) audience education
(d) audience income

20. Post-modernism is associated with
(a) Newspapers (b) Magazines
(c) Radio (d) Television

21. Didactic communication is
(a) intra-personal (b) inter-personal
(c) organisational (d) relational

22. In communication, the language is
(a) the non-verbal code
(b) the verbal code
(c) the symbolic code
(d) the iconic code

23. Identify the correct sequence of the following:
(a) Source, channel, message, receiver
(b) Source, receiver, channel, message
(c) Source, message, receiver, channel
(d) Source, message, channel, receiver

24. **Assertion (A):** Mass media promote a culture of violence in the society.
Reason (R): Because violence sells in the market as people themselves are violent in character.
(a) Both (A) and (R) are true and (R) is the correct explanation of (A).
(b) Both (A) and (R) are true, but (R) is not the correct explanation of (A).
(c) (A) is true, but (R) is false.
(d) Both (A) and (R) are false.

25. When an error of 1% is made in the length of a square, the percentage error in the area of a square will be
(a) 0 (b) 1/2
(c) 1 (d) 2

26. On January 12, 1980, it was a Saturday. The day of the week on January 12, 1979 was
(a) Thursday (b) Friday
(c) Saturday (d) Sunday

27. If water is called food, food is called tree, tree is called earth, earth is called world, which of the following grows a fruit?
(a) Water (b) Tree
(c) World (d) Earth

28. E is the son of A, D is the son of B, E is married to C, C is the daughter of E. How is D related to E?
(a) Brother (b) Uncle
(c) Father-in-law (d) Brother-in-law

29. If INSURANCE is coded as ECNARUSNI, how HINDRANCE will be coded?
(a) CADNIHWCE (b) HANODEINR
(c) AENIRHDCN (d) ECNARDNIH

30. Find the next number in the following series: 2, 5, 10, 17, 26, 37, 50.
(a) 63 (b) 65
(c) 67 (d) 69

31. Which of the following is an example of circular argument?
(a) God created man in his image and man created God in his own image.
(b) God is the source of a scripture and the scripture is the source of our knowledge of God.
(c) Some of the Indians are great because India is great.
(d) Rama is great because he is Rama.

32. Lakshmana is a morally good person because
    (a) he is religious (b) he is educated
    (c) he is rich (d) he is rational

33. Two statements I and II given below are followed by two conclusions (a) and (b). Supposing the statements are true, which of the following conclusions can logically follow?

    Statements:

    I. Some religious people are morally good.

    II. Some religious people are rational.

    Conclusions:

    (A) Rationally religious people are good morally.

    (B) Non-rational religious persons are not morally good.

    (a) Only (A) follows
    (b) Only (B) follows
    (c) Both (A) and (B) follow
    (d) Neither (A) nor (B) follows

34. Certainty is
    (a) an objective fact
    (b) emotionally satisfying
    (c) logical
    (d) ontological

Questions from 35 to 36 are based on the following diagram in which there are three intersecting circles I, S and P where circle I stands for Indians, circle S stands for Scientists and circle P for Politicians. Different regions of the figure are lettered from a to g.

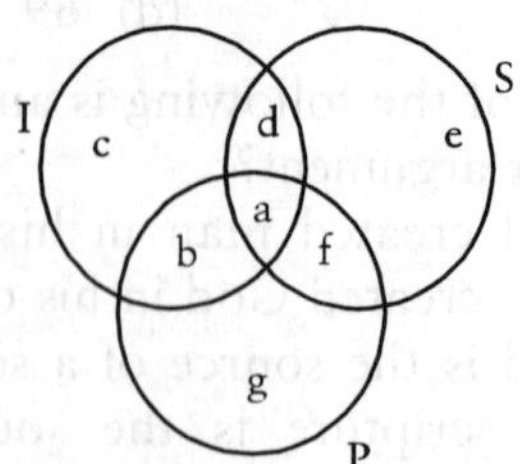

35. The region which represents non-scientists who are politicians.
    (a) f (b) d
    (c) a (d) c

36. The region which represents politicians who are Indians as well as scientists.
    (a) b (b) c
    (c) a (d) d

37. The population of a city is plotted as a function of time (years) in graphic form below:

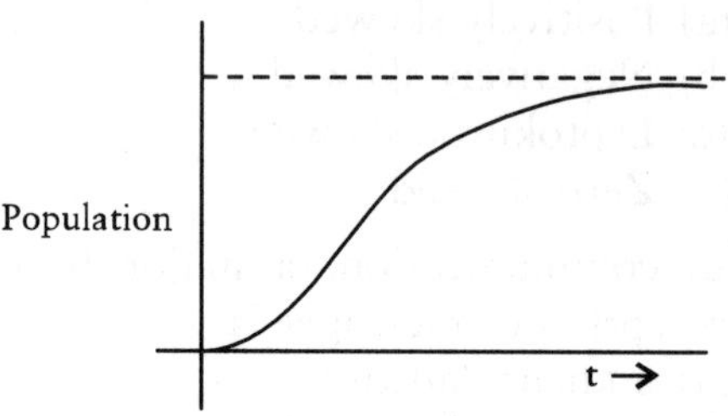

Which of the following inference can be drawn from above plot?

(a) The population increases exponentially.
(b) The population increases in parabolic fashion.
(c) The population initially increases in a linear fashion and then stabilises.
(d) The population initially increases exponentially and then stabilises.

In the following chart, the price of logs is shown in per cubic metre and that of Plywood and Saw Timber in per tonnes. Study the chart and answer the following questions 38, 39 and 40.

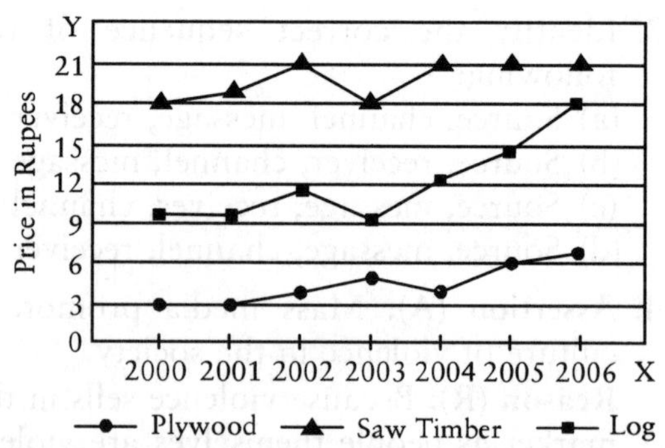

38. Which product shows the maximum percentage increase in price over the period?

(a) Saw timber (b) Plywood
(c) Log (d) None of these

39. What is the maximum percentage increase in price per cubic metre of log?
(a) 6 (b) 12
(c) 18 (d) None of these

40. In which year the prices of two products decreased and that of the third increased?
(a) 2000 (b) 2002
(c) 2003 (d) 2006

41. Which one of the following is the oldest Archival source of data in India?
(a) National Sample Surveys
(b) Agricultural Statistics
(c) Census
(d) Vital Statistics

42. In a large random data set following normal distribution, the ratio (%) of number of data points which are in the range of (mean ± standard deviation) to the total number of data points, is
(a) ~ 50% (b) ~ 67%
(c) ~ 97% (d) ~ 47%

43. Which number system is usually followed in a typical 32-bit computer?
(a) 2 (b) 8
(c) 10 (d) 16

44. Which one of the following is an example of Operating System?
(a) Microsoft Word
(b) Microsoft Excel
(c) Microsoft Access
(d) Microsoft Windows

45. Which one of the following represent the binary equivalent of the decimal number 23?
(a) 01011 (b) 10111
(c) 10011 (d) None of these

46. Which one of the following is different from other members?
(a) Google (b) Windows
(c) Linux (d) Mac

47. Where does a computer add and compare its data?
(a) CPU (b) Memory
(c) Hard disk (d) Floppy disk

48. Computers on an internet are identified by
(a) e-mail address
(b) street address
(c) IP address
(d) None of the above

49. The Right to Information Act, 2005 makes the provision of
(a) Dissemination of all types of information by all public authorities to any person
(b) Establishment of Central, State and District Level Information Commissions as an appellate body
(c) Transparency and accountability in Public authorities
(d) All of the above

50. Which type of natural hazards cause maximum damage to property and lives?
(a) Hydrological
(b) Hydro-meteorological
(c) Geological
(d) Geo-chemical

51. Dioxins are produced from
(a) Wastelands
(b) Power plants
(c) Sugar factories
(d) Combustion of plastics

52. The slogan "A tree for each child" was coined for
(a) Social forestry program
(b) Clean air program
(c) Soil conservation program
(d) Environmental protection program

53. The main constituents of biogas are

(a) Methane and Carbon dioxide
(b) Methane and Nitric oxide
(c) Methane, Hydrogen and Nitric oxide
(d) Methane and Sulphur dioxide

54. **Assertion (A):** In the world as a whole, the environment has degraded during past several decades.
Reason (R): The population of the world has been growing significantly.
(a) (A) is correct, (R) is correct and (R) is the correct explanation of (A).
(b) (A) is correct, (R) is correct and (R) is not the correct explanation of (A).
(c) (A) is correct, but (R) is false.
(d) (A) is false, but (R) is correct.

55. Climate change has implications for
1. soil moisture 2. forest fires
3. biodiversity 4. groundwater
Identify the correct combination according to the code:
Codes:
(a) 1 and 3 (b) 1, 2 and 3
(c) 1, 3 and 4 (d) 1, 2, 3 and 4

56. The accreditation process by National Assessment and Accreditation Council (NAAC) differs from that of National Board of Accreditation (NBA) in terms of
(a) Disciplines covered by both being the same, there is duplication of efforts.
(b) One has institutional grading approach and the other has program grading approach.
(c) Once get accredited by NBA or NAAC, the institution is free from renewal of grading, which is not a progressive decision.
(d) This accreditation amounts to approval of minimum standards in the quality of education in the institution concerned.

57. Which option is not correct?
(a) Most of the educational institutions of National repute in scientific and technical sphere fall under 64th entry of Union list.
(b) Education, in general, is the subject of concurrent list since 42nd Constitutional Amendment Act 1976.
(c) Central Advisory Board on Education (CABE) was first established in 1920.
(d) India had implemented the right to Free and Compulsory Primary Education in 2002 through 86th Constitutional Amendment.

58. Which statement is not correct about the "National Education Day" of India?
(a) It is celebrated on 5th September every year.
(b) It is celebrated on 11th November every year.
(c) It is celebrated in the memory of India's first Union Minister of Education, Dr. Abul Kalam Azad.
(d) It is being celebrated since 2008.

59. Match List I with List II and select the correct answer from the codes given below:
List I (Articles of the Constitution)
A. Article 280 B. Article 324
C. Article 323 D. Article 315
List II (Institutions)
1. Administrative Tribunals
2. Election Commission of India
3. Finance Commission at Union level
4. Union Public Service Commission

Codes:	A	B	C	D
(a)	1	2	3	4
(b)	3	2	1	4
(c)	2	3	4	1
(d)	2	4	3	1

60. Deemed Universities declared by UGC under Section 3 of the UGC Act 1956, are not permitted to

(a) offer programs in higher education and issue degrees
(b) give affiliation to any institute of higher education
(c) open off-campus and off-shore campus anywhere in the country and overseas respectively without the permission of the UGC
(d) offer distance education programs without the approval of the Distance Education Council

ANSWERS

1. (b)	2. (c)	3. (c)	4. (b)	5. (c)
6. (a)	7. (c)	8. (a)	9. (a)	10. (c)
11. (b)	12. (a)	13. (c)	14. (c)	15. (d)
16. (c)	17. (c)	18. (d)	19. (c)	20. (d)
21. (b)	22. (b)	23. (d)	24. (d)	25. (d)
26. (b)	27. (c)	28. (d)	29. (d)	30. (b)
31. (b)	32. (a)	33. (d)	34. (c)	35. (a)
36. (c)	37. (d)	38. (c)	39. (d)	40. (b)
41. (c)	42. (b)	43. (a)	44. (d)	45. (b)
46. (b)	47. (a)	48. (c)	49. (d)	50. (c)
51. (d)	52. (d)	53. (a)	54. (b)	55. (d)
56. (c)	57. (a)	58. (a)	59. (b)	60. (b)

PAPER–II

Note: This paper contains fifty (50) objective type questions, each question carrying two (2) marks. All questions are compulsory.

1. Following is not an essential amino acid.
(a) Lysine (b) Methionine
(c) Alanine (d) Phenyl alanine

2. To reduce the risk of atherosclerosis, the LDL and HDL levels should be
(a) LDL below 200 mg %, and HDL above 40 mg %
(b) LDL below 240 mg %, and HDL above 50 mg %
(c) LDL below 200 mg %, and HDL below 40 mg %
(d) LDL below 240 mg %, and HDL above 40 mg %

3. The record of food store inventory is kept in
(a) Ledger (b) Stock Register
(c) Cash Book (d) Journal

4. The iron requirement for a pregnant mother is
(a) 30 mg (b) 32 mg
(c) 38 mg (d) 36 mg

5. The enzyme responsible for digestibility of fats in human body is
(a) Lipase (b) Amylase
(c) Renin (d) Protease

6. Degree of polymerization for polyester ranges between
(a) 50 – 70 (b) 90 – 115
(c) 115 – 140 (d) 140 – 165

7. Which of the following dart is drawn till the pivot point?
(a) French dart
(b) Fish dart
(c) Designers' dart
(d) Dressmakers' dart

8. The pocket that is applied on the surface of the garment is
(a) Kangaroo pocket (b) Welt pocket
(c) Yoke pocket (d) Bound pocket

9. The standards for space to be provided all around a building is referred to as
(a) Set back (b) Ventilation
(c) Open space (d) Landscape

10. The scientific study of man and his working environment is

(a) Demography
(b) Ergonomics
(c) Work simplication
(d) Occupational health

11. An example of cross-sectional study is
(a) Comparing individuals of various ages at the same time.
(b) Continued observations of the same individuals.
(c) Careful description by the researcher.
(d) One that requires no manipulation.

12. Dyslexic refers to individual who have difficulty in
(a) Learning to express
(b) Learning to stand
(c) Learning to read and write
(d) Learning to speak

13. The type of communication best suited to address an audience is
(a) Group communication
(b) Interpersonal communication
(c) Mass communication
(d) Cosmopolite communication

14. Expansion of IEC is
(a) Information, Electronics and Communication
(b) International Export Council
(c) Information, Education and Communication
(d) Indian Economic Council

15. Which among these can be used for demonstration purposes?
(a) Flat pictures (b) Exhibit
(c) Flannel Boards (d) Displays

16. The most appropriate statistical test for analysing quantitative data is
(a) chi square (b) sign test
(c) t-test (d) median test

17. Two variables are said to be (+)vly correlated if
(a) The change in one variable results in a corresponding change in the other variable.
(b) The change of the variables is in the opposite directions.
(c) The two variables are similar in nature.
(d) The two variables are dissimilar.

18. Which of the following method is used to test reliability of a measurement instrument?
(a) Observation (b) Test retest
(c) Interview (d) Split half

19. **Assertion (A):** Consumption of plenty of fruits and vegetables protects individuals from certain cancers.
Reason (R): The antioxidants present in fruits and vegetables help in the removal of free radicals.
(a) Both (A) and (R) are false.
(b) (A) is true and (R) is false.
(c) Both (A) and (R) are true.
(d) (A) is false and (R) is true.

20. **Assertion (A):** Green leafy vegetables turn brown in colour on cooking.
Reason (R): Chlorophyll pigment gets converted to phenophytin on application of heat.
(a) Both (A) and (R) are false.
(b) Both (A) and (R) are true.
(c) (A) is true, but (R) is false.
(d) (A) is false, but (R) is true.

21. **Assertion (A):** A Kwashiorkor child shows oedema of the lower limbs.
Reason (R): The kidneys are not able to excrete sodium thus causing water retention.
(a) (A) is true and (R) is false.
(b) Both (A) and (R) are true.
(c) (A) is false and (R) is true.
(d) Both (A) and (R) are false.

22. **Assertion (A):** Surface designing includes printing.
Reason (R): Printing is a form of applying colour all over the fabric.
(a) (A) is true, but (R) is false.
(b) (A) is false, but (R) is true.
(c) Both (A) and (R) are false.
(d) Both (A) and (R) are true.

23. **Assertion (A):** In a seam notches are given in an outward curve.
Reason (R): Smaller area falls over bigger area.
(a) (A) is true, but (R) is false.
(b) (A) is false, but (R) is true.
(c) Both (A) and (R) are true.
(d) Both (A) and (R) are false.

24. **Assertion (A):** The quality of decisions determine the quality of management.
Reason (R): Decision making occurs when there is a problem to solve or some choice to make.
(a) Both (A) and (R) are true.
(b) (A) is true, but (R) is false.
(c) (A) is true, but (R) is only partly true.
(d) Both (A) and (R) are false.

25. **Assertion (A):** One of the best styles of parental discipline is democratic pattern.
Reason (R): Both parent and the child discuss and take decision.
(a) Both (A) and (R) are false.
(b) Both (A) and (R) are true.
(c) (A) is true and (R) is false.
(d) (A) is false and (R) is true.

26. **Assertion (A):** The effectiveness of audio visuals rely upon the skill of the user.
Reason (R): The AV aids are selected on the basis of the criteria used for teaching and learning.
(a) (A) is false and (R) is correct.
(b) Both (A) and (R) are true.
(c) (A) is true, but (R) is partially true.
(d) Both (A) and (R) are false.

27. **Assertion (A):** Campaigning which is an educational extension activity helps to mobilize and solve the problems of a community.
Reason (R): It is done to seek emotional participation of the community for adopting new practices.
(a) Both (A) and (R) are correct.
(b) (A) is correct, but (R) is false.
(c) Both (A) and (R) are false.
(d) (A) is correct, but (R) is partially correct.

28. Give the correct sequence of steps involved in bread making.
A. Making dough with flour
B. Adding yeast to warm milk
C. Punching the dough
D. Rising the dough
E. Proofing
F. Baking
(a) A, B, C, D, E, F (b) A, B, D, E, C, F
(c) B, A, D, C, E, F (d) B, A, D, E, C, F

29. Give the correct sequence of foods in decreasing order of protein content.
A. Suji B. Moong dal
C. Green peas D. Sweet potato
(a) B, C, A, D (b) C, B, D, A
(c) A, B, C, D (d) D, A, C, B

30. Give the correct sequence of appearance of iron deficiency anaemia (IDA).
A. Fall in serum ferritin level.
B. Decrease in stainable iron in bone marrow.
C. Fall in hemoglobin level.
D. Exhaustion of body iron reserves.
(a) A, B, C, D (b) D, B, A, C
(c) B, C, D, A (d) C, D, B, A

31. Give the correct sequence of preparation of fabric for cutting.
(a) Blocking, straightening, marking, pressing.
(b) Pressing, blocking, straightening, marking.

(c) Straightening, blocking, pressing, marking.
(d) Marking, pressing, straightening, blocking.

32. Give the correct sequence of processing the linen fibre.
(a) Rippling, Retting, Scutching, Hackling.
(b) Retting, Rippling, Scutching, Hackling.
(c) Scutching, Rippling, Retting, Hackling.
(d) Hackling, Rippling, Retting, Scutching.

33. Arrange the level of mental retardation in ascending order:
(a) Moderate, profound, mild and severe.
(b) Profound, mild, severe and moderate.
(c) Mild, moderate, severe and profound.
(d) Severe, profound, moderate and mild.

34. Give the right sequence of Home Management Process.

i. Energising | ii. Evaluation
iii. Planning | iv. Adjusting
v. Checking

Codes:

(a) iii, i, v, iv, ii | (b) i, ii, iv, iii, v
(c) iv, ii, i, iii, v | (d) v, iv, iii, ii, i

35. The sequential order of communication is

i. Message | ii. Sender
iii. Decoder | iv. Encoder
v. Receiver

(a) ii, i, iv, iii, v | (b) i, ii, iv, iii, v
(c) ii, i, iv, v, iii | (d) iv, ii, iii, i, v

36. Arrange in the correct sequence from the lowest to the highest scale of measurement.

A. Interval scale | B. Ordinal scale
C. Ratio scale | D. Nominal scale

(a) D, B, A, C | (b) A, B, D, C
(c) B, A, C, D | (d) B, D, C, A

37. Match List I with List II:

List I

(A) Cyclic Menu | (B) A La Carte Menu
(C) Table d | (D) Dujour Menu

List II

i. Menu of the day
ii. Set menu
iii. Choice of dishes
iv. Menu rotated at definite interval

Codes:	**A**	**B**	**C**	**D**
(a)	iv	iii	ii	i
(b)	i	ii	iii	iv
(c)	ii	i	iii	iv
(d)	iii	iv	ii	i

38. Match the Hormones in List I with Diseases in List II:

List I (Hormones)

(A) Insulin | (B) TSH
(C) Renin-Angiotensin | (D) Cortisol

List II (Diseases)

i. Goitre
ii. Hypertension
iii. Cushing syndrome
iv. Diabetes

Codes:	**A**	**B**	**C**	**D**
(a)	i	ii	iii	iv
(b)	iii	iv	i	ii
(c)	iv	i	ii	iii
(d)	iv	ii	i	iii

39. Match the deficiency disease/symptom in List I with nutrient in List II.

List I (Deficiency Disease/Symptom)

(A) Pellagra | (B) Beriberi
(C) Koilonechia | (D) Xerophthalmia

List II (Nutrient)

i. Iron | ii. Niacin
iii. Ascorbic acid | iv. Retinol
v. Thiamine

Codes:	**A**	**B**	**C**	**D**
(a)	v	iv	iii	ii
(b)	ii	v	i	iv
(c)	i	ii	iii	iv
(d)	ii	v	iii	iv

40. Match the description given in Column II with the terms given in Column I.

Column I	Column II
(A) Ciré	i. Fabrics with wavy pattern
(B) Plissé	ii. Wrinkled fabric
(C) Suede	iii. Highly polished fabric
(D) Moire	iv. Fuzzed surface fabric

Codes:	A	B	C	D
(a)	i	iii	ii	iv
(b)	iii	ii	iv	i
(c)	ii	iv	i	iii
(d)	iv	i	iii	ii

41. Match the collars given in Column I with their types given in Column II.

Column I	Column II
(A) Peterpan	i. Convertible
(B) Stand and fall	ii. Stand
(C) Roll	iii. Non-convertible
(D) Shawl	iv. Grown-on

Codes:	A	B	C	D
(a)	ii	iii	iv	i
(b)	iii	i	ii	iv
(c)	i	iv	iii	ii
(d)	iv	ii	i	iii

42. Match the effect given in Column II to the finish mentioned in Column I.

Column I	Column II
(A) Parchmentization	i. alter lustre
(B) Beetling	ii. alter drape
(C) Embossing	iii. raises fibre surface
(D) Gigging	iv. creates textures

Codes:	A	B	C	D
(a)	i	iv	iii	ii
(b)	iii	ii	i	iv
(c)	ii	i	iv	iii
(d)	iv	iii	ii	i

43. Match the List I of Mundel's classes of change with List II of activities.

List I

(A) Change in raw material
(B) Change in finished product
(C) Change in equipment and workplace
(D) Change in hand and body motion

List II

i. Making use of Mixer grinder
ii. Instant Dosa mix powder
iii. working in standing position
iv. square puri instead of round

Codes:	A	B	C	D
(a)	ii	iv	iii	i
(b)	ii	iv	i	iii
(c)	iii	iv	ii	i
(d)	ii	i	iv	iii

44. Match the following List I with List II.

List I (Age in Months)

(A) 4 months (B) 5 months
(C) 8 months (D) 9 months

List II (Pattern of Development of Hand Coordination)

i. Pincer grasp perfected
ii. See but cannot contact
iii. A cube in each hand
iv. Palmar scoop

Codes:	A	B	C	D
(a)	iii	i	ii	iv
(b)	iv	iii	i	ii
(c)	ii	iv	iii	i
(d)	i	iv	ii	iii

45. Match the statistical test in List I with the description in List II.

List I

(A) t-test (B) F-test
(C) Chi square (D) Pearson's

List II

i. testing difference in means of more than two groups
ii. data is in frequencies
iii. bivariate distribution
iv. testing mean against population mean

Codes:	A	B	C	D
(a)	iii	iv	ii	i
(b)	iv	i	ii	iii
(c)	i	ii	iii	iv
(d)	iv	iii	ii	i

46. Match the following items in List I with List II.

List I

(A) CD ROM
(B) Video Conferencing
(C) Satellite technology
(D) Mime & Puppetry

List II

i. Interactive Multimedia
ii. Folk media
iii. Computer stored media
iv. Global Networking media

Codes:	A	B	C	D
(a)	ii	iv	iii	i
(b)	iii	i	iv	ii
(c)	i	ii	iii	iv
(d)	iii	iv	i	ii

47. Match the following items in List I with List II.

List I	List II
(A) Slide	i. Non-projected visual aid
(B) Radio	ii. Projected audio-visual aid
(C) Chart	iii. Audio aid
(D) Video	iv. Projected visual aid

Codes:	A	B	C	D
(a)	iv	iii	i	ii
(b)	iv	i	ii	iii
(c)	i	iii	ii	iv
(d)	iii	iv	i	ii

Read the passage below and answer the questions that follow based on your understanding of the passage:

Poverty underlies the poor health status of most of the Indian population, and women represent a disproportionate share of the poor. Women's relatively low status and the risks associated with reproduction exacerbate what is already an unfavourable overall health situation. Reliable and disaggregated statistics on health are difficult to comeby, and this difficulty is acute regarding women's health. Official health records are not comprehensive or up-to-date, and so-called "female health conditions" are not considered health problems, either by health care professionals or by women themselves. Reproductive health problems fall into the realm of "private and unspoken diseases," leading to a culture of silence. Consequently, most diseases go unreported. The fact that a majority of health care professionals in rural areas are men adds to the hesitation to seek medical help. The social distance between women and the health care service center or provider because of gender, caste, or class is even greater than the geographic distance, which itself is a deterrent. Millions of women simply lack the freedom to go out and seek medical help. According to the second National Family Health Survey, (International Institute for Population Sciences, 1998–1999), only 52 percent of women in India are ever consulted on about their own health. 100 times more likely to die of maternity-related causes than is a woman in the industrialized world. About 15 percent of pregnant women in India develop life-threatening complications (Mahbub ul Haq Development Centre, 2000: 127). Maternal mortality in India, estimated at 407 maternal deaths per 100,000 live births, results primarily from infection, haemorrhage, eclampsia, obstructed labor, abortion, and anemia. Lack of appropriate care during pregnancy and childbirth, especially the inadequacy of services for detecting and managing complications, explains most maternal deaths. In rural areas, over 80 percent of deliveries occur at home, assisted by older household women and traditional birth attendants (dais). The unhygienic conditions in which rural deliveries usually occur often lead to infection in mothers and newborns. Infection and excessive bleeding are the largest causes of maternal deaths. Iron-deficiency anemia is widespread among Indian girls and women and affects 50 percent to 90 percent of pregnant women. Childbirth closely follows marriage, which tends to occur at a young age: 30 percent of Indian females between the ages of 15 and 19 are married. Child bearing during adolescence poses significantly greater health risks than it does during the peak reproductive years and contributes to high rates of population growth.

48. Match the following items in List I with the items in List II.

List I	List II
(A) 15%	i. Delivery at home
(B) 50 – 90%	ii. Develop life threatening complications
(C) 52%	iii. Anaemia
(D) 80%	iv. Never sought medical help.

Codes:	A	B	C	D
(a)	ii	iii	iv	i
(b)	i	ii	iii	iv
(c)	ii	i	iii	iv
(d)	iv	iii	i	ii

49. **Assertion (A):** Female reproductive health problems generally are well reported.

Reason (R): Reproductive health problems fall under the category of "private and unspoken diseases".
(a) (A) is true, but (R) is false.
(b) (A) is false, but (R) is true.
(c) Both (A) and (R) are false.
(d) Both (A) and (R) are true.

50. A major determinant of the social distance between women and health care services is
(a) Geographic distance
(b) Caste
(c) Age factor
(d) Family

ANSWERS

1. (c)	2. (c)	3. (b)	4. (c)	5. (a)
6. (d)	7. (b)	8. (a)	9. (c)	10. (b)
11. (a)	12. (c)	13. (c)	14. (c)	15. (d)
16. (a)	17. (c)	18. (d)	19. (c)	20. (b)
21. (b)	22. (a)	23. (a)	24. (b)	25. (b)
26. (c)	27. (d)	28. (c)	29. (a)	30. (d)
31. (b)	32. (b)	33. (c)	34. (a)	35. (a)
36. (a)	37. (a)	38. (c)	39. (c)	40. (b)
41. (b)	42. (c)	43. (b)	44. (c)	45. (b)
46. (b)	47. (a)	48. (a)	49. (a)	50. (d)

DECEMBER–2009

Note: This paper contains Sixty (60) multiple choice questions, each question carrying two (2) marks. Candidate is expected to answer any Fifty (50) questions. In case more than Fifty (50) questions are attempted, only the first Fifty (50) questions will be evaluated.

PAPER–I

1. The University which telecasts interaction educational programs through its own channel is
   (a) Osmania University
   (b) University of Pune
   (c) Annamalai University
   (d) Indira Gandhi National University (IGNOU)

2. Which of the following skills are needed for present-day teacher to adjust effectively with the classroom teaching?
   1. Knowledge of technology
   2. Use of technology in teaching learning
   3. Knowledge of students' needs
   4. Content mastery

   (a) 1 and 3 (b) 2 and 3
   (c) 2, 3 and 4 (d) 2 and 4

3. Who has signed as MoU for Accreditation of Teacher Education Institutions in India?
   (a) NAAC and UGC
   (b) NCTE and NAAC
   (c) UGC and NCTE
   (d) NCTE and IGNOU

4. The primary duty of the teacher is to
   (a) raise the intellectual standard of the students
   (b) improve the physical standard of the students
   (c) help all-round development of the students
   (d) imbibe value system in the students

5. Micro teaching is more effective
   (a) during the preparation for teaching-practice
   (b) during the teaching-practice
   (c) after the teaching-practice
   (d) always

6. What quality the students like the most in a teacher?
   (a) Idealist philosophy
   (b) Compassion
   (c) Discipline
   (d) Entertaining

7. A null hypothesis is
   (a) when there is no difference between the variables
   (b) the same as research hypothesis
   (c) subjective in nature
   (d) when there is difference between the variables

8. The research which is exploring new facts through the study of the past is called
   (a) Philosophical research
   (b) Historical research
   (c) Mythological research
   (d) Content analysis

9. Action research is
   (a) An applied research
   (b) A research carried out to solve immediate problems
   (c) A longitudinal research
   (d) Simulative research

10. The process not needed in Experimental Researches is
(a) Observation (b) Manipulation
(c) Controlling (d) Content Analysis

11. Manipulation is always a part of
(a) Historical research
(b) Fundamental research
(c) Descriptive research
(d) Experimental research

12. Which correlation co-efficient best explains the relationship between creativity and intelligence?
(a) 1.00 (b) 0.6
(c) 0.5 (d) 0.3

Read the following passage and answer the Question Nos. 13 to 18:

The decisive shift in British Policy really came about under mass pressure in the autumn and winter of 1945 to 46—the months which Penderel Moon while editing Wavell's Journal has perceptively described as 'The Edge of a Volcano'. Very foolishly, the British initially decided to hold public trials of several hundreds of the 20,000 I.N.A. prisoners (as well as dismissing from service and detaining without trial no less than 7,000). They compounded the folly by holding the first trial in the Red Fort, Delhi in November 1945, and putting on the dock together a Hindu, a Muslim and a Sikh (P.K. Sehgal, Shah Nawaz, Gurbaksh Singh Dhillon). Bhulabhai Desai, Tejbahadur Sapru and Nehru appeared for the defence (the latter putting on his barrister's gown after 25 years), and the Muslim League also joined the countrywide protest. On 20 November, an Intelligence Bureau note admitted that "there has seldom been a matter which has attracted so much Indian public interest and, it is safe to say, sympathy...this particular brand of sympathy cuts across communal barriers". A journalist (B. Shiva Rao) visiting the Red Fort prisoners on the same day reported that 'There is not the slightest feeling among them of Hindu and Muslim.... A majority of the men now awaiting trial in the Red Fort is Muslim. Some of these men are bitter that Mr. Jinnah is keeping alive a controversy about Pakistan.' The British became extremely nervous about the I.N.A. spirit spreading to the Indian Army, and in January the Punjab Governor reported that a Lahore reception for released I.N.A. prisoners had been attended by Indian soldiers in uniform.

13. Which heading is more appropriate to assign to the above passage?
(a) Wavell's Journal
(b) Role of Muslim League
(c) I.N.A. Trials
(d) Red Fort Prisoners

14. The trial of P.K. Sehgal, Shah Nawaz and Gurbaksh Singh Dhillon symbolises
(a) communal harmony
(b) threat to all religious persons
(c) threat to persons fighting for the freedom
(d) British reaction against the natives

15. I.N.A. stands for
(a) Indian National Assembly
(b) Indian National Association
(c) Inter-national Association
(d) Indian National Army

16. 'There has seldom been a matter which has attracted so much Indian Public Interest and, it is safe to say, sympathy... this particular brand of sympathy cuts across communal barriers.' Who sympathises to whom and against whom?
(a) Muslims sympathised with Shah Nawaz against the British
(b) Hindus sympathised with P.K. Sehgal against the British
(c) Sikhs sympathised with Gurbaksh Singh Dhillon against the British
(d) Indians sympathised with the persons who were to be trialled

17. The majority of people waiting for trial outside the Red Fort and criticising Jinnah were the
(a) Hindus
(b) Muslims
(c) Sikhs
(d) Hindus and Muslims both
18. The sympathy of Indian soldiers in uniform with the released I.N.A. prisoners at Lahore indicates
(a) Feeling of Nationalism and Fraternity
(b) Rebellion nature of Indian soldiers
(c) Simply to participate in the reception party
(d) None of the above
19. The country which has the distinction of having the two largest circulated newspapers in the world is
(a) Great Britain
(b) The United States
(c) Japan
(d) China
20. The chronological order of non-verbal communication is
(a) Signs, symbols, codes, colours
(b) Symbols, codes, signs, colours
(c) Colours, signs, codes, symbols
(d) Codes, colours, symbols, signs
21. Which of the following statements is not connected with communication?
(a) Medium is the message.
(b) The world is an electronic cocoon.
(c) Information is power.
(d) Telepathy is technological.
22. Communication becomes circular when
(a) the decoder becomes an encoder
(b) the feedback is absent
(c) the source is credible
(d) the channel is clear
23. The site that played a major role during the terrorist attack on Mumbai (26/11) in 2008 was
(a) Orkut (b) Facebook
(c) Amazon.com (d) Twitter
24. **Assertion (A):** For an effective classroom communication at times it is desirable to use the projection technology.
Reason (R): Using the projection technology facilitates extensive coverage of course contents.
(a) Both (A) and (R) are true, and (R) is the correct explanation.
(b) Both (A) and (R) are true, but (R) is not the correct explanation.
(c) (A) is true, but (R) is false.
(d) (A) is false, but (R) is true.
25. January 1, 1995 was a Sunday. What day of the week lies on January 1, 1996?
(a) Sunday (b) Monday
(c) Wednesday (d) Saturday
26. When an error of 1% is made in the length and breadth of a rectangle, the percentage error (%) in the area of a rectangle will be
(a) 0 (b) 1
(c) 2 (d) 4
27. The next number in the series 2, 5, 9, 19, 37, ? will be
(a) 74 (b) 75
(c) 76 (d) None of these
28. There are 10 true-false questions in an examination. Then these questions can be answered in
(a) 20 ways (b) 100 ways
(c) 240 ways (d) 1024 ways
29. What will be the next term in the following?
DCXW, FEVU, HGTS, ?
(a) AKPO (b) ABYZ
(c) JIRQ (d) LMRS
30. Three individuals X, Y, Z hired a car on a sharing basis and paid ₹ 1,040. They used it for 7, 8, 11 hours, respectively.

What are the charges paid by Y?
(a) ₹ 290 (b) ₹ 320
(c) ₹ 360 (d) ₹ 440

31. Deductive argument involves
(a) sufficient evidence
(b) critical thinking
(c) seeing logical relations
(d) repeated observation

32. Inductive reasoning is based on or presupposes
(a) uniformity of nature
(b) God created the world
(c) unity of nature
(d) laws of nature

33. To be critical, thinking must be
(a) practical
(b) socially relevant
(c) individually satisfying
(d) analytical

34. Which of the following is an analogous statement?
(a) Man is like God
(b) God is great
(c) Gandhiji is the Father of the Nation
(d) Man is a rational being

Questions from 35-36 are based on the following diagram in which there are three intersecting circles. H representing The Hindu, I representing Indian Express and T representing The Times of India. A total of 50 persons were surveyed and the number in the Venn diagram indicates the number of persons reading the newspapers.

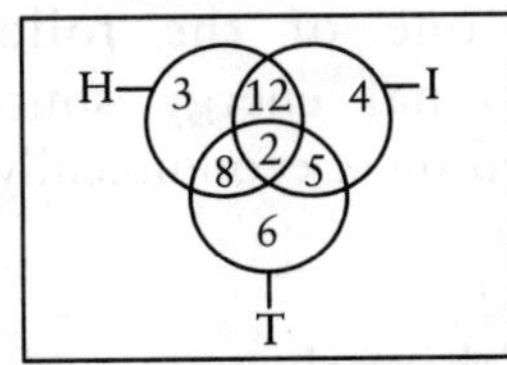

35. How many persons would be reading at least two newspapers?
(a) 23 (b) 25
(c) 27 (d) 29

36. How many persons would be reading almost two newspapers?
(a) 23 (b) 25
(c) 27 (d) 48

37. Which of the following graphs does not represent regular (periodic) behaviour of the variable f(t)?

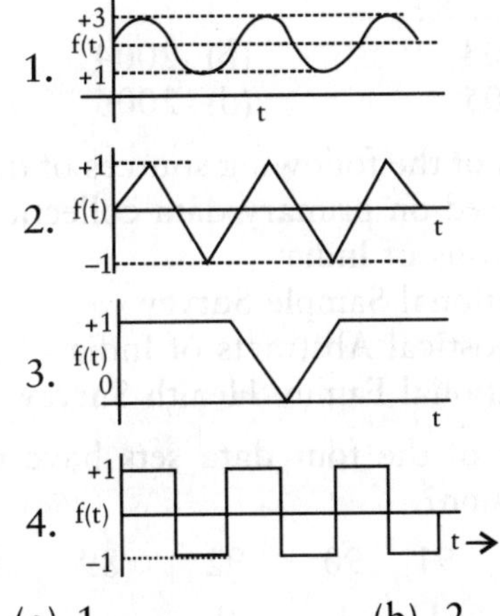

(a) 1 (b) 2
(c) 3 (d) 4

Study the following graph and answer the questions 38 to 40.

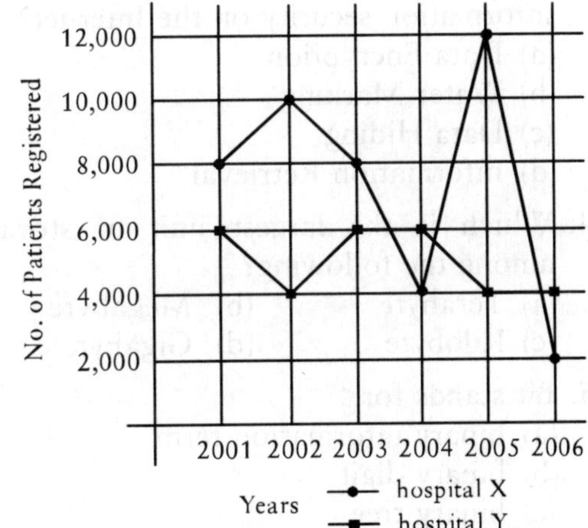

38. In which year total number of patients registered in hospital X and hospital Y was the maximum?

(a) 2003 (b) 2004
(c) 2005 (d) 2006

39. What is the maximum dispersion in the registration of patients in the two hospitals in a year?
(a) 8000 (b) 6000
(c) 4000 (d) 2000

40. In which year there was maximum decrease in registration of patients in hospital X?
(a) 2003 (b) 2004
(c) 2005 (d) 2006

41. Which of the following sources of data is not based on primary data collection?
(a) Census of India
(b) National Sample Survey
(c) Statistical Abstracts of India
(d) National Family Health Survey

42. Which of the four data sets have more dispersion?

(a)	88	91	90	92	89	91
(b)	0	1	1	0	–1	–2
(c)	3	5	2	4	1	5
(d)	0	5	8	10	–2	–8

43. Which of the following is not related to information security on the Internet?
(a) Data Encryption
(b) Water Marking
(c) Data Hiding
(d) Information Retrieval

44. Which is the largest unit of storage among the following?
(a) Terabyte (b) Megabyte
(c) Kilobyte (d) Gigabyte

45. Bit stands for
(a) binary information term
(b) binary digit
(c) binary tree
(d) Bivariate Theory

46. Which one of the following is not a linear data structure?
(a) Array (b) Binary Tree
(c) Queue (d) Stack

47. Which one of the following is not a network device?
(a) Router (b) Switch
(c) Hub (d) CPU

48. A compiler is used to convert the following to object code which can be executed
(a) High-level language
(b) Low-level language
(c) Assembly language
(d) Natural language

49. The great Indian Bustard bird is found in
(a) Thar Desert of Rajasthan
(b) Malabar Coast
(c) Coastal regions of India
(d) Delta regions

50. The Sagarmanthan National Park has been established to preserve the eco-system of which mountain peak?
(a) Kanchenjunga (b) Mount Everest
(c) Annapurna (d) Dhaulavira

51. Maximum soot is released from
(a) Petrol vehicles
(b) CNG vehicles
(c) Diesel vehicles
(d) Thermal Power Plants

52. Surface Ozone is produced from
(a) Transport sector
(b) Cement plants
(c) Textile industry
(d) Chemical industry

53. Which one of the following non-conventional energy sources can be exploited most economically?
(a) Solar
(b) Wind
(c) Geo-thermal
(d) Ocean Thermal Energy Conversion (OTEC)

54. The most recurring natural hazard in India is
(a) Earthquakes (b) Floods
(c) Landslides (d) Volcanoes

55. The recommendation of National Knowledge Commission for the establishment of 1500 Universities is to
(a) create more teaching jobs
(b) ensure increase in student enrolment in higher education
(c) replace or substitute the privately managed higher education institutions by public institutions
(d) enable increased movement of students from rural areas to urban areas

56. According to Article 120 of the Constitution of India, the business in Parliament shall be transacted in
(a) Only English
(b) Only Hindi
(c) Both English and Hindi
(d) All the languages included in Eighth Schedule of the Constitution

57. Which of the following is more interactive and student centric?
(a) Seminar
(b) Workshop
(c) Lecture
(d) Group Discussion

58. The Parliament in India is composed of
(a) Lok Sabha and Rajya Sabha
(b) Lok Sabha, Rajya Sabha and Vice President
(c) Lok Sabha, Rajya Sabha and President
(d) Lok Sabha, Rajya Sabha with their Secretariats

59. The enrolment in higher education in India is contributed both by Formal System of Education and by System of Distance Education. Distance education contributes
(a) 50% of formal system
(b) 25% of formal system
(c) 10% of the formal system
(d) Distance education system's contribution is not taken into account while considering the figures of enrolment in higher education

60. **Assertion (A):** The UGC Academic Staff Colleges came into existence to improve the quality of teachers.
Reason (R): University and college teachers have to undergo both orientation and refresher courses.
(a) Both (A) and (R) are true and (R) is the correct explanation.
(b) Both (A) and (R) are correct but (R) is not the correct explanation of (A).
(c) (A) is correct and (R) is false.
(d) (A) is false and (R) is correct.

ANSWERS

1. (d)	2. (c)	3. (b)	4. (c)	5. (b)
6. (c)	7. (a)	8. (b)	9. (b)	10. (b)
11. (c)	12. (b)	13. (c)	14. (a)	15. (d)
16. (d)	17. (b)	18. (a)	19. (c)	20. (a)
21. (d)	22. (a)	23. (a)	24. (a)	25. (b)
26. (c)	27. (b)	28. (d)	29. (c)	30. (b)
31. (c)	32. (a)	33. (b)	34. (a)	35. (c)
36. (d)	37. (c)	38. (c)	39. (a)	40. (d)
41. (c)	42. (d)	43. (d)	44. (a)	45. (b)
46. (b)	47. (d)	48. (a)	49. (a)	50. (b)
51. (d)	52. (a)	53. (a)	54. (b)	55. (b)
56. (c)	57. (d)	58. (c)	59. (b)	60. (a)

PAPER–II

Note: This paper contains fifty (50) objective type questions, each question carrying two (2) marks. All questions are compulsory.

1. The Emulsifying agent found in food is
   (a) Gluten (b) Trypsin
   (c) Lecithin (d) Caffeine
2. The iso electric point of milk is
   (a) 6.6 (b) 5.6
   (c) 5.2 (d) 4.6
3. Following is a sulphur containing amino acid:
   (a) Lysine (b) Methionine
   (c) Phenyl alanine (d) Valine
4. Strict restriction of carbohydrates is not done in a diabetic diet because it can lead to
   (a) Constipation (b) Glycos uria
   (c) Ketosis (d) Steatorrhoea
5. BARS is a tool used for
   (a) Checking quality of food
   (b) Designing layout plan
   (c) Performance appraisal
   (d) Feedback communication
6. 'Prime method' of pricing includes
   (a) attempt to add profit to food cost.
   (b) considers actual labour cost.
   (c) method used for labour intensive products.
   (d) adds profit to individual item price.
7. A dress is most visually pleasing if it is divided into
   (a) two equal parts
   (b) three equal parts
   (c) unequal parts
   (d) four equal parts
8. Drapability of the costume is more pleasing with
   (a) straight grain (b) off grain
   (c) true bias grain (d) None of these
9. Spandex fibre is
   (a) Crease resistant fibre
   (b) Water proof fibre
   (c) Elastomeric fibre
   (d) Flame retardant fibre
10. Shrinkage of cotton fabrics is reduced by the process
    (a) Felting (b) Mercerisation
    (c) Sanforization (d) Calendering
11. Students arrange books on their desk in an order as per subjects in Time Table is
    (a) change in hand and body motion.
    (b) change in work, storage space and equipment.
    (c) change in production process.
    (d) change in raw materials.
12. Analogous colour scheme makes use of following colours in a colour wheel:
    (a) Two or three colours adjacent to each other
    (b) Two colours opposite to each other
    (c) Three colours forming a triangle
    (d) Half of colour wheel
13. Which of the following statements is an example of a causal statement?
    (a) Both boys and girls participate in sports activities.
    (b) The incidence of childhood diseases decreases as the adolescent years approach.
    (c) Young children may talk out loud without realizing it.
    (d) When a woman in the first trimester of pregnancy contracts rubella, she may give birth to a deaf and blind baby.
14. Erikson's stage of development of trust versus mistrust most closely matches Freud's

(a) Genital stage
(b) Differentiation stage
(c) Oral stage
(d) Oedipal stage

15. Non-formal education should not be
(a) Democratic
(b) Abstract and theoretical
(c) Environmental friendly
(d) Teacher oriented

16. According to Lee Thayer (1968) the categories of the functions of communication are
(a) Six (b) Four
(c) Three (d) Five

17. Extension education as a discipline has its historical roots in
(a) India (b) U.S.A
(c) U.K. (d) Sri Lanka

18. Educational movies are generally long
(a) 10 mm (b) 7 mm
(c) 16 mm (d) 15 mm

19. To plot Histogram from frequency distribution the following are used on X-axis:
(a) Real limits of class intervals.
(b) Apparent limits of class intervals.
(c) Mid-points of class intervals.
(d) Upper limits of class intervals.

20. Which one of the following is a non-probability sampling technique?
(a) Random sampling
(b) Snowball sampling
(c) Systemic random sampling
(d) Cluster sampling

21. **Assertion (A):** Scorching of milk happen on prolonged boiling.
Reason (R): The sugar and protein in milk react to give the burnt taste.
(a) Both (A) and (R) are true.
(b) (A) is true (R) is false.
(c) (A) is false (R) is true.
(d) Both (A) and (R) are false.

22. **Assertion (A):** Hypertension is a risk factor for CHD.
Reason (R): High blood pressure leads to raised cholesterol levels.
(a) Both (A) and (R) are false.
(b) Both (A) and (R) are true.
(c) (A) is false, but (R) is true.
(d) (A) is true, but (R) is false.

23. **Assertion (A):** A prospectus is a formal summary of proposed work.
Reason (R): It is an evaluation tool used by professional for assessment.
(a) Both (A) and (R) are correct.
(b) (A) is correct but (R) is false.
(c) Both (A) and (R) are false.
(d) (A) is false but (R) is correct.

24. **Assertion (A):** In pattern making waist line dart can be shifted to any location without changing the fit of the garment.
Reason (R): Angle of the dart changes accordingly.
(a) (A) and (R) are true.
(b) (A) and (R) are false.
(c) (A) is true but (R) is false.
(d) (A) is false but (R) is true.

25. **Assertion (A):** Direct dyes bleed while washing.
Reason (R): Therefore direct dyed fabrics are after treated with cationic agents.
(a) (A) and (R) are true.
(b) (A) is true, (R) is false.
(c) (A) and (R) are false.
(d) (A) is false, (R) is true.

26. **Assertion (A):** Polyurethane foam is used as insulating material in refrigerators these days.
Reason (R): As it is in liquid state and set in walls of refrigerator evenly.
(a) (A) is true but (R) is false.
(b) (A) and (R) are true.
(c) (A) and (R) are false.
(d) (A) is false but (R) is true.

27. **Assertion (A):** Authoritative mother is responsive, attentive, patient and sensitive to the child's need.
Reason (R): Authoritative mother makes reasonable demands for maturity and consistently enforces and explains things to the children.
(a) Both (A) and (R) are correct.
(b) (A) is true but (R) is false.
(c) Both (A) and (R) are false.
(d) (A) is false but (R) is true.

28. **Assertion (A):** Good teaching helps individual to live independently and happily in a socially constructive way.
Reason (R): Teaching is a two-way communication in which teacher explains clearly and students learn the same way as desired by teacher.
(a) Both (A) and (R) are wrong.
(b) Both (A) and (R) are correct.
(c) (A) is correct but (R) is wrong.
(d) (A) is wrong but (R) is correct.

29. **Assertion (A):** All types of puppets used for educational purposes should be of prominent colour and appropriate size.
Reason (R): Being attractive puppets motivate learners.
(a) Both (A) and (R) are wrong.
(b) Both (A) and (R) are correct.
(c) (A) is wrong and (R) is correct.
(d) (A) is correct and (R) is wrong.

30. Arrange in the right sequence the stages of sugar cookery.
(i) Firm ball (ii) Soft crack
(iii) Thread (iv) Brown liquid
(v) Clear liquid
Codes:
(a) (i), (iii), (ii), (iv), (v)
(b) (iii), (i), (ii), (v), (iv)
(c) (ii), (iv), (v), (i), (iii)
(d) (iv), (v), (i), (ii), (iii)

31. Arrange the following foods in ascending order of their iron content.
(i) egg (ii) leafy vegetable
(iii) liver (iv) milk
Codes:
(a) (iv), (ii), (i), (iii) (b) (iii), (i), (ii), (iv)
(c) (iii), (ii), (iv), (i) (d) (i), (iii), (iv), (ii)

32. Arrange the employment process in the right sequence.
(i) Induction
(ii) Application forms
(iii) Other tests
(iv) Interview
(v) Contract Negotiations
Codes:
(a) (i), (iii), (iv), (ii), (v)
(b) (ii), (i), (iii), (iv), (v)
(c) (iv), (v), (ii), (i), (iii)
(d) (ii), (iv), (iii), (v), (ii)

33. Write down the correct sequence in preparation of fabric for clothing construction.
(i) Blocking (ii) Shrinking
(iii) Pressing (iv) Straightening
Codes:
(a) (i), (ii), (iii), (iv) (b) (ii), (iv), (i), (iii)
(c) (iv), (i), (ii), (iii) (d) (iii), (iv), (i), (ii)

34. Correct the sequence for the preparation of screen for printing.
(i) Tracing the design and application of printing ink.
(ii) Exposure to Sunlight/Artificial light.
(iii) Coating with emulsion and drying.
(iv) Washing the screen.
Codes:
(a) (ii), (iii), (i), (iv) (b) (i), (ii), (iv), (iii)
(c) (i), (iii), (ii), (iv) (d) (ii), (i), (iii), (iv)

35. Arrange different methods of resolving conflict according to the level of satisfaction (less to more).
(i) Compromise
(ii) Dominance
(iii) Integration
(iv) Voluntary Submission

Codes:

(a) (ii), (iii), (i), (iv) (b) (iv), (i), (ii), (iii)
(c) (ii), (i), (iii), (iv) (d) (ii), (iv), (i), (iii)

36. Write the correct sequence of Piaget's cognitive stages.
(i) Preoperational (ii) Sensorimotor
(iii) Concrete (iv) Formal

Codes:

(a) (ii), (i), (iii), (iv) (b) (ii), (iii), (i), (iv)
(c) (iii), (iv), (i), (ii) (d) (i), (ii), (iii), (iv)

37. Write the steps of extension educational process in sequence:
(i) Objectives (ii) Teaching
(iii) Evaluation (iv) Situation
(v) Reconsideration

Codes:

(a) (iv), (i), (ii), (iii), (v)
(b) (iv), (i), (ii), (v), (iii)
(c) (v), (iii), (iv), (ii), (i)
(d) (iii), (ii), (i), (iv), (v)

38. Arrange them in descending order in order of retaining in memory from various teaching aids.
(i) Reading
(ii) Listening
(iii) Looking at charts/diagrams
(iv) Watching a film
(v) Watching a demonstration

Codes:

(a) (iv), (v), (ii), (i), (iii)
(b) (v), (iv), (iii), (ii), (i)
(c) (i), (iii), (ii), (v), (iv)
(d) (i), (iv), (ii), (iii), (v)

39. Identify the statement giving the correct sequence of steps in data analysis.
(a) Coding, tabulation, data entry, interpretation
(b) Coding, data entry, tabulation, interpretation
(c) Interpretation, tabulation, coding, data entry
(d) Tabulation, coding, data entry, interpretation

40. Match the items in List I with List II:

List I	List II
(A) Milk	(i) Rigor Mortis
(B) Apple	(ii) Maillard reaction
(C) Egg	(iii) Gelatinization
(D) Meat	(iv) Rancidity
(E) Cereal	(v) Poaching
	(vi) Browning reaction

Codes:	A	B	C	D	E
(a)	(i)	(iii)	(iv)	(v)	(ii)
(b)	(ii)	(vi)	(v)	(i)	(iii)
(c)	(iii)	(i)	(ii)	(vi)	(v)
(d)	(iv)	(v)	(vi)	(i)	(ii)

41. Match the items in List I with List II:

List I
(A) Spectrophotometer
(B) Soxlet Apparatus
(C) HPLC
(D) Muffle furnace

List II
(i) Retinol
(ii) Iron
(iii) Total inorganic content
(iv) Oil

Codes:	A	B	C	D
(a)	(iii)	(iv)	(i)	(ii)
(b)	(i)	(iv)	(ii)	(iii)
(c)	(ii)	(iv)	(i)	(iii)
(d)	(ii)	(i)	(iv)	(iii)

42. Match the following food service units in List I with types of service in List II:

List I	List II
(A) Airlines	(i) Decentralized
(B) Hostel	(ii) Counter
(C) Hospital	(iii) Portable
(D) Cafeteria	(iv) Scramble
(E) Fast food unit	(v) Waiter
	(vi) Drive in

Codes:	A	B	C	D	E
(a)	(iii)	(ii)	(i)	(iv)	(vi)
(b)	(i)	(iii)	(v)	(vi)	(ii)

(c)	(ii)	(iv)	(v)	(iii)	(i)
(d)	(iv)	(i)	(ii)	(vi)	(v)

43. Match the items in List I with items in List II:

List I

(A) Drafting requires
(B) Softness or roughness
(C) Fabric suitable for travel
(D) Coir is obtained from

List II

(i) Coconut (ii) Details
(iii) Texture (iv) Nylon

Codes:	A	B	C	D
(a)	(i)	(ii)	(iii)	(iv)
(b)	(iv)	(iii)	(ii)	(i)
(c)	(ii)	(iii)	(iv)	(i)
(d)	(iii)	(i)	(iv)	(ii)

44. Match List I with List II:

List I

(A) Polyamide fibre
(B) Yarn number
(C) Pile weave
(D) Strand of long fibres

List II

(i) Filament (ii) Nylon
(iii) Count (iv) Velvet

Codes:	A	B	C	D
(a)	(i)	(ii)	(iii)	(iv)
(b)	(ii)	(i)	(iii)	(iv)
(c)	(iv)	(ii)	(i)	(iii)
(d)	(ii)	(iii)	(iv)	(i)

45. Match List I with List II:

List I

(A) Economic decision
(B) Individual decision
(C) Habitual decision
(D) Group decision

List II

(i) Automatic type
(ii) Not good as may lead to conflicting situation
(iii) Allocation and exchange of resource use
(iv) Easy to make
(v) Good quality but conflict may occur

Codes:	A	B	C	D
(a)	(iii)	(ii)	(iv)	(v)
(b)	(iv)	(i)	(ii)	(iii)
(c)	(ii)	(i)	(iii)	(iv)
(d)	(iii)	(iv)	(i)	(v)

46. Match the items in List I with List II:

List I

(A) Weschsler scale
(B) The perspective of the social group is considered
(C) Think of one aspect of a relationship at a time
(D) Defects which are results of alcohol consumption during pregnancy

List II

(i) Intelligence
(ii) Centring
(iii) Social conventional role thinking
(iv) Fetal alcohol syndrome (FAS)

Codes:	A	B	C	D
(a)	(ii)	(iii)	(i)	(iv)
(b)	(iv)	(ii)	(iii)	(i)
(c)	(iii)	(i)	(ii)	(iv)
(d)	(iii)	(ii)	(i)	(iv)

47. This consists of two lists of statements regarding educational aids. Match the List A with List B:

List A

(A) Flannel Board (B) Illustrations
(C) Lettering (D) Colours

List B

(i) Big, bold and simple
(ii) Plywood, Hardwood or Cardboard
(iii) Large, bold and printed
(iv) Few and pleasing

Codes:	A	B	C	D
(a)	(ii)	(i)	(iii)	(iv)
(b)	(i)	(iii)	(ii)	(iv)

(c)	(iv)	(ii)	(i)	(iii)
(d)	(i)	(ii)	(iv)	(iii)

48. Match the symbols in List I with formulas in List II:

List I	List II
(A) Σx	(i) $\frac{\sigma}{\sqrt{n}}$
(B) Z	(ii) $(\Sigma X)^2 - \frac{\Sigma X^2}{n}$
(C) $\sigma_{\bar{X}}$	(iii) $\frac{(\Sigma X - \bar{X})^2}{n}$
(D) S^2	(iv) $\Sigma X^2 - \frac{(\Sigma X)^2}{n}$
	(v) $\frac{X - \bar{X}}{S}$

Codes:	A	B	C	D
(a)	(ii)	(v)	(i)	(iii)
(b)	(iv)	(v)	(i)	(iii)
(c)	(ii)	(v)	(iii)	(i)
(d)	(iv)	(iii)	(i)	(ii)

Read the passage below and answer the questions that follow based on your understanding of the passage.

Inclusive education means welcoming all children without discrimination, into regular or ordinary schools. It refers to the process of educating all children in their neighbourhood school, regardless of the nature of their disabilities. Students participating in an inclusion programme follow the same schedule as their classmates and participate in age appropriate academic classes. They don't receive special education services in separated or isolated places. Students with disabilities are not required to be "ready" and don't have to "earn" their way into regular classrooms based upon their academic skills. A well-run inclusion programme provides an appropriate inclusion programme for all students. It does not ignore children's individual needs or parents' concerns. It doesn't sacrifice the education of students with special needs nor that of the general run of students.

49. Inclusive education means
    - (a) Educating children in their neighbourhood school.
    - (b) Educating disabled and normal children in the same school.
    - (c) Following same schedule for allchildren.
    - (d) All of the above.

50. Main purpose of inclusive education is
    - (a) that children with disabilities have not to earn their way into regular class rooms based on their academic skills.
    - (b) that children with disability need special schooling.
    - (c) that children with disability participate in age appropriate academic classes.
    - (d) that it sacrifices the education of general students.

ANSWERS

1. (c)	2. (a)	3. (b)	4. (c)	5. (c)
6. (b)	7. (a)	8. (d)	9. (b)	10. (c)
11. (b)	12. (a)	13. (b)	14. (a)	15. (b)
16. (c)	17. (b)	18. (c)	19. (c)	20. (a)
21. (a)	22. (d)	23. (c)	24. (d)	25. (b)
26. (c)	27. (b)	28. (b)	29. (c)	30. (a)
31. (c)	32. (b)	33. (c)	34. (d)	35. (b)
36. (a)	37. (a)	38. (b)	39. (b)	40. (d)
41. (d)	42. (d)	43. (d)	44. (d)	45. (b)
46. (c)	47. (a)	48. (b)	49. (d)	50. (a)

JUNE–2009

Note: This paper contains Fifty (50) multiple choice questions, each question carrying two (2) marks. Attempt all of them.

PAPER–I

1. Good evaluation of written material should not be based on
   (a) Linguistic expression
   (b) Logical presentation
   (c) Ability to reproduce whatever is read
   (d) Comprehension of subject

2. Why do teachers use teaching aid?
   (a) To make teaching fun-filled
   (b) To teach within understanding level of students
   (c) For students' attention
   (d) To make students attentive

3. Attitudes, concepts, skills and knowledge are products of
   (a) Learning (b) Research
   (c) Heredity (d) Explanation

4. Which among the following gives more freedom to the learner to interact?
   (a) Use of film
   (b) Small group discussion
   (c) Lectures by experts
   (d) Viewing country-wide classroom program on TV

5. Which of the following is not a product of learning?
   (a) Attitudes (b) Concepts
   (c) Knowledge (d) Maturation

6. How can the objectivity of the research be enhanced?
   (a) Through its impartiality
   (b) Through its reliability
   (c) Through its validity
   (d) All of these

7. Action-research is
   (a) An applied research
   (b) A research carried out to solve immediate problems
   (c) A longitudinal research
   (d) All the above

8. The basis on which assumptions are formulated
   (a) Cultural background of the country
   (b) Universities
   (c) Specific characteristics of the castes
   (d) All of these

9. Which of the following is classified in the category of the developmental research?
   (a) Philosophical research
   (b) Action research
   (c) Descriptive research
   (d) All the above

10. We use Factorial Analysis
    (a) To know the relationship between two variables
    (b) To test the Hypothesis
    (c) To know the difference between two variables
    (d) To know the difference among the many variables

Read the following passage and answer the questions 11 to 15:

While the British rule in India was detrimental to the economic development of the country, it did help in starting of the process of modernising Indian society and formed several progressive institutions during that process. One of the most beneficial institutions, which were initiated by the British, was democracy. Nobody can dispute that despite its many shortcomings, democracy was and is far better alternative to the arbitrary rule of the rajas and nawabs, which prevailed in India in the pre-British days.

However, one of the harmful traditions of British democracy inherited by India was that of conflict instead of cooperation between elected members. This was its essential feature. The party, which got the support of the majority of elected members, formed the Government while the others constituted a standing opposition. The existence of the opposition to those in power was and is regarded as a hallmark of democracy.

In principle, democracy consists of rule by the people; but where direct rule is not possible, it's rule by persons elected by the people. It is natural that there would be some differences of opinion among the elected members as in the rest of the society.

Normally, members of any organisations have differences of opinion between themselves on different issues but they manage to work on the basis of a consensus and they do not normally form a division between some who are in majority and are placed in power, while treating the others as in opposition.

The members of an organisation usually work on consensus. Consensus simply means that after an adequate discussion, members agree that the majority opinion may prevail for the time being. Thus persons who form a majority on one issue and whose opinion is allowed to prevail may not be on the same side if there is a difference on some other issue.

It was largely by accident that instead of this normal procedure, a two-party system came to prevail in Britain and that is now being generally taken as the best method of democratic rule.

Many democratically inclined persons in India regret that such a two-party system was not brought about in the country. It appears that to have two parties in India—of more or less equal strength—is a virtual impossibility. Those who regret the absence of a two-party system should take the reasons into consideration.

When the two-party system got established in Britain, there were two groups among the rulers (consisting of a limited electorate) who had the same economic interests among themselves and who therefore formed two groups within the selected members of Parliament.

There were members of the British aristocracy (which landed interests and consisting of lord, barons, etc.) and members of the new commercial class consisting of merchants and artisans. These groups were more or less of equal strength and they were able to establish their separate rule at different times.

Answer the following questions:

11. In pre-British period, when India was ruled by the independent rulers
    (a) Peace and prosperity prevailed in the society
    (b) People were isolated from political affairs
    (c) Public opinion was inevitable for policy making
    (d) Law was equal for one and all
12. What is the distinguishing feature of the democracy practised in Britain?
    (a) End to the rule of might is right.
    (b) Rule of the people, by the people and for the people.
    (c) It has stood the test of time.
    (d) Cooperation between elected members.

13. Democracy is practised where
    (a) Elected members form a uniform opinion regarding policy matter.
    (b) Opposition is more powerful than the ruling combine.
    (c) Representatives of masses.
    (d) None of these.

14. Which of the following is true about the British rule in India?
    (a) It was behind the modernisation of the Indian society.
    (b) India gained economically during that period.
    (c) Various establishments were formed for the purpose of progress.
    (d) None of these.

15. Who became the members of the new commercial class during that time?
    (a) British Aristocrats
    (b) Lord and Barons
    (c) Political Persons
    (d) Merchants and Artisans

16. Which one of the following Telephonic Conferencing with a radio link is very popular throughout the world?
    (a) TPS (b) Telepresence
    (c) Video conference (d) Video teletext

17. Which is not 24 hours news channel?
    (a) NDTV 24×7
    (b) ZEE News
    (c) Aajtak
    (d) Lok Sabha Channel

18. The main objective of FM station in radio is
    (a) Information, Entertainment and Tourism
    (b) Entertainment, Information and Interaction
    (c) Tourism, Interaction and Entertainment
    (d) Entertainment only

19. In communication chatting on internet is
    (a) Verbal communication
    (b) Non-verbal communication
    (c) Parallel communication
    (d) Grapevine communication

20. Match List I with List II and select the correct answer using the codes given below:

    List I (Artists)
    A. Pandit Jasraj B. Kishan Maharaj
    C. Ravi Shankar D. Udai Shankar

    List II (Art)
    1. Hindustani vocalist
    2. Sitar
    3. Tabla
    4. Dance

Codes:	A	B	C	D
(a)	1	2	3	4
(b)	1	3	4	2
(c)	1	3	2	4
(d)	3	2	1	4

21. Insert the missing number in the following.
    3, 8, 18, 23, 33, ?, 48
    (a) 37 (b) 40
    (c) 38 (d) 45

22. In a certain code, CLOCK is written as KCOLC. How would STEPS be written in that code?
    (a) SPEST (b) SPSET
    (c) SPETS (d) SEPTS

23. The letters in the first set have a certain relationship. On the basis of this relationship mark the right choice for the second set
    BDFH : OMKI :: GHIK : ?
    (a) FHJL (b) RPNL
    (c) LNPR (d) LJHF

24. What was the day of the week on 1st January 2001?
    (a) Friday (b) Monday
    (c) Sunday (d) Wednesday

25. Find out the wrong number in the sequence.
    52, 51, 48, 43, 34, 27, 16
    (a) 27 (b) 34
    (c) 43 (d) 48

26. In a deductive argument conclusion is
    (a) Summing up of the premises
    (b) Not necessarily based on premises
    (c) Entailed by the premises
    (d) Additional to the premises

27. 'No man are mortal' is contradictory of
    (a) Some man are mortal
    (b) Some man are not mortal
    (c) All men are mortal
    (d) No mortal is man

28. A deductive argument is valid if
    (a) premises are false and conclusion is true
    (b) premises are false and conclusion is also false
    (c) premises are true and conclusion is false
    (d) premises are true and conclusion is true

29. Structure of logical argument is based on
    (a) Formal validity
    (b) Material truth
    (c) Linguistic expression
    (d) Aptness of examples

30. Two ladies and two men are playing bridge and seated at North, East, South and West of a table. No lady is facing East. Persons sitting opposite to each other are not of the same sex. One man is facing South. Which direction are the ladies facing to?
    (a) East and West
    (b) North and West
    (c) South and East
    (d) None of these

Questions 31 and 32 are based on the following Venn diagram in which there are three intersecting circles representing Hindi knowing persons, English knowing persons and persons who are working as teachers. Different regions so obtained in the figure are marked as a, b, c, d, e, f and g.

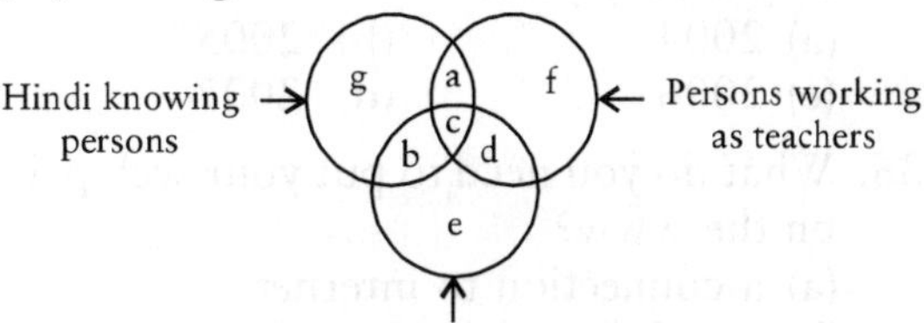

31. If you want to select Hindi and English knowing teachers, which of the following is to be selected?
    (a) g (b) b
    (c) c (d) e

32. If you want to select persons, who do not know English and are not teachers, which of the region is to be selected?
    (a) e (b) g
    (c) b (d) a

Study the following graph carefully and answer questions 33 to 35.

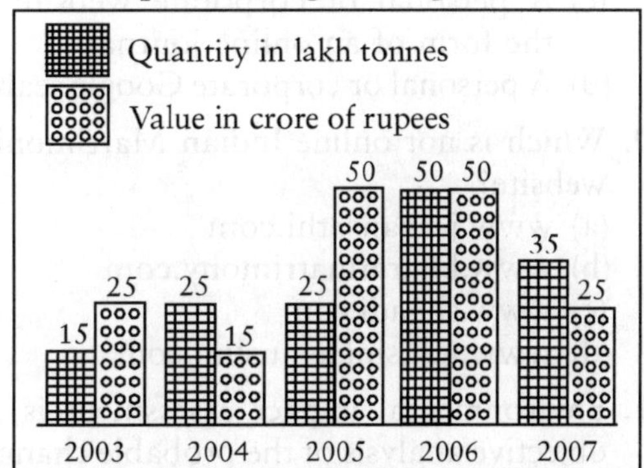

33. In which year the quantity of engineering goods' exports was maximum?
    (a) 2005 (b) 2006
    (c) 2004 (d) 2007

34. In which year the value of engineering goods decreased by 50 percent compared to the previous year?

(a) 2004 (b) 2007
(c) 2005 (d) 2006

35. In which year the quantity of exports was 100 percent higher than the quantity of previous year?
(a) 2004 (b) 2005
(c) 2006 (d) 2007

36. What do you need to put your web pages on the www?
(a) a connection to internet
(b) a web browser
(c) a web server
(d) All of the above

37. Which was the first company to launch mobile phone services in India?
(a) Essar (b) BPL
(c) Hutchison (d) Airtel

38. Chandrayan I was launched on 22nd October, 2008 in India from
(a) Bangalore (b) Sri Harikota
(c) Chennai (d) Ahmedabad

39. What is blog?
(a) Online music
(b) Intranet
(c) A personal or corporate website in the form of an online journal
(d) A personal or corporate Google search

40. Which is not online Indian Matrimonial website?
(a) www.jeevansathi.com
(b) www.bharatmatrimony.com
(c) www.shaadi.com
(d) www.u.k.singlemuslim.com

41. Environmental impact assessment is an objective analysis of the probable changes in
(a) physical characteristics of the environment
(b) biophysical characteristics of the environment
(c) socio-economic characteristics of the environment
(d) All of the above

42. Bog is a wetland that receives water from
(a) nearby water bodies
(b) melting
(c) Only rainfall
(d) Only sea

43. Which of the following region is in the very high risk zone of earthquakes?
(a) Central Indian Highland
(b) Coastal region
(c) Himalayan region
(d) Indian desert

44. Match List I with List II and select the correct answer using the codes given below.

List I (Institutes)
A. Central Arid Zone Institute
B. Space Application Centre
C. Indian Institute of Public Administration
D. Headquarters of Indian Science Congress

List II (Cities)
1. Kolkata 2. New Delhi
3. Ahmedabad 4. Jodhpur

Codes:	A	B	C	D
(a)	4	3	2	1
(b)	4	2	1	3
(c)	3	1	2	4
(d)	1	2	4	3

45. Indian coastal areas experienced Tsunami disaster in the year
(a) 2005 (b) 2004
(c) 2006 (d) 2007

46. The Kothari Commission's report was entitled on
(a) Education and National Development
(b) Learning to be adventure
(c) Diversification of Education
(d) Education and socialisation in democracy

47. Which of the following is not a Dual mode University?
(a) Delhi University
(b) Bangalore University

(c) Madras University
(d) Indira Gandhi National Open University

48. Which part of the Constitution of India is known as "Code of Administrators"?
(a) Part I (b) Part II
(c) Part III (d) Part IV

49. Which article of the Constitution provides safeguards to Naga Customary and their social practices against any act of Parliament?
(a) Article 371 A
(b) Article 371 B
(c) Article 371 C
(d) Article 263

50. Which one of the following is not the tool of good governance?
(a) Right to Information
(b) Citizens' Charter
(c) Social Auditing
(d) Judicial Activism

ANSWERS

1. (a)	2. (a)	3. (a)	4. (b)	5. (d)
6. (d)	7. (b)	8. (a)	9. (d)	10. (d)
11. (b)	12. (d)	13. (a)	14. (c)	15. (a)
16. (b)	17. (d)	18. (b)	19. (b)	20. (c)
21. (c)	22. (c)	23. (b)	24. (b)	25. (b)
26. (c)	27. (c)	28. (d)	29. (b)	30. (b)
31. (c)	32. (b)	33. (b)	34. (b)	35. (c)
36. (d)	37. (d)	38. (b)	39. (c)	40. (d)
41. (d)	42. (a)	43. (b)	44. (a)	45. (b)
46. (a)	47. (d)	48. (d)	49. (a)	50. (d)

PAPER–II

Note: This paper contains fifty (50) objective type questions, each question carrying two (2) marks. All questions are compulsory.

1. The protective covering on the egg shell is called:
(a) Pericarp (b) Rennin
(c) Cuticle (d) Epimyosin

2. The active component in clove is:
(a) Allicin (b) Eugenol
(c) Currcumin (d) Theaflavin

3. Additional Energy and Protein requirement during pregnancy is as follows:
(a) 700 keal, 30 g (b) 300 keal, 15 g
(c) 350 keal, 15 g (d) 300 keal, 30 g

4. To reduce the risk of complication, the Systolic and Diastolic Blood Pressure should be:
(a) < 120 mm Hg and < 85 mm Hg
(b) < 125mm Hg and < 80 mm Hg
(c) < 80 mm Hg and < 120 mm Hg
(d) < 120 mm Hg and < 80 mm Hg

5. The store room inventory is recorded in:
(a) Journal (b) Cash book
(c) Ledger (d) Bincards

6. Contingency approach of Management holds:
(a) that job should be segmented.
(b) that organisation should be seen as whole.
(c) that activities to be adjusted to suit situations.
(d) that productivity is increased by opportunity.

7. Bright coloured clothes express:
   (a) Confidence
   (b) Disturbed mind
   (c) Happiness
   (d) Lack of confidence
8. Shears are used for cutting:
   (a) Paper (b) Leaf
   (c) Cloth (d) Metal
9. Jute is called as:
   (a) Silver fibre
   (b) Copper fibre
   (c) Golden fibre
   (d) Aluminium fibre
10. The part of pineapple plant used for fabric manufacturing process is:
    (a) Root (b) Stem
    (c) Flowers (d) Leaf
11. Doing many activities together is called:
    (a) Grouping (b) Dovetailing
    (c) Combining (d) All the above
12. The insulating material used in refrigerator these days is:
    (a) Fiber glass
    (b) Mica
    (c) Asbestos sheet
    (d) Polyurethane foam
13. Which mother is most likely to give birth to a down's syndrome baby?
    (a) A mother who is tall, under weight, 25 years old, and who takes narcotics.
    (b) A mother who is 30 years old, overweight, and who drinks wine and smokes.
    (c) A mother who is a jogger, in good health, 45 years old, and who neither smokes nor drinks.
    (d) A mother who is Rh-negative, overweight, 20 years old, and who neither drinks nor smokes.
14. Mrs. Singh wants to teach her preschool class not to fight over toys. What does your knowledge suggests as a good method?
    (a) Punish the grabbing behaviour.
    (b) Show the children alternatives to aggressive behaviour.
    (c) Make sure she has only one toy of each type for every child.
    (d) Ignore the aggression.
15. Non-formal education programme can be organized wherever:
    (a) classrooms are available
    (b) teachers are available
    (c) most convenient to learners
    (d) classrooms and teachers both are available
16. The curriculum of non-formal education should be:
    (a) Formally approved
    (b) Flexible
    (c) Need specific of learner
    (d) Culturally based
17. Home Science is a field of knowledge and service primarily concerned with:
    (a) Strengthening family life
    (b) Empowering women
    (c) Empowering women and children
    (d) Strengthening society
18. The three-dimensional recognisable limitation of an object is known as:
    (a) Mock-ups (b) Film
    (c) Specimen (d) Poster
19. F-test is used:
    (a) To check the design of experiment
    (b) To text the difference between means of two or more groups
    (c) To design a randomization model
    (d) To make an estimate of the population
20. Which of the following scales is "summated rating scale" used to measure attitudes:
    (a) Likert's scale (b) Bogardus scale
    (c) Thurstone scale (d) Guttman's scale

21. **Assertion (A):** The preservative added to dark coloured fruit juices is potassium meta bisulphite.
Reason (R): This preservative is used to enhance colour.
(a) Both (A) and (R) are correct
(b) (A) is correct (R) is wrong
(c) (A) is wrong (R) is correct
(d) Both (A) and (R) are wrong

22. **Assertion (A):** Both iron and vitamin C are required for correction/prevention of anaemia.
Reason (R): Vitamin C helps in absorption of iron in the gut.
(a) (A) is true, but (R) is false
(b) (A) is false, but (R) is true
(c) Both (A) and (R) are true
(d) Both (A) and (R) are false

23. **Assertions (A):** Menu is considered as an essential tool in food service planning.
Reason (R): Menu is a detailed list of food items served that will attract customers.
(a) Both (A) and (R) are correct
(b) (A) is true and (R) is false
(c) Both (A) and (R) are false
(d) (A) is false and (R) is true

24. **Assertion (A):** Puckering takes place while machine stitching.
Reason (R): Use of improper needle and thread tension.
(a) (A) and (R) are true
(b) (A) is true and (R) is false
(c) (A) is false and (R) is true
(d) (A) and (R) is true but (R) is not the correct explanation

25. **Assertion (A):** Value addition includes Dyeing.
Reason (R): Dyeing is a form of applying colour using blocks.
(a) (A) and (R) are true
(b) (A) is true (R) is false
(c) (A) and (R) are false
(d) (A) is false (R) is true

26. **Assertion (A):** With increase in family income the proportionate expenditure on food will increase.
Reason (R): As family income increases the family will be spending more money on food.
(a) (A) is true but (R) is false
(b) Both (A) and (R) are true
(c) (A) and (R) both are false
(d) (A) is false but (R) is true

27. **Assertion (A):** A secondary circular reaction involves an action that has an effect on an object in the infant's environment.
Reason (R): Secondary circular reaction is the only process which involves symbolic play.
(a) Both (A) and (R) correct
(b) (A) is true but (R) is false
(c) Both (A) and (R) are false
(d) (A) is false but (R) is true

28. **Assertion (A):** The success of an extension programme depends on the involvement of the leader in the programme.
Reason (R): An active mass following and participation makes any programme success.
(a) Both (A) and (R) are wrong
(b) Both (A) and (R) are correct
(c) (A) is correct but (R) is wrong
(d) (R) is correct but (A) is wrong

29. **Assertion (A):** Integrated Rural Development Programme ensures that beneficiaries have an opportunity to earn.
Reason (R): Any women oriented programme improves nutritional, educational and financial status of the family.
(a) Both (A) and (R) wrong
(b) Both (A) and (R) correct

(c) (A) is correct but (R) is wrong
(d) (A) is wrong but (R) is correct

30. **Assertion (A):** The research study must start with the formulation of hypothesis.
Reason (R): Hypothesis will help to extrapolate the sample results to the population.
(a) (A) is true, but (R) is false
(b) (A) is false, but (R) is true
(c) Both (A) and (R) are true
(d) Both (A) and (R) are false

31. Arrange the activities in the right sequence for making cheese:
(i) Add lactic acid
(ii) Pasteurise milk
(iii) Add salt
(iv) Add bacteria or fungus
(v) Add rennin
Codes:
(a) (i), (ii), (iii), (iv), (v)
(b) (ii), (i), (v), (iii), (iv)
(c) (iii), (iv), (i), (ii), (v)
(d) (iv), (i), (ii), (iii), (v)

32. Identify statement giving the correct sequence of foods in decreasing order of calcium content:
(a) Ragi, Rice, Milk, Spinach
(b) Milk, Ragi, Spinach, Rice
(c) Spinach, Milk, Rice, Ragi
(d) Milk, Spinach, Ragi, Rice

33. Give the correct sequence of the purchasing schedule:
(i) Select the market
(ii) Develop purchase order
(iii) Identify needs
(iv) Receive and inspect deliveries
(v) Write specification
Codes:
(a) (i), (ii), (v), (iv), (iii)
(b) (iii), (v), (ii), (i), (iv)
(c) (i), (ii), (v), (iv), (iii)
(d) (ii), (iv), (v), (i), (iii)

34. Garment Construction includes the sequence of:
(i) Body measurement
(ii) Surface enrichment
(iii) Drafting and pattern making
(iv) Joining of front and back
(v) Insertion of darts and fullness
Codes:
(a) (v), (ii), (iii), (i), (iv)
(b) (i), (iii), (iv), (v), (ii)
(c) (ii), (iii), (iv), (i), (v)
(d) (v), (ii), (i), (iii), (iv)

35. Arrange the correct sequence of weaving process:
(i) Shedding (ii) Picking
(iii) Take up (iv) Beating
Codes:
(a) (i), (ii), (iii), (iv) (b) (iv), (iii), (ii), (i)
(c) (ii), (iii), (iv), (i) (d) (i), (ii), (iv), (iii)

36. Arrange class of change in sequence as given by Mundel:
(i) Change in raw material
(ii) Change in production sequence
(iii) Change in body position and number and type of motions
(iv) Change in finished product
(v) Change in working arrangement and equipment
Codes:
(a) (iii), (iv), (v), (i), (ii)
(b) (iii), (v), (ii), (iv), (i)
(c) (i), (iii), (ii), (iv), (v)
(d) (iii), (iv), (ii), (i), (v)

37. Give the correct sequence of cognitive process:
(i) Reflexes
(ii) Primary circular reactions
(iii) Secondary circular reactions
(iv) Mental combinations
Codes:
(a) (i), (ii), (iii), (iv) (b) (ii), (iii), (iv), (i)
(c) (iii), (iv), (i), (ii) (d) (iv), (ii), (iii), (i)

38. Write the steps given by Wilson and Gallup (1954) of Home science extension teaching in a sequence:
(i) Interest (ii) Conviction
(iii) Attention (iv) Action
(v) Desire (vi) Satisfaction
Codes:
(a) (iii), (i), (v), (ii), (iv), (vi)
(b) (vi), (iii), (ii), (i), (iv), (v)
(c) (ii), (iii), (i), (iv), (v), (vi)
(d) (v), (iii), (ii), (i), (iv), (vi)

39. Write the elements of communication process in a sequence:
(i) Channel (ii) Treatment
(iii) Sender (iv) Message
(v) Receiver
Codes:
(a) (vi), (iii), (ii), (i), (iv)
(b) (iii), (iv), (ii), (i), (v)
(c) (v), (iii), (ii), (iv), (i)
(d) (i), (ii), (iii), (v), (iv)

40. Give the correct sequence in writing a research article:
(i) Review of literature
(ii) Bibliography
(iii) Introduction
(iv) Methodology
(v) Objectives
(vi) Results and conclusion
Codes:
(a) (i), (ii), (iii), (iv), (v), (vi)
(b) (i), (v), (iii), (iv), (vi), (ii)
(c) (iii), (v), (i), (iv), (vi), (ii)
(d) (iii), (v), (i), (iv), (ii), (vi)

41. Match the items in List I with List II:

List I	List II
(A) Blanching	(i) oil
(B) Foaming	(ii) milk
(C) Emulsion	(iii) wheat
(D) Homogenization	(iv) egg
(E) Gluten formation	(v) green leaves
	(vi) sugar

Codes:	A	B	C	D	E
(a)	(iii)	(ii)	(iv)	(i)	(vi)
(b)	(ii)	(i)	(iv)	(iii)	(v)
(c)	(i)	(ii)	(v)	(iv)	(iii)
(d)	(v)	(iv)	(i)	(ii)	(iii)

42. Match the diseases in List I with organs in List II:

List I	List II
(A) Diabetes	(i) Liver
(B) Celiac disease	(ii) Kidney
(C) Nephritis	(iii) Gall bladder
(D) Cholelithiasis	(iv) Pancreas
	(v) Intestines

Codes:	A	B	C	D
(a)	(iv)	(i)	(v)	(iii)
(b)	(v)	(i)	(ii)	(iv)
(c)	(i)	(iii)	(ii)	(v)
(d)	(iv)	(v)	(ii)	(iii)

43. Match the following Equipment in List I with food items which use them in List II:

List I	List II
(A) Bainmaric	(i) mutton curry
(B) Salamander	(ii) chapati
(C) Steam cooker	(iii) pizza
(D) Food processor	(iv) rice
(E) Griddles	(v) vegetables
	(vi) ice cream

Codes:	A	B	C	D	E
(a)	(iii)	(ii)	(i)	(iv)	(vi)
(b)	(i)	(iii)	(iv)	(v)	(ii)
(c)	(iv)	(v)	(iii)	(ii)	(i)
(d)	(vi)	(ii)	(i)	(v)	(iii)

44. Match the following items in List I with List II:
List I
(A) Bias binding (B) Under stitching
(C) Notches (D) Stay stitching
List II
(i) Turning the seam easily
(ii) Finishing the raw edges

(iii) Removing extra fullness from the seam
(iv) To retain the shape

Codes:	A	B	C	D
(a)	(iv)	(ii)	(i)	(iii)
(b)	(i)	(ii)	(iii)	(iv)
(c)	(ii)	(i)	(iii)	(iv)
(d)	(iii)	(iv)	(ii)	(i)

45. Match the following List I with List II:

List I	List II
(A) Acrylic	(i) Modified Basic dyes
(B) Silk	(ii) Disperse dyes
(C) Polyester	(iii) Direct dyes
(D) Cotton	(iv) Acid dyes
	(v) Pigment dyes

Codes:	A	B	C	D
(a)	(i)	(ii)	(iii)	(v)
(b)	(i)	(iv)	(ii)	(iii)
(c)	(ii)	(iii)	(v)	(iv)
(d)	(iii)	(iv)	(v)	(i)

46. Match the items in List I with List II:

List I
(A) Resources
(B) Human Resources
(C) Economic Resources
(D) Non-human Resources

List II
(i) Ability, skill
(ii) Materials and human abilities
(iii) Tangible resources
(iv) Knowledge, time, community resources
(v) Resources used in production and distribution

Codes:	A	B	C	D
(a)	(i)	(ii)	(iii)	(v)
(b)	(ii)	(i)	(v)	(iii)
(c)	(ii)	(iv)	(v)	(iii)
(d)	(iii)	(i)	(iv)	(ii)

47. Match the items in List I with List II:

List I
(A) Soft spot in infant's skull
(B) One word utterances expressing a more complex thought
(C) Care giver used a base for exploration
(D) Disorder involving extreme weight loss

List II
(i) Anorexia Nervosa (ii) Holophrase
(iii) Secure attachment (iv) Fontanelle

Codes:	A	B	C	D
(a)	(iv)	(ii)	(iii)	(i)
(b)	(ii)	(iii)	(iv)	(i)
(c)	(i)	(ii)	(iii)	(iv)
(d)	(iii)	(ii)	(i)	(iv)

48. This consists of two lists of statements, name of the books and authors Match the List I with List II:

List I (Name of the Authors)
(A) Directorate of Extension
(B) Chandra, Arvind and Shah, Anupama
(C) Dahama, O.P. and Bhatnagar, O.P.
(D) Chakraborty, Sujit K.

List II (Name of Books)
(i) *Audio-Visual Education in India*
(ii) *Education and Communication for Development*
(iii) *Non-formal Education for All*
(iv) *Extension Education in Community Development*

Codes:	A	B	C	D
(a)	(iv)	(iii)	(i)	(ii)
(b)	(iv)	(iii)	(ii)	(i)
(c)	(i)	(iii)	(iv)	(ii)
(d)	(ii)	(i)	(iii)	(iv)

Read the passage below and answer the questions that follow based on your understanding of the passage:

The gap which exists between the literacy rates of the two sexes also exists between the enrolment of girls and boys at all levels of education. Right from the primary school to the university, we find that the number of girl students is considerably lower than the number of boy students. According to Article 45 of the Constitution universal compulsory and free education until the age of 14 was to be achieved by the year 1960. Looking at the present condition of primary education in villages, it seems doubtful that 100 per cent enrolment of girls can be achieved by the end of this century. There is no doubt that we have made great headway in the education of women in the last century. It is unfortunately true of our society that children are sent to school not according to their intelligence or aptitude but according to their sex. Such attitude need to be changed without further delay if we want to achieve 100 per cent enrolment of the primary school-going children.

49. Article 45 of the Constitution states:
   (a) Compulsory education to be achieved by 1960
   (b) Universal compulsory and free education up to the age of 14
   (c) Compulsory and free education up to primary school only
   (d) Compulsory and free education for girls

50. Gap between the literacy rates of boys and girls exists because of:
   (a) Preference given to boys for schooling
   (b) Economic reasons
   (c) Children sent to school based on intelligence
   (d) None of the above

ANSWERS

1. (c)	2. (b)	3. (b)	4. (d)	5. (c)
6. (d)	7. (c)	8. (c)	9. (c)	10. (d)
11. (a)	12. (d)	13. (b)	14. (c)	15. (d)
16. (b)	17. (a)	18. (b)	19. (d)	20. (d)
21. (c)	22. (c)	23. (a)	24. (d)	25. (b)
26. (b)	27. (d)	28. (b)	29. (c)	30. (b)
31. (b)	32. (b)	33. (b)	34. (b)	35. (a)
36. (b)	37. (a)	38. (a)	39. (b)	40. (c)
41. (d)	42. (d)	43. (b)	44. (c)	45. (b)
46. (c)	47. (a)	48. (b)	49. (b)	50. (a)

DECEMBER–2008

Note: This paper contains Fifty (50) multiple choice questions, each question carrying two (2) marks. Attempt all of them.

PAPER–I

1. According to Swami Vivekananda, teacher's success depends on
   (a) His renunciation of personal gain and service to others
   (b) His professional training and creativity
   (c) His concentration on his work and duties with a spirit of obedience to God
   (d) His mastery on the subject and capacity in controlling the students

2. Which of the following teacher will be liked most?
   (a) A teacher of high idealistic attitude
   (b) A loving teacher
   (c) A teacher who is disciplined
   (d) A teacher who often amuses his students

3. A teacher's most important challenge is
   (a) To make students do their home work
   (b) To make teaching-learning process enjoyable
   (c) To maintain discipline in the class-room
   (d) To prepare the question paper

4. Value-education stands for
   (a) making a student healthy
   (b) making a student to get a job
   (c) inculcation of virtues
   (d) all-round development of personality

5. When a normal student behaves in an erratic manner in the class, you would
   (a) pull up the student then and there
   (b) talk to the student after the class
   (c) ask the student to leave the class
   (d) ignore the student

6. The research is always
   (a) verifying the old knowledge
   (b) exploring new knowledge
   (c) filling the gap between knowledge
   (d) All of these

7. The research that applies the laws at the time of field study to draw more and more clear ideas about the problem is
   (a) Applied research
   (b) Action research
   (c) Experimental research
   (d) None of these

8. When a research problem is related to heterogeneous population, the most suitable sampling method is
   (a) Cluster Sampling
   (b) Stratified Sampling
   (c) Convenient Sampling
   (d) Lottery Method

9. The process not needed in experimental research is:
   (a) Observation
   (b) Manipulation and replication
   (c) Controlling
   (d) Reference collection

10. A research problem is not feasible only when

(a) it is researchable
(b) it is new and adds something to knowledge
(c) it consists of independent and dependent variables
(d) it has utility and relevance

Read the following passage carefully and answer the questions 11 to 15:

Radically changing monsoon patterns, reduction in the winter rice harvest and a quantum increase in respiratory diseases all part of the environmental doomsday scenario which is reportedly playing out in South Asia. According to a United Nations Environment Program report, a deadly three-kilometer deep blanket of pollution comprising a fearsome, cocktail of ash, acids, aerosols and other particles has enveloped in this region. For India, already struggling to cope with a drought, the implication of this are devastating and further crop failure will amount to a life and death question for many Indians. The increase in premature deaths will have adverse social and economic consequences and a rise in morbidities will place an unbearable burden on our crumbling health system. And there is no one to blame but ourselves. Both official and corporate India has always been allergic to any mention of clean technology. Most mechanical two wheelers roll of the assembly line without proper pollution control system. Little effort is made for R&D on simple technologies, which could make a vital difference to people's lives and the environment.

However, while there is no denying that South Asia must clean up its act, skeptics might question the timing of the haze report. The Kyoto meet on climate change is just two weeks away and the stage is set for the usual battle between the developing world and the West, particularly the Unites States of America. President Mr. Bush has adamantly refused to sign any protocol, which would mean a change in American consumption level. U.N. environment report will likely find a place in the U.S. arsenal as it plants an accusing finger towards controls like India and China. Yet the U.S.A. can hardly deny its own dubious role in the matter of erasing trading quotas.

Richer countries can simply buy up excess credits from poorer countries and continue to pollute. Rather than try to get the better of developing countries, who undoubtedly have taken up environmental shortcuts in their bid to catch up with the West, the USA should take a look at the environmental profigacy, which is going on within. From opening up virgin territories for oil exploration to relaxing the standards for drinking water, Mr. Bush's policies are not exactly beneficial, not even to America's interests. We realise that we are all in this together and that pollution anywhere should be a global concern otherwise there will only be more tunnels at the end of the tunnel.

11. Both official and corporate India is allergic to
(a) Failure of Monsoon
(b) Poverty and Inequality
(c) Slowdown in Industrial Production
(d) Mention of Clean Technology

12. If the rate of premature death increases it will
(a) Exert added burden on the crumbling economy
(b) Have adverse social and economic consequences
(c) Make positive effect on our effort to control population
(d) Have less job aspirants in the society

13. According to the passage, the two-wheeler industry is not adequately concerned about
(a) Passenger safety on the roads
(b) Life cover insurance of the vehicle owner

(c) Pollution control system in the vehicle
(d) Rising cost of the two wheelers

14. What could be the reason behind timing of the haze report just before the Kyoto meet?
(a) United Nations is working hand-in-glove with U.S.A.
(b) Organisers of the forthcoming meet to teach a lesson to the U.S.A.
(c) Drawing attention of the world towards devastating effects of environment degradation.
(d) U.S.A. wants to use it as a handle against the developing countries in the forthcoming meet.

15. Which of the following is the indication of environmental degradation in South Asia?
(a) Social and economic inequality
(b) Crumbling health care system
(c) Inadequate pollution control system
(d) Radically changing monsoon pattern

16. Community Radio is a type of radio service that caters to the interest of
(a) Local audience (b) Education
(c) Entertainment (d) News

17. Orkcut is a part of
(a) Intrapersonal Communication
(b) Mass Communication
(c) Group Communication
(d) Interpersonal Communication

18. Match List I with List II and select the correct answer using the codes given below.

List I (Artists)
A. Amrita Shergill
B. T. Swaminathan Pillai
C. Bhimsen Joshi
D. Padma Subramaniyam

List II (Art)
1. Flute 2. Classical Song
3. Painting 4. Bharat Natyam

Codes:	A	B	C	D
(a)	3	1	2	4
(b)	2	3	1	4
(c)	4	2	3	1
(d)	1	4	2	3

19. Which is not correct in latest communication award?
(a) Salman Rushdie - Booker's Prize—July 20, 2008
(b) Dilip Sanghavi - Business Standard CEO Award, July 22, 2008
(c) Tapan Sinha - Dada Saheb Falke Award, July 21, 2008
(d) Gautam Ghosh - Osians Lifetime Achievement Award, July 11, 2008

20. Firewalls are used to protect a communication network system against
(a) Unauthorised attacks
(b) Virus attacks
(c) Data-driven attacks
(d) Fire-attacks

21. Insert the missing number in the following

$\frac{2}{7}, \frac{4}{7}, ?, \frac{11}{21}, \frac{16}{31}$

(a) $\frac{10}{8}$ (b) $\frac{6}{10}$
(c) $\frac{5}{10}$ (d) $\frac{7}{13}$

22. In a certain code, GAMESMAN is written as AGMEMSAN. How would DISCLOSE be written in that code?
(a) IDSCOLSE (b) IDCSOLES
(c) IDSCOLES (d) IDSCLOSE

23. The letters in the first set have a certain relationship. On the basis of this relationship mark the right choice for the second set : AST : BRU :: NQV: ?

(a) ORW (b) MPU
(c) MRW (d) OPW

24. On what dates of April, 1994 did Sunday fall?
(a) 2, 9, 16, 23, 30
(b) 3, 10, 17, 24
(c) 4, 11, 18, 25
(d) 1, 8, 15, 22, 29

25. Find out the wrong number in the sequence
125, 127, 130, 135, 142, 153, 165
(a) 130 (b) 142
(c) 153 (d) 165

26. There are five books A, B, C, D and E. The book C lies above D, the book E is below A and B is below E. Which is at the bottom?
(a) E (b) B
(c) A (d) C

27. Logical reasoning is based on
(a) Truth of involved propositions
(b) Valid relation among the involved propositions
(c) Employment of symbolic language
(d) Employment of ordinary language

28. Two propositions with the same subject and predicate terms but different in quality are
(a) Contradictory (b) Contrary
(c) Subaltern (d) Identical

29. The premises of a valid deductive argument
(a) Provide some evidence for its conclusion
(b) Provide no evidence for its conclusion
(c) Are irrelevant for its conclusion
(d) Provide conclusive evidence for its conclusion

30. Syllogistic reasoning is
(a) Deductive (b) Inductive
(c) Experimental (d) Hypothetical

Study the following Venn diagram and answer questions nos. 31 to 33.

Three circles representing Graduates, Clerks and Government Employees are intersecting. The intersections are marked A, B, C, e, f, g and h. Which part best represents the statements in questions 31 to 33?

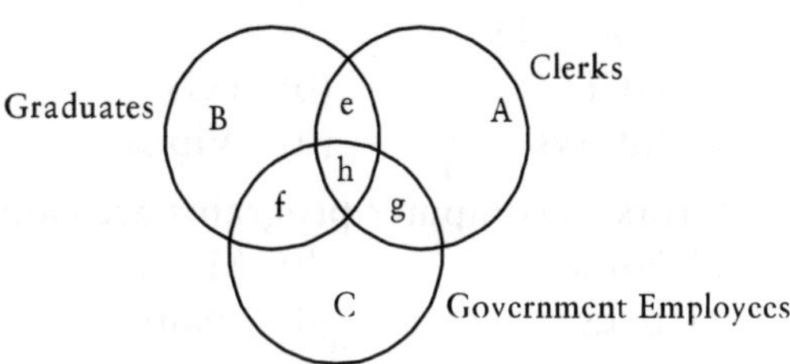

31. Some Graduates are Government employees but not as Clerks.
(a) h (b) g
(c) f (d) e

32. Clerks who are graduates as well as government employees.
(a) e (b) f
(c) g (d) h

33. Some graduates are Clerks but not Government employees.
(a) f (b) g
(c) h (d) e

Study the following graph and answer questions numbers from 34 to 35

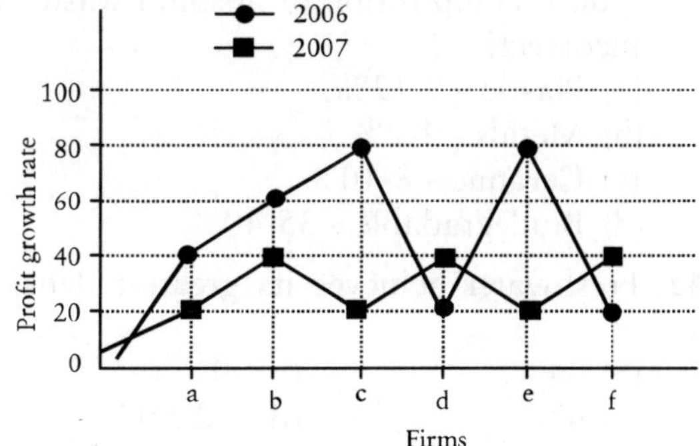

34. Which of the firms got maximum profit growth rate in the year 2006.

(a) ab (b) ce
(c) cd (d) ef

35. Which of the firms got maximum profit growth rate in the year 2007.
(a) bdf (b) acf
(c) bed (d) ace

36. The accounting software 'Tally' was developed by
(a) HCL (b) TCS
(c) Infosys (d) Wipro

37. Errors in computer programs are called
(a) Follies (b) Mistakes
(c) Bugs (d) Spam

38. HTML is basically used to design
(a) Webpage
(b) Website
(c) Graphics
(d) Tables and Frames

39. 'Micro Processing' is made for
(a) Computer
(b) Digital System
(c) Calculator
(d) Electronic Goods

40. Information, a combination of graphics, text, sound, video and animation is called
(a) Multiprogram (b) Multifacet
(c) Multimedia (d) Multiprocess

41. Which of the following pairs regarding typical composition of hospital wastes is incorrect?
(a) Plastic - 9-12%
(b) Metals - 1-2%
(c) Ceramic - 8-10%
(d) Biodegradable - 35-40%

42. Freshwater achieves its greatest density at
(a) –4°C (b) 0°C
(c) 4°C (d) –2.5°C

43. Which one of the following is not associated with earthquakes?
(a) Focus (b) Epicenter
(c) Seismograph (d) Swells

44. The tallest trees in the world are found in the region
(a) Equatorial region
(b) Temperate region
(c) Monsoon region
(d) Mediterranean region

45. Match List I with List II and select the correct answer from the codes given below.

List I (National Parks)
A. Periyar
B. Nandan Kanan
C. Corbett National Park
D. Sariska Tiger Reserve

List II (States)
1. Orissa
2. Kerala
3. Rajasthan
4. Uttarakhand

Codes:	A	B	C	D
(a)	2	1	4	3
(b)	1	2	4	3
(c)	3	2	1	4
(d)	1	2	3	4

46. According to Radhakrishnan Commission, the aim of Higher Education is
(a) To develop the democratic values, peace and harmony
(b) To develop great personalities who can give their contributions in politics, administration, industry and commerce
(c) Both (a) and (b)
(d) None of these

47. The National Museum at New Delhi is attached to
(a) Delhi University
(b) a Deemed University

(c) a Subordinate Office of the JNU
(d) Part of Ministry of Tourism and Culture

48. Match List I with List II and select the correct answer from the code given below.

List I (Institutions)
A. National Law Institute
B. Indian Institute of Advanced Studies
C. National Judicial Academy
D. National Savings Institute

List II (Locations)
1. Shimla
2. Bhopal
3. Hyderabad
4. Nagpur

Codes:	**A**	**B**	**C**	**D**
(a)	3	2	4	1
(b)	1	2	3	4
(c)	4	3	1	2
(d)	3	1	2	4

49. Election of Rural and Urban local bodies are conducted and ultimately supervised by
(a) Election Commission of India
(b) State Election Commission
(c) District Collector and District Magistrate
(d) Concerned Returning Officer

50. Which opinion is not correct?
(a) Education is a subject of concurrent list of VII schedule of Constitution of India
(b) University Grants Commission is a statutory body
(c) Patent, inventions, design, copyright and trade marks are the subject of concurrent list
(d) Indian Council of Social Science Research is a statutory body related to research in social sciences

ANSWERS

1. (d)	2. (c)	3. (b)	4. (c)	5. (b)
6. (d)	7. (a)	8. (b)	9. (d)	10. (b)
11. (d)	12. (b)	13. (c)	14. (c)	15. (d)
16. (a)	17. (d)	18. (a)	19. (b)	20. (a)
21. (d)	22. (a)	23. (d)	24. (b)	25. (d)
26. (b)	27. (b)	28. (a)	29. (d)	30. (a)
31. (c)	32. (d)	33. (d)	34. (b)	35. (a)
36. (b)	37. (c)	38. (a)	39. (a)	40. (c)
41. (d)	42. (c)	43. (d)	44. (b)	45. (a)
46. (c)	47. (d)	48. (d)	49. (b)	50. (c)

JUNE–2008

Note: This paper contains Fifty (50) multiple choice questions, each question carrying two (2) marks. Attempt all of them.

PAPER–I

1. The teacher has been glorified by the phrase "Friend, philosopher and guide" because
   (a) He has to play all vital roles in the context of society
   (b) He transmits the high value of humanity to students
   (c) He is the great reformer of the society
   (d) He is a great patriot
2. The most important cause of failure for teacher lies in the area of
   (a) interpersonal relationship
   (b) lack of command over the knowledge of the subject
   (c) verbal ability
   (d) strict handling of the students
3. A teacher can establish rapport with his students by
   (a) becoming a figure of authority
   (b) impressing students with knowledge and skill
   (c) playing the role of a guide
   (d) becoming a friend to the students
4. Education is a powerful instrument of
   (a) Social transformation
   (b) Personal transformation
   (c) Cultural transformation
   (d) All of the above
5. A teacher's major contribution towards the maximum self-realisation of the student is affected through
   (a) Constant fulfilment of the students' needs
   (b) Strict control of classroom activities
   (c) Sensitivity to students' needs, goals and purposes
   (d) Strict reinforcement of academic standards
6. Research problem is selected from the stand point of
   (a) Researcher's interest
   (b) Financial support
   (c) Social relevance
   (d) Availability of relevant literature
7. Which one is called non-probability sampling?
   (a) Cluster sampling
   (b) Quota sampling
   (c) Systematic sampling
   (d) Stratified random sampling
8. Formulation of hypothesis may not be required in
   (a) Survey method
   (b) Historical studies
   (c) Experimental studies
   (d) Normative studies
9. Field-work based research is classified as
   (a) Empirical (b) Historical
   (c) Experimental (d) Biographical
10. Which of the following sampling method is appropriate to study the prevalence of AIDS amongst male and female in India in 1976, 1986, 1996 and 2006?

(a) Cluster sampling
(b) Systematic sampling
(c) Quota sampling
(d) Stratified random sampling

Read the following passage and answer the questions 11 to 15:

The fundamental principle is that Article 14 forbids class legislation but permits reasonable classification for the purpose of legislation which classification must satisfy the twin tests of classification being founded on an intelligible differentia which distinguishes persons or things that are grouped together from those that are left out of the group and that differentia must have a rational nexus to the object sought to be achieved by the Statute in question. The thrust of Article 14 is that the citizen is entitled to equality before law and equal protection of laws. In the very nature of things the society being composed of unequals a welfare State will have to strive by both executive and legislative action to help the less fortunate in society to ameliorate their condition so that the social and economic inequality in the society may be bridged. This would necessitate a legislative application to a group of citizens otherwise unequal and amelioration of whose lot is the object of state affirmative action. In the absence of the doctrine of classification such legislation is likely to flounder on the bedrock of equality enshrined in Article 14. The Court realistically appraising the social and economic inequality and keeping in view the guidelines on which the State action must move as constitutionally laid down in Part IV of the Constitution evolved the doctrine of classification. The doctrine was evolved to sustain a legislation or State action designed to help weaker sections of the society or some such segments of the society in need of succour. Legislative and executive action may accordingly be sustained if it satisfies the twin tests of reasonable classification and the rational principle correlated to the object sought to be achieved.

The concept of equality before the law does not involve the idea of absolute equality among human beings which is a physical impossibility. All that Article 14 guarantees is a similarity of treatment contra-distinguished from identical treatment. Equality before law means that among equals the law should be equal and should be equally administered and that the likes should be treated alike. Equality before the law does not mean that things which are different shall be as though they are the same. It of course means denial of any special privilege by reason of birth, creed or the like. The legislation as well as the executive government, while dealing with diverse problems arising out of an infinite variety of human relations must of necessity have the power of making special laws, to attain any particular object and to achieve that object it must have the power of selection or classification of persons and things upon which such laws are to operate.

11. Right to equality, one of the fundamental rights, is enunciated in the constitution under Part III, Article
(a) 12 (b) 13
(c) 14 (d) 15

12. The main thrust of Right to Equality is that it permits
(a) class legislation
(b) equality before law and equal protection under the law
(c) absolute equality
(d) special privilege by reason of birth

13. The social and economic inequality in the society can be bridged by
(a) executive and legislative action
(b) universal suffrage
(c) identical treatment
(d) None of the above

14. The doctrine of classification is evolved to
    (a) Help weaker sections of the society
    (b) Provide absolute equality
    (c) Provide identical treatment
    (d) None of the above
15. While dealing with diverse problems arising out of an infinite variety of human relations, the government
    (a) must have the power of making special laws
    (b) must not have any power to make special laws
    (c) must have power to withdraw equal rights
    (d) None of the above
16. Communication with oneself is known as
    (a) Group communication
    (b) Grapevine communication
    (c) Interpersonal communication
    (d) Intrapersonal communication
17. Which broadcasting system for TV is followed in India?
    (a) NTSE (b) PAL
    (c) SECAM (d) NTCS
18. All India Radio before 1936 was known as
    (a) Indian Radio Broadcasting
    (b) Broadcasting Service of India
    (c) Indian State Broadcasting Service
    (d) All India Broadcasting Service
19. The biggest news agency of India is
    (a) PTI
    (b) UNI
    (c) NANAP
    (d) Samachar Bharati
20. Prasar Bharati was launched in the year
    (a) 1995 (b) 1997
    (c) 1999 (d) 2001
21. A statistical measure based upon the entire population is called parameter while measure based upon a sample is known as
    (a) Sample parameter
    (b) Inference
    (c) Statistics
    (d) None of these
22. The importance of the correlation co-efficient lies in the fact that
    (a) There is a linear relationship between the correlated variables
    (b) It is one of the most valid measure of statistics
    (c) It allows one to determine the degree or strength of the association between two variables
    (d) It is a non-parametric method of statistical analysis
23. The F-test
    (a) is essentially a two tailed test
    (b) is essentially a one tailed test
    (c) can be one tailed as well as two tailed depending on the hypothesis
    (d) can never be a one tailed test
24. What will be the next letters in the following series
    DCXW, FEVU, HGTS, ______?
    (a) AKPO (b) JBYZ
    (c) JIRQ (d) LMRS
25. The following question is based on the diagram given below. If the two small circles represent formal classroom education and distance education and the big circle stands for university system of education, which figure represents the university systems?

(a) 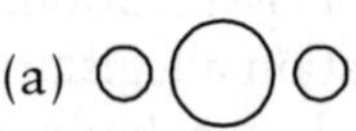 (b) 

(c) (d) 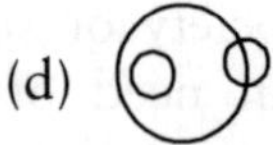

26. The statement, 'To be non-violent is good' is a

(a) Moral judgement
(b) Factual judgement
(c) Religious judgement
(d) Value judgement

27. **Assertion (A):** Man is a rational being.
Reason (R): Man is a social being.
(a) Both (A) and (R) are true and (R) is the correct explanation of (A)
(b) Both (A) and (R) are true but (R) is not the correct explanation of (A)
(c) (A) is true but (R) is false
(d) (A) is false but (R) is true

28. Value Judgements are
(a) Factual Judgements
(b) Ordinary Judgements
(c) Normative Judgements
(d) Expression of public opinion

29. Deductive reasoning proceeds from
(a) general to particular
(b) particular to general
(c) one general conclusion to another general conclusion
(d) one particular conclusion to another particular conclusion

30. AGARTALA is written in code as 14168171, the code for AGRA is
(a) 1641 (b) 1416
(c) 1441 (d) 1461

31. Which one of the following is the most comprehensive source of population data?
(a) National Family Health Surveys
(b) National Sample Surveys
(c) Census
(d) Demographic Health Surveys

32. Which one of the following principles is not applicable to sampling?
(a) Sample units must be clearly defined
(b) Sample units must be dependent on each other
(c) Same units of sample should be used throughout the study
(d) Sample units must be chosen in a systematic and objective manner

33. If January 1st, 2007 is Monday, what was the day on 1st January 1995?
(a) Sunday (b) Monday
(c) Friday (d) Saturday

34. Insert the missing number in the following series
4 16 8 64 ? 256
(a) 16 (b) 24
(c) 32 (d) 20

35. If an article is sold for ₹ 178 at a loss of 11%; what would be its selling price in order to earn a profit of 11%?
(a) ₹ 222.50 (b) ₹ 267
(c) ₹ 222 (d) ₹ 220

36. WYSIWYG—describes the display of a document on screen as it will actually print
(a) What you state is what you get
(b) What you see is what you get
(c) What you save is what you get
(d) What you suggest is what you get

37. Which of the following is not a Computer language?
(a) PASCAL (b) UNIX
(c) FORTRAN (d) COBOL

38. A keyboard has at least
(a) 91 keys (b) 101 keys
(c) 111 keys (d) 121 keys

39. An E-mail address is composed of
(a) two parts (b) three parts
(c) four parts (d) five parts

40. Corel Draw is a popular
(a) Illustration program
(b) Programming language
(c) Text program
(d) None of the above

41. Human ear is most sensitive to noise in which of the following ranges
(a) 1-2 kHz (b) 100-500 Hz
(c) 10-12 kHz (d) 13-16 kHz

42. Which one of the following units is used to measure intensity of noise?
(a) Decible (b) Hz
(c) Phon (d) Watts/m^2

43. If the population growth follows a logistic curve, the maximum sustainable yield
(a) is equal to half the carrying capacity
(b) is equal to the carrying capacity
(c) depends on growth rates
(d) depends on the initial population

44. Chemical weathering of rocks is largely dependent upon
(a) high temperature
(b) strong wind action
(c) heavy rainfall
(d) glaciation

45. Structure of earth's system consists of the following: Match List I with List II and give the correct answer.
List I (Zone)
A. Atmosphere B. Biosphere
C. Hydrosphere D. Lithosphere
List II (Chemical Character)
1. Inert gases
2. Salt, freshwater, snow and ice
3. Organic substances, skeleton matter
4. Light silicates

Codes:	**A**	**B**	**C**	**D**
(a)	2	3	1	4
(b)	1	3	2	4
(c)	2	1	3	4
(d)	3	1	2	4

46. NAAC is an autonomous institution under the aegis of
(a) ICSSR (b) CSIR
(c) AICTE (d) UGC

47. National Council for Women's Education was established in
(a) 1958 (b) 1976
(c) 1989 (d) 2000

48. Which one of the following is not situated in New Delhi?
(a) Indian Council of Cultural Relations
(b) Indian Council of Scientific Research
(c) National Council of Educational Research and Training
(d) Indian Institute of Advanced Studies

49. Autonomy in higher education implies freedom in
(a) Administration
(b) Policy-making
(c) Finance
(d) Curriculum development

50. Match List I with List II and select the correct answer from the code given below
List I (Institutions)
A. Dr. Hari Singh Gour University
B. S.N.D.T. University
C. M.S. University
D. J.N. Vyas University
List II (Locations)
1. Mumbai 2. Baroda
3. Jodhpur 4. Sagar

Codes:	**A**	**B**	**C**	**D**
(a)	4	1	2	3
(b)	1	2	3	4
(c)	3	1	2	4
(d)	2	4	1	3

ANSWERS

1. (b)	2. (b)	3. (b)	4. (d)	5. (c)
6. (c)	7. (b)	8. (b)	9. (a)	10. (d)
11. (c)	12. (b)	13. (a)	14. (a)	15. (a)
16. (d)	17. (b)	18. (c)	19. (a)	20. (b)
21. (a)	22. (c)	23. (c)	24. (c)	25. (b)
26. (a)	27. (b)	28. (c)	29. (a)	30. (d)
31. (c)	32. (b)	33. (d)	34. (a)	35. (c)
36. (b)	37. (b)	38. (b)	39. (a)	40. (a)
41. (b)	42. (a)	43. (a)	44. (c)	45. (b)
46. (d)	47. (a)	48. (d)	49. (c)	50. (a)

PAPER–II

Note: This paper contains fifty (50) objective type questions, each question carrying two (2) marks. All questions are compulsory.

1. The textile fibre products identification act defines it as a manufactured fibre in which the fibre forming substance is any long chain synthetic polymer composed of at least 85% by weight of ethylene propylene or other olefin units except amorphous polyeolefins
   (a) Saran (b) Olefin
   (c) Vinyon (d) None
2. The sports of clustridum botulinum and Clostridium perfingers are destroyed by
   (i) Heat (ii) Underpressure
   (iii) Refrigeration (iv) Drying
   (a) i, ii, iii, iv (b) i, ii, iii
   (c) i, ii (d) i, iv
3. The process of guidance towards occupational, adjustment includes .... while, still in school
   (a) Adequate job preparation
   (b) Wise selection of vocation
   (c) Placement according to specialization
   (d) All of these
4. State which is/are true
   (a) Appendices in report is the statements or original documents on the basis of which the generalizations have been formed.
   (b) Footnotes are generally used as reference guide or short explanations to the points under discussion.
   (c) Suggestion in report is given when the investigation is not for purely research purpose.
   (d) Suggestions are needed for reformations or creative steps.
   (e) All of the above.
5. Before costing a report the researcher has to take into consideration
   (i) Whom the report is meant
   (ii) Language
   (iii) Clarity
   (iv) Level of knowledge
   (a) i, ii, iii, iv (b) i, ii, iii
   (c) i, ii (d) i, iv
6. Match the following:

   List I
   (A) Clear liquid diet
   (B) Tea lemon cereal extracts strained fruit juices carbonated beverages dal extract fat-free both
   (C) Avoid foods which produce gas like cabbage, beans, peas, etc.
   (D) Heart disease occurs
   (E) Arrhythmia, Ischzcuric, chronic Valvaller are

   List II
   (i) Clear fluid diet
   (ii) In heart disease
   (iii) Common heart diseases
   (iv) replaces the fluids lost by the body preventing dehydration,
   (v) Heredity, diabetes, faf abnormalities, cigarette smoking, lack of exercise emotionally stressful life.

Codes:	A	B	C	D	E
(a)	iv	i	ii	v	iii
(b)	iii	ii	i	iv	v
(c)	v	iv	iii	i	ii
(d)	ii	iii	i	v	i

7. The causes of discipline problem found in the nature of school organization
   (i) Unsympathetic staff
   (ii) No curricular activities
   (iii) Heavy assignment
   (iv) Inadequate facilities
   (a) i, ii, iii, iv (b) i, ii, iii
   (c) i, ii (d) i, iv
8. Variables are the characteristic of conditions that are .... by the experimenter

(a) Manipulated (b) Controlled
(c) Observed (d) All of these

9. In experimental research variables are classified into
(i) Dependent (ii) Independent
(iii) Continuous (iv) Broken
(a) i, ii, iii, iv (b) i, ii, iii
(c) i, ii (d) i, iv

10. Who stated "A purposive selection denotes the method of selecting a number of groups of units in such a way that selected groups together yield as nearly as possible the same averages or proportion as the totality with respect of those characteristic which are already a matter of statistical knowledge."?
(a) Adolph Jenson (b) Smith and Whyte
(c) P.V. Young (d) None

11. Which of the following is/are the Criticism advanced by Snedecor for purposive selection.
(i) The knowledge of the population must be available in advance which is mostly not possible
(ii) The controls are often not effective and a biased sample is selected
(iii) Estimate of sampling error rests upon hypothesis which are seldom if ever met in practice
(iv) It is a hopeless method
(a) i, ii, iii, iv (b) i, ii, iii
(c) i, ii (d) i, iv

12. What could be kept in mind regarding a questionnaire?
(i) Size (ii) Appearance
(iii) Clarity (iv) Catching
(a) i, ii, iii, iv (b) i, ii, iii
(c) i, ii (d) i, iv

13. The advantages of questionnaire method could be
(i) Low cost
(ii) Large coverage
(iii) Repetitive information
(iv) Rapidity
(a) i, ii, iii, iv (b) i, ii, iii
(c) i, ii (d) i, iv

14. The comparison with controlled group shows
(a) Occurence of effect frequency
(b) Cause occurred before an effect or not
(c) Others factors determining conditions
(d) All of these

15. Research is a "Careful and critical query or examination in seeking facts or principles diligent investigation in order to ascertain something."
(a) Websters International Dictionary
(b) Prot Clifford Moody
(c) Stephenson
(d) None of these

16. Which of the coloured vegetables should be boiled gently to preserve their shape
(i) Carrots (ii) Potatoes
(iii) Turnips (iv) Peas
(a) i, ii, iii, iv (b) i, ii, iii
(c) i, ii (d) i, iv

17. Cooking of food in water for a long time on low heat is
(a) Grilling (b) Boiling
(c) Stewing (d) Baking

18. The pan in stewing is covered for
(i) Quick result
(ii) Save fuel
(iii) Minimum evaporation
(iv) Conserve nutrients and flavour
(a) i, ii, iii, iv (b) i, ii, iv
(c) i, ii (d) i, iv

19. The heat provided in stewing is
(i) Slow (ii) Steady
(iii) Moist (iv) Tenderizing
(a) i, ii, iii, iv (b) i, ii, iii
(c) i, ii (d) i, iv

20. In stewing food should be cut into small equal pieces for
 (a) Beauty
 (b) Exposure to softening power of boiling water
 (c) Makes bigger dish
 (d) None

21. Enzymes in meat are responsible of the increased .... that occurs in it during storage
 (a) Haemoglobin (b) Extracts
 (c) Water retention (d) Tenderness

22. The optimum temperature at which most enzymes act rapidly is about
 (a) 600°C (b) 490°C
 (c) 370°C (d) 240°C

23. Before freezing or canning foods the enzymes in them are inactivated by
 (i) Scalding (ii) Blanching
 (iii) Vacuum (iv) Oxygen addition
 (a) i, ii, iii, iv (b) i, ii, iii
 (c) i, ii (d) i, iv

24. Insect which commonly cause damage to food is/are
 (i) Worms and bugs
 (ii) Weevils and fruit flies
 (iii) Moth
 (iv) Other insects
 (a) i, ii, iii, iv (b) i, ii, iii
 (c) i, ii (d) i, iv

25. A running account of the behavior of a particular child for a stated period of time. It is
 (a) Diary records
 (b) Anecdotal records
 (c) Self reports
 (d) None of these

26. Which of the following is/are true?
 (i) With practice only one learns to record the most significant events that relate to a child's use of objects and materials in his environment.
 (ii) A wise producer for diary records is to record as accurately and completely as possible for not more than 5 minutes at a time following by brief rest period.
 (iii) One of the important key of observation is that of raising question in the observer's mind which can lead to further attempts to understand child.
 (iv) The very process of formulating a 'significant' question is a key in the direction of greater understanding.
 (a) i, ii, iii, iv (b) i, ii, iii
 (c) i, ii (d) i, iv

27. Diary records should be completely factual with conscientious efforts to eliminate
 (a) Opinions
 (b) Value judgement
 (c) Personal attitudes
 (d) All of these

28. In a country like India the problem and difficulty faced in assignment method is
 (a) Distance
 (b) Well-equipped library
 (c) Conveyance
 (d) Time

29. Criteria of good project should include
 (i) Purposeful
 (ii) Selected by students and teacher
 (iii) Challenging
 (iv) Feasible
 (a) i, ii, iii, iv (b) i, ii, iii
 (c) i, ii (d) i, iv

30. In audio-visual aid teaching students can
 (a) Discuss (b) Questions
 (c) Comment (d) All

31. There are different types of chalk boards which have been suggested from time to time
 (a) Hinged
 (b) Fixed-wall board

(c) Roller board
(d) All of these

32. Charts try to explain
(a) How of event
(b) Express a product
(c) Symbolise matter
(d) All of these

33. Charts using, is an advantage in
(i) Information in gist
(ii) Facts and figures clear
(iii) Information interesting
(iv) Logical combination
(a) i, ii, iii, iv (b) i, ii, iii
(c) i, ii (d) i, iv

34. The media were for Learner powerful tools for changing people's
(a) Perceptions (b) Attitudes
(c) Aspirations (d) All of these

35. Any idea, practice or product which an individual perceives to be new. It is
(a) Adoption (b) Different
(c) Innovation (d) None of these

36. State which is/are true
(a) In business a shorter adoption period means a quicker payback on new products
(b) The adoption process views the mental stages an individual goes through in adopting an innovation
(c) The diffusion process is concerned with the broader scope of adoption within groups of a social system
(d) Those who recognize an innovation early have a higher level of education
(e) All of these

37. Erickson, Williamson, Wrenn, Hahn and Mclean propose the type of counselling
(a) Non-directive (b) Directive
(c) Electric (d) None of these

38. Rogers, Poter Snyder philosophy was _____ type of counselling.
(a) Directive (b) Non-directive
(c) Electric (d) None

39. Both organization and administration demand a very high level of
(i) Competence
(ii) Imagination
(iii) Firesight
(iv) Executive capacity
(a) i, ii, iii, iv (b) i, ii, iii
(c) i, ii (d) i, iv

40. Gulick has mentioned which of the following activities involved in organization and administration
(i) Planning, Organizing
(ii) Staffing, Directing
(iii) Coordinating, Reporting
(iv) Budgeting
(a) i, ii, iii, iv (b) i, ii, iii
(c) i, ii (d) i, iv

41. Who wrote curriculum and community in Wales?
(a) Fred Clarks (b) Rousseau
(c) Durkheim (d) None

42. Many of the setbacks of curriculum development since the World War II are to be attributed less to the intrinsic character of new methods and content more to
(a) Status
(b) Understanding
(c) Social roles acceptance
(d) None of these

43. Children engage in symbolic play in which they pretend that one object and in which they imagine increasingly complex sequences of events and actions at the age of
(a) 3-4 (b) 4-5
(c) 5-6 (d) 6-7

44. Contextual theories suggest that in order to understand development we must consider .... in which people live

(i) Social environment
(ii) Cultural environment
(iii) Emotional environment
(iv) Cognitive environment
(a) i, ii, iii, iv (b) i, ii, iii
(c) i, ii (d) i, iv

45. At what stage are we most influenced by the evens occurring in our society?
(i) Adolescents (ii) Young adults
(iii) Middle age (iv) Old age
(a) i, ii, iii, iv (b) i, ii, iii
(c) i, ii (d) i, iv

46. Which physical changes occur during early and middle adulthood?
(i) Reduced physical functioning
(ii) Decreased vigor
(iii) Appearance
(iv) Reproductive system
(a) i, ii, iii, iv (b) i, ii, iii
(c) i, ii (d) i, iv

47. Compared to water food is cooked ....
(a) Slowing (b) Quicker
(c) Same time (d) None of these

48. Compared to boiling and baking fried foods are
(a) Attractive (b) Tasty
(c) Higher energy (d) All of these

49. Which of the following is/are true
(i) Development is due to maturational changes that take place in a sequence.
(ii) Development is a complex process of integrating many structures and functions.
(iii) There are two essentially antagonistic processes in development which take place simultaneously throughout life-growth or evolution and atrophy or involution.
(iv) Atrophic changes occur as early as embryonic life.
(a) i, ii, iii, iv (b) i, ii, iii
(c) i, ii (d) i, iv

50. After birth increase in body continues at a progressively slower rate until late teens when growth
(a) Retards
(b) Comes to a standstill
(c) Growth spurts
(d) None of these

ANSWERS

1. (b)	2. (c)	3. (d)	4. (e)	5. (d)
6. (a)	7. (a)	8. (d)	9. (a)	10. (a)
11. (b)	12. (a)	13. (a)	14. (d)	15. (a)
16. (b)	17. (c)	18. (b)	19. (a)	20. (b)
21. (d)	22. (c)	23. (c)	24. (a)	25. (a)
26. (a)	27. (d)	28. (b)	29. (a)	30. (d)
31. (d)	32. (d)	33. (a)	34. (d)	35. (c)
36. (e)	37. (b)	38. (b)	39. (a)	40. (a)
41. (a)	42. (c)	43. (c)	44. (c)	45. (c)
46. (a)	47. (b)	48. (d)	49. (a)	50. (b)

DECEMBER–2007

Note: This paper contains Fifty (50) multiple choice questions, each question carrying two (2) marks. Attempt all of them.

PAPER–I

1. Verbal guidance is least effective in the learning of
   (a) Aptitudes (b) Skills
   (c) Attitudes (d) Relationship
2. Which is the most important aspect of the teacher's role in learning?
   (a) The development of insight into what consititutes an adequate performance
   (b) The development of insight into what consititutes the pitfalls and dangers to be avoided
   (c) The provision of encouragement and moral support
   (d) The provision of continuous diagnostic and remedial help
3. The most appropriate purpose of learning is
   (a) personal adjustment
   (b) modification of behaviour
   (c) social and political awarness
   (d) preparing oneself for employment
4. The students who keep on asking questions in the class should be
   (a) encouraged to find answer independently
   (b) advised to meet the teacher after the class
   (c) encouraged to continue questioning
   (d) advised not to disturb during the lecture
5. Maximum participation of students is possible in teaching through
   (a) discussion method
   (b) lecture method
   (c) audio-visual aids
   (d) textbook method
6. Generalised conclusion on the basis of a sample is technically known as
   (a) Data analysis and interpretation
   (b) Parameter inference
   (c) Statistical inference
   (d) All of the above
7. The experimental study is based on
   (a) The manipulation of variables
   (b) Conceptual parameters
   (c) Replication of research
   (d) Survey of literature
8. The main characteristic of scientific research is
   (a) Empirical (b) Theoretical
   (c) Experimental (d) All of the above
9. Authenticity of a research finding is its
   (a) Originality (b) Validity
   (c) Objectivity (d) All of the above
10. Which technique is generally followed when the population is finite?
    (a) Area Sampling Technique
    (b) Purposive Sampling Technique
    (c) Systematic Sampling Technique
    (d) None of the above

Read the following passage and answer the questions 11 to 15:

Gandhi's overall social and environmental philosophy is based on what human beings need rather than what they want. His early introduction to the teachings of Jains, Theosophists, Christian sermons, Ruskin and Tolstoy, and most significantly the *Bhagavad Gita*, were to have profound impact on the development of Gandhi's holistic thinking on humanity, nature and their ecological interrelation. His deep concern for the disadvantaged, the poor and rural population created an ambience for an alternative social thinking that was at once far-sighted, local and immediate. For Gandhi was acutely aware that the demands generated by the need to feed and sustain human life, compounded by the growing industrialisation of India, far outstripped the finite resources of nature. This might nowadays appear naive or commonplace, but such pronouncements were as rare as they were heretical a century ago. Gandhi was also concerned about the destruction, under colonial and modernist designs, of the existing infrastructures which had more potential for keeping a community flourishing within ecologically-sensitive traditional patterns of subsistence, especially in the rural areas, than did the incoming Western alternatives based on nature-blind technology and the enslavement of human spirit and energies.

Perhaps the moral principle for which Gandhi is best known is that of active non-violence, derived from the traditional moral restraint of not injuring another being. The most refined expression of this value is in the great epic of the *Mahabharata*, (c. 100 BCE to 200 CE), where moral development proceeds through placing constraints on the liberties, desires and acquisitiveness endemic to human life. One's action is judged in terms of consequences and the impact it is likely to have on another. Jainas had generalised this principle to include all sentient creatures and biocommunities alike. Advanced Jaina monks and nuns will sweep their path to avoid harming insects and even bacteria. Non-injury is a non-negotiable universal prescription.

11. Which one of the following have a profound impact on the development of Gandhi's holistic thinking on humanity, nature and their ecological interrelations?
    (a) Jain teachings
    (b) Christian sermons
    (c) *Bhagavad Gita*
    (d) Ruskin and Tolstoy

12. Gandhi's overall social and environmental philosophy is based on human beings'
    (a) Need (b) Desire
    (c) Wealth (d) Welfare

13. Gandhiji's deep concern for the disadvantaged, the poor and rural population created an ambience for an alternative
    (a) rural policy
    (b) social thinking
    (c) urban policy
    (d) economic thinking

14. Colonial policy and modernisation led to the destruction of
    (a) major industrial infrastructure
    (b) irrigation infrastructure
    (c) urban infrastructure
    (d) rural infrastructure

15. Gandhi's active non-violence is derived from
    (a) Moral restraint of not injuring another being
    (b) Having liberties, desires and acquisitiveness
    (c) Freedom of action
    (d) Nature-blind technology and enslavement of human spirit and energies

16. DTH service was started in the year
    (a) 2000 (b) 2002
    (c) 2004 (d) 2006

17. National Press day is celebrated on
    (a) 16th November (b) 19th November
    (c) 21st November (d) 30th November

18. The total number of members in the Press Council of India are
(a) 28 (b) 14
(c) 17 (d) 20

19. The right to impart and receive information is guaranteed in the Constitution of India by Article
(a) 19(2)(a) (b) 19(16)
(c) 19(2) (d) 19(1)(a)

20. Use of radio for higher education is based on the presumption of
(a) Enriching curriculum based instruction
(b) Replacing teacher in the long run
(c) Everybody having access to a radio set
(d) Other means of instruction getting outdated

21. Find out the number which should come at the place of question mark which will complete the following series.
5, 4, 9, 17, 35, ? = 139
(a) 149 (b) 79
(c) 49 (d) 69

Questions 22 to 24 are based on the following diagram in which there are three interlocking circles I, S and P, where circle I stands for Indians, circle S for Scientists and circle P for Politicians. Different regions in the figure are lettered from a to f.

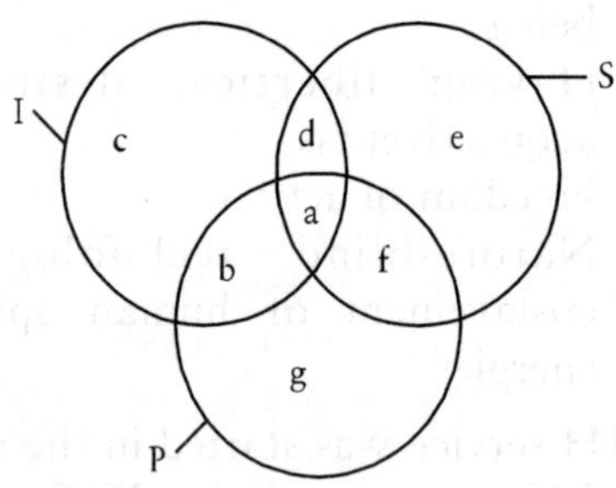

22. The region which represents Non-Indian Scientists who are Politicians.
(a) f (b) d
(c) a (d) c

23. The region which represents Indians who are neither Scientists nor Politicians.
(a) g (b) c
(c) f (d) a

24. The region which represents Politicians who are Indians as well as Scientists.
(a) b (b) c
(c) a (d) d

25. Which number is missing in the following series?
2, 5, 10, 17, 26, 37, 50, ?
(a) 63 (b) 65
(c) 67 (d) 69

26. The function of measurement includes.
(a) Prognosis (b) Diagnosis
(c) Prediction (d) All of the above

27. Logical arguments are based on
(a) Scientific reasoning
(b) Customary reasoning
(c) Mathematical reasoning
(d) Syllogistic reasoning

28. Insert the missing number 4 : 17 :: 7 : ?
(a) 48 (b) 49
(c) 50 (d) 51

29. Choose the odd word.
(a) Nun (b) Knight
(c) Monk (d) Priest

30. Choose the number which is different from others in the group.
(a) 49 (b) 63
(c) 77 (d) 81

31. Probability sampling implies.
(a) Stratified Random Sampling
(b) Systematic Random Sampling
(c) Simple Random Sampling
(d) All of the above

32. Insert the missing number.
$\frac{36}{62}, \frac{39}{63}, \frac{43}{61}, \frac{48}{64}, ?$

(a) $\frac{51}{65}$ (b) $\frac{56}{60}$

(c) $\frac{54}{65}$ (d) $\frac{33}{60}$

33. At what time between 3 and 4 O'clock will the hands of a watch point in opposite directions?
    (a) 40 minutes past three
    (b) 45 minutes past three
    (c) 50 minutes past three
    (d) 55 minutes past three

34. Mary has three children. What is the probability that none of the three children is a boy?
    (a) $\frac{1}{2}$ (b) $\frac{1}{3}$
    (c) $\frac{3}{4}$ (d) 1

35. If the radius of a circle is increased by 50 percent. Its area is increased by
    (a) 125 percent (b) 100 percent
    (c) 75 percent (d) 50 percent

36. CD ROM stands for
    (a) Computer Disk Read Only Memory
    (b) Compact Disk Read Over Memory
    (c) Compact Disk Read Only Memory
    (d) Computer Disk Read Over Memory

37. The 'brain' of a computer which keeps peripherals under its control is called
    (a) Common Power Unit
    (b) Common Processing Unit
    (c) Central Power Unit
    (d) Central Processing Unit

38. Data can be saved on backing storage medium known as
    (a) Compact Disk Recordable
    (b) Computer Disk Rewritable
    (c) Compact Disk Rewritable
    (d) Computer Data Rewritable

39. RAM means
    (a) Random Access Memory
    (b) Rigid Access Memory
    (c) Rapid Access Memory
    (d) Revolving Access Memory

40. www represents
    (a) who what and where
    (b) weird wide web
    (c) word wide web
    (d) world wide web

41. Deforestation during the recent decades has led to
    (a) Soil erosion
    (b) Landslides
    (c) Loss of bio-diversity
    (d) All of the above

42. Which one of the following natural hazards is responsible for causing highest human disaster?
    (a) Earthquakes
    (b) Volcanic eruptions
    (c) Snowstorms
    (d) Tsunami

43. Which one of the following is appropriate for natural hazard mitigation?
    (a) International AID
    (b) Timely Warning System
    (c) Rehabilitation
    (d) Community Participation

44. Slums in metro city are the result of
    (a) Rural to urban migration
    (b) Poverty of the city-scape
    (c) Lack of urban infrastructure
    (d) Urban-governance

45. The great Indian Bustard bird is found in
    (a) Thar Desert of India
    (b) Coastal regions of India
    (c) Temperate Forests in the Himalaya
    (d) Tarai zones of the Himalayan Foot

46. The first Indian Satellite for serving the educational sector is known as
    (a) SATEDU (b) INSAT-B
    (c) EDUSAT (d) INSAT-C

47. Exclusive educational channel of IGNOU is known as
   (a) Gyan Darshan (b) Gyan Vani
   (c) Door Darshan (d) Prasar Bharati

48. The headquarter of Mahatma Gandhi Antarrashtriya Hindi Vishwavidyalaya is situated in
   (a) Sevagram (b) New Delhi
   (c) Wardha (d) Ahmedabad

49. Match List I with List II and select the correct answer using the codes given below.

   List I (Institutes)
   A. Central Institute of English and Foreign Languages
   B. Gramodaya Vishwavidyalaya
   C. Central Institute of Higher Tibetan Studies
   D. IGNOU

   List II (Locations)
   1. Chitrakoot 2. Hyderabad
   3. New Delhi 4. Dharmasala

Codes:	A	B	C	D
(a)	2	1	4	3
(b)	4	3	2	1
(c)	3	4	1	2
(d)	1	2	4	3

50. The aim of vocationalisation of education is
   (a) preparing students for a vocation along with knowledge
   (b) converting liberal education into vocational education
   (c) giving more importance to vocational than general education
   (d) making liberal education job-oriented

ANSWERS

1. (b)	2. (a)	3. (b)	4. (a)	5. (a)
6. (c)	7. (c)	8. (c)	9. (d)	10. (c)
11. (c)	12. (a)	13. (b)	14. (c)	15. (a)
16. (d)	17. (a)	18. (a)	19. (d)	20. (b)
21. (d)	22. (a)	23. (b)	24. (d)	25. (b)
26. (d)	27. (d)	28. (c)	29. (b)	30. (c)
31. (d)	32. (c)	33. (c)	34. (d)	35. (a)
36. (c)	37. (d)	38. (c)	39. (a)	40. (d)
41. (d)	42. (a)	43. (b)	44. (a)	45. (a)
46. (c)	47. (a)	48. (c)	49. (a)	50. (d)

PAPER–II

Note: This paper contains fifty (50) objective type questions, each question carrying two (2) marks. All questions are compulsory.

1. Which of the following is/are true?
   (i) The tasks of acquiring pupil with vocational opportunities help them in their vocational choices locating jobs.
   (ii) An alert teacher who on recognizing a pupil's need for out-of-classroom help refers him to an appropriate counselor
   (iii) The vocational counselor works closely with pupil in attempting to discover their vocational potentialities and interests
   (iv) Vocational guidance usually is interpreted as the assistance given to leaders to choose, prepare for and progress in an occupation
   (a) i, ii, iii, iv (b) i, ii, iii
   (c) i, ii (d) i, iv

2. If a business woman orders a market survey to be conducted for her product. The report submitted must be
   (a) Elaborate (b) Simple
   (c) Non-technical (d) None

3. A report may be technical but it cannot afford to be
   (a) Incomplete
   (b) Ambiguous
   (c) Sweeping remarks
   (d) All of these
4. Measure of variation is useful because
   (a) Tell us how representative the average is
   (b) Provides a yardstick on how much variability
   (c) Gives representative value
   (d) All of these
5. Structured questionnaire contains .... questions
   (i) Definite
   (ii) Concrete
   (iii) Preordinated
   (iv) Additional questions to elicit response
   (a) i, ii, iii, iv (b) i, ii, iii
   (c) i, ii (d) i, iv
6. Non-structured questionnaire often known as interview guide is used for ...... interviews.
   (a) Focused (b) Depth
   (c) Non-directive (d) All of these
7. Which of the following can be included in the general qualities of good research worker
   (i) Scientific attitude, perseverantt
   (ii) Imagination and insight
   (iii) A quick grasping power
   (iv) Clarity of thinking
   (a) i, ii, iii, iv (b) i, ii, iii
   (c) i, ii (d) i, iv
8. If food is kept at _____ temp then the risk of micro-organism infection is not there below
   (a) 5°C and above 40°C
   (b) Below 7°C and above 45°C
   (c) Below 8°C and above 55°C
   (d) Below 10°C and above 60°C
9. Moulds do not grow in
   (a) Acetic Acid (b) Lemon Juice
   (c) Vinegar (d) None of these
10. The musty smell of spoiled grapes is due to
    (a) Bacteria (b) Moulds
    (c) Yeast (d) Enzymes
11. Foods likely to be spoiled by yeast is/are
    (i) Fruit juices and syrups
    (ii) Molasses
    (iii) Honey
    (iv) Jams and Jellies
    (a) i, ii, iii, iv (b) i, ii, iii
    (c) i, ii (d) i, iv
12. Many yeasts grow best in
    (i) Acid medium
    (ii) Ample oxygen
    (iii) Alkaline medium
    (iv) Ample carbon-di-oxide
    (a) i, ii, iii, iv (b) i, ii, iii
    (c) i, ii (d) i, iv
13. Yeast cells convert sugar into alcohol. For food industry this reaction is used in making
    (i) Vinegar (ii) Bread
    (iii) Beer (iv) Wine
    (a) i, ii, iii, iv (b) i, ii, iii
    (c) i, ii (d) i, iv
14. The nectar of flowers and the exuding sap of trees and plant may contain large number of .... which are carried to distinct places by wind and insects.
    (a) Bacteria (b) Yeast
    (c) Moulds (d) Enzymes
15. The gravy of the stew should not have
    (i) A lot of thickness
    (ii) Fat laden
    (iii) To be thrown away
    (iv) Spicy
    (a) i, ii (b) ii, iii
    (c) iii, iv (d) i, iv

16. The food does not come in contact with water while cooking. It is
    (a) Frying (b) Grilling
    (c) Steaming (d) None of these
17. Idlis and dhoklas are good example of
    (a) Direct steaming
    (b) Indirect steaming
    (c) Pressure cooking
    (d) None of these
18. Custards and pudding which are steamed are examples of
    (a) Direct steaming
    (b) Indirect steaming
    (c) Pressure cooking
    (d) None of these
19. Steaming foods are best for invalids as
    (i) Light
    (ii) Easily digestible
    (iii) No over cooking
    (iv) Enhance flavour
    (a) i, ii, iii, iv (b) i, ii, iii
    (c) i, ii (d) i, iv
20. Observation as the oldest most commonly used instrument of research becomes scientific when
    (i) Objective
    (ii) Meaning attached to observation
    (iii) Answer's question
    (iv) Relationship perceived
    (a) i, ii, iii, iv (b) i, ii, iii
    (c) i, ii (d) i, iv
21. The observation over a period of time can determine the child's characteristic
    (i) Pattern of response
    (ii) Feeling
    (iii) Convictions
    (iv) Perception
    (a) i, ii, iii, iv (b) i, ii, iii
    (c) i, ii (d) i, iv
22. Who made the statement on Keertana as a weapon of social education. "If I were not a journalist, I would have been a Keertanakar."?
    (a) Lok Manya Tilak
    (b) Kabir
    (c) Tukaram
    (d) None of these
23. Who stated this on satellite and its impact on distance education "In some cases hermes (The satellite) brought people together in a way that was every bit as emotionally moving as it was intellectually stimulating. In other cases students became bored technical problems made effective interaction impossible information seemed colourless and static."?
    (a) Rajiv Gandhi (b) Sam Pitroda
    (c) Geoff Potter (d) None of these
24. Charts are being used to teach
    (i) Reading (ii) Working
    (iii) Maths tables (iv) Practicals
    (a) i, ii, iii, iv (b) i, ii, iii
    (c) i, ii (d) i, iv
25. Match the following:

List I

(A) The very diversity of folk tradition
(B) Mass opinion created by 'Barrakatha' a popular folk form in Andhra Pradesh
(C) Folk media and personal contact
(D) Three important aspects of folk media
(E) Radio advertisement jingles

List II

(i) During Telangana movement
(ii) Use them as vehicles for communication
(iii) Personal contact, demonstration interaction
(iv) Utilized to communicate message
(v) Based on folk tunes promoting agricultural products

Codes:	A	B	C	D	E
(a)	ii	i	iv	iii	v
(b)	v	iv	iii	i	ii

(c) ii iii v iv i
(d) v ii iii i iv

26. Puppetry becomes a valuable .... only if the message to be communicated is developed in dramatic terms.
(a) Art (b) Visual aid
(c) Guzzet (d) None

27. Puppet historians tell us that nearly .... years ago in ancient India the only form of theatre was the puppet theatre.
(a) 2000 (b) 1500
(c) 1000 (d) 500

28. The type of receiver influences the communicator's decisions regarding
(i) Message content (ii) Tone
(iii) Channel (iv) Timing
(a) i, ii, iii, iv (b) i, ii, iii
(c) i, ii (d) i, iv

29. Which of the following is/are applicable to mass communication
(i) Indirect
(ii) Impersonal
(iii) Lack means of immediate feedback
(iv) One-way
(a) i, ii, iii, iv (b) i, ii, iii
(c) i, ii (d) i, iv

30. The technical attributes of a stimulus play an important role in attracting a receiver's attention for one message several of actors are interacting simultaneously to gain receiver's attention. These could be
(i) Size, movement, intensity
(ii) Novelty, contrast, colour
(iii) Position, suddenness, shape
(iv) Isolation, multi-sensory like perform use
(a) i, ii, iii, iv (b) i, ii, iii
(c) i, ii (d) i, iv

31. Selective attention is based on two sets of factors
(i) Stimulus (ii) Individual
(iii) Company (iv) Channel
(a) i, ii, iii, iv (b) i, ii, iii
(c) i, ii (d) i, iv

32. Individual factors are inherent in humans or are learned and stored in their perceptual fields. They are
(i) Permanent interests
(ii) Immediate concerns
(iii) Attitudes and opinions
(iv) Needs
(a) i, ii, iii, iv (b) i, ii, iii
(c) i, ii (d) i, iv

33. State true or false
Fundamental principal of perception include
(a) Perception depends upon structural characteristic
(b) Perception depends upon receiver characteristic
(c) Perception is selective
(d) Perception is organized and has structure
(e) All of these

34. Which of the following is/are true? According to Andrews and Willy the basic assumptions of the directive counseling can be
(a) Counsellor has superior training, experience and information
(b) The maladjustment of an individual does not entirely impair the intellectual ability of the client
(c) Because of such factor as bias the client is not always capable of solving his problems
(d) The objectives of counselling are achieved primarily through solving problems
(e) All of these

35. The role of the counsellor in directive counselling

(i) Analysis (ii) Synthesis
(iii) Diagnosis (iv) prognosis
(a) i, ii, iii, iv (b) i, ii, iii
(c) i, ii (d) i, iv

36. State which is/are false
(a) Administration of education is an activity which is independent of other activities of society
(b) Educational activity based on certain principles will enable educators to formulate educational objectives, procedures and methods, and evaluate tools and techniques
(c) The educational administrator is a practising social scientist and administration of education is social statesmanship
(d) Educational administration demands a very high level of educational engineering skill which is the result of natural genius, training, study and experience

37. Educational administrators to do their job will have to acquire a good deal of
(i) Training (ii) Foreign trips
(iii) Media espouser (iv) Experience
(a) i, ii, iii, iv (b) i, ii, iii
(c) i, ii (d) i, iv

38. Curriculum is a means to realize
(i) Educational philosophy
(ii) Objectives
(iii) Needs
(iv) Values
(a) i, ii, iii, iv (b) i, ii, iii
(c) i, ii (d) i, iv

39. The pattern and organization of the curriculum will primarily, determine
(i) Efficacy of instruction
(ii) Objectives
(iii) Social cultural relevance
(iv) Needs of community
(a) i, ii, iii, iv (b) i, ii, iii
(c) i, ii (d) i, iv

40. According to the views of Karl Marx education aims at producing
(a) Employed person
(b) Businessman
(c) Fully developed
(d) None of these

41. A rudimentary literate achieves a standard which a child reaches after .... years.
(a) 3 or 4 years (b) 4 or 5 years
(c) 5 or 6 years (d) 6 or 7 years

42. Which of the country succeeded in eradication illiteracy in less than 20 years?
(a) Pakistan (b) India
(c) Russia (d) USA

43. Which of the following depends on maturation?
(i) Reflex (ii) Walberg
(iii) Rejection (iv) Acceptance
(a) i, ii, iii, iv (b) i, ii, iii
(c) i, ii (d) i, iv

44. Which of the following is/are true?
(i) According to Erickson the part of the body on which their attention is focused, and the life tasks which preoccupy them change radically from one stage to another.
(ii) A key word to describe children's thought by Praget is "unsystematic".
(iii) Preoperational children tend to focus their attention only on the most compelling aspect of an event.
(iv) Perceptual constancies appear early in infancy but object, constancy develop relatively slowly.
(a) i, ii, iii, iv (b) i, ii, iii
(c) i, ii (d) i, iv

45. Cognitive development in the elementary school years is
(a) Systematic (b) Rational
(c) Predictable (d) All

46. Praget noted other important characteristic of thought in the preoperational period which is/are

(i) Ego centrism
(ii) Animism
(iii) Realism
(iv) Magic omnipotence
(a) i, ii, iii, iv (b) i, ii, iii
(c) i, ii (d) i, iv

47. Physical changes occurring later in life include
(i) Sensory abilities
(ii) Slowing of reflexes
(iii) Mood swings
(iv) Depression
(a) i, ii, iii, iv (b) i, ii, iii
(c) i, ii (d) i, iv

48. According to Erickson what is the most important crisis faced by adolescents,
(i) Identity confusion
(ii) Physical growth
(iii) Voice
(iv) Role confusion
(a) i, ii, iii, iv (b) i, ii, iii
(c) i, ii (d) i, iv

49. In a baby, gain in weight comes partly from increase in
(i) Neural (ii) Glandular
(iii) Muscle tissue (iv) Physical activity
(a) i, ii, iii, iv (b) i, ii, iii
(c) i, ii (d) i, iv

50. Heating milk results in a floating payer on top cooking meat show drippings are examples of
(a) Improving texture
(b) Improving flavour
(c) Fat has tendency to separate from food when heated
(d) None of these

ANSWERS

1. (a)	2. (c)	3. (d)	4. (d)	5. (a)
6. (d)	7. (a)	8. (d)	9. (a)	10. (c)
11. (a)	12. (c)	13. (a)	14. (b)	15. (a)
16. (c)	17. (a)	18. (b)	19. (a)	20. (a)
21. (a)	22. (a)	23. (c)	24. (c)	25. (a)
26. (b)	27. (a)	28. (a)	29. (a)	30. (a)
31. (c)	32. (a)	33. (e)	34. (e)	35. (a)
36. (a)	37. (d)	38. (c)	39. (a)	40. (c)
41. (a)	42. (c)	43. (c)	44. (a)	45. (d)
46. (a)	47. (c)	48. (d)	49. (b)	50. (c)

JUNE–2007

Note: This paper contains Fifty (50) multiple choice questions, each question carrying two (2) marks. Attempt all of them.

PAPER–I

1. Teacher uses visual-aids to make learning
   (a) Simple
   (b) More knowledgeable
   (c) Quicker
   (d) Interesting
2. The teacher's role at the higher educational level is to
   (a) provide information to students
   (b) promote self-learning in students
   (c) encourage healthy competition among students
   (d) help students to solve their personal problems
3. Which one of the following teachers would you like the most?
   (a) Punctual
   (b) Having research aptitude
   (c) Loving and having high idealistic philosophy
   (d) Who often amuses his students
4. Micro teaching is most effective for the student-teacher
   (a) during the practice-teaching
   (b) after the practice-teaching
   (c) before the practice-teaching
   (d) None of the above
5. Which is the least important factor in teaching?
   (a) Punishing the students
   (b) Maintaining discipline in the class
   (c) Lecturing in impressive way
   (d) Drawing sketches and diagrams on the blackboard
6. To test null hypothesis, a researcher uses
   (a) t-test (b) ANOVA
   (c) χ^2 (d) factorial analysis
7. A research problem is feasible only when
   (a) it has utility and relevance
   (b) it is researchable
   (c) it is new and adds something to knowledge
   (d) All of the above
8. Bibliography given in a research report
   (a) shows vast knowledge of the researcher
   (b) helps those interested in further research
   (c) has no relevance to research
   (d) All of the above
9. Fundamental research reflects the ability to
   (a) Synthesise new ideals
   (b) Expound new principles
   (c) Evaluate the existing material concerning research
   (d) Study the existing literature regarding various topics
10. The study in which the investigators attempt to trace an effect is known as
    (a) Survey Research
    (b) *Ex-post Facto* Research

(c) Historical Research
(d) Summative Research

Read the following passage and answer the questions 11 to 15:

All political systems need to mediate the relationship between private wealth and public power. Those that fail risk a dysfunctional government captured by wealthy interests. Corruption is one symptom of such failure with private willingness-to-pay trumping public goals. Private individuals and business firms pay to get routine services and to get to the head of the bureaucratic queue. They pay to limit their taxes, avoid costly regulations, obtain contracts at inflated prices and get concessions and privatised firms at low prices. If corruption is endemic, public officials—both bureaucrats and elected officials—may redesign programs and propose public projects with few public benefits and many opportunities for private profit. Of course, corruption, in the sense of bribes, pay-offs and kickbacks, is only one type of government failure. Efforts to promote 'good governance' must be broader than anti-corruption campaigns. Governments may be honest but inefficient because no one has an incentive to work productively, and narrow elites may capture the state and exert excess influence on policy. Bribery may induce the lazy to work hard and permit those not in the inner circle of cronies to obtain benefits. However, even in such cases, corruption cannot be confined to 'functional' areas. It will be a temptation whenever private benefits are positive. It may be a reasonable response to a harsh reality but, over time, it can facilitate a spiral into an even worse situation.

11. The governments which fail to focus on the relationship between private wealth and public power are likely to become
(a) Functional
(b) Dysfunctional
(c) Normal functioning
(d) Good governance

12. One important symptom of bad governance is
(a) Corruption
(b) High taxes
(c) Complicated rules and regulations
(d) High prices

13. When corruption is rampant, public officials always aim at many opportunities for
(a) Public benefits (b) Public profit
(c) Private profit (d) Corporate gains

14. Productivity linked incentives to public/private officials is one of the indicatives for
(a) Efficient government
(b) Bad governance
(c) Inefficient government
(d) Corruption

15. The spiralling corruption can only be contained by promoting
(a) Private profit
(b) Anti-corruption campaign
(c) Good governance
(d) Pay-offs and kickbacks

16. Press Council of India is located at
(a) Chennai (b) Mumbai
(c) Kolkata (d) Delhi

17. Adjusting the photo for publication by cutting is technically known as
(a) Photo cutting
(b) Photo bleeding
(c) Photo cropping
(d) Photo adjustment

18. Feedback of a message comes from
(a) Satellite (b) Media
(c) Audience (d) Communicator

19. Collection of information in advance before designing communication strategy is known as

(a) Feedback (b) Feed-forward
(c) Research study (d) Opinion poll

20. The aspect ratio of TV screen is
(a) 4:3 (b) 4:2
(c) 3:5 (d) 2:3

21. Which is the number that comes next in the sequence?
9, 8, 8, 8, 7, 8, 6, __
(a) 5 (b) 6
(c) 8 (d) 4

22. If in a certain language PUNCTUAL is coded as 16598623, how would ACTUPULN be coded?
(a) 834536 (b) 29861635
(c) 834530 (d) 834539

23. The question to be answered by factorial analysis of the quantitative data does not explain one of the following
(a) Is 'X' related to 'Y'?
(b) How is 'X' related to 'Y'?
(c) How does 'X' affect the dependent variable 'Y' at different levels of another independent variable 'K' or 'M'?
(d) How is 'X' by 'K' related to 'M'?

24. January 12, 1980 was Saturday, what day was January 12, 1979?
(a) Saturday (b) Friday
(c) Sunday (d) Thursday

25. How many Mondays are there in a particular month of a particular year, if the month ends on Wednesday?
(a) 5 (b) 4
(c) 3 (d) None of these

26. From the given four statements, select the two which cannot be true but yet both can be false. Choose the right pair.
1. All men are mortal
2. Some men are mortal
3. No man is mortal
4. Some men are not mortal
(a) 1 and 2 (b) 3 and 4
(c) 1 and 3 (d) 2 and 4

27. A Syllogism must have
(a) Three terms (b) Four terms
(c) Six terms (d) Five terms

28. Copula is that part of proposition which denotes the relationship between
(a) Subject and predicate
(b) Known and unknown
(c) Major premise and minor premise
(d) Subject and object

29. "E" denotes
(a) Universal Negative Proposition
(b) Particular Affirmative Proposition
(c) Universal Affirmative Proposition
(d) Particular Negative Proposition

30. 'A' is the father of 'C' and 'D' is the son of 'B'. 'E' is the brother of 'A'. If 'C' is the sister of 'D' how is 'B' related to 'E'?
(a) Daughter (b) Husband
(c) Sister-in-law (d) Brother-in-law

31. Which of the following methods will you choose to prepare choropleth map of India showing urban density of population?
(a) Quartiles (b) Quintiles
(c) Mean and SD (d) Break-point

32. Which of the following methods is best suited to show on a map the types of crops being grown in a region?
(a) Choropleth (b) Chorochromatic
(c) Choroschematic (d) Isopleth

33. A ratio represents the relation between
(a) Part and Part
(b) Part and Whole
(c) Whole and Whole
(d) All of the above

34. Out of four numbers, the average of the first three numbers is thrice the fourth number. If the average of the four numbers is 5, the fourth number is

(a) 4.5 (b) 5
(c) 2 (d) 4

35. Circle graphs are used to show
(a) How various sections share in the whole
(b) How various parts are related to the whole
(c) How one whole is related to other wholes
(d) How one part is related to other parts

36. On the keyboard of computer each character has an "ASCII" value which stands for
(a) American Stock Code for Information Interchange
(b) American Standard Code for Information Interchange
(c) African Standard Code for Information Interchange
(d) Adaptable Standard Code for Information Change

37. Which part of the Central Processing Unit (CPU) performs calculation and makes decisions
(a) Arithmetic Logic Unit
(b) Alternating Logic Unit
(c) Alternate Local Unit
(d) American Logic Unit

38. "Dpi" stands for
(a) Dots per inch
(b) Digits per unit
(c) Dots pixel inch
(d) Diagrams per inch

39. The process of laying out a document with text, graphics, headlines and photographs is involved in
(a) Deck Top Publishing
(b) Desk Top Printing
(c) Desk Top Publishing
(d) Deck Top Printing

40. Transfer of data from one application to another line is known as
(a) Dynamic Disk Exchange
(b) Dodgy Data Exchange
(c) Dogmatic Data Exchange
(d) Dynamic Data Exchange

41. Tsunami occurs due to
(a) Mild earthquakes and landslides in the oceans
(b) Strong earthquakes and landslides in the oceans
(c) Strong earthquakes and landslides in mountains
(d) Strong earthquakes and landslides in deserts

42. Which of the natural hazards have big effect on Indian people each year?
(a) Cyclones (b) Floods
(c) Earthquakes (d) Landslides

43. Comparative Environment Impact Assessment study is to be conducted for
(a) the whole year
(b) three seasons excluding monsoon
(c) any three seasons
(d) the worst season

44. Sea level rise results primarily due to
(a) Heavy rainfall
(b) Melting of glaciers
(c) Submarine volcanism
(d) Seafloor spreading

45. The plume rise in a coal based power plant depends on
1. Buoyancy
2. Atmospheric stability
3. Momentum of exhaust gases identify

Codes:
(a) Both (1) and (2) (b) Both (2) and (3)
(c) Both (1) and (3) (d) (1), (2) and (3)

46. Value education makes a student
(a) Good citizen
(b) Successful businessman

(c) Popular teacher
(d) Efficient manager

47. Networking of libraries through electronic media is known as
(a) Inflibnet (b) Libinfnet
(c) Internet (d) HTML

48. The University which telecasts interactive educational programs through its own channel is
(a) B.R. Ambedkar Open University, Hyderabad
(b) I.G.N.O.U.
(c) University of Pune
(d) Annamalai University

49. The Government established the University Grants Commission by an Act of Parliament in the year
(a) 1980 (b) 1948
(c) 1950 (d) 1956

50. Universities having central campus for imparting education are called
(a) Central Universities
(b) Deemed Universities
(c) Residential Universities
(d) Open Universities

ANSWERS

1. (d)	2. (a)	3. (a)	4. (b)	5. (a)
6. (c)	7. (d)	8. (b)	9. (b)	10. (b)
11. (b)	12. (a)	13. (c)	14. (a)	15. (c)
16. (d)	17. (c)	18. (c)	19. (d)	20. (a)
21. (c)	22. (b)	23. (c)	24. (b)	25. (d)
26. (b)	27. (a)	28. (b)	29. (a)	30. (d)
31. (b)	32. (c)	33. (b)	34. (c)	35. (a)
36. (a)	37. (a)	38. (a)	39. (c)	40. (d)
41. (b)	42. (b)	43. (a)	44. (b)	45. (d)
46. (a)	47. (a)	48. (b)	49. (d)	50. (b)

PAPER–II

Note: This paper contains fifty (50) objective type questions, each question carrying two (2) marks. All questions are compulsory.

1. Individual interest is of primary importance in vocational selection but the development of a particular vocational interest is interwoven with
(i) physical condition including health
(ii) degree of mental activity
(iii) dominant urges
(iv) environmental conditions
(a) i, ii, iii, iv (b) i, ii, iii
(c) i, ii (d) i, iv

2. The sources of case data is/are
(i) Diaries, memories
(ii) Letters
(iii) Life history
(iv) Autobiography
(a) i, ii, iii, iv (b) i, ii, iii
(c) i, ii (d) i, iv

3. The defects of questionnaire method could possibly be
(a) Ambiguous format
(b) Half-hearted information
(c) Biased interpretation
(d) All of these

4. P.V. Young has classified questionnaires into
(i) Structured questionnaire
(ii) Non-structured questionnaires
(iii) Telephone questionnaire
(iv) Computer questionnaire
(a) i, ii, iii, iv (b) i, ii, iii
(c) i, ii (d) i, iv

5. Who stated "Research may or may not come to success; it may or may not all anything to what is already known. It is sufficient that its objectives be new

knowledge or at least a new mode or orientation of knowledge."?
(a) F.A. Ogg
(b) Rodman and Morey
(c) Stephenson
(d) None of these

6. Thermophilic bacteria affect the
(a) Refrigerated food
(b) Milk processing
(c) Pickle making
(d) None of these

7. Aerobic and anaerobic bacteria may cause
(a) Food spoilage
(b) Food Poisoning
(c) Disease borne via food
(d) All of these

8. State which is/are true
(a) The worth of a research generally depends not on the work but on results produced
(b) The drafting of report is an art
(c) Report writing requires a grasp over the subject but also a command over the language
(d) In a report facts and inference should be interwoven into a theory or hypothesis thus leading to some concrete results
(e) All of these

9. By means of report
(a) Small research coordinated
(b) Small research consolidated
(c) One single theory produced
(d) All of these

10. The best characteristic of Pressure Cooker is
(a) Its sturdy body
(b) Time-borne cooking
(c) High temp reduces cooking time
(d) Saves energy

11. Frying is suitable for
(a) Invalids
(b) Foods that take short time to cook
(c) Taste
(d) None of these

12. It is not a good method of cooking
(a) Difficult to digest
(b) Flattening
(c) Absorbs a lot of fat
(d) All of these

13. Toxic produced by mould's growing on groundnuts and other agricultural products
(a) Mycotoxin (b) Enzymes
(c) Aflatoxin (d) None

14. State whether all true or false
(a) If agricultural products are not dried as soon as they are harvested moulds produce aflatoxins
(b) Some micro organisms can exist both in vegetative and spore form
(c) Spores are more resistant to destruction by heat and other agents
(d) Foods that have high moisture content are highly susceptible to spoilage
(e) All of these

15. Yeast produce during their metabolism
(a) Undesirable chemical products
(b) Pigments
(c) Toxin
(d) All of these

16. Steamed food can be soddened because of
(a) Moist heat
(b) Condensation of vapour
(c) Addition of sugar/salt
(d) None of these

17. The basic characteristic of pressure cooker
(a) Aluminum alloy
(b) Withstand heat
(c) Temperature around food higher than 100°C
(d) All of these

18. State which is false
Cooking by pressure cooker.
   (a) Cooker should be only 2/3rd filled.
   (b) Fire high till pressure of steam built up then reduced to slow till cooked.
   (c) Do not open till cooled down.
   (d) Idli is cooked by pressure.

19. Cheese like cedar surss brick is ripened by
   (a) Yeast (b) Mould
   (c) Bacteria (d) All of these

20. State which is/are true
   (a) Bacteria are responsible for rising bread, production of vinegar from fermented sugar solution like grape juice
   (b) Most bacteria grow best at a pH near neutrality
   (c) Some moulds will grow in sunlight
   (d) Most moulds produce toxic substance

21. Radio experiments in the use of radio for promoting literacy and education was conducted as early as
   (a) 1900s (b) 1920s
   (c) 1930s (d) 1940s

22. State which is/are true
   (a) Television was introduced into India by the Nehru Govt., with the primary aim of exploiting the medium for distance education
   (b) Today Doordarshan devotes at least 10% of its telecast time to educational or enrichment programmes for farmers school children, youth and other groups
   (c) Mahatma Gandhi spoke just once over radio and was able to mobilize the masses
   (d) Kheda communication project chalked out a path in the use of television for development
   (e) All of these

23. Folk forms of the local regions have been utilized both by voluntary social action groups and by govt supported literacy campaigns in the state of
   (a) Kerala
   (b) Maharashtra
   (c) Andhra Pradesh
   (d) All of these

24. Charts can be
   (i) Pictorial
   (ii) Organizational, flow chart
   (iii) Suspense chart
   (iv) Strip tease chart
   (a) i, ii, iii, iv (b) i, ii, iii
   (c) i, ii (d) i, iv

25. State which is/are true
   (a) Posters are generally used in the awareness stage
   (b) A poster has to be bold in design, simple to understand and attractive in colour
   (c) The components of a poster may be picture or illustration, the words, colour and space
   (d) While preparing illustrations keep in mind the experience of the audience and use objects familiar to them
   (e) All of these

26. Caption in a poster
   (i) Small
   (ii) 5-word
   (iii) Unbroken caption
   (iv) Write vertically
   (a) i, ii, iii, iv (b) i, ii, iii
   (c) i, ii (d) i, iv

27 .... is used as a leavening in bread making. It gives the required flavor and sponginess to the bread.
   (a) Bacteria (b) Mould
   (c) Yeast (d) Enzymes

28. Drying will not kill all bacteria. Upon hydrating certain dehydrated foods may lead to

(a) Better flavour
(b) Better textile
(c) Less cooking time
(d) Spoilage

29. The life of every cell of plant or animal tissue depends upon the chemical reactions activated by
(a) Pigments (b) Oxygen
(c) Enzymes (d) None

30. One usually comes across the art of puppetry used mostly in the presentation of historical or mythological stories. This medium can be effectively used to bring out some basic facts and scientific aspects on
(i) Cleanliness
(ii) Nutrition
(iii) Educational topics
(iv) None of these
(a) i, ii, iii, iv (b) i, ii, iii
(c) i, ii (d) i, iv

31. State which is/are true
(a) Non-verbal signs communicate feelings preferences and likings and either to supports or to contracted verbal communication
(b) Individuals tend to relax their positive move with a low-status person
(c) Although we use signs to share thought or meaning with others the two terms i.e. signs and meaning are not synonymous
(d) Good communicators are people who select words that they feel will elicit the intended meaning
(e) All of these

32. A connotative meaning is the relationship between a
(a) Snig (b) Object
(c) Person (d) All of these

33. Why it is so important to quote people in order to understand what someone means
(a) Denotative meaning
(b) Connotative meaning
(c) Contextual meaning
(d) Structural meaning

34. The communications threshold follows which of the following
(i) Non-communicative behaviour
(ii) Communicative behaviour
(iii) A combination of communicative and non-communicative behaviour
(iv) Storage of the need state in the perceptual field for later action
(a) i, ii, iii, iv (b) i, ii, iii
(c) i, ii (d) i, iv

35. Non-Directive counseling is also known as
(i) Permissive counseling
(ii) Client-oriented counseling
(iii) Goal-oriented counseling
(iv) Objective counseling
(a) i, ii, iii, iv (b) i, ii, iii
(c) i, ii (d) i, iv

36. Which of the following is/are true?
The basic assumptions in non-directive counselling according to Snyder
(a) The client has the right to select his own life goals.
(b) The client will be given opportunity to choose for himself the goals most likely to result in the greatest possible happiness.
(c) In a reasonably short time the counselling situation should develop to a point at which the client will be able to operate independently.
(d) An emotional disturbance is the primary cause preventing an individual from adjusting properly.
(e) All of these.

37. Educational planning is a .... process.
(a) Strenuous (b) Cumbersome
(c) Dynamic (d) None of these

38. Planning is an intellectual activity which needs knowledge of affairs and resources and other situations required for planning is/are
    (i) Sufficient reasoning
    (ii) Insight and imagination
    (iii) Professional skill
    (iv) Specialized knowledge
    (a) i, ii, iii, iv (b) i, ii, iii
    (c) i, ii (d) i, iv

39. State which is/are true
    (a) Planning is retrospective. It looks forward to see how things take shape and materialise
    (b) At the end of the activity planning looks backward to see how far the desired results have been attainable and what limitations hindered their execution
    (c) Planning is the initiating process
    (d) In a democratic society any plan of education must correspond to the ideals of a democratic philosophy
    (e) All of these

40. Democratic control does not imply regimentation of dictatorship. It is sufficiently flexible based not on the rule of the rod but on
    (i) Rule of law
    (ii) Professional and personal ethics
    (iii) Demand of social properties
    (iv) Need of objectives
    (a) i, ii, iii, iv (b) i, ii, iii
    (c) i, ii (d) i, iv

41. Control over people can be organized in many ways such as
    (i) Rules, Contracts
    (ii) Schedules, Checkbooks
    (iii) Logbooks
    (iv) Supervision
    (a) i, ii, iii, iv (b) i, ii, iii
    (c) i, ii (d) i, iv

42. The liquidation of mass illiteracy is necessary not only for promoting participation in the working of democratic institutions but, for .... specially for farmers.
    (a) Education (b) Finance
    (c) Production (d) None of these

43. People who reappraise emotion producing situation with ...... may find that they are able to reduce the intensity of disturbing emotional feelings.
    (a) Denial
    (b) Intellectualization
    (c) Reaction formation
    (d) Any one

44. Which of the following is/are covered by developmental psychology?
    (i) Perception (ii) Physiology
    (iii) Learning (iv) Cognition
    (a) i, ii, iii, iv (b) i, ii, iii
    (c) i, ii (d) i, iv

45. Changes which occur mainly as a result of experience are said to be a product of
    (a) Learning (b) Maturation
    (c) Guidance (d) None of these

46. Changes regulated by inner time clock refers to
    (a) Learning (b) Maturation
    (c) Glands (d) None of these

47. According to Kubler-Ross what stages do terminally ill persons pass through when confronting their own death.
    (i) Denial, anger (ii) Bargaining
    (iii) Depression (iv) Acceptance
    (a) i, ii, iii, iv (b) i, ii, iii
    (c) i, ii (d) i, iv

48. The stages of bereavement include
    (i) stock
    (ii) protest and yearning
    (iii) despair
    (iv) detachment and recovery

(a) i, ii, iii, iv (b) i, ii, iii
(c) i, ii (d) i, iv

49. In childhood the gain in weight comes principally from
(i) Bone (ii) Blood
(iii) Harmones (iv) Muscle tissue
(a) i, ii, iii, iv (b) i, ii, iii
(c) i, ii (d) i, iv

50. Collagen and elastic proteins in animal food on being roasted at high temperature
(i) Toughens (ii) Become chewy
(iii) Tasty (iv) Attractive
(a) i, ii, iii, iv (b) i, ii, iii
(c) i, ii (d) i, iv

ANSWERS

1. (a)	2. (a)	3. (d)	4. (c)	5. (a)
6. (b)	7. (d)	8. (e)	9. (d)	10. (c)
11. (b)	12. (d)	13. (c)	14. (e)	15. (d)
16. (b)	17. (d)	18. (d)	19. (c)	20. (c)
21. (c)	22. (e)	23. (d)	24. (a)	25. (e)
26. (b)	27. (c)	28. (d)	29. (c)	30. (a)
31. (e)	32. (d)	33. (c)	34. (c)	35. (c)
36. (e)	37. (c)	38. (a)	39. (e)	40. (a)
41. (a)	42. (c)	43. (d)	44. (a)	45. (a)
46. (b)	47. (a)	48. (a)	49. (d)	50. (a)

DECEMBER–2006

Note: This paper contains fifty (50) objective type questions, each question carrying two (2) marks. All questions are compulsory.

PAPER–I

1. Which of the following is not instructional material?
   (a) Over Head Projector
   (b) Audio Casset
   (c) Printed Material
   (d) Transparency

2. Which of the following statement is not correct?
   (a) Lecture Method can develop reasoning
   (b) Lecture Method can develop knowledge
   (c) Lecture Method is one way process
   (d) During Lecture Method students are passive

3. The main objective of teaching at Higher Education Level is:
   (a) To prepare students to pass examination
   (b) To develop the capacity to take decisions
   (c) To give new information
   (d) To motivate students to ask questions during lecture

4. Which of the following statement is correct?
   (a) Reliability ensures validity
   (b) Validity ensures reliability
   (c) Reliability and validity are independent of each other
   (d) Reliability does not depend on objectivity

5. Which of the following indicates evaluation?
   (a) Ram got 45 marks out of 200
   (b) Mohan got 38 percent marks in English
   (c) Shyam got First Division in final examination
   (d) All the above

6. Research can be conducted by a person who:
   (a) has studied research methodology
   (b) holds a postgraduate degree
   (c) possesses thinking and reasoning ability
   (d) is a hard worker

7. Which of the following statements is correct?
   (a) Objectives of research are stated in first chapter of the thesis
   (b) Researcher must possess analytical ability
   (c) Variability is the source of problem
   (d) All the above

8. Which of the following is not the Method of Research?
   (a) Observation (b) Historical
   (c) Survey (d) Philosophical

9. Research can be classified as:
   (a) Basic, Applied and Action Research
   (b) Quantitative and Qualitative Research
   (c) Philosophical, Historical, Survey and Experimental Research
   (d) All the above

10. The first step of research is:
    (a) Selecting a problem
    (b) Searching a problem
    (c) Finding a problem
    (d) Identifying a problem

Read the following passage and answer the question nos. 11 to 15:

After almost three decades of contemplating Swarovski-encrusted navels on increasing flat abs, the Mumbai film industry is on a discovery of India and itself. With budgets of over 30 crore each, four soon to be released movies by premier directors are exploring the idea of who we are and redefining who the other is. It is a fundamental question which the bling-bling, glam-sham and disham-disham tends to avoid. It is also a question which binds an audience when the lights go dim and the projector rolls: as a nation, who are we? As a people, where are we going?

The Germans coined a word for it, zeitgeist, which perhaps Yash Chopra would not care to pronounce. But at 72, he remains the person who can best capture it. After being the first to project the diasporic Indian on screen in *Lamhe* in 1991, he has returned to his roots in a new movie. *Veer Zaara*, set in 1986, where Pakistan, the traditional other, the part that got away, is the lover and the saviour. In Subhas Ghai's *Kisna*, set in 1947, the other is the English woman. She is not a memsahib, but a mehbooba. In Ketan Mehta's *The Rising*, the East India Englishman is not the evil oppressor of countless cardboard characterisations, which span the spectrum from *Jewel in the Crown* to *Kranti*, but an honourable friend.

This is Manoj Kumar's *Desh Ki Dharti* with a difference: there is culture, not contentious politics; balle balle, not bombs: no dooriyan (distance), only nazdeekiyan (closeness).

All four films are heralding a new hero and heroine. The new hero is fallible and vulnerable, committed to his dharma, but also not afraid of failure—less of a boy and more of a man. He even has a grown up name : Veer Pratap Singh in *Veer-Zaara* and Mohan Bhargav in *Swades*. The new heroine is not a babe, but often a bebe, dressed in traditional Punjabi clothes, often with the stereotypical body type as well, as in Bride and Prejudice of Gurinder Chadha.

11. Which word Yash Chopra would not be able to pronounce?
    (a) Bling + bling (b) Zeitgeist
    (c) Montaz (d) Dooriyan
12. Who made *Lambe* in 1991?
    (a) Subhash Ghai (b) Yash Chopra
    (c) Aditya Chopra (d) Sakti Samanta
13. Which movie is associated with Manoj Kumar?
    (a) *Jewel in the Crown*
    (b) *Kisna*
    (c) *Zaara*
    (d) *Desh Ki Dharti*
14. Which is the latest film by Yash Chopra?
    (a) *Deewar*
    (b) *Kabhi Kabhi*
    (c) *Dilwale Dulhaniya Le Jayenge*
    (d) *Veer Zaara*
15. Which is the dress of the heroine in *Veer-Zaara*?
    (a) Traditional Gujarati Clothes
    (b) Traditional Bengali Clothes
    (c) Traditional Punjabi Clothes
    (d) Traditional Madrasi Clothes
16. Which one of the following can be termed as verbal communication?
    (a) Prof. Sharma delivered the lecture in the classroom.
    (b) Signal at the cross-road changed from green to orange.
    (c) The child was crying to attract the attention of the mother.
    (d) Dipak wrote a letter for leave application.

17. Which is the 24 hours English Business news channel in India?
(a) Zee News (b) NDTV 24×7
(c) CNBC (d) India News

18. Consider the following statements in communication:
(i) Hema Malini is the Chairperson of the Children's Film Society, India.
(ii) Yash Chopra is the Chairman of the Central Board of Film Certification of India.
(iii) Sharmila Tagore is the Chairperson of National Film Development Corporation.
(iv) Dilip Kumar, Raj Kapoor and Preeti Zinta have all been recipients of Dada Saheb Phalke Award.

Which of the statements given above is/are correct?
(a) (i) and (iii) (b) (ii) and (iii)
(c) (iv) only (d) (iii) only

19. Which of the following pair is not correctly matched?
(a) N. Ram : The Hindu
(b) Barkha Dutt : Zee News
(c) Pranay Roy : NDTV 24×7
(d) Prabhu Chawla : Aajtak

20. "Because you deserve to know" is the punchline used by:
(a) *The Times of India*
(b) *The Hindu*
(c) *Indian Express*
(d) *Hindustan Times*

21. In the sequence of numbers 8, 24, 12, X, 18, 54 the missing number X is:
(a) 26 (b) 24
(c) 36 (d) 32

22. If A stands for 5, B for 6, C for 7, D for 8 and so on, then the following numbers stand for 17, 19, 20, 9 and 8:
(a) PLANE (b) MOPED
(c) MOTOR (d) TONGA

23. The letters in the first set have certain relationship. On the basis of this relationship what is the right choice for the second set?

AST : BRU :: NQV : ?
(a) ORW (b) MPU
(c) MRW (d) OPW

24. In a certain code, PAN is written as 31 and PAR as 35. In this code PAT is written as:
(a) 30 (b) 37
(c) 38 (d) 39

25. The sides of a triangle are in the ratio of $\frac{1}{2}:\frac{1}{3}:\frac{1}{4}$. If its perimeter is 52 cm, the length of the smallest side is:
(a) 9 cm (b) 10 cm
(c) 11 cm (d) 12 cm

26. Which one of the following statements is completely non-sensical?
(a) He was a bachelor, but he married recently.
(b) He is a bachelor, but he married recently.
(c) When he married, he was not a bachelor.
(d) When he was a bachelor, he was not married.

27. Which of the following statements are mutually contradictory?
(i) All flowers are not fragrant.
(ii) Most flowers are not fragrant.
(iii) None of the flowers is fragrant.
(iv) Most flowers are fragrant.

Choose the correct answer from the code given below:

Code:
(a) (i) and (ii) (b) (i) and (iii)
(c) (ii) and (iii) (d) (iii) and (iv)

28. Which of the following statements say the same thing?
   (i) "I am a teacher" (said by Arvind)
   (ii) "I am a teacher" (said by Binod)
   (iii) "My son is a teacher" (said by Binod's father)
   (iv) "My brother is a teacher" (said by Binod's sister)
   (v) "My brother is a teacher" (said by Binod's only sister)
   (vi) "My sole enemy is a teacher" (said by Binod's only enemy)

   Choose the correct answer from the code given below:

   Codes:
   (a) (i) and (ii)
   (b) (ii), (iii), (iv) and (v)
   (c) (ii) and (vi)
   (d) (v) and (vi)

29. Which of the following are correct ways of arguing?
   (i) There can be no second husband without a second wife.
   (ii) Anil is a friend of Bob, Bob is a friend of Raj, hence Anil is a friend of Raj.
   (iii) A is equal to B, B is equal to C, hence A is equal to C.
   (iv) If everyone is a liar, then we cannot prove it.

   Choose the correct answer from the code given below:

   Codes:
   (a) (iii) and (iv)
   (b) (i), (iii) and (iv)
   (c) (ii), (iii) and (iv)
   (d) (i), (ii), (iii) and (iv)

30. Which of the following statement/s are ALWAYS FALSE?
   (i) The sun will not rise in the East some day.
   (ii) A wooden table is not a table.
   (iii) Delhi city will be drowned under water.
   (iv) Cars run on water as fuel.

   Choose the correct answer from the code given below:

   Codes:
   (a) (i), (iii) and (iv) (b) (iii) only
   (c) (i), (ii) and (iii) (d) (ii) only

Study the following graph and answer question numbers 31 to 33:

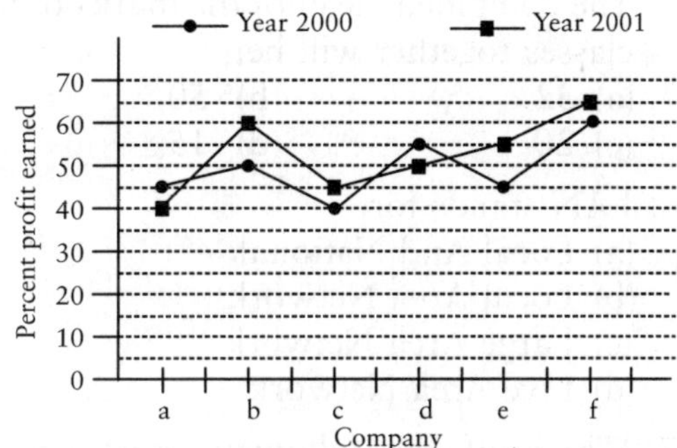

31. In the year 2000, which of the following Companies earned maximum percent profit?
   (a) a (b) b
   (c) d (d) f

32. In the year 2001, which of the following Companies earned minimum percent profit?
   (a) a (b) c
   (c) d (d) e

33. In the years 2000 and 2001, which of the following Companies earned maximum average percent profit?
   (a) f (b) e
   (c) d (d) b

34. Human Development Report for 'each' of the year at global level has been published by:
   (a) UNDP (b) WTO
   (c) IMF (d) World Bank

35. The number of students in four classes A, B, C, D and their respective mean marks obtained by each of the class are given below:

	Class A	Class B	Class C	Class D
Number of students	10	40	30	20
Arithmetic mean	20	30	50	15

The combined mean of the marks of four classes together will be:
(a) 32 (b) 50
(c) 20 (d) 15

36. LAN stands for:
(a) Local And National
(b) Local Area Network
(c) Large Area Network
(d) Live Area Network

37. Which of the following statements is correct?
(a) Modem is a software
(b) Modem helps in stabilizing the voltage
(c) Modem is the operating system
(d) Modem converts the analog signal into digital signal and vice-versa

38. Which of the following is the appropriate definition of a computer?
(a) Computer is a machine that can process information.
(b) Computer is an electronic device that can store, retrieve and process both qualitative and quantitative data quickly and accurately.
(c) Computer is an electronic device that can store, retrieve and quickly process only quantitative data.
(d) Computer is a machine that can store, retrieve and process quickly and accurately only qualitative information.

39. Information and Communication Technology includes:
(a) On line learning
(b) Learning through the use of EDUSAT
(c) Web Based Learning
(d) All the above

40. Which of the following is the appropriate format of URL of e-mail?
(a) www_mail.com
(b) www@mail.com
(c) WWW@mail.com
(d) www.mail.com

41. The most significant impact of volcanic eruption has been felt in the form of:
(a) change in weather
(b) sinking of islands
(c) loss of vegetation
(d) extinction of animals

42. With absorption and decomposition of CO_2 in ocean water beyond desired level, there will be:
(a) decrease in temperature
(b) increase in salinity
(c) growth of phyto plankton
(d) rise in sea level

43. Arrange column II in proper sequence so as to match it with column I and choose the correct answer from the code given below:

Column I (Water Quality)	**Column II (pH Value)**
(A) Neutral	(i) 5
(B) Moderately acidic	(ii) 7
(C) Alkaline	(iii) 4
(D) Injurious	(iv) 8

Codes:	**A**	**B**	**C**	**D**
(a)	(ii)	(iii)	(i)	(iv)
(b)	(i)	(iii)	(ii)	(iv)
(c)	(ii)	(i)	(iv)	(iii)
(d)	(iv)	(ii)	(iii)	(i)

44. The maximum emission of pollutants from fuel sources in India is caused by:
(a) Coal
(b) Firewood
(c) Refuse burning
(d) Vegetable waste product

45. The urbanisation process accounts for the wind in the urban centres during nights to remain:
(a) faster than that in rural areas
(b) slower than that in rural areas
(c) the same as that in rural areas
(d) cooler than that in rural areas

46. The University Grants Commission was constituted on the recommendation of:
(a) Dr. Sarvapalli Radhakrishnan Commission
(b) Mudaliar Commission
(c) Sargent Commission
(d) Kothari Commission

47. Which one of the following Articles of the Constitution of India safeguards the rights of Minorities to establish and run educational institutions of their own liking?
(a) Article 19 (b) Article 29
(c) Article 30 (d) Article 31

48. Match List I (Institutions) with List II (Functions) and select the correct answer by using the code given below:

List I (Institutions)
(A) Parliament
(B) C & A.G.
(C) Ministry of Finance
(D) Executing Departments

List II (Functions)
(i) Formulation of Budget
(ii) Enactment of Budget
(iii) Implementation of Budget
(iv) Legality of expenditure
(v) Justification of Income

Codes:	A	B	C	D
(a)	(iii)	(iv)	(ii)	(i)
(b)	(ii)	(iv)	(i)	(iii)
(c)	(v)	(iii)	(iv)	(ii)
(d)	(iv)	(ii)	(iii)	(v)

49. Foundation training to the newly recruited IAS (Probationers) is imparted by:
(a) Indian Institute of Public Administration
(b) Administrative Staff College of India
(c) L.B.S. National Academy of Administration
(d) Centre for Advanced Studies

50. Electoral disputes arising out of Presidential and Vice-Presidential Elections are settled by:
(a) Election Commission of India
(b) Joint Committee of Parliament
(c) Supreme Court of India
(d) Central Election TribunalAnswers

ANSWERS

1. (d)	2. (a)	3. (b)	4. (b)	5. (d)
6. (c)	7. (d)	8. (b)	9. (d)	10. (d)
11. (b)	12. (b)	13. (d)	14. (d)	15. (c)
16. (c)	17. (c)	18. (d)	19. (b)	20. (d)
21. (c)	22. (b)	23. (d)	24. (b)	25. (d)
26. (b)	27. (b)	28. (b)	29. (a)	30. (d)
31. (d)	32. (a)	33. (a)	34. (a)	35. (a)
36. (b)	37. (d)	38. (b)	39. (d)	40. (b)
41. (a)	42. (c)	43. (c)	44. (c)	45. (b)
46. (a)	47. (c)	48. (b)	49. (c)	50. (c)

PAPER–II

1. The approach towards vocational selection should be
(a) Scientific
(b) Well founded judgement
(c) Knowledge
(d) All of these

2. The purpose of the report
(a) Dissipation of knowledge
(b) Broadcasting of generalization

(c) Widest use in public
(d) All of these

3. The survey is sometimes conducted at the instance of a third party that has some stake in the problem such surveys deal with
(a) Market research
(b) Market poll
(c) Results not meant for general public
(d) All of these

4. The report should also mention
(a) Sampling method
(b) Size of sample
(c) Criteria for selection
(d) All of these

5. The one variable about which the experimenter makes a prediction
(a) Independent (b) Dependent
(c) Continuous (d) None of these

6. The variable which is manipulated measured and selected by the experimenter for the purpose of producing observable change in behavioural measure
(a) Continuous (b) Discontinuous
(c) Independent (d) None of these

7. State which is/are true
(a) The independent variable is the variable on the basis of which the prediction about dependent variable is made
(b) The variable must be selected in view of the scope of design of the experiment
(c) Most commonly used measure of variability is the standard deviation
(d) In psychological research the dependent variable variation is usually some measures of the subjects behaviour
(e) All of these

8. Who stated "The interview of perhaps the most ubiquitous method of obtaining information from the people."?
(a) Goode and Hart
(b) Fred N. Kerlinger
(c) Gibbons
(d) None of these

9. "Interviewing has become of greater importance in contemporary research because of reassessment of qualitative research"
(a) Goode and Hatt
(b) Bogardiss
(c) Galton
(d) None of these

10. Specific qualities that should be present in a research worker
(i) Knowledge of the subject, technique of research
(ii) Personal taste in the study
(iii) Familiarity about the informants
(iv) Unbiased attitude
(a) i, ii, iii, iv (b) i, ii, iii
(c) i, ii (d) i, iv

11. Match the following:

(A)	Lemon Juice	(i)	Tartaric acid
(B)	Vinegar	(ii)	Citric acid
(C)	Tamarind extract	(iii)	Acetic acid
(D)	Organic acid	(iv)	Used in preparation for acidity they contribute
(E)	Tomato juice	(v)	Slow down bacterial action

Codes:	A	B	C	D	E
(a)	ii	iii	i	v	iv
(b)	i	ii	iv	iii	v
(c)	v	iv	iii	i	ii
(d)	iii	v	ii	iv	i

12. Blanching of vegetables done before freezing
(a) To wash it
(b) To inactivate enzyme
(c) For taste
(d) For texture

13. The term food processing is used in canning industry means
    (a) Heating or cooling of canned foods to inactivate bacteria
    (b) Determining the right temp to eliminate bacterial growth
    (c) Duration of cooking
    (d) All of these

14. The role of salt in food preparation
    (a) Seasoning
    (b) Draws out water
    (c) Binds water in solution
    (d) All of these

15. The organic acids used in food preparation
    (i) Lemon juice
    (ii) Vinegar
    (iii) Tamarind extract
    (iv) Cocum extract
    (a) i, ii, iii, iv (b) i, ii, iii
    (c) i, ii (d) i, iv

16. The % of sugar in candy is
    (a) 25% (b) 50%
    (c) 75% (d) 100%

17. In a ready to serve murraba the % sugar is
    (a) 30% (b) 40%
    (c) 60% (d) 70%

18. Fruits and vegetables by
    (i) By hand or with knife
    (ii) By machine
    (iii) By heat treatment
    (iv) By eye solution i.e. caustic soda solution
    (a) i, ii, iii, iv (b) i, ii, iii
    (c) i, ii (d) i, iv

19. Treatment of fruits and vegetables with boiling water or steam for short periods followed by cooling is
    (a) Washing (b) Blanching
    (c) Syruping (d) None

20. Clinching is
    (a) Intentional escape of air from loose lid
    (b) Seality of cans
    (c) Adding syrup or brine to a can
    (d) None of these

21. The three types of cookers used for canning of fruits include
    (a) Open cookers
    (b) Continuous non-agitating cookers
    (c) Continuous agitating cookers
    (d) All of these

22. In food industry moulds are used in making
    (i) Curing cheese (ii) Soya sauce
    (iii) Curd (iv) Idli
    (a) i, ii, iii, iv (b) i, ii, iii
    (c) i, ii (d) i, iv

23. Yeast fermentation produces chemical changes in which enzymes produced by the yeast cells convert
    (a) Alcohol into sugar
    (b) Protein into amino acid
    (c) Fats into fatty acids
    (d) Sugar into alcohol

24. Bread, vinegar, beer and wine are produced with the help of
    (a) Mould (b) Bacteria
    (c) Yeast (d) Enzymes

25. Yeasts are undersirable when they grow and ferment
    (i) Fruit
    (ii) Fruit juices
    (iii) Syrups
    (iv) Honey and molasses
    (a) i, ii, iii, iv (b) i, ii, iii
    (c) i, ii (d) i, iv

26. Thermophilic bacteria cause problem in
    (a) Banking industry
    (b) Hotel industry
    (c) Catering industry
    (d) Canning industry

27. Psychrophilic bacteria are a source of concern to
    (i) Tiffin industry
    (ii) Cold storage people

(iii) Housewife who uses refrigerator
(iv) Food preservation
(a) i, ii, iii, iv (b) ii, iii
(c) i, ii (d) i, iv

28. Kneaded dough left in the refrigerator show grey or black specks due to the activity of
(a) Psychrophilic (b) Mesophilic
(c) Thermophilic (d) None

29. Which of the following is/are true?
(i) In making observations of naturally occurring behavior anecdotes may be substituted for genuine observation or interpretation for descriptions
(ii) Observation methods have been brought into the laboratory
(iii) Case histories are important sources of data for studying individuals
(iv) Case histories may also be based on a longitudinal study
(a) i, ii, iii, iv (b) i, ii, iii
(c) i, ii (d) i, iv

30. The advantage of a longitudinal study is that it does not depend on
(a) Observer (b) Memories
(c) Time schedule (d) None

31. The two characteristic in which a behaviour can be termed as normal or problem are its
(i) Frequency
(ii) Intensity
(iii) Distraction
(iv) Counter productiveness
(a) i, ii, iii, iv (b) i, ii, iii
(c) i, ii (d) i, iv

32. State which is/are true
(a) Gossip groups are micro-groups
(b) Modern mass media are processes and must not be mistaken for the phenomenon of communication itself
(c) Traditional community media like the keertana the treasure house of folksong, folk dance and folk theatre are the real organs of mass media in India
(d) Modern mass media are produced and distributed like other consumers and industrial products-on a mass scale
(e) All of these

33. Daniel Lorner terms them 'mobility multiplies and Wilbur Schramm considers them to be' mobility multipliers.
(a) Mass media
(b) Group communication
(c) Individual communication
(d) None of these

34. The system in a language providing for the orderly presentation of words is called
(a) Grammar sequence
(b) Syntax
(c) Comprehension
(d) None of these

35. Some non-verbal forms include
(i) Smiles (ii) Tears
(iii) Gestures (iv) Body movement
(a) i, ii, iii, iv (b) i, ii, iii
(c) i, ii (d) i, iv

36. State which is/are true
(a) The responsibility in respect to coordination of work in education starts from the individual workers and extends to the highest top administrators in the country
(b) Scope of coordination covers personnel methods, material, purposes, procedures, programmes policies etc.
(c) Control puts a break to an activity and then looks back to appraise and evaluate the results
(d) Control is not only concerned with the evaluation it is also contained with the resources used
(e) All of these

37. Control establishes a relationship between
(i) Aims and materials
(ii) Aims and methods
(a) (i) only (b) (ii) only
(c) Both (i) and (ii) (d) None of these

38. Carl Rogers has outlined the role of counselor in non-directive counselor
(i) Defines problematic situation
(ii) Recognizes and classifies the negative and positive feelings
(iii) Reflects and clarifies new feeling of he client
(iv) Watch for signs for counseling termination
(a) i, ii, iii, iv (b) i, ii, iii
(c) i, ii (d) i, iv

39. In electric counseling
(i) Counselor and counselee active
(ii) Counselor and counselee cooperative
(iii) Both talk turn by turn
(iv) Problem jointly solved
(a) i, ii, iii, iv (b) i, ii, iii
(c) i, ii (d) i, iv

40. Characteristic of counseling process
(i) Professional service
(ii) Centre-problem of client
(iii) Client-made discussions
(iv) Based on accuracy of counselor's predication
(a) i, ii, iii, iv (b) i, ii, iii
(c) i, ii (d) i, iv

41. Literacy programmes should be linked to all development plans of the country whether these be economic, social, political or cultural in character according to .... report.
(a) Kothari (b) Teheran
(c) Mark Blaug (d) None of these

42. Which of the following is/are true?
(i) The traditional subjects of the curriculum are like eggs in a crate, each fitting snugly into pre-designed space, isolated from the rest.
(ii) Curriculum development can encourage the notion that the curriculum is the natural care for initial and in-service training courses for teachers so that it becomes the reason for inclusion of selected topics from separate disciplines and the integrating force for all elements of the course.
(iii) The definition of curriculum used by Elizabeth Maccia of Ohio University is presented as instructional content.
(iv) Instruction is taken to be very specifically as a function of relation between teacher behaviour and pupil behavior.
(a) i, ii, iii, iv (b) i, ii, iii
(c) i, ii (d) i, iv

43. Satellite educational programme has much less to offer you if you believe in
(i) Learning by being
(ii) Learning by personal exploration
(iii) Learning by role
(iv) Learning by conditioning
(a) i, ii, iii, iv (b) i, ii, iii
(c) i, ii (d) i, iv

44. Learning through satellite is basically learning by
(a) Guidance (b) Unitation
(c) Seeing (d) None

45. The role of co-ordination in a satellite programme is
(a) Crucial (b) Difficult
(c) Time consuming (d) Expensive

46. Media have a role and a function in society which could be
(a) Stabilise
(b) Reinforce
(c) Maintain the consensus
(d) All of these

47. Charts are utilized
(a) To show relationship
(b) Classification

(c) Development of an aspect
(d) All of these

48. In the adult years the gain in weight is from
(a) Accumulation of fat tissue
(b) Lack of activity
(c) Blood
(d) Hormones

49. Match the following:

List I
(A) Physical decline
(B) The pattern of human life development
(C) At no time can development curve
(D) Plateau period of long and short duration
(E) The basic personality pattern

List II
(i) is that of a bell-shaped curve
(ii) Precedes mental
(iii) found in the curves for different capacities
(iv) represented by a straight line
(v) is set during the early years of life

Codes:	A	B	C	D	E
(a)	ii	i	iv	iii	v
(b)	i	ii	iii	v	iv
(c)	i	v	iv	ii	iii
(d)	v	iv	i	ii	iii

50. Which of the following is/are true?
(i) The child who does not learn tasks at periods of readiness may have great difficulty learning them later.
(ii) Serious behavior problems cause abruptly in adolescence but trace their organ to maladjustment in the early years.
(iii) In the pattern of intellectual development memory precedes reasoning with abstract reasoning following concrete.
(iv) Within the pattern of development there is a marked correlation between physical and psychological development.

(a) i, ii, iii, iv (b) i, ii, iii
(c) i, ii (d) i, iv

ANSWERS

1. (d)	2. (d)	3. (d)	4. (d)	5. (b)
6. (c)	7. (e)	8. (b)	9. (a)	10. (a)
11. (a)	12. (b)	13. (d)	14. (d)	15. (a)
16. (c)	17. (d)	18. (a)	19. (b)	20. (a)
21. (d)	22. (c)	23. (d)	24. (c)	25. (a)
26. (d)	27. (b)	28. (a)	29. (a)	30. (b)
31. (c)	32. (e)	33. (a)	34. (b)	35. (a)
36. (e)	37. (c)	38. (a)	39. (a)	40. (a)
41. (b)	42. (a)	43. (c)	44. (a)	45. (c)
46. (d)	47. (d)	48. (a)	49. (a)	50. (a)

JUNE–2006

Note: This paper contains fifty (50) objective type questions, each question carrying two (2) marks. All questions are compulsory.

PAPER–I

1. Which of the following comprise teaching skill:
   (a) Blackboard writing
   (b) Questioning
   (c) Explaining
   (d) All the above
2. Which of the following statements is most appropriate?
   (a) Teachers can teach.
   (b) Teachers help can create in a student a desire to learn.
   (c) Lecture Method can be used for developing thinking.
   (d) Teachers are born.
3. The first Indian chronicler of Indian history was:
   (a) Megasthanese (b) Fahiyan
   (c) Huan Tsang (d) Kalhan
4. Which of the following statements is correct?
   (a) Syllabus is a part of curriculum.
   (b) Syllabus is an annexure to curriculum.
   (c) Curriculum is the same in all educational institutions affiliated to a particular university.
   (d) Syllabus is not the same in all educational institutions affiliated to a particular university.
5. Which of the two given options is of the level of understanding?
   (I) Define noun.
   (II) Define noun in your own words.
   (a) Only I (b) Only II
   (c) Both I and II (d) Neither I nor II
6. Which of the following options are the main tasks of research in modern society?
   (I) to keep pace with the advancement in knowledge.
   (II) to discover new things.
   (III) to write a critique on the earlier writings.
   (IV) to systematically examine and critically analyse the investigations/sources with objectivity.
   (a) IV, II and I (b) I, II and III
   (c) I and III (d) II, III and IV
7. Match List I (Interviews) with List II (Meaning) and select the correct answer from the code given below:

   List I (Interviews)
   (A) Structured interviews
   (B) Unstructured interviews
   (C) Focussed interviews
   (D) Clinical interviews

   List II (Meaning)
   (i) greater flexibility approach
   (ii) attention on the questions to be answered
   (iii) individual life experience
   (iv) Pre determined question
   (v) non-directive

Codes:	A	B	C	D
(a)	(iv)	(i)	(ii)	(iii)
(b)	(ii)	(iv)	(i)	(iii)
(c)	(v)	(ii)	(iv)	(i)
(d)	(i)	(iii)	(v)	(iv)

8. What do you consider as the main aim of inter disciplinary research?
   (a) To bring out holistic approach to research.
   (b) To reduce the emphasis of single subject in research domain.
   (c) To over simplify the problem of research.
   (d) To create a new trend in research methodology.
9. One of the aims of the scientific method in research is to:
   (a) improve data interpretation
   (b) eliminate spurious relations
   (c) confirm triangulation
   (d) introduce new variables
10. The depth of any research can be judged by:
   (a) title of the research.
   (b) objectives of the research.
   (c) total expenditure on the research.
   (d) duration of the research.

Read the following passage and answer the questions 11 to 15:

The superintendence, direction and control of preparation of electoral rolls for, and the conduct of, elections aims to Parliament and State Legislatures and elections to the offices of the President and the Vice-President of India are vested in the Election Commission of India. It is an independent constitutional authority.

Independence of the Election Commission and its insulation from executive interference is ensured by a specific provision under Article 324(5) of the Constitution that the chief Election Commissioner shall not be removed from his office except in like manner and on like grounds as a Judge of the Supreme Court and conditions of his service shall not be varied to his disadvantage after his appointment.

In C.W.P. No. 4912 of 1998 (Kushra Bharat Vs. Union of India and others), the Delhi High Court directed that information relating to Government dues owed by the candidates to the departments dealing with Government accommodation, electricity, water, telephone and transport etc. and any other dues should be furnished by the candidates and this information should be published by the election authorities under the commission.

11. The text of the passage reflects or raises certain questions:
   (a) The authority of the commission can not be challenged.
   (b) This would help in stopping the criminalization of Indian politics.
   (c) This would reduce substantially the number of contesting candidates.
   (d) This would ensure fair and free elections.
12. According to the passage, the Election Commission is an independent Constitutional authority. This is under Article No.:
   (a) 324 (b) 356
   (c) 246 (d) 161
13. Independence of the Commission means:
   (a) have a constitutional status.
   (b) have legislative powers.
   (c) have judicial powers.
   (d) have political powers.
14. Fair and free election means:
   (a) transparency
   (b) to maintain law and order
   (c) regional considerations
   (d) role for pressure groups
15. The Chief Election Commissioner can be removed from his office under Article:
   (a) 125 (b) 352
   (c) 226 (d) 324
16. The function of mass communication of supplying information regarding the processes, issues, events and societal developments is known as:

(a) content supply (b) surveillance
(c) gratification (d) correlation

17. The science of the study of feedback systems in humans, animals and machines is known as:
(a) cybernetics
(b) reverse communication
(c) selectivity study
(d) response analysis

18. Networked media exist in inter-connected:
(a) social environments
(b) economic environments
(c) political environments
(d) technological environments

19. The combination of computing, telecommunications and media in a digital atmosphere is referred to as:
(a) online communication
(b) integrated media
(c) digital combine
(d) convergence

20. A dialogue between a human-being and a computer programme that occurs simultaneously in various forms is described as:
(a) man-machine speak
(b) binary chat
(c) digital talk
(d) interactivity

21. Insert the missing number:

$\frac{16}{32}, \frac{15}{33}, \frac{17}{31}, \frac{14}{34}, ?$

(a) $\frac{19}{35}$ (b) $\frac{19}{30}$
(c) $\frac{18}{35}$ (d) $\frac{18}{30}$

22. Monday falls on 20th March 1995. What was the day on 3rd November 1994?
(a) Thursday (b) Sunday
(c) Tuesday (d) Saturday

23. The average of four consecutive even numbers is 27. The largest of these numbers is
(a) 36 (b) 32
(c) 30 (d) 28

24. In a certain code, FHQK means GIRL. How will WOMEN be written in the same code?
(a) VNLDM (b) FHQKN
(c) XPNFO (d) VLNDM

25. At what time between 4 and 5 O'clock will the hands of a watch point in opposite directions?
(a) 45 min. past 4
(b) $40\frac{4}{11}$ min. past 4
(c) 50 min. past 4
(d) $54\frac{6}{11}$ min. past 4

26. Which of the following conclusions is logically valid based on statement given below ?
Statement: Most teachers are hard working.
Conclusions: (I) Some teachers are hard working.
(II) Some teachers are not hard working.
(a) Only (I) is implied
(b) Only (II) is implied
(c) Both (I) and (II) are implied
(d) Neither (I) nor (II) is implied

27. Who among the following can be asked to make a statement in Indian Parliament?
(a) Any MLA
(b) Chief of Army Staff
(c) Solicitor General of India
(d) Mayor of Delhi

28. Which of the following conclusions is logically valid based on statement given below?

Statement : Most of the Indian states existed before independence.

Conclusions : (I) Some Indian States existed before independence.

(II) All Indian States did not exist before independence.

(a) only (I) is implied
(b) only (II) is implied
(c) Both (I) and (II) are implied
(d) Neither (I) nor (II) is implied

29. Water is always involved with landslides. This is because it:
(a) reduces the shear strength of rocks
(b) increases the weight of the overburden
(c) enhances chemical weathering
(d) is a universal solvent

30. Direction for this question:
Given below are two statements (a) and (b) followed by two conclusions (i) and (ii). Considering the statements to be true, indicate which of the following conclusions logically follow from the given statements by selecting one of the four response alternatives given below the conclusion:

Statements: (a) All businessmen are wealthy.

(b) All wealthy people are hard working.

Conclusions: (i) All businessmen are hard working.

(ii) All hardly working people are not wealthy.

(a) Only (i) follows
(b) Only (ii) follows
(c) Both (i) and (ii) follow
(d) Neither (i) nor (ii) follows

31. Using websites to pour out one's grievances is called:
(a) cyberventing (b) cyber ranting
(c) web hate (d) web plea

32. In web search, finding a large number of documents with very little relevant information is termed:
(a) poor recall
(b) web crawl
(c) poor precision rate
(d) poor web response

33. The concept of connect intelligence is derived from:
(a) virtual reality
(b) fuzzy logic
(c) bluetooth technology
(d) value added networks

34. Use of an ordinary telephone as an Internet appliance is called:
(a) voicenet (b) voice telephone
(c) voice line (d) voice portal

35. Video transmission over the Internet that looks like delayed livecasting is called:
(a) virtual video
(b) direct broadcast
(c) video shift
(d) real-time video

36. Which is the smallest North-east State in India?
(a) Tripura (b) Meghalaya
(c) Mizoram (d) Manipur

37. Tamil Nadu coastal belt has drinking water shortage due to:
(a) high evaporation
(b) sea water flooding due to tsunami
(c) over exploitation of ground water by tubewells
(d) seepage of sea water

38. While all rivers of Peninsular India flow into the Bay of Bengal, Narmada and Tapti flow into the Arabian Sea because these two rivers:
(a) Follow the slope of these rift valleys
(b) The general slope of the Indian peninsula is from east to west

(c) The Indian peninsula north of the Satpura ranges, is tilted towards the west
(d) The Indian peninsula south of the Satpura ranges is tilted towards east

39. Soils in the Mahanadi delta are less fertile than those in the Godavari delta because of:
(a) erosion of top soils by annual floods
(b) inundation of land by sea water
(c) traditional agriculture practices
(d) the derivation of alluvial soil from red-soil hinterland

40. Which of the following institutions in the field of education is set up by the MHRD Government of India?
(a) Indian council of world Affair, New Delhi
(b) Mythic Society, Bangalore
(c) National Bal Bhawn, New Delhi
(d) India International Centre, New Delhi

41. **Assertion (A):** Aerosols have potential for modifying climate.
Reason (R): Aerosols interact with both short waves and radiation.
(a) Both (A) and (R) are true, and (R) is the correct explanation of (A)
(b) Both (A) and (R) are true, but (R) is not the correct explanation of (A)
(c) (A) is true, but (R) is false
(d) (A) is false, but (R) is true

42. 'SITE' stands for:
(a) System for International technology and Engineering
(b) Satellite Instructional Television Experiment
(c) South Indian Trade Estate
(d) State Institute of Technology and Engineering

43. What is the name of the Research station established by the Indian Government for 'Conducting Research at Antarctic'?
(a) Dakshin Gangotri
(b) Yamunotri
(c) Uttari Gangotri
(d) None of the above

44. Ministry of Human Resource Development (HRD) includes:
(a) Department of Elementary Education and Literacy
(b) Department of Secondary Education and Higher Education
(c) Department of Women and Child Development
(d) All the above

45. Parliament can legislate on matters listed in the State list:
(a) With the prior permission of the President.
(b) Only after the Constitution is amended suitably.
(c) In case of inconsistency among State legislatures.
(d) At the request of two or more States.

The below pie chart indicates the expenditure of a country on various sports during a particular year. Study the pie chart and answer Question Numbers 46 to 50.

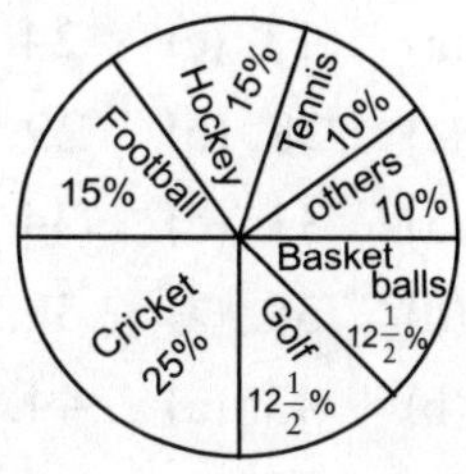

46. The ratio of the total expenditure on football to that of expenditure on hockey is:
(a) 1 : 15 (b) 1 : 1
(c) 15 : 1 (d) 3 : 20

47. If the total expenditure on sports during the year was Rs. 1,20,000,00 how much was spent on basket ball?

(a) Rs. 9,50,000 (b) Rs. 10,00,000
(c) Rs. 12,00,000 (d) Rs. 15,00,000

48. The chart shows that the most popular game of the country is:
(a) Hockey (b) Football
(c) Cricket (d) Tennis

49. Out of the following country's expenditure is the same on:
(a) Hockey and Tennis
(b) Golf and Basket ball
(c) Cricket and Football
(d) Hockey and Golf

50. If the total expenditure on sport during the year was Rs. 1,50,00,000 the expenditure on cricket and hockey together was:
(a) Rs. 60,00,000 (b) Rs. 50,00,000
(c) Rs. 37,50,000 (d) Rs. 25,00,000

ANSWERS

1. (d)	2. (b)	3. (d)	4. (a)	5. (b)
6. (a)	7. (a)	8. (a)	9. (b)	10. (b)
11. (d)	12. (a)	13. (a)	14. (b)	15. (d)
16. (a)	17. (a)	18. (d)	19. (d)	20. (d)
21. (d)	22. (a)	23. (c)	24. (c)	25. (d)
26. (c)	27. (c)	28. (b)	29. (b)	30. (a)
31. (a)	32. (a)	33. (d)	34. (c)	35. (d)
36. (c)	37. (d)	38. (a)	39. (a)	40. (c)
41. (a)	42. (b)	43. (a)	44. (d)	45. (d)
46. (b)	47. (a)	48. (c)	49. (b)	50. (a)

PAPER–II

1. Apart from individual abilities and assets, vocational selection usually is made in light of
(i) expected financial returns
(ii) working condition
(iii) distance from home
(iv) prestige value
(a) i, ii, iii, iv (b) i, ii, iii
(c) i, ii (d) i, iv

2. Data to be analysed is presented in the form of
(i) Bar Charts
(ii) Graphic
(iii) Tabular
(iv) Pictorial Presentation
(a) i, ii, iii, iv (b) i, ii, iii
(c) i, ii (d) i, iv

3. Out of some generalizations some conclusions are drawn
(i) Deductive method
(ii) Inductive method
(a) Only i (b) Only ii
(c) Both i and ii (d) None of these

4. It is the spread between the highest and the lowest score
(a) Standard deviation
(b) Range
(c) Ratio
(d) None of these

5. In interview method because of personal presence of the researcher the researcher is/are
(i) Reliable and dependable
(ii) Can judge attitudes
(iii) Test the veracity of facts
(iv) Proper conclusion drawn
(a) i, ii, iii, iv (b) i, ii, iii
(c) i, ii (d) i, iv

6. The interview method depends on individual researcher's
(a) Ability
(b) Capability
(c) Communication
(d) Sensitivity to situation

7. The basic assumption in case study is/are
(i) Totally of the being
(ii) Underlying unity

(iii) Complexity of social phenomena
(iv) Influence of time
(a) i, ii, iii, iv (b) i, ii, iii
(c) i, ii (d) i, iv

8. According to John Dewey scientific attitude is linked with
(a) Curiosity
(b) Fertile imagination
(c) Love of experimental enquiry
(d) All of these

9. Sir Francis Galton states this "an inherent stimulus to climb the path that leads to knowledge with strength to reach the summit" about
(a) Imagination (b) Scientific attitude
(c) Perseverance (d) Grasping power

10. Which of the following is used to tenderize meat
(i) Heat (ii) Spices
(iii) Oil (iv) Papain
(a) i, ii, iii, iv (b) i, ii, iii
(c) i, ii (d) i, iv

11. State which is/are true
(a) Rennin is used to coagulate milk protein in cheese making.
(b) Sugars mineral salts organic acids and salts are the flavour components in fruits and vegetables
(c) Salt sugar acid herbs and spices are used in food preparation to modify or enhance the natural flavour
(d) To stew cooked meat takes 3-4 hours for cooking
(e) All of these

12. The boiling point of most of fats and oil is
(a) 300°-350°F (b) 350°-400°F
(c) 425°-475°F (d) None of these

13. When fat is heated above 380°F it gives out
(a) Heat (b) Smoke
(c) Acroline (d) All of these

14. At high temperature the chemical constituents of fat i.e. glycerol and fatty acid.
(a) Form a bond
(b) Separate out
(c) Chemically react
(d) None of these

15. State which is/are true
(a) About 45% of fruit and 55% of sugar are usually combined together so that the final concentration of soluble solids is not less than 68.5% in jams
(b) Tropical fruits which are good for making jams are papaya, pineapple, raw mangoes and gooseberry
(c) A perfect jelly should be transparent well set with original flavour
(d) All of these

16. The steps involved in drying turnip are
(a) Cut
(b) 2-3 minute blanch
(c) Dip in 1% solution sulphide
(d) All of these

17. The nutritional loss of canned fruit and vegetables include
(i) Vit C (ii) Vit B group
(iii) Vit A (iv) Vit E
(a) i, ii, iii, iv (b) i, ii, iii
(c) i, ii (d) i, iv

18. State which is/are true
(a) To make coloured vinegar white vinegar is mixed with burnt sugar or colour
(b) Compared to freezing B group vitamins loss is more in canning
(c) The loss of nutrients is maximum in sun drying
(d) Vit C and A are destroyed in sun drying by oxidation
(e) All of these

19. Studies have shown that by sun drying the green leafy vegetables show loss of

(a) Protein 3-3.2%
(b) Vit C 39-63%
(c) Vitamin A 48-49%
(d) All of these

20. Staphylococci causes
(a) Septic throat (b) By injury
(c) Heart attack (d) None of these

21. Cordials are prepared with
(a) 25% sour juicy fruits
(b) 50% sugar
(c) preservative
(d) All of these

22. Murraba and candy is made by
(a) Apple raw mango, pear
(b) Ginger
(c) Petha
(d) Anyone of them

23. Externalizing problems are disruptive behaviour that are often a nuisance to other, these are
(i) Aggression (ii) Hyperactivity
(iii) Impulsivity (iv) Inattention
(a) i, ii, iii, iv (b) i, ii, iii
(c) i, ii (d) i, iv

24. Child experiencing difficulty in interacting with peers or problems with expressing their wishes and needs to other can be labelled as
(a) Externalizing problems
(b) Internalizing problems
(c) Normal growth
(d) All of these

25. Who stated "Interviewing is not a simple way to conversation between an interrogator and informant. Gestures, glances, facial expressions, pauses often reveal subtle feelings."?
(a) Maclver (b) Goode and Hatt
(c) P.V. Yaing (d) None of these

26. .... has said about interview that "In other words it is a purposive conservation whose purpose may vary widely to include for example, a meeting undertaking to collect information".
(a) John Madge
(b) Fred and Kerlinger
(c) Vivien
(d) None of these

27. The groups which are taken into account for communication is/are
(i) Cultural groups
(ii) Social groups
(iii) Family groups
(iv) Reference group
(a) i, ii, iii, iv (b) i, ii, iii
(c) i, ii (d) i, iv

28. "The complex of values ideas attitudes and other meaningful symbols created by man to shape human behaviour and the artifacts of that behaviour as they are transmitted from one generation to the next."
(a) Culture (b) Civilization
(c) Adoption (d) None of these

29. State which is/are true
(a) Since perception is largely determined by cultured people of different cultures often perceive the same phenomenon in different fashions
(b) Social groups provide guidance to individuals in many diverse situations
(c) The factors cause the pressure as individual feels to conform to groups he is a member include, (i) information and trust (ii) deviancy (iii) Characteristics of group (iv) characteristic of the situation (v) characteristic of the individual
(d) People respond differently to various levels of "newness" of an idea, practice or product
(e) All of these

30. Yeast is a rich sources of
(a) Vit. C (b) Vit. D
(c) Vit. B (d) Vit. A

31. State true or false
   (a) In interpersonal communication feedback is instantaneous it is not so in group communication
   (b) Public speaking is more necessary at the group level than at the interpersonal level
   (c) In group communication particularly where the group is large deception and pretence cannot be detected immediately
   (d) 'Gossip group' and other traditional groups come together either regularly or occasionally for sharing information
   (e) All of these

32. The theatre, religions services, dance performances, carnival, the kumbh mela, Ram Lila, Rasa Lila and folk events are examples of
   (a) Focused interaction
   (b) Unfocused interaction
   (c) Group communication
   (d) Interpersonal communication

33. Village markets, bazaars and melas are instances of
   (a) Formal group communication
   (b) Informal group communication
   (c) Focused
   (d) Unfocused

34. These groups communicate among and within themselves in terms of their status and the nature of their relationships
   (a) Macro groups
   (b) Micro groups
   (c) Gossip groups
   (d) None of these

35. Counselling process should result in assisting the individual to become
   (i) Autonomous (ii) Self-directing
   (iii) Self-disciplined (iv) Egoist
   (a) i, ii, iii, iv (b) i, ii, iii
   (c) i, ii (d) i, iv

36. Duties that a counsellor should never perform
   (i) Clerical
   (ii) Substitute teaching
   (iii) Checking absence
   (iv) Sponsoring extra curricular duties
   (a) i, ii, iii, iv (b) i, ii, iii
   (c) i, ii (d) i, iv

37. Perhaps most important of all as a form of guidance are the—child sees in his parents
   (a) Love
   (b) Respect
   (c) Behavioral models
   (d) Conflict

38. State which is/are true
   (a) Mother milk has lactalbumin protein which is easily digestible than casein.
   (b) Maternal diet is reflected in the milk by fat and fatty acid content
   (c) Linoleic acid content amounts over 10% of the total fatty acid present in human milk.
   (d) Most Vit. D preparation given to infant contain Vit. A. which is essential as a growth promoter.
   (e) All of these.

39. Breast feeding prolongs the period of natural immunity to viral infections like
   (a) Mumps and measles
   (b) Polio
   (c) Some kinds of pneumonia and diarrhoeas
   (d) All of above

40. Match of the following
   List I
   (A) Babies fed on breast milk
   (B) Bottle feeding results in
   (C) Breast feeding discontinued
   (D) First solid discontinued
   (E) A baby

List II

(i) increased infant sickness and mortality
(ii) less likely to develop constipation and allergies
(iii) 5-6 months of age
(iv) doubles its birth weight between 4-6 months and triples by end of 10-12 months
(v) when mother suffers from chronic illnesses, infant is weak.

Codes:	A	B	C	D	E
(a)	ii	i	v	iii	iv
(b)	i	v	iv	ii	iii
(c)	i	ii	v	iv	iii
(d)	v	iv	iii	ii	i

41. Planning should be
(i) Flexible (ii) Adaptable
(iii) Consistent (iv) Stable
(a) i, ii, iii, iv (b) i, ii, iii
(c) i, ii (d) i, iv

42. Organisation in administration is
(i) Arrangement of Material
(ii) Arrangement of individuals
(a) Only (i) (b) Only (ii)
(c) Both (i) and (ii) (d) None of these

43. The description of imitation is given by "self conscious assumption of another's acts or roles"
(a) MacIver (b) Hurlock
(c) Mead (d) None of these

44. Language and pronunciation are acquired by the child through
(a) Suggestion (b) Imitation
(c) Identification (d) None of these

45. "It is the process of communication resulting in the acceptance with conviction of the communicated proposition in the absence of logically adequate grounds for its acceptance." It is
(a) Imitation (b) Identification
(c) Suggestion (d) None of these

46. Suggestion is conveyed through
(a) Language (b) Pictures
(c) Similar medium (d) All of these

47. The foundations are laid during the early years. Changes can and do occur as the life cycle progress. Changes are likely to occur
(a) By guidance
(b) Change in attitude towards the treatment of the individual
(c) Self-motivation
(d) All of these

48. Variations in the pattern of physical and intellectual growth may be due to
(a) Health
(b) Emotional climate
(c) Cultural atmosphere
(d) All of these

49. Dry heat method of cooking meat
(i) Roasting (ii) Broiling
(iii) Pan Broiling (iv) Frying
(a) i, ii, iii, iv (b) i, ii, iii
(c) i, ii (d) i, iv

50. The technique employed for most heat cooking of meat include
(a) Braising
(b) Stewing
(c) Pressure Cooking
(d) All of these

ANSWERS

1. (d)	2. (a)	3. (a)	4. (b)	5. (a)
6. (a)	7. (a)	8. (d)	9. (b)	10. (d)
11. (e)	12. (b)	13. (d)	14. (b)	15. (d)
16. (d)	17. (c)	18. (e)	19. (d)	20. (a)
21. (d)	22. (d)	23. (a)	24. (b)	25. (c)
26. (a)	27. (a)	28. (a)	29. (e)	30. (c)
31. (e)	32. (c)	33. (b)	34. (b)	35. (b)
36. (a)	37. (c)	38. (e)	39. (d)	40. (a)
41. (a)	42. (c)	43. (a)	44. (b)	45. (c)
46. (d)	47. (d)	48. (d)	49. (a)	50. (d)

DECEMBER–2005

Note: This paper contains fifty (50) objective type questions, each question carrying two (2) marks. All questions are compulsory.

PAPER–I

1. Team teaching has the potential to develop:
   (a) Competitive spirit
   (b) Cooperation
   (c) The habit of supplementing the teaching of each other
   (d) Highlighting the gaps in each other's teaching
2. Which of the following is the most important characteristic of Open Book Examination system?
   (a) Students become serious.
   (b) It improves attendance in the classroom.
   (c) It reduces examination anxiety amongst students.
   (d) It compels students to think.
3. Which of the following methods of teaching encourages the use of maximum senses?
   (a) Problem-solving method
   (b) Laboratory method
   (c) Self-study method
   (d) Team teaching method
4. Which of the following statement is correct?
   (a) Communicator should have fine senses
   (b) Communicator should have tolerance power
   (c) Communicator should be soft spoken
   (d) Communicator should have good personality
5. An effective teacher is one who can:
   (a) control the class
   (b) give more information in less time
   (c) motivate students to learn
   (d) correct the assignments carefully
6. One of the following is not a quality of researcher:
   (a) Unison with that of which he is in search
   (b) He must be of alert mind
   (c) Keenness in enquiry
   (d) His assertion to outstrip the evidence
7. A satisfactory statistical quantitative method should not possess one of the following qualities:
   (a) Appropriateness (b) Measurability
   (c) Comparability (d) Flexibility
8. Books and records are the primary sources of data in:
   (a) historical research
   (b) participatory research
   (c) clinical research
   (d) laboratory research
9. Which of the following statement is correct?
   (a) Objectives should be pin-pointed
   (b) Objectives can be written in statement or question form
   (c) Another word for problem is variable
   (d) All of the above
10. The important pre-requisites of a researcher in sciences, social sciences and humanities are:

(a) laboratory skills, records, supervisor, topic
(b) Supervisor, topic, critical analysis, patience
(c) archives, supervisor, topic, flexibility in thinking
(d) topic, supervisor, good temperament, pre-conceived notions

Read the following passage and answer the questions 11 to 15:

Knowledge creation in many cases requires creativity and idea generation. This is especially important in generating alternative decision support solutions. Some people believe that an individual's creative ability stems primarily from personality traits such as inventiveness, independence, individuality, enthusiasm, and flexibility. However, several studies have found that creativity is not so much a function of individual traits as was once believed, and that individual creativity can be learned and improved. This understanding has led innovative companies to recognise that the key to fostering creativity may be the development of an idea-nurturing work environment. Idea-generation methods and techniques, to be used by individuals or in groups, are consequently being developed. Manual methods for supporting idea generation, such as brainstorming in a group, can be very successful in certain situations. However, in other situations, such an approach is either not economically feasible or not possible. For example, manual methods in group creativity sessions will not work or will not be effective when : (1) there is no time to conduct a proper idea-generation session; (2) there is a poor facilitator (or no facilitator at all; (3) it is too expensive to conduct an idea-generation session; (4) the subject matter is too sensitive for a face-to-face session; or (5) there are not enough participants, the mix of participants is not optimal, or there is no climate for idea generation. In such cases, computerised idea-generation methods have been tried, with frequent success.

Idea-generation software is designed to help stimulate a single user or a group to produce new ideas, options and choices. The user does all the work, but the software encourages and pushes, something like a personal trainer. Although idea-generation software is still relatively new, there are several packages on the market. Various approaches are used by idea-generating software to increase the flow of ideas to the user. Idea Fisher, for example, has an associate lexicon of the English language that cross-references words and phrases. These associative links, based on analogies and metaphors, make it easy for the user to be fed words related to a given theme. Some software packages use questions to prompt the user towards new, unexplored patterns of thought. This helps users to break out of cyclical thinking patterns, conquer mental blocks, or deal with bouts of procrastination.

11. The author, in this passage has focussed on
(a) knowledge creation
(b) idea-generation
(c) creativity
(d) individual traits

12. Fostering creativity needs an environment of
(a) decision support systems
(b) idea-nurturing
(c) decision support solutions
(d) alternative individual factors

13. Manual methods for the support of idea-generation, in certain occasions,
(a) are alternatively effective
(b) can be less expensive
(c) do not need a facilitator
(d) require a mix of optimal participants

14. Idea-generation software works as if it is a:
(a) stimulant
(b) knowledge package
(c) user-friendly trainer
(d) climate creator

15. Mental blocks, bouts of procrastination and cyclical thinking patterns can be won when:
(a) innovative companies employ electronic thinking methods
(b) idea-generation software prompts questions
(c) manual methods are removed
(d) individuals acquire a neutral attitude towards the software

16. Level C of the effectiveness of communication is defined as:
(a) channel noise
(b) semantic noise
(c) psychological noise
(d) source noise

17. Recording a television programme on a VCR is an example of:
(a) time-shifting
(b) content reference
(c) mechanical clarity
(d) media synchronisation

18. A good communicator is the one who offers to his audience:
(a) plentiful of information
(b) a good amount of statistics
(c) concise proof
(d) repetition of facts

19. The largest number of newspapers in India is published from the state of:
(a) Kerala (b) Maharashtra
(c) West Bengal (d) Uttar Pradesh

20. Insert the missing number:
8 24 12 ? 18 54
(a) 26 (b) 24
(c) 36 (d) 32

21. January 1, 1995 was Sunday. What day of the week lies on January 1, 1996?
(a) Sunday (b) Monday
(c) Saturday (d) None of these

22. The sum of a positive number and its reciprocal is twice the difference of the number and its reciprocal. The number is:
(a) $\sqrt{2}$ (b) $\frac{1}{\sqrt{2}}$
(c) $\sqrt{3}$ (d) $\frac{1}{\sqrt{3}}$

23. In a certain code, ROUNDS is written as RONUDS. How will PLEASE will be written in the same code:
(a) LPAESE (b) PLAESE
(c) LPAEES (d) PLASEE

24. At what time between 5.30 and 6.00 will the hands of an clock be at right angles?
(a) $43\frac{5}{11}$ min. past 5
(b) $43\frac{7}{11}$ min. past 5
(c) 40 min. past 5
(d) 45 min past 5

25. **Statements:** I All students are ambitious
II All ambitious persons are hard working
Conclusions: (i) All students are hard-working
(ii) All hardly working people are not ambitious
Which of the following is correct?
(a) Only (i) is correct
(b) Only (ii) is correct
(c) Both (i) and (ii) are correct
(d) Neither (i) nor (ii) is correct

26. **Statement:** Most students are intelligent
Conclusions: (i) Some students are intelligent
(ii) All students are not intelligent

Which of the following is implied?
(a) Only (i) is implied
(b) Only (ii) is implied
(c) Both (i) and (ii) are implied
(d) Neither (i) nor (ii) is implied

27. **Statement:** Most labourers are poor
Conclusions: (i) Some labourers are poor
(ii) All labourers are not poor
Which of the following is implied?
(a) Only (i) is implied
(b) Only (ii) is implied
(c) Both (i) and (ii) are implied
(d) Neither (i) nor (ii) is implied

28. Line access and avoidance of collision are the main functions of:
(a) the CPU
(b) the monitor
(c) network protocols
(d) wide area networks

29. In the hypermedia database, information bits are stored in the form of:
(a) Signals (b) Cubes
(c) Nodes (d) Symbols

30. Communications bandwidth that has the highest capacity and is used by microwave, cable and fibre optics lines is known as:
(a) Hyper-link (b) Broadband
(c) Bus width (d) Carrier wave

31. An electronic bill board that has a short text or graphical advertising message is referred to as:
(a) Bulletin (b) Strap
(c) Bridge line (d) Banner

32. Which of the following is not the characteristic of a computer?
(a) Computer is an electrical machine
(b) Computer cannot think of its own
(c) Computer processes information error free
(d) Computer can hold data for any length of time

33. Bitumen is obtained from:
(a) Forests and plants
(b) Kerosene oil
(c) Crude oil
(d) Underground mines

34. Malaria is caused by:
(a) bacterial infection
(b) viral infection
(c) parasitic infection
(d) fungal infection

35. The cloudy nights are warmer compared to clear nights (without clouds) during winter days. This is because:
(a) clouds radiate heat towards the earth
(b) clouds prevent cold wave from the sky, descend on earth
(c) clouds prevent escaping of the heat radiation from the earth
(d) clouds being at great heights from earth absorb heat from the sun and send towards the earth

36. Largest soil group of India is:
(a) Red soil (b) Black soil
(c) Sandy soil (d) Mountain soil

37. Main pollutant of the Indian coastal water is:
(a) oil spill
(b) municipal sewage
(c) industrial effluents
(d) aerosols

38. Human ear is most sensitive to noise in the following frequency ranges:
(a) 1-2 kHz (b) 100-500 Hz
(c) 10-12 kHz (d) 13-16 kHz

39. Which species of chromium is toxic in water:
(a) Cr + 2 (b) Cr + 3
(c) Cr + 6 (d) Cr is non-toxic element

40. Match List I (Dams) with List II (River) in the following:

List I (Dams)	List II (Rivers)
(A) Bhakra	(i) Krishna
(B) Nagarjunasagar	(ii) Damodar
(C) Panchet	(iii) Sutlej
(D) Hirakud	(iv) Bhagirathi
(E) Tehri	(v) Mahanadi

Codes:	A	B	C	D	E
(a)	v	iii	iv	ii	i
(b)	iii	i	ii	v	iv
(c)	i	ii	iv	iii	v
(d)	ii	iii	iv	i	v

41. A negative reaction to a mediated communication is described as:
(a) flak
(b) fragmented feedback
(c) passive response
(d) non-conformity

42. The launch of satellite channel by IGNOU on 26th January 2003 for technological education for the growth and development of distance education is:
(a) Eklavya channel
(b) Gyandarshan channel
(c) Rajrishi channel
(d) None of these

43. Match List I with List II and select the correct answer from the code given below:

List I (Institutions)	List II (Locations)
(A) The Indian Council of Historical Reasearch (ICHR)	(i) Shimla
(B) The Indian Institute of Advanced Studies (IIAS)	(ii) New Delhi
(C) The Indian Council of Philosophical Research (ICPR)	(iii) Banglore
(D) The Central Institute of Coastal Engineering for fisheries	(iv) Lucknow

Codes:	A	B	C	D
(a)	ii	i	iv	iii
(b)	i	ii	iii	iv
(c)	ii	iv	i	iii
(d)	iv	iii	ii	i

44. Which of the following is not a Fundamental Right?
(a) Right to equality
(b) Right against exploitation
(c) Right to freedom of speech and expression
(d) Right of free compulsory education of all children upto the age of 14

45. The Lok-Sabha can be dissolved before the expiry of its normal five year term by:
(a) The Prime Minister
(b) The Speaker of Lok Sabha
(c) The President on the recommendation of the Prime Minister
(d) None of the above

Study the following graph carefully and answer Q.No. 46 to 50 given below it:

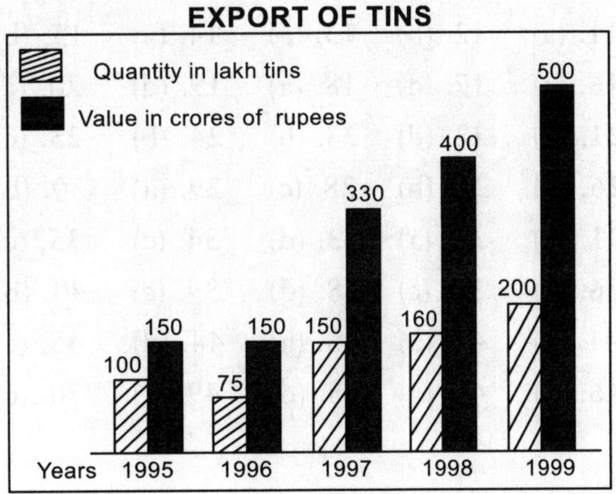

46. In which year the value per tin was minimum?

(a) 1995 (b) 1996
(c) 1998 (d) 1999

47. What was the difference between the tins exported in 1997 and 1998?
(a) 10 (b) 1000
(c) 100000 (d) 1000000

48. What was the approximate percentage increase in export value from 1995 to 1999?
(a) 350 (b) 330.3
(c) 433.3 (d) None of these

49. What was the percentage drop in export quantity from 1995 to 1996?
(a) 75 (b) 50
(c) 25 (d) None of these

50. If in 1998, the tins were exported at the same rate per tin as that in 1997, what would be the value (in crores of rupees) of export in 1998?
(a) 400 (b) 375
(c) 352 (d) 330

ANSWERS

1. (c)	2. (d)	3. (b)	4. (a)	5. (c)
6. (d)	7. (d)	8. (a)	9. (a)	10. (b)
11. (a)	12. (b)	13. (a)	14. (a)	15. (b)
16. (a)	17. (d)	18. (a)	19. (d)	20. (c)
21. (b)	22. (d)	23. (b)	24. (b)	25. (c)
26. (b)	27. (b)	28. (c)	29. (a)	30. (b)
31. (b)	32. (a)	33. (d)	34. (c)	35. (c)
36. (a)	37. (c)	38. (d)	39. (c)	40. (b)
41. (c)	42. (a)	43. (a)	44. (d)	45. (c)
46. (a)	47. (a)	48. (d)	49. (c)	50. (c)

PAPER–II

1. A person may shift from one orderly career progression to another but, when the shifts become frequent and lose direction, the career progression is said to be
(a) Orderly (b) Stagnant
(c) Disorderly (d) None of these

2. Some facts are collected and on the basis of those facts some conclusions in the broader and wider sense are drawn
(i) Deductive method
(ii) Inductive method
(a) Only i (b) Only ii
(c) Both i and ii (d) None of these

3. State true or false
(a) The student's t-distribution obtained by W.S. Gosset was published under the pen name of "Student" in 1908
(b) Gosset was a statistician for a brewery and that the management did not want him to publish his scholarly theoretical work under his real name and bring shame to his employer
(c) The 't' and 'F' distribution are defined in terms of number of degrees of freedom
(d) The number of degree of freedom usually denoted by the Greek symbol ν (read as nu) can be interpreted as the number of useful items of information generated by a sample of given size with respect to the estimation of a given population parameter
(e) All of these

4. Some important applications of the t-distribution is/are
   (i) Test of Hypothesis about the population mean
   (ii) Test of Hypothesis concerning the difference between two means
   (iii) Test of Hypothesis concerning the difference between two means with dependent samples
   (iv) Test of Hypothesis concerning coefficient of correlation
   (a) i, ii, iii, iv (b) i, ii, iii
   (c) i, ii (d) i, iv

5. Who stated that "mode of production determines the character of the social political and intellectual life."?
   (a) M. Page
   (b) Marx and Engels
   (c) M. Weber
   (d) None of these

6. Sampling method could be a disadvantage when
   (i) Bias
   (ii) Lack of representative sample
   (iii) Need for specialized knowledge, difficulties in sticking to sample
   (iv) Impossibility of sampling
   (a) i, ii, iii, iv (b) i, ii, iii
   (c) i, ii (d) i, iv

7. The entire group from which sample is chosen is known as
   (a) The population (b) Universe
   (c) Supply (d) All of these

8. It can be said that the design tells us
   (a) What observation to make
   (b) How to analyze the quantitative representation of the observation
   (c) How to make observation
   (d) All of these

9. State which is/are true
   (a) A research design will always help us in knowing successive stages.
   (b) Research design will help identifying the importance of each step in the whole scheme of things.
   (c) The design help in making the research know as to why is he studying the issue and what types of data will be needed, how data will be found.
   (d) Design will also help in finding out what total time the study is likely to take and what time each step in the study is likely to consume.
   (e) All of these.

10. The design tells us about the universe of the study. It means
   (a) How many cases will be covered?
   (b) What manner will these cases be picked?
   (c) How will cases be identified?
   (d) All of these

11. India's oldest newspaper is
   (a) *Bombay Samachar*
   (b) *Hindustant Times*
   (c) *Times of India*
   (d) None of these

12. One of the earliest examples of interpersonal communication obeying Denis McQuail's model must be between
   (a) Laila and Majnu
   (b) Juliet and Caesar
   (c) Ram and Sita
   (d) Adam and Eve

13. Frying pan of which of the following are considered best for cooking?
   (a) Aluminium (b) Steel
   (c) Iron (d) All of these

14. The boiling ghee or oil acts on utensil
   (i) Melts solder of tin
   (ii) Destroy enamel layer
   (a) Only i (b) Only ii
   (c) Both i and ii (d) None of these

15. The electric frying pan is made of
   (a) Steel (b) Iron
   (c) Enamel (d) Span Steel

16. The roasting of caschewnut bring about
    (a) Browning (b) Taste
    (c) Loss of thiamine (d) All of these
17. Moderate roasting of peanut leads to
    (a) Thiamine loses
    (b) Trypsin inhibitor destroyed
    (c) Improved NV of protein
    (d) All of these
18. Canned fruit juice nutritive value
    (a) 20-40% ascorbic acid lose
    (b) Loss of Vitamin B
    (c) Taste
    (d) All of these
19. State which is/are true
    (a) Raw pack method is suitable for delicate fruits like berries. Large pieces of fruits of apples, pears can also be packed
    (b) In hot pack canning food is heated in syrup, water, steam or extracted juice before being packed into containers
    (c) Hot pack method helps to wilt or shrink some plant tissues and allows closer packing and slightly shortens the processing time
    (d) Acid fruits and tomatoes are processed by putting the containers in boiling water and a pressure canner is used for vegetable meat fish and poultry
    (e) All of these
20. The signs of spoilage apparent in canning can be
    (a) Microorganisms
    (b) Flat sour and hydrogen swell
    (c) Metallic salts and discolouration
    (d) All of these
21. Souring or turning acidic is due to
    (a) Growth of micro-organisms
    (b) Micro-organisms attack carbohydrates
    (c) Produce acid
    (d) All of these
22. Made by boiling fruit pulp with sufficient quantity of sugar to a reasonably thick consistency till it forms enough to hold the fruit tissues in position.
    (a) Jam (b) Jelly
    (c) Murabba (d) None of these
23. The technique to prevent DB developing into CD. What the psychologist does is
    (a) Teach new social skills
    (b) Assist in solving social conflict
    (c) Parents are trained for effective discipline
    (d) All of these
24. A study conducted on ADHD in 1994 by Streissguth pinpointed which of the following factor as being the cause of ADHD
    (i) low birth weight
    (ii) Oxygen deprivation at birth
    (iii) Alcohol Consumption by expectant mother
    (iv) Poverty.
    (a) i, ii, iii, iv (b) i, ii, iii
    (c) i, ii (d) i, iv
25. State which is/are true
    (a) Radio provides the communicator with the opportunity to reach local communities and audiences segmented by age
    (b) Radio is low-cost medium
    (c) Billboard provide an opportunity for repetitive exposure of a well-executed but static message
    (d) Posters are miniature billboards whose main advantage are lower cost and greater flexibility of placement
    (e) All of these
26. Television is medium with its own psychological and emotional appeal able to transcend barriers of

(i) Time (ii) Place
(iii) Disciplines (iv) Personalities
(a) i, ii, iii, iv (b) i, ii, iii
(c) i, ii (d) i, iv

27. A person spends about .... of his active time communicating.
(a) 20-30% (b) 30-40%
(c) 45-50% (d) 50-60%

28. In which order does a person spend his time communicating
(i) Listening (ii) Speaking
(iii) Reading (iv) Writing
(a) i, ii, iii, iv (b) i, ii, iii
(c) i, ii (d) i, iv

29. When using colour in a poster
(i) Bright attractive
(ii) Highlight centre core
(iii) Not more than 3 colour
(iv) Highlight prominent word
(a) i, ii, iii, iv (b) i, ii, iii
(c) i, ii (d) i, iv

30. State which is/are true
(a) Interpersonal exchanges can be used by tricksters and common to throw wool over people's eyes.
(b) Only the ones who have our trust and have proved themselves are allowed to cross the barriers of an intimate relationship.
(c) Communication does not generally imply intimacy nor does constant gazing into each other's eyes.
(d) In European cultures it is considered bad manners and bad communication to get too close.
(e) All of these.

31. Buddhism has four social emotions that should guide interpersonal communication
(i) Metta (loving kindness)
(ii) Karuna (compassion)
(iii) Murdita (sympathetic joy)
(iv) Upekkha (equanimity)
(a) i, ii, iii, iv (b) i, ii, iii
(c) i, ii (d) i, iv

32. An unfocused interaction is usually all set off by
(a) Sound
(b) Smell
(c) Eye contact
(d) Physical closeness

33. Professional discussions rarely go beyond
(a) Phatic stage
(b) Personal stage
(c) Intimate stage
(d) None of these

34. Robert Shuter states "In this stage communications reveal their innermost thoughts and feelings—their fear and joys, weaknesses and strengths. The stage is
(a) Phatic stage
(b) Personal stage
(c) Intimate stage
(d) None of these

35. The degree of directness and intimacy in group communication depends upon
(a) Size
(b) Place of meeting
(c) Relationship between members
(d) Group leader

36. The organization of men will involve
(i) Staff
(ii) Student
(iii) Boards of Management
(iv) Experts in society
(a) i, ii, iii, iv (b) i, ii, iii
(c) i, ii (d) i, iv

37. What does it indicate in administration "That affects the decision, gives the signal to act indicates what action is to be and when it is to start and stop. It is authority on the move."?
(a) Organization (b) Direction
(c) Coordination (d) None of these

38. Parents and other adults may also guide a child by structuring his environment in such a way as to provide certain kinds of
   (i) Experiences
   (ii) Incentives
   (iii) Satisfaction
   (iv) Reinforcements
   (a) i, ii, iii, iv (b) i, ii, iii
   (c) i, ii (d) i, iv

39. The need for competent and understanding adult-guidance is often increased during critical periods of development for example.
   (i) Child starts school
   (ii) Child is scolded
   (iii) Approaches other adults
   (iv) Approaches adolescence
   (a) i, ii, iii, iv (b) i, ii, iii
   (c) i, ii (d) i, iv

40. We take it for granted that a child needs help in learning to read and work arithmetic problems, but we are less likely to realize that he also needs guidance in
   (i) Learning non-academic skills
   (ii) Developing emotional competencies
   (iii) Developing social competencies
   (iv) Acquiring sound value system
   (a) i, ii, iii, iv (b) i, ii, iii
   (c) i, ii (d) i, iv

41. Many discipline problems involve
   (i) Angry feelings
   (ii) Angry acts
   (a) Only (i) (b) Only (ii)
   (c) Both (i) and (ii) (d) None of these

42. Most of the curriculum revision attempted so far has been of an adhoc character—not generally preceded by
   (i) Careful research
   (ii) Not based on adequate expertise
   (iii) Preparation of learning materials
   (iv) Orientation of teachers
   (a) i, ii, iii, iv (b) i, ii, iii
   (c) i, ii (d) i, iv

43. Which of the following is/are true?
   (i) Our model of curriculum theory must include an element of true—awareness of past, future.
   (ii) While, making curriculum we have to take into account cultural time-lag.
   (iii) The curriculum theorist builds a theory which is relevant to a particular kind of social situation—which change, a change which is considered a good thing.
   (iv) The three interacting dimensions of curriculum—content teaching methods and purpose—gives operational curriculum.
   (a) i, ii, iii, iv (b) i, ii, iii
   (c) i, ii (d) i, iv

44. Which of the following is/are true?
   (i) The process by which individuals learn the culture of their society is known as socialization
   (ii) Primary socialization probably the important aspect of the socialization process takes place during infancy usually within the family
   (iii) Socialization is confined to growing up years
   (iv) Other important agencies of socialization include the educational system the occupational group and the peer group
   (a) i, ii, iii, iv (b) i, ii, iii
   (b) i, ii (d) i, iv

45. Which of the following processes are fundamental to the equilibrium of the social system an order in society?
   (i) Socialization (ii) Rationalization
   (iii) Language (iv) Social Control
   (a) i, ii, v, iv (b) i, ii, iii
   (c) i, ii (d) i, iv

46. "Socialization will mean the process of inducting the individual into the social and cultural world of making him a particular member in society and its various groups and inducting him to accept the norms and values of that society—Socialization is definitely a matter of learning and not of biological inheritance." This definition is given by
(a) Maclver (b) Kimball Young
(c) Green (d) Lundberg

47. It is now possible to set up standards to know what to anticipate in the development level of a given individual at any chronological age by assessing
(i) age-height
(ii) age-weight
(iii) mental age
(iv) social-development age scales
(a) i, ii, iii, iv (b) i, ii, iii
(c) i, ii (d) i, iv

48. Individual differences are significant because they are responsible for individuality in personality make up. Individuality
(i) makes people interesting
(ii) social progress possible
(iii) makes better adjustment
(iv) gives emotional stability
(a) i, ii, iii, iv (b) i, ii, iii
(c) i, ii (d) i, iv

49. Stewing method cooking in meat preparation
(i) Longtime
(ii) Temperature below boiling point
(iii) Protein not coagulated
(iv) Extracts mix with gravy
(a) i, ii, iii, iv (b) i, ii, iii
(c) i, ii (d) i, iv

50. Poultry can be preserved and stored
(a) Canning
(b) Dehydration and Chilling
(c) Freezing
(d) All of these

ANSWERS

1. (c)	2. (b)	3. (e)	4. (a)	5. (b)
6. (a)	7. (d)	8. (d)	9. (e)	10. (d)
11. (a)	12. (d)	13. (d)	14. (c)	15. (d)
16. (d)	17. (d)	18. (d)	19. (e)	20. (d)
21. (d)	22. (a)	23. (d)	24. (b)	25. (e)
26. (a)	27. (d)	28. (a)	29. (a)	30. (e)
31. (a)	32. (c)	33. (b)	34. (c)	35. (a)
36. (a)	37. (b)	38. (d)	39. (d)	40. (a)
41. (c)	42. (a)	43. (a)	44. (a)	45. (d)
46. (b)	47. (a)	48. (c)	49. (a)	50. (d)

JUNE–2005

Note: This paper contains fifty (50) objective type questions, each question carrying two (2) marks. All questions are compulsory.

PAPER–II

1. V.P. Acharya Narendra Deo committee in 1953 stated with regards to examinations
   (i) Monthly, quarterly, half-early examinations
   (ii) Internal examiner for assessment
   (iii) Grade system
   (iv) One language formula
   (a) i, ii, iii, iv (b) i, ii, iii
   (c) i, ii (d) i, iv

2. Math the following:
   List I
   (A) Z^2 (princed as chi-square test)
   (B) Z^2 is a random variable
   (C) The exact shape of Z^2 distribution depends upon
   (D) Most widely used non para-metric test in statistical work
   (E) With the help of Z^2 test we can know
   List II
   (i) That cannot assume negative values
   (ii) Is based on Z^2 distribution which was first used by Karl Person in 1900
   (iii) Z^2 test
   (iv) Whether a given discrepancy between theory and observation can be attributed to chance or inadequacy of the theory
   (v) The number of degrees of freedom

Codes:	A	B	C	D	E
(a)	ii	i	v	iii	iv
(b)	i	v	iii	iv	ii
(c)	v	iv	i	ii	iii
(d)	iv	i	iii	v	ii

3. This study determines frequency with which something occurs with something else:
   (a) Diagnostic (b) Experimental
   (c) Descriptive (d) None of these

4. Studies which accurately portray the characteristics of a particular situation or groups or individual are
   (a) Exploratory (b) Descriptive
   (c) Experimental (d) None of these

5. The basis of sampling is on the assumptions
   (a) Underlying homogeneity amidst complexity
   (b) Possibility of representative selection
   (c) Absolute accuracy not essential
   (d) All of these

6. Sampling becomes the best alternative in case of social studies due to
   (i) Vastness of the population
   (ii) Difference of contacting people
   (iii) High refuse rate
   (iv) Difficulties of ascertaining the universe making sampling
   (a) i, ii, iii, iv (b) i, ii, iii
   (c) i, ii (d) i, iv

7. The list of advantages of sampling could be
   (i) Saving of time, money
   (ii) Detailed study

(iii) Accuracy of result, administrative convenience
(iv) Impossibility of the use of census method
(a) i, ii, iii, iv (b) i, ii, iii
(c) i, ii (d) i, iv

8. State which is/are true
(a) The technology oriented media has come to influence every form of communication
(b) The mass media has interlaced media and intertwined itself inextricably with the social fabric by weaving new designs and patterns of thought by taking a yarn or a fabric every aspect of our personal life
(c) It is aptly said that the children of yesteryears remained cocooned in an adult world
(d) Technology and the rest of society are intimately related
(e) All of these

9. What controls technology
(i) Economics
(ii) Political institutions
(iii) Social change
(iv) Social control
(a) i, ii, iii, iv (b) i, ii, iii
(c) i, ii (d) i, iv

10. The loss of vitamins during dehydration is affected by
(a) Method of drying
(b) Stability of the vitamin
(c) Effect of air and heat
(d) All of these

11. State which is/are true in case of Lathyrism Acton (1922) stated
(a) First stage characterized by weakness of the lower limbs with spasticity of leg muscles
(b) Flexion of the knee is more marked and there is a certain amount of inversion of foot with a tendency to walk on toes
(c) Person can walk only with the help of crutches of sticks
(d) Walking becomes impossible
(e) All of these

12. The process in which small new shoots come out of pulses or cereals certain controlled conditions thereby improving their nutrient content is
(a) Fermentation (b) Germination
(c) Agriculture (d) None of these

13. The germination takes longer when
(a) In air tight container
(b) Dried
(c) Temp is low
(d) None of these

14. Toasting as a method of cooking has the benefit
(i) Taste
(ii) Trypsin destroyed
(iii) Growth inhibitors destroyed
(iv) Better protein NV
(a) i, ii, iii, iv (b) i, ii, iii
(c) i, ii (d) i, iv

15. The affect of emulsifying agents on products
(a) Volume
(b) Uniformity and fineness
(c) Keeping quality
(d) All of these

16. Emulsifiers are also known as
(i) Surfactants
(ii) Surface action agents
(iii) Homogenitizer
(iv) Stabilisers
(a) i, ii, iii, iv (b) i, ii, iii
(c) i, ii (d) i, iv

17. Generally salt or sugar is added to foods being canned. It depends on
(a) Degree of sweetness required
(b) Type of fruit

(c) Acidity of fruit
(d) All of these

18. Jelmeter is a machine or an instrument for
(a) Measuring the pH of food
(b) Measuring the temperature of food
(c) Determines pectin content of juices
(d) None of these

19. The method of canning includes
(a) Raw pack method
(b) Hot pack canning
(c) Hot pack method
(d) All of these

20. Psychological factors contributing ADHD include
(i) Parental intrusiveness
(ii) Overestimation
(iii) Rejection
(iv) Pampering
(a) i, ii, iii, iv (b) i, ii, iii,
(c) i, ii (d) i, iv

21. The cause of phobia could be
(a) Social
(b) Emotional
(c) Classical conditioning
(d) None of these

22. A child with learning disabilities is likely to have difficulties with
(i) Math
(ii) Reading
(iii) Illegible handwriting
(iv) English
(a) i, ii, iii, iv (b) i, ii, iii
(c) i, ii (d) i, iv

23. An Italian Engineer was the first to demonstrate the actual transmission and reception of message. He was
(a) G. Marconi (b) Hartoz
(c) Maxwell (d) None of these

24. Who stated "Radio is not addition to education. Radio is not something to be placed on top of education. Rather, radio is education."?
(a) Reynolds R.G. (b) George Watson
(c) F. Wittis (d) None of these

25. Radio is a means of ______ the material of textbooks.
(i) Supplementing (ii) Vitalizing
(iii) Correlating (iv) Modernizing
(a) i, ii, iii, iv (b) i, ii, iii
(c) i, ii (d) i, iv

26. State which is/are true
(a) Blackboard is helpful in meeting and group discussion
(b) For village programmes 30″ × 40″ in size best
(c) Blackboard can be painted black or green
(d) The lighting arrangement should not cause glaze
(e) All of these

27. In the communication process the sender may
(i) Speak (ii) Act
(iii) Draw (iv) Write
(a) i, ii, iii, iv (b) i, ii, iii
(c) i, ii (d) i, iv

28. Receiver receives communication by
(a) Listening (b) Observing
(c) Reading (d) All of these

29. Visual take the forms of
(i) Picture (ii) Blue-prints
(iii) Posters (iv) Charts
(a) i, ii, iii, iv (b) i, ii, iii
(c) i, ii (d) i, iv

30. Numbers and numerical language useful for decision-making and comparative judgement could be
(i) Mathematics (ii) Statistics
(iii) Abacus (iv) Cardinals
(a) i, ii, iii, iv (b) i, ii, iii
(c) i, ii (d) i, iv

31. Face-to-face communication between two persons
   (i) Highest form of communication
   (ii) Persuasive and influential
   (iii) Interplay of word and gestures
   (iv) Involve all five senses
   (a) i, ii, iii, iv (b) i, ii, iii
   (c) i, ii (d) i, iv

32. Curriculum is "all the learning which is planned and guided by the school, whether it is carried on in groups or individually, inside or outside the school." According to this definition which are the interrelated components?
   (i) Curriculum objectives
   (ii) Knowledge
   (iii) Learning experience
   (iv) Curriculum evaluation
   (a) i, ii, iii, iv (b) i, ii, iii
   (c) i, ii (d) i, iv

33. Professor Bantock was helpful to curriculum builders when he said that the ultimate purpose of education is the clarification of the world of nature including
   (i) The world of form
   (ii) The world of man
   (iii) Internal world of sensation
   (iv) Reflection of emotion and cognition.
   (a) i, ii, iii, iv (b) i, ii, iii
   (c) i, ii (d) i, iv

34. Feelings have to be
   (i) Identified
   (ii) Clarified
   (iii) Accepted
   (iv) Worked through
   (a) i, ii, iii, iv (b) i, ii, iii
   (c) i, ii (d) i, iv

35. Acts may have to be
   (a) Controlled (b) Limited
   (c) Redirected (d) All of these

36. Children grow and function best in a clearly structured environment-one which is orderly and consistent. Key elements of structure involve
   (a) Clearly defined standards and limits
   (b) Adequately defined roles
   (c) Established method of handling
   (d) All of these

37. Who described interview at the heart of counseling process to which other techniques are contributory?
   (a) Mathur (b) Ruth Strang
   (c) Hilgard (d) None of these

38. The two things to be avoided during counselling session
   (i) Moralizing (iii) Humour
   (ii) Compliment (iv) Condemnation
   (a) i, ii, iii, iv (b) i, ii, iii
   (c) i, ii (d) i, iv

39. State which is/are true
   (a) In a democratic set up, the authority of law is the final controlling power an authority that has the sanction ol people
   (b) Direction requires a very high level of competence knowledge, qualities of leadership, foresight, and imagination
   (c) Direction in a democratic set-up stands for distribution and decentralization of authority
   (d) Much of the dissatisfaction mounting in educational system is due to lack of coordination between units
   (e) All of them

40. Bring things together in harmonious relationships to the end that they would function together effectively
   (a) Co-ordinates (b) Control
   (c) Organisation (d) None of these

41. Lack of coordination brings about
   (a) Conflict (b) Friction
   (c) Overlapping (d) Duplications

(a) i, ii, iii, iv (b) i, ii, iii
(c) i, ii (d) i, iv

42. Included in the agencies of socialization are
(a) Family (b) Peers, school
(c) Organizations (d) Media
(a) i, ii, iii, iv (b) i, ii, iii
(c) i, ii (d) i, iv

43. Secondary socialization has its beginning at
(a) Later stage of childhood
(b) Adolescence
(c) Maturity
(d) None of these

44. "Socialization is the process by which the child acquires a cultural content along with selfhood and personality", it is stated by
(a) Green
(b) Horton and Hunt
(c) Lundberg
(d) None of these

45. Which of the following are factor in socialization?
(i) Unitation (ii) Suggestions
(iii) Identification (iv) Language
(a) i, ii, iii, iv (b) i, ii, iii
(c) i, ii (d) i, iv

46. Preservation and fish storage method include
(i) Canning and chilling
(ii) Freezing and curing
(iii) Pickling or smoking
(iv) Salting and drying
(a) i, ii, iii, iv (b) i, ii, iii
(c) i, ii (d) i, iv

47. Meat is coated with bread besan or maida because
(i) To give enhance taste
(ii) Lessen the effect of high temp
(iii) Lessen fat absorption
(iv) Shelf life
(a) i, ii, iii, iv (b) i, ii, iii
(c) i, ii (d) i, iv

48. In which of the following Parget's theory underestimates the importance
(a) Cognitive abilities
(b) Importance of language
(c) Importance of social interactions
(d) All of these

49. The attachment is measured by
(a) Mother-child relationship
(b) Strange situation test
(c) Child's reaction
(d) None of these

50. Attachment is influenced by which of the following factor(s) on infant
(a) Infant's temperament
(b) Contact comfort
(c) Parents responsiveness to needs
(d) All of these

ANSWERS

1. (c)	2. (a)	3. (a)	4. (b)	5. (d)
6. (a)	7. (a)	8. (e)	9. (c)	10. (d)
11. (e)	12. (b)	13. (c)	14. (a)	15. (d)
16. (c)	17. (d)	18. (c)	19. (d)	20. (c)
21. (c)	22. (a)	23. (a)	24. (b)	25. (a)
26. (e)	27. (a)	28. (d)	29. (a)	30. (c)
31. (a)	32. (a)	33. (a)	34. (a)	35. (d)
36. (d)	37. (b)	38. (d)	39. (e)	40. (a)
41. (a)	42. (a)	43. (a)	44. (a)	45. (a)
46. (a)	47. (c)	48. (d)	49. (b)	50. (d)

PRACTICE PAPERS

MOCK TEST–1
PAPER–I

1. A teacher is called the leader of the class because
   (a) he is autocratic emperor of his class
   (b) he masters the art of oratory like a political leader
   (c) he is a maker of the future of his students
   (d) he belongs to a recognised teachers' union
2. The aim of introducing career courses in schools and colleges is to
   (a) increase G.K. in students
   (b) develop the ability to make the intelligent choice of jobs
   (c) provide professional knowledge to students
   (d) All of the above
3. The most effective attribute for a teacher is
   (a) Teaching skills (b) Knowledge
   (c) Feedback (d) Management
4. Those teachers are preferred most by students who
   (a) are themselves disciplined
   (b) give important questions before examination
   (c) dictate notes in the class
   (d) can clear their difficulties regarding subject-matter
5. The qualities of a teacher is/are
   (i) He must not give any false promise
   (ii) He must not have any bad habits
   (iii) He should be mentally and physically fit
   (iv) He must not be superstitious about his class and students
   (a) (iii), (iv) and (ii)
   (b) (iv), (i) and (ii)
   (c) (i), (iii) and (iv)
   (d) All of the above
6. A teacher is more effective who can
   (a) motivate students to learn
   (b) control the class
   (c) correct the assignments carefully
   (d) give more information in less time
7. A teacher ought to know the problems prevalent in the field of education because
   (a) he can tell the government about it
   (b) with this knowledge, he can have information about education
   (c) he can tell about the same to another teacher
   (d) only he can do something about solving them
8. We can judge the quality of a research by the
   (a) experience of researcher
   (b) relevance of research
   (c) depth of the research
   (d) methodology followed in conducting the research
9. The theory or model developed through the fundamental research to the actual solution of the problems is applied in
   (a) educational research
   (b) action research
   (c) applied research
   (d) basic research

10. A write-up based on studies of the census data of a given area is called
(a) Research paper (b) Article
(c) Research report (d) Thesis

Direction: (11-16) Study the following passage and give answer to the questions based on it.

Knowledge creation in many cases requires creativity and idea generation. This is especially important in generating alternative decision support solutions. Some people believe that an individual's creative ability stems primarily from personality traits such as inventiveness, independence, individuality, enthusiasm, and flexibility. However, several studies have found that creativity is not so much a function of individual traits as was once believed, and that individual creativity can be learned and improved. This understanding has led innovative companies to recognise that the key to fostering creativity may be the development of an idea-nurturing work environment. Idea-generation methods and techniques, to be used by individuals or in groups, are consequently being developed. Manual methods for supporting idea generation, such as brain-storming in a group, can be very successful in certain situations. However, in other situations, such an approach is either not economically feasible or not possible. For example, manual methods in group creativity sessions will not work or will not be effective when: (a) there is no time to conduct a proper idea-generation session; (b) there is a poor facilitator (or no facilitator at all; (c) it is too expensive to conduct an idea-generation session; (d) the subject matter is too sensitive for a face-to-face session; or (e) there are not enough participants, the mix of participants is not optimal, or there is no climate for idea generation. In such cases, computerised idea-generation methods have been tried, with frequent success. Idea-generation software is designed to help stimulate a single user or a group to produce new ideas, options and choices. The user does all the work, but the software encourages and pushes, something like a personal trainer. Although idea-generation software is still relatively new, there are several packages on the market. Various approaches are used by idea-generating software to increase the flow of ideas to the user. Idea Fisher, for example, has an associate lexicon of the English language that cross-references words and phrases. These associative links, based on analogies and metaphors, make it easy for the user to be fed words related to a given theme. Some software packages use questions to prompt the user towards new, unexplored patterns of thought. This helps users to break out of cyclical thinking patterns, conquer mental blocks, or deal with bouts of procrastination.

11. The author, in this passage has focused on
(a) individual traits
(b) knowledge creation
(c) creativity
(d) idea-generation

12. Idea-generation software works as if it is a
(a) user-friendly trainer
(b) stimulant
(c) climate creator
(d) knowledge package

13. Which among the following personality traits is not believed to be a factor contributing to an individual's creative ability?
(a) Flexibility (b) Individuality
(c) Sophistication (d) Enthusiasm

14. In certain occasions, manual methods for the support of idea-generation
(a) can be less expensive
(b) do not need a facilitator
(c) require a mix of optimal participants
(d) are alternatively effective

15. Mental blocks, bouts of procrastination and cyclical thinking patterns can be won when
    (a) idea-generation software prompts questions
    (b) individuals acquire a neutral attitude towards the software
    (c) manual methods are removed
    (d) innovative companies employ electronic thinking methods
16. Fostering creativity needs an environment of
    (a) decision support systems
    (b) alternative individual factors
    (c) idea-nurturing
    (d) decision support solutions
17. For controlling noise in a classroom, the best method of communication is
    (a) remaining calm and just looking at student
    (b) saying 'don't talk'
    (c) continue teaching without caring for noise
    (d) raising one's voice above students voice
18. In India, Education TV was first introduced in the year
    (a) 1978 (b) 1959
    (c) 1987 (d) 1998
19. The failure of the teacher to communicate his ideas well to students may result into:
    I. Classroom indiscipline.
    II. Decrease in attendance in class.
    III. Loss of student's interest in class.
    (a) II only (b) III only
    (c) I only (d) All of these
20. Visualisation in the instructional process cannot increase
    (a) curiosity and concentration
    (b) interest and motivation
    (c) stress and boredom
    (d) retention and adaptation
21. Communication helps in
    (a) entertainment
    (b) integration of country
    (c) cultural promotion
    (d) All of these
22. "Because you deserve to know" is the punchline used by
    (a) *Hindustan Times*
    (b) *The Telegraph*
    (c) *The Times of India*
    (d) *India Today*
23. Find the odd man out from the following groups of letters.
    (a) UlmnE (b) AbcdE
    (c) ApqrL (d) IfghO
24. The ambitious computerisation program of the Government of India aimed at connecting 60,000 government schools through internet is known as
    (a) Vidya Vahini (b) Gyan Vahini
    (c) Kalpana project (d) Vidya Vani
25. Find the wrong number in the following sequence.
    225, 336, 447, 557, 669, 771
    (a) 669 (b) 557
    (c) 336 (d) 771
26. In this question two words are given which have certain relationship followed by four paired lettered words. Select the paired words, that has the same relation as original pair.
    ROOF : FOUNDATION
    (a) Plateau : Valley
    (b) Peak : Valley
    (c) Mountain : Grassland
    (d) Hill : Mountain
27. "Communication is a verbal process by which we understand each other and reduce uncertainty through the use of symbol." Who is the author of this statement?

(a) David K. Barlo
(b) Dance
(c) P.S.K. Serichavenko
(d) K.J. Newman

28. Find out the missing number:
8 24 12 ? 18 54
(a) 28 (b) 32
(c) 36 (d) 38

29. A D C F
C F E H
O R ? ?
(a) JK (b) RN
(c) SU (d) QT

30. 3, 12, 27, 48, 75, ?, 147.
(a) 111 (b) 108
(c) 117 (d) 122

31. In this question four words have been given, out of which three are alike in some manner and the fourth one is different. Choose the odd one out.
(a) Epigraphy (b) Ecology
(c) Archaeology (d) Palaeontology

32. Which of the following figures will represent the right relationship between, societies, societies who run schools, DPS society.

(a) 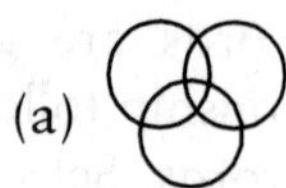 (b) 

(c)  (d) 

33. **Statements:**
I. All students are ambitious.
II. All ambitious persons are hard working.
Conclusions:
(i) All students are hard-working.
(ii) All hardly working people are not ambitious.
Which of the following is correct?
(a) Only (i) is correct
(b) Only (ii) is correct
(c) Both (i) and (ii) are correct
(d) Neither (i) nor (ii) is correct

34. In a certain code language:
'pit dit mit' means: 'Reena went to Delhi'.
'dit ket set' means: 'Delhi is closing'.
'mit set un' means: 'Reena' is educated.
Then what is the code for 'went'?
(a) dit (b) mit
(c) pit (d) None of these

35. EDITOR : MAGAZINE
Choose the pair from the answer choices that best expresses the relationship similar to that expressed by the question pair.
(a) Novel : Writer
(b) Director : Film
(c) Poem : Poet
(d) Chair : Carpenter

36. Should education in India be made free?
Arguments:
I. Yes, this is the only way to improve the level of literacy.
II. No, this would add already heavy burden on the exchequer.
(a) Only argument I is strong
(b) Only argument II is strong
(c) Both the arguments are strong
(d) None of these

Direction: (37-41) Study the table and answer the questions:

Export of Pulses and Import of Onion (in ₹ crores)

Year	Export of Pulses (in ₹ crores)	Import of Onion (in ₹ crores)
1998-99	44	58
1999-00	45	50
2000-01	60	54

2001-02	56	60
2002-03	92	68
2003-04	100	78
2004-05	68	60

37. During which year there was a maximum fall in export?
(a) 2004-05 (b) 2001-02
(c) 2003-04 (d) None of these

38. The percent of increase of imports in 2003-04 over 2002-03 is
(a) 14.9% (b) 14.7%
(c) 18.4% (d) 18.9%

39. In 1999-2000, the ratio of export to the import is
(a) 19:11 (b) 11:9
(c) 13:17 (d) 9:10

40. During which year there was maximum increase in import over its preceding year?
(a) 2003-04 (b) 2000-01
(c) 2001-02 (d) 2002-03

41. During which year there was minimum increase in import over its preceding year?
(a) 2003-04 (b) 2002-03
(c) 2001-02 (d) None of these

42. The sum of a positive number and its reciprocal is twice the difference of the number and its reciprocal. The number is:
(a) $\sqrt{3}$ (b) $\sqrt{2}$
(c) $\frac{1}{\sqrt{2}}$ (d) $\frac{1}{\sqrt{3}}$

43. Which one of the following states has the maximum number of Wildlife Sanctuaries (National Park and Sanctuaries)?
(a) Madhya Pradesh
(b) Rajasthan
(c) Uttar Pradesh
(d) West Bengal

Directions: (44-48) Answer the following questions based on the graph given below:

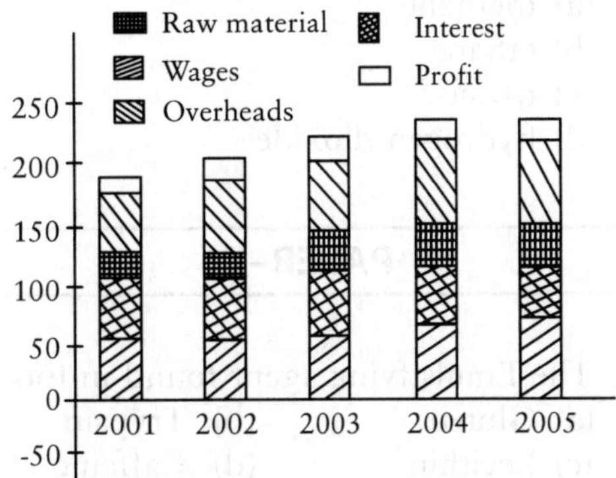

44. Which component of the cost of production has remained almost unchanged over the period 2001-05?
(a) Wages (b) Interest
(c) Raw material (d) Overheads

45. In which year was the increase in raw material maximum?
(a) 2004 (b) 2002
(c) 2003 (d) 2001

46. What percent of costs did the profits form over the period?
(a) 7% (b) 5%
(c) 2% (d) 1%

47. In which period was the change in profit maximum?
(a) 2002-03 (b) 2001-02
(c) 2004-05 (d) 2003-04

48. If the interest component is not included in the total cost calculation, which year would show the maximum profit per unit cost?
(a) 2001 (b) 2002
(c) 2003 (d) 2005

49. How many types of emergencies have been envisaged by the constitution?
(a) One (b) Two
(c) Three (d) Four

50. Photocopying and other electrical equipments produce
    (a) methane
    (b) ethane
    (c) ozone
    (d) hydrogen dioxide

PAPER–II

1. The Emulsifying agent found in food is
   (a) Gluten (b) Trypsin
   (c) Lecithin (d) Caffeine
2. Students arrange books on their desk in an order as per subjects in Time Table is
   (a) change in hand and body motion.
   (b) change in work, storage space and equipment.
   (c) change in production process.
   (d) change in raw materials.
3. What is the primary reason for blanching food?
   (a) Cleans the food
   (b) Prevents pest infestation
   (c) Inactivates enzymes in food
   (d) Prevents food from drying
4. Strict restriction of carbohydrates is not done in a diabetic diet because it can lead to
   (a) Constipation (b) Glycos uria
   (c) Ketosis (d) Steatorrhoea
5. Which of the following statements is an example of a causal statement?
   (a) Both boys and girls participate in sports activities.
   (b) The incidence of childhood diseases decreases as the adolescent years approach.
   (c) Young children may talk out loud without realizing it.
   (d) When a woman in the first trimester of pregnancy contracts rubella, she may give birth to a deaf and blind baby.
6. Which of the following does not represent Kasuti Embroidery?
   (a) Menthi (b) Aari
   (c) Gavanti (d) Murgi
7. ABC of Poster
   (a) Attractive, Brief, Clear
   (b) Attention, Brief, Clarity
   (c) Attractive, Bold, Clear
   (d) Attractive, Bold, Colourful
8. Chi-square test is used
   (a) When there are only two groups for comparison
   (b) When the data is in frequencies
   (c) To check accuracy of data
   (d) When there are three or more groups for comparison
9. Which of the following is not a design repeat?
   (a) Drop (b) Mirror
   (c) Rotary (d) Satin
10. HDL is synthesized and secreted from
    (a) Pancreas (b) Liver
    (c) Kidneys (d) Muscles
11. Arrange constituent processes of observational learning in correct sequence:
    (i) Production (ii) Motivation
    (iii) Retention (iv) Attention
    Codes:
    (a) (iii), (iv), (i) and (ii)
    (b) (iv), (iii), (i) and (ii)
    (c) (ii), (i), (iii) and (iv)
    (d) (i), (ii), (iii) and (iv)
12. Write the steps of extension educational process in sequence:
    (i) Objectives (ii) Teaching
    (iii) Evaluation (iv) Situation
    (v) Reconsideration
    Codes:
    (a) (iv), (i), (ii), (iii), (v)
    (b) (iv), (i), (ii), (v), (iii)
    (c) (v), (iii), (iv), (ii), (i)
    (d) (iii), (ii), (i), (iv), (v)

13. Give the correct sequence for applying the following in a garment:
(A) Interlining (B) Interfacing
(C) Underlining (D) Lining
Codes:
(a) (A), (B), (C), (D) (b) (B), (C), (A), (D)
(c) (C), (D), (B), (A) (d) (D), (A), (C), (B)

14. Language development in children is promoted through:
(i) Story telling
(ii) Conversation
(iii) Social participation
(iv) Solitary play
Codes:
(a) (i) and (iii) are correct.
(b) (ii) and (iii) are correct.
(c) (i), (ii) and (iii) are correct.
(d) (ii), (iii) and (iv) are correct.

15. Correct the sequence for the preparation of screen for printing.
(i) Tracing the design and application of printing ink.
(ii) Exposure to Sunlight/Artificial light.
(iii) Coating with emulsion and drying.
(iv) Washing the screen.
Codes:
(a) (ii), (iii), (i), (iv) (b) (i), (ii), (iv), (iii)
(c) (i), (iii), (ii), (iv) (d) (ii), (i), (iii), (iv)

16. Arrange in the right sequence the stages of sugar cookery.
(i) Firm ball (ii) Soft crack
(iii) Thread (iv) Brown liquid
(v) Clear liquid
Codes:
(a) (i), (iii), (ii), (iv), (v)
(b) (iii), (i), (ii), (v), (iv)
(c) (ii), (iv), (v), (i), (iii)
(d) (iv), (v), (i), (ii), (iii)

17. Which of the following equipments are not used in the kitchen?
(A) Oven (B) Cooking range
(C) Tally machine (D) Baine mar
(E) Blender (F) Potato peeler
Codes:
(a) (A) and (D) (b) (A) and (C)
(c) (C) and (D) (d) (E) and (F)

18. Give the sequential involvement of enzymes for the digestion of food in the GIT.
(A) Iso maltase (B) Pepsin
(C) Ptylin (D) Amylase
Codes:
(a) (A), (B), (D), (C) (b) (C), (B), (D), (A)
(c) (D), (A), (B), (C) (d) (B), (A), (C), (D)

19. Match the following in List I with List II:
List I
(A) Use of goods and services
(B) Handling money
(C) Income generation
(D) Values
List II
(i) Parker (ii) Entrepreneur
(iii) Standard of living (iv) Budget

Codes:	**A**	**B**	**C**	**D**
(a)	(iii)	(iv)	(ii)	(i)
(b)	(i)	(ii)	(iii)	(iv)
(c)	(ii)	(i)	(iv)	(iii)
(d)	(iv)	(iii)	(ii)	(i)

20. The most appropriate statistical test for analysing qualitative data is
(i) Pearson's r
(ii) Sign test
(iii) Kruskal-Wallis test
(iv) F-test
Codes:
(a) Both (i) and (ii) are correct
(b) Both (iii) and (iv) are correct
(c) Both (i) and (iii) are correct
(d) Both (ii) and (iii) are correct

21. Match the foods in List I with its rich nutrients in List II:
List I (Food) **List II (Nutrients)**
(A) Papaya (i) Iron
(B) Orange (ii) Calcium

(C) Dates		(iii) Vitamin C		
(D) Ragi		(iv) Vitamin A		
Codes:	**A**	**B**	**C**	**D**
(a)	(i)	(ii)	(iii)	(iv)
(b)	(ii)	(iii)	(iv)	(i)
(c)	(iv)	(iii)	(i)	(ii)
(d)	(iii)	(ii)	(iv)	(i)

22. Match List I with List II:

List I

(A) Wale (B) Weft
(C) Warp (D) Courses

List II

(i) Series of loops extending crosswise
(ii) Longitudinal yarns
(iii) Crosswise yarns
(iv) Column loops parallel to length

Codes:	**A**	**B**	**C**	**D**
(a)	(i)	(iv)	(iii)	(ii)
(b)	(ii)	(i)	(iv)	(iii)
(c)	(iv)	(iii)	(ii)	(i)
(d)	(iii)	(ii)	(i)	(iv)

23. Non-formal education is
(i) an organised
(ii) systematic
(iii) highly institutionalised
(iv) an educational activity

Codes:
(a) (i), (ii) and (iv) are correct
(b) (i) and (ii) are correct
(c) (i), (ii) and (iii) are correct
(d) (ii), (iii) and (iv) are correct

24. **Assertion (A):** The existence of a correlation between two variables can be shown to exist only when there is variability.

Reason (R): If one of the variables is a constant, with no variability, then the correlation coefficient is not even defined.

Codes:
(a) Both (A) and (R) are true and (R) is the correct explanation.
(b) Both (A) and (R) are not true.
(c) (A) is true and (R) is false.
(d) (A) is false and (R) is true.

25. **Assertion (A):** Cross dyeing and union dyeing are same.

Reason (R): Both may produce multicoloured effects.

Codes:
(a) Both (A) and (R) are false.
(b) (A) is true and (R) is false.
(c) Both (A) and (R) are true.
(d) (A) is false and (R) is true.

26. **Assertion (A):** Pasteurization in milk is done to destroy the microbes.

Reason (R): It is tested for the presence of lactic acid in milk.

Codes:
(a) Both (A) and (R) are false.
(b) Both (A) and (R) are true.
(c) (A) is true but (R) is false.
(d) (A) is false but (R) is true.

27. **Assertion (A):** Confidentiality is an essential quality of the counsellor.

Reason (R): Counselling relationship will be effective only if the counsellor maintain confidentiality.

Codes:
(a) Both (A) and (R) are true.
(b) Both (A) and (R) are false.
(c) (A) is true, but (R) is false.
(d) (A) is false, but (R) is true.

28. Arrange the stages of Psycho-Social development in correct sequence
(i) Generativity Vs. Stagnation
(ii) Identity Vs. Role confusion
(iii) Ego Integrity Vs. Despair
(iv) Initiative Vs. Guilt

Codes:
(a) (i), (ii), (iii) and (iv)
(b) (iv), (ii), (i) and (iii)
(c) (iii), (ii), (iv) and (i)
(d) (ii), (iv), (i) and (iii)

29. **Assertion (A):** Large food service institutions use formal competitive bid buying.
Reason (R): Here the purchaser goes to the whole sale market and bids the price.
Codes:
(a) Both (A) and (R) are true.
(b) Both (A) and (R) are false.
(c) (A) is true, but (R) is false.
(d) (A) is false, but (R) is true.

30. Which of the following methods of printing are currently practised largely in the Indian textile industry?
(i) Screen Printing (ii) Digital
(iii) Roller Printing (iv) Block Printing
Codes:
(a) (ii), (iii) and (iv) are correct
(b) (i), (ii) and (iii) are correct
(c) (i), (iii) and (iv) are correct
(d) (i), (ii) and (iv) are correct

31. Match the foods in List I to it's pigments in List II.

List I (Food)	**List II (Pigments)**
(A) Beet root	i. Flavones
(B) Carrot	ii. Betalin
(C) Onions	iii. Chlorophyll
(D) Spinach	iv. Carotenoids

Codes:	**A**	**B**	**C**	**D**
(a)	i	ii	iii	iv
(b)	ii	iv	i	iii
(c)	iii	ii	iv	i
(d)	iv	iii	i	ii

32. Match the traditional methods of communication with the State in India.

List I	**List II**
(A) Odissi	i. Kerala
(B) Oyil Attam	ii. Karnataka
(C) Kathakali	iii. Tamil Nadu
(D) Yakshgana	iv. Orissa

Codes:	**A**	**B**	**C**	**D**
(a)	iv	iii	i	ii
(b)	ii	i	iv	iii
(c)	iv	ii	i	iii
(d)	iii	iv	ii	i

33. Match the items in List I with List II.
List I
(A) Spectrophotometer
(B) Soxlet Apparatus
(C) HPLC
(D) Muffle furnace
List II
(i) Retinol
(ii) Iron
(iii) Total inorganic content
(iv) Oil

Codes:	**A**	**B**	**C**	**D**
(a)	(iii)	(iv)	(i)	(ii)
(b)	(i)	(iv)	(ii)	(iii)
(c)	(ii)	(iv)	(i)	(iii)
(d)	(ii)	(i)	(iv)	(iii)

34. Match the items in List I with List II.
List I
I. Clay Modelling
II. Pre basic education
III. International Women's day
IV. Beneficiaries of Supplementary nutrition in ICDS.
List II
1. M.K. Gandhi
2. 6 months–72 months children
3. Imagination & creativity
4. 8th March
5. 8th July

Codes:	**I**	**II**	**III**	**IV**
(a)	3	2	5	1
(b)	2	5	4	3
(c)	3	1	4	2
(d)	1	3	2	4

35. This consists of two lists of statements regarding educational aids. Match the List A with List B:
List A
(A) Flannel Board (B) Illustrations
(C) Lettering (D) Colours

List B

(i) Big, bold and simple
(ii) Plywood, Hardwood or Cardboard
(iii) Large, bold and printed
(iv) Few and pleasing

Codes:	A	B	C	D
(a)	(ii)	(i)	(iii)	(iv)
(b)	(i)	(iii)	(ii)	(iv)
(c)	(iv)	(ii)	(i)	(iii)
(d)	(i)	(ii)	(iv)	(iii)

36. Match List I with List II:

List I

(A) Polyamide fibre
(B) Yarn number
(C) Pile weave
(D) Strand of long fibres

List II

(i) Filament (ii) Nylon
(iii) Count (iv) Velvet

Codes:	A	B	C	D
(a)	(i)	(ii)	(iii)	(iv)
(b)	(ii)	(i)	(iii)	(iv)
(c)	(iv)	(ii)	(i)	(iii)
(d)	(ii)	(iii)	(iv)	(i)

37. **Assertion (A):** In pattern making waist line dart can be shifted to any location without changing the fit of the garment.
Reason (R): Angle of the dart changes accordingly.
Codes:
(a) (A) and (R) are true.
(b) (A) and (R) are false.
(c) (A) is true but (R) is false.
(d) (A) is false but (R) is true.

38. **Assertion (A):** Direct dyes bleed while washing.
Reason (R): Therefore direct dyed fabrics are after treated with cationic agents.
Codes:
(a) (A) and (R) are true.
(b) (A) is true, (R) is false.
(c) (A) and (R) are false.
(d) (A) is false, (R) is true.

39. **Assertion (A):** Scorching of milk happens on prolonged boiling.
Reason (R): The sugar and protein in milk react to give the burnt taste.
Codes:
(a) Both (A) and (R) are true.
(b) (A) is true (R) is false.
(c) (A) is false (R) is true.
(d) Both (A) and (R) are false.

40. To meet the individual differences the curriculum should be:
I. Lengthy II. Formal
III. Informal IV. Flexible
Codes:
(a) I and II are correct.
(b) II and III are correct.
(c) I, II and IV are correct.
(d) II and IV are correct.

41. Power of statistical test of a mean depends on:
I. Particular H_A that is assumed true if H_0 is false.
II. Value of α chosen
III. Size of sample
IV. Variability of the population under study.
Codes:
(a) I & II (b) I, III & IV
(c) II & III (d) All of the above

42. **Assertion (A):** People choose to dress in the style that makes a statement about their personalities.
Reason (R): As per their wish to be perceived by the outside society.
Codes:
(a) (A) is correct, but (R) is wrong.
(b) (A) is wrong, but (R) is correct.
(c) Both (A) and (R) are correct.
(d) Both (A) and (R) are wrong.

43. **Assertion (A):** Test retest is the method used to test the reliability of the measurement instrument.
Reason (R): The measurement instrument to collect data should have both reliability and validity.
Codes:
(a) (A) is true, but (R) is false.
(b) Both (A) and (R) are false.
(c) Both (A) and (R) are true, but (R) is not the correct explanation of (A).
(d) (A) is false but (R) is true.

44. Give the correct sequence in the processing of textiles:
(A) Singeing (B) Scouring
(C) Bleaching (D) Designing
(E) Mercerization
Codes:
(a) (B), (A), (E), (C), (D)
(b) (A), (D), (B), (C), (E)
(c) (A), (E), (B), (D), (C)
(d) (D), (C), (A), (E), (B)

45. Give the correct sequence of the procedure to be adopted in organising audio-visual programme:
I. Planning II. Presentation
III. Follow-up IV. Preparation
Codes:
(a) I, II, IV, III (b) I, IV, II, III
(c) IV, I, II, III (d) III, IV, II, I

46. Match List I correctly with List II:
List I
A. Over-protectiveness
B. Permissiveness
C. Rejection
D. Acceptance
List II
i. Aggressiveness
ii. Over dependency
iii. Confident
iv. Irresponsible
v. Inferior

Codes:	**A**	**B**	**C**	**D**
(a)	iv	i	ii	iii
(b)	ii	iv	i	iii
(c)	iii	ii	iv	v
(d)	v	iii	iv	ii

47. Match the equipment given in List I with the end products for which they are used given in List II:

List I	**List II**
A. Pad steam range	i. Fibre
B. Crimp tester	ii. Dyeing
C. Air permeability	iii. Yarn
D. Hairiness meter	iv. Fabric

Codes:	**A**	**B**	**C**	**D**
(a)	i	ii	iii	iv
(b)	iii	iv	i	ii
(c)	ii	i	iv	iii
(d)	iv	iii	ii	i

Read the following passage and answer the questions 48 to 50:

The genesis of service tax emanates from the ongoing structural transformation of the Indian economy, whereby presently more than one-half of GDP originates from the services sector. Despite the growing presence of the services sector in the Indian economy it remained out of the tax net prior to 1994-95, leading to a steady deterioration in tax-GDP ratio. The service tax was introduced in 1994-95 on a select category of services at a low rate of five percent. While the service tax rate and the coverage of services being taxed have increased ever since, the combined tax-GDP ratio of the Centre and States, nevertheless, deteriorated from 16.4 percent in 1985-86 to 14.1 percent in 1999-2000. It may be noted that between 1990-91 and 1998-99, the share of industrial sector in GDP dropped by 6.4 percentage points whereas almost 64 percent of the tax revenue was generated by indirect taxes for which industrial sector continues to be the principal tax base. On the other hand, during the same period, the share of services sector in

GDP has increased by 10 percentage points and this sector has still remained poorly taxed.

The rationale for service tax, therefore, lies not only in arresting the falling tax-GDP ratio but also in *ipso facto* improving allocative efficiency in the economy as well as promoting equity. Against this backdrop, the service tax needs to be designed taking into account the fact that (i) the share of services in GDP is expanding; (ii) failure to tax services distorts consumer choices and encourages spending on services at the expense of goods; (iii) untaxed service traders are unable to claim Value Added Tax (VAT) on service inputs, which encourages businesses to develop in-house services, creating further distortions; and (iv) most services that are likely to become taxable are positively correlated with expenditure of high-income households and, therefore, service tax improves equity.

In the Indian context, taxation of services assumes importance in the wake of the need for improving the revenue system, ensuring a measure of neutrality in taxation between goods and services and eventually helping to evolve an efficient system of domestic trade taxes, both at the Central and the State levels.

48. What, according to the passage, was the impact of exclusion of service tax till the first half of the last decade of the past century?
    (a) Service sector used to flourish exorbitantly
    (b) There was no impact as there was no service tax
    (c) There was a steady deterioration in the GDP
    (d) Tax-GDP ratio had steadily and gradually aggravated

49. The origin of service tax is attributed to
    (a) metamorphosis of our country's economy
    (b) increase in Gross Domestic Product (GDP)
    (c) existence of service sector
    (d) tax of the future

50. Which of the following factors helps service tax to improve fairness across different economic strata of society?
    (a) It improves revenue system
    (b) Taxable services are mostly those that are utilised by the rich
    (c) Untaxed service traders are prevented from claiming value added tax
    (d) Encouragement to in-house services is effected

PAPER–III

1. Mens sana is corpore sana is a Latin saying which means
   (a) A sound mind in healthy body
   (b) Healthy body only
   (c) All men are same
   (d) Men give strict punishment

2. Chemical compound in foods which perform one more specific function in the body
   (a) Food (b) Food groups
   (c) Nutrients (d) None of these

3. On hearing a sad event in the family we
   (a) Retard appetite (b) Lose appetite
   (c) Gain appetite (d) None of these

4. Multipurpose food are
   (a) Specially prepared
   (b) Nutritious
   (c) Cheap
   (d) All of the above

5. Vitamin A is not destroyed by the action of
   (a) Dry heat (b) Steam
   (b) Acid (d) Alkali

6. Man is ...... host in case of T. Saginata and T. Solium.

(a) Primary (b) Secondary
(c) Tertiary (d) None of these

7. Infectious hepatitis
(a) Viral Infection through food
(b) Mycotoxins
(c) Micro-organism
(d) Utensils

8. Passive artificial immunity in infants derived from maternal antibodies lasts only for months.
(a) 2 weeks (b) 1 month
(c) 2 months (d) 3-6 months

9. Weight in kg divided by height is $(\text{meters})^2$ is a formula to calculate
(a) DC (b) BMR
(c) RDA (d) BMI

10. Find odd one out.
(a) NPU (b) BV
(c) Douglas Bag (d) NPR

11. Oral fluids does not include
(a) Whey water (b) Bear
(c) Fruit Punch (d) None of these

12. Fibres help in large intestine to
(i) Maintain muscle tone
(ii) By their capacity to bind water
Codes:
(a) (i) only (b) Both (i) and (ii)
(c) (ii) only (d) None of these

13. Which among them is a polysaccharides?
(a) Pentosans, Pectins
(b) Fructosans, galactans
(c) Cellulose, Hemicelluloses
(d) All of the above

14. Which among the following is called animal starch?
(a) Caramel (b) Cellulose
(c) Dextrins (d) Glycogen

15. What is $C_{27}H_{45}OH$?
(a) Cholesterol (b) Stearic acid
(c) Oleic acid (d) None of these

16. The blood of normal human contains .... of cholesterol.
(a) 120-250 mg/100 mL
(b) 175-300 mg/100 mL
(c) 150-250 mg/100 mL
(d) 10-200 mg/100 mL

17. Which psychoanalyst stated 'family is dead except for the first year or two of child raising?
(a) Max Weber (b) K. Kautilya
(c) William Wolf (d) William J. Goode

18. Reality orientation makes the elder aware of
(a) Person (b) Place
(c) Time (d) All of these

19. In ancient India, according to Dr. Altekar Village Panchayat worked for ..... for the village ......
i. the defence
ii. collected the revenue of the state
iii. fought bottles
iv. arranged marriage
Codes:
(a) i and ii (b) i and iv
(c) i, ii, iii and iv (d) i, ii, and iii

20. **Assertion (A):** The theory and hypotheses of Argyris suggest no relationship between personal development of the individual and the organisational situation.
Reason (R): The principles and the characteristics of a formal organisation, in the opinion of Argyris, are incorgruent to the needs of adult human beings.
Codes:
(a) (A) and (R) are true and (R) is the correct explanation of (A)
(b) (A) and (R) are true, but (R) does not explain (A)
(c) (A) is true but (R) is false
(d) (A) is false but (R) is true

21. The Scientific Management stressed upon
1. Rationality
2. Specialisation

3. Technical competence
4. Predictability

Codes:

(a) 1 and 2 (b) 1, 2 and 3
(c) 2, 3 and 4 (d) All of these

22. In a men's casual shirt, the chest size 116 corresponds to a neck size of
(a) 44.6 (b) 42
(c) 40 (d) 45

23. Feed mechanism does not include the operator
(a) Compound feed (b) Drop feed
(c) Needle feed (d) None of these

24. A pocket which is stitched on garment piece as a patch
(a) Patch pocket (b) Inseam pocket
(c) Bound pocket (d) Welt pocket

25. The most widely used bleaches are
(a) Chlorine bleaches
(b) Hydrogen peroxide bleaches
(c) Both (a) and (b)
(d) None of these

26. Olive green colour of Azo dyes is a combination of
(a) AS – GR + Blue B salt
(b) CT + Red B salt
(c) MN + GP salt
(d) AT + Yellow salt

27. The Largest cotton growing areas are in
i. India
ii. China
iii. USA and USSR
vi. Egypt and Brazil

Codes:

(a) ii and iii (b) i and iii
(c) i, ii, iii and iv (d) i, ii and iii

28. Match the following in List I with List II:

List I

A. In drawing of cotton fibre
B. Roving machine puts
C. Spinning of cotton is
D. Under microscope cotton fibre
E. Convolutions of cotton

List II

(i) Cuticle, cell wall lumen
(ii) Cotton fibres inside the cotton ball are cylinderical in shape when balls open they collapse and twist. This is the name given to it
(iii) Elongation of the silver and decrease in its diameter
(iv) Puts a slight twist on cotton fibre and winds the roving on a bobin roving
(v) A continuous, simultaneous, twisting and winding operations

Codes:	A	B	C	D	E
(a)	(iii)	(v)	(ii)	(iv)	(i)
(b)	(i)	(ii)	(v)	(iii)	(iv)
(c)	(iii)	(iv)	(v)	(i)	(ii)
(d)	(i)	(iv)	(v)	(ii)	(iii)

29. India ranks .... among the top cotton produced in the world.
(a) 3rd (b) 4th
(c) 1st (d) 2nd

30. Cotton textile in India comprise
(a) Mill-made fabrics
(b) Blended yarn
(c) Cotton
(d) All of these

31. The average production of handloom of 7 meters of cloth per day is done at
i. Karnataka
ii. Kerala
iii. Andhra Pradesh
iv. Tamil Nadu

Codes:

(a) i and iii (b) i and iv
(c) i, ii, iii and iv (d) i, ii and iii

32. Flax shows its adverse reaction to acids by
i. Frays ii. Shrinks
iii. Holes iv. Discoloration

Codes:
(a) i and ii (b) i and ii
(c) i, ii, iii and iv (d) i, ii and iii

33. Match the following in List I with List II:
List I
A. A predominance more of square and oblong forms
B. A predominance of oval and circular forms
C. The rough texture
D. A smooth surface
E. Wall finish rugs wood work, an painting a ceramic urn, wood
List II
(i) Absorbs light
(ii) Textures in home
(iii) Suited for masculine rooms
(iv) Best for feminine rooms
(v) Reflect light

Codes:	A	B	C	D	E
(a)	(iii)	(i)	(iv)	(v)	(ii)
(b)	(ii)	(iv)	(v)	(iii)	(i)
(c)	(iii)	(iv)	(i)	(v)	(ii)
(d)	(iv)	(v)	(ii)	(i)	(iii)

34. Line movements create
(i) Rhythm (ii) Confusion
(a) (i) only (b) (ii) only
(c) Both (i) and (ii) (d) None of these

35. Emphasis applies in several ways to the exterior of a house. which of the options wil create it?
i. One large dominate block
ii. Wings smaller
iii. One surface material dominates
iv. Wings lower than the main body
Codes:
(a) i and ii (b) i and iv
(c) i, ii, iii and iv (d) i, ii and iii

36. Fundamental or primary colour(s) is/are
(a) Blue (b) Yellow
(c) Red (d) All of them

37. *Designing and Decorating Interiors* is a book by
(a) David B. Van Dommelen
(b) Alexander Pope
(c) Mary Jean Alexander
(d) Anna Hong Rutt

38. A specialist for child who help in study of child's behaviour and feelings?
(a) Child psychologist
(b) Paediatrics
(c) Anthropologist
(d) Child specialist

39. FAS is a short form of
(a) fetus adult stage
(b) fetus alcohol syndrome
(c) fetal accident stress
(d) None of these

40. A process of change which is relatively independent of experiences.
(a) Maturity
(b) Congnitive development
(c) Learning
(d) Motor development

41. In the baby, gain in weight commes partly from increase in
i. Neural ii. Glandular
iii. Muscle tissue iv. Physical activity
Codes:
(a) i and ii (b) i and iv
(c) i, ii, iii and iv (d) i, ii and iii

42. Individual differences are significant because they are responsible for individuality in personality make up. Individuality
i. makes people interesting
ii. social progress possible
iii. makes better adjustment
iv. gives emotional stability
Codes:
(a) i and ii (b) i and iv
(c) i, ii, iii and iv (d) i, ii and iii

43. According to Humpherys Traxier, and North which are the field of counselling?

i. Eudcational
ii. Personal and Social
iii. Vocational
iv. Health

Codes:
(a) i and ii (b) i and iv
(c) i, ii, iii and iv (d) i, ii and iii

44. The role of the counsellor in directive counselling—
i. Analysis ii. Systhesis
iii. Diagnosis iv. Prognosis

Codes:
(a) i and ii (b) i and iv
(c) i, ii, iii and iv (d) i, ii and iii

45. Who defines rapport during interview "personal relationship of mutual trust and respect based on a feeling of confidence and secuirty in other person"?
(a) Symonds (b) Ruth Strang
(c) Hilgard (d) Mussen

46. Who wrote curriclum and community in Wales?
(a) Durkheim (b) MacIver
(c) Fred Clarks (d) Rousseau

47. In the communication process the sender may—
i. Speak ii. Act
iii. Draw iv. Write

Codes:
(a) i and ii (b) i and iv
(c) i, ii, iii and iv (d) i, ii and iii

48. Match the following in List I with List II:

List I
A. A line graph or curve graph
B. Area graph
C. Solid graph
D. Pie graph or circle graph or sector graph
E. Tutorial

List II
(i) Two dimensional shapes to compare 2 or 3 items
(ii) Three dimensional geometrical symbols of any shape used for comparison
(iii) Total numerical amoung each slice a specific percentage ideal for fractional relation
(iv) Two related data in an exact and complete manner
(v) Method invented by Socrates

Codes:	A	B	C	D	E
(a)	(i)	(ii)	(v)	(iv)	(iii)
(b)	(iii)	(v)	(iv)	(ii)	(i)
(c)	(iv)	(i)	(ii)	(iii)	(v)
(d)	(v)	(ii)	(iii)	(i)	(iv)

49. Specific qualities that should be present in a research worker—
i. Knowledge of the subject, technique of research
ii. Personal taste in the study
iii. Familiaity about the information
iv. Unbiased attitude

Codes:
(a) i and ii (b) i and iv
(c) i, ii, iii and iv (d) i, ii and iii

50. The advantages of questionanarie method could be—
i. Low cost
ii. Large coverage
iii. Repetitive information
iv. Rapidity

Codes:
(a) i and ii (b) i and iv
(c) i, ii, iii and iv (d) i, ii and iii

ANSWER SHEET

PAPER—I

1. (c)	2. (c)	3. (a)	4. (d)	5. (d)
6. (a)	7. (d)	8. (b)	9. (c)	10. (b)
11. (d)	12. (a)	13. (c)	14. (c)	15. (a)
16. (c)	17. (a)	18. (b)	19. (a)	20. (c)
21. (d)	22. (a)	23. (c)	24. (a)	25. (b)

26. (b)	27. (b)	28. (c)	29. (d)	30. (b)
31. (b)	32. (c)	33. (a)	34. (c)	35. (b)
36. (b)	37. (a)	38. (b)	39. (d)	40. (a)
41. (d)	42. (c)	43. (a)	44. (b)	45. (c)
46. (b)	47. (d)	48. (b)	49. (c)	50. (c)

PAPER—II

1. (c)	2. (b)	3. (c)	4. (c)	5. (b)
6. (b)	7. (a)	8. (b)	9. (c)	10. (b)
11. (b)	12. (a)	13. (b)	14. (c)	15. (d)
16. (a)	17. (c)	18. (b)	19. (a)	20. (d)
21. (c)	22. (c)	23. (a)	24. (a)	25. (d)
26. (c)	27. (a)	28. (b)	29. (c)	30. (c)
31. (b)	32. (a)	33. (d)	34. (c)	35. (a)
36. (d)	37. (d)	38. (b)	39. (a)	40. (d)
41. (a)	42. (c)	43. (c)	44. (d)	45. (b)
46. (b)	47. (c)	48. (d)	49. (a)	50. (b)

PAPER—III

1. (a)	2. (c)	3. (b)	4. (d)	5. (b)
6. (a)	7. (a)	8. (d)	9. (d)	10. (c)
11. (c)	12. (b)	13. (d)	14. (a)	15. (a)
16. (c)	17. (c)	18. (d)	19. (a)	20. (d)
21. (d)	22. (d)	23. (d)	24. (a)	25. (c)
26. (a)	27. (b)	28. (c)	29. (b)	30. (d)
31. (c)	32. (b)	33. (c)	34. (c)	35. (c)
36. (d)	37. (a)	38. (b)	39. (b)	40. (a)
41. (d)	42. (a)	43. (c)	44. (c)	45. (a)
46. (c)	47. (c)	48. (c)	49. (c)	50. (c)

MOCK TEST–2
PAPER–I

1. Minimum program of guidance includes
   (a) occupational information service
   (b) data collector service
   (c) counselling service
   (d) All of these

2. If majority of students in a class is weak, a teacher should
   (a) not care about intelligent students
   (b) keep his speed of teaching fast so that students comprehension level may increase
   (c) keep his teaching slow which can also be helpful to bright students
   (d) keep his teaching slow along with some extra guidance to bright students

3. If the principal of your institution is not satisfied with your performance and charge you with the act of negligence of duties, how would you behave with him?
   (a) You would neglect him
   (b) You would take revenge by giving physical and mental agony to him
   (c) You would keep yourself alert and make his efforts unfruitful
   (d) You would take a tough stand against the charges

4. What makes people to undertake research?
   (a) Desire to get intellectual joy of doing some creative work
   (b) Desire to get a research degree along with its consequential benefits
   (c) Desire to face the challenge in solving the unsolved problems
   (d) All of these

5. Which of the following aims at probing into the phenomenon to formulate a more precise research problem or to develop a new hypothesis?
   (a) Descriptive research
   (b) Conclusive research
   (c) Diagnostic research
   (d) Exploratory research
6. Which of the following is not instructional material?
   (a) Transparency
   (b) Overhead projector
   (c) Printed material
   (d) Audio cassette
7. Of great importance in determining the amount of transference that occurs in the process of learning is the
   (a) knowledge of the teacher
   (b) IQ of the teacher
   (c) presence of identical elements
   (d) use of appropriate elements
8. The characteristic(s) of hypothesis is/are:
   I. It can be tested.
   II. It must consist of known facts.
   III. It must be objective and specific.
   Codes:
   (a) I and III (b) I and II
   (c) I only (d) All of these
9. The guide for the research requires which of the following qualities?
   (a) Interdisciplinary expertise
   (b) Subject matter expertise
   (c) Methodological expertise
   (d) All of these
10. Which of the following indicates evaluation?
    (a) Seema got 195 marks out of 200
    (b) Sapna got 72 percent marks in English
    (c) Asha got First Division in final examination
    (d) All of the above

Direction: (11-16) Study the following passage and give answer to the questions based on it.

Much of the theoretical literature of archeology in the 1980s devotes considerable energy to bashing the 1970s, and the target often turns out to be the so-called New or Processual Archeology. While many of the attacks come from recent theorists who are attempting to replace it with post-processual archeology, some criticism comes from within what was New Archeology even from the hand of its original champion, Lewis Binford. If scholars from both outside and inside the theoretical developments of the 1970s are rejecting the New Archeology, why am I defending its importance to us today? The answer is very simple...for better or worse, it is us! As Alison Whylie has recently said the New Archeology of the 1960s quickly became everybody's archeology in the 1970s. Most of today's faculty members and senior archeologists were the people who, in one way or another, adopted the teachings of New Archeology. Although most archeologists did not claim to agree with all aspects of New Archeology nor could more than two or three people agree on what it was, virtually one rejected it outright. Typically, each one presented her or his version, often using a New Archeology text as a starting point for pedagogical purposes. Few wanted to be left out of the exciting new theoretical movement of those years, and New Archeology was passed on to the succeeding generation of students who reached maturity in the 1980s and are today's young professionals.

Criticisms now levelled against the New Archeology of the seventies do have merit, but by discounting that era as misguided, critics have overlooked its crucial importance. New Archeology has an important historical role in the developments of the field we have today and it has continuing importance because it is still guiding archeology's trajectory into the future. Equally troubling is that some critics ask us to reject the basic tenets of New Archeology and to replace them with a system often called post processualist archeology. I believe this is rhetoric that not only misrepresents the achievements of the New Archeology of the seventies, but also does not successfully articulate the potential contributions of its own position.

To put the New Archeology of the seventies into perspective, it is important to review the decades leading up to its development. In the first years following World War II, archeology was still a small field, but by the fifties and the sixties, it was expanding rapidly and taking itself quite seriously. Since the launching of Sputnik in 1957 there had emerged a frenzy in the United States to make all disciplines more scientific. Great strides were made in bringing science into archeology through new dating techniques a multidisciplinary approach, early experiments with the use of statistics, and devoting substantial attention to increasing the precision of artifact classification. The sixties provided the nation with both the optimistic Kennedy years, with an emphasis on science and the conviction that we were capable of accomplishing wondrous; things, and the cynical Vietnam era. Coming on the heels of a decade of civil rights unrest, the widespread dissatisfaction with the Vietnam conflict in the late sixties molded a generation of young Americans who were distrustful of established authority. In academic life, there was an increasing emphasis on environment, other cultures, and people-oriented disciplines. Anthropology and archeology grew markedly because of these trends. Archeologists were urged to become concerned with sociological issues—the people behind the artifacts.

It was during these decades of rapid change that many of the core concepts of the New Archeology entered the literature. However, they were not, at first, assembled into a program for action that attracted a solid following. Water Taylor advocated the conjuctive approach with little effect, while Leslie White's evolutionism and Julian Styeward's cultural ecology attracted some attention, but largely among cultural anthropologists. Albert Spaulding led a one-man campaign to bring science and statistics into archeology. But the individual whose work catalyzed the New Archeology movement was Lewis Binford, who incorporated these earlier lines of thinking together with an explicit concern for scientific methods and field research designs. Much of Binford's thinking probably crystallised while he was at the University of Michigan, but was during his relatively few years at the University of Chicago that he changed the direction of modern archeology.

11. New Archeology refers to
    (a) newer techniques used in Archeology
    (b) newer inventions used in Archeology
    (c) newer theoretical foundations in Archeology
    (d) None of these

12. The author defends the Archeology of the 1970s because
    (a) he has a nostalgic feeling about it
    (b) it has research value
    (c) it paved way for newer traditions
    (d) it has historical value

13. The author suggests that
    (a) We should respect new Archeology as a movement in Archeology
    (b) We should go back to the tenets of processual Archeology
    (c) We should treat tenets of new Archeology with respect
    (d) All of the above

14. The importance of Archeology arose from
    (a) the end of World War II
    (b) an increasing scientific outlook

(c) the launch of Sputnik in 1957
(d) All of these

15. Which one of the following is not an area of focus for archeologist?
(a) Study the interaction of people of small group
(b) Studying cultures of other people
(c) Study the social structure of the past societies
(d) Study the man-environment relationship in the past

16. An archeologist is concerned with
(a) classification of artefacts
(b) maintenance of museums
(c) digging of ancient cities
(d) All of these

17. Rhetorics means
(a) study of the technique and rules for using language effectively
(b) using language effectively to please or persuade
(c) excessive use of verbal ornamentation
(d) All of the above

18. If a receiver replying on 'hmm-mm' or 'I see'. This type of reply is known as
(a) positive feedback
(b) ambiguous feedback
(c) negative feedback
(d) None of these

19. Which of the following FM radio stations is owned by the Times of India group?
(a) AIR
(b) Radio Rainbow
(c) Radio Mirchi
(d) Red FM

20. Find the next number in the following sequence:
9, 8, 25, 12, 49, 18, 121, 26, ?, ?
(a) 142, 36 (b) 169, 36
(c) 225, 36 (d) 196, 36

21. **Statement:** Should there be complete ban on pouched tobacco products (like Gutka) in India?

Arguments:
(i) Yes, it is the most important cause of mouth cancer and mouth ulcer in our country.
(ii) No, there are many people employed in this industry right from manufacturing to retailing. This ban will hamper their livelihood.
(a) Only argument (i) is strong
(b) Only argument (ii) is strong
(c) Both the arguments (i) and (ii) are strong
(d) Neither (i) nor (ii) is strong

22. The relationship between Animal, Cows, Dogs can be shown by

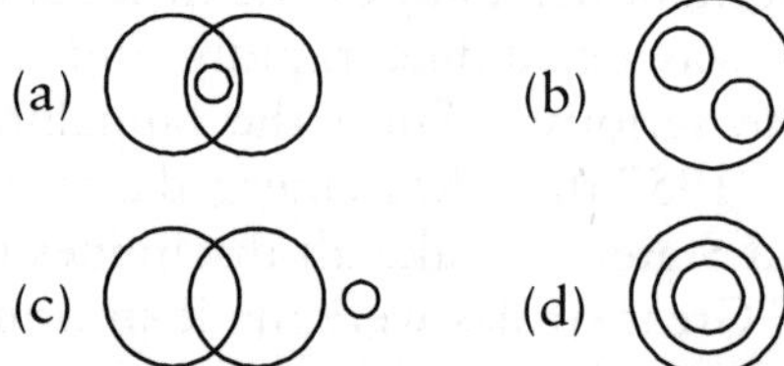

23. If in a certain code:
'nso prt kli chn' means 'Sharma gets marriage gift'.
'pit lnm wop chn' means 'wife gives marriage gift'. 'tti wop nhi' means 'he gives nothing'. What would mean gives:
(a) kli (b) tti
(c) wop (d) lnm

24. Characteristics of all informal and formal communications are
(a) Same (b) Structured
(c) Different (d) None of these

25. Three of the following four are alike in a certain way and so form a group. Find the one which doesn't belong to that group?
(a) Dog (b) Tiger
(c) Horse (d) Lion

26. What is research design?
(a) The methods used in analysis and finding the final conclusion is known as research design

(b) A researcher needs to prepare a plan of action for his study which is known as research design
(c) The presentation of final data is known as research design
(d) None of these

27. Recording a television program on a Set Top Box is an example of
(a) content reference
(b) time-shifting
(c) media synchronisation
(d) mechanical clarity

28. Which of the following statements say the same thing?
(i) "I am a teacher" (said by Arvind)
(ii) "I am a teacher" (said by Binod)
(iii) "My son is a teacher" (said by Binod's father)
(iv) "My brother is a teacher" (said by Binod's sister)
(v) "My brother is a teacher" (said by Binod's only sister)
(vi) "My sole enemy is a teacher" (said by Binod's only enemy)
Choose the correct answer from the codes given below:
Codes:
(a) (v) and (vi)
(b) (i) and (ii)
(c) (ii) and (vi)
(d) (ii), (iii), (iv) and (v)

29. In this question there are two statements followed by four conclusions numbered I, II, III and IV.
Statements:
A. All books are trees.
B. All trees are lions.
Conclusions:
I. All books are lions.
II. All lions are books.
III. All trees are books.
IV. Some lions are books.
Choose the correct answer.
(a) I and IV follow
(b) II and III follow
(c) None of conclusions follow
(d) All conclusion follows

Directions: (30-34) Answer the questions based on following table.

Machines X and Y can independently produce either product P or product Q. The time taken by machines X and Y (in minutes) to produce one unit of product P and Q are given in the table below. (Each machine works 8 hours per day.)

Product	X	Y
P	10	8
Q	6	6

30. If the number of units of P is to be three times that of Q, what is the maximum idle time to maximise total units manufactured?
(a) 8 minutes (b) 0 minute
(c) 12 minutes (d) None of these

31. If X works at half its normal efficiency, what is the maximum number of units produced, if at least one unit of each must be produced?
(a) 119 (b) 135
(c) 127 (d) 136

32. What is the maximum number of units that can be manufactured in one day?
(a) 250 (b) 160
(c) 270 (d) 195

33. If equal quantities of both are to be produced, then out of four choice given below the least efficient way would be
(a) 59 of each with 8 min. idle
(b) 71 of each with 9 min. idle
(c) 53 of each with 10 min. idle
(d) 48 of each with 4 min. idle

34. What is the least number of machine hours required to produce 30 pieces of P and 25 pieces of Q respectively?

(a) 6 hr 30 min. (b) 9 hr 30 min.
(c) 6 hr 40 min. (d) 8 hr 30 min.

35. Telematic is a combination of
(a) Telecommunication and computer
(b) Telecommunication and information
(c) Television and computer
(d) All of the above

36. Following is a part of balance sheet of Timas Pvt. Ltd. Study the table and give answer to the question given below:

(All values in ₹ crore)

Year	Expenditure	Income
1990	3400	4000
1995	3800	4500
2000	4500	5400
2005	6400	8000

Which of the following conclusions is not true?
(a) There has been a steady growth in % profit of the company
(b) There is around 90% increase in expenditure of the firm from 1990 to 2005
(c) Income of the company is doubled in 15 years
(d) Percentage profit in 2000 was 18%

37. If EFGHUK is coded as VUTSRQ then LIMIT can be coded as
(a) KNRNC (b) ORNRG
(c) JKOKG (d) RSTSG

38. The more is 'Resolution Power' of a printer better is its
(a) Speed (b) Colour
(c) Memory (d) Quality

39. Laterite soil develops due to
(a) deposits of alluvial
(b) deposition of loess
(c) leaching
(d) continued vegetation cover

40. Line access and avoidance of collision are the main functions of
(a) network protocols
(b) wide area networks
(c) the CPU
(d) the monitor

41. Communication satellites are placed in
(a) Geostationary Orbit
(b) Polar Orbit
(c) Both (a) and (b)
(d) None of these

42. DLL stands for
(a) Data Deriving Language
(b) Data Definition Language
(c) Data Design Language
(d) All of the above

43. Transistors were first used in
(a) 2nd generation computers
(b) 3rd generation computers
(c) 4th generation computers
(d) None of these

44. Which of the following is not provided in the Constitution?
(a) Planning Commission
(b) Election Commission
(c) Finance Commission
(d) Public Service Commission

45. The first satellite launched in space was
(a) Early Bird (b) Sputnik-1
(c) Skylab (d) Aryabhatta-1

46. At what time between 5.30 and 6.00 will the hands of a clock be at right angles?
(a) 45 minutes past 5
(b) $43\frac{5}{11}$ minutes past 5
(c) $43\frac{7}{11}$ minutes past 5
(d) 40 minutes past 5

47. A person can be a member of Council of Ministers without being a member of Parliament for a maximum period of
(a) 45 days (b) 90 days
(c) 180 days (d) One year

48. Many engineers and architects use a different type of pen called a
(a) Pointer pen (b) Computer pen
(c) Light pen (d) Logical pen

49. Which of the following are wrongly matched?

Name of Volcano	Country
(a) Mt. Spur	USA
(b) Mt. Fuego	Guatemala
(c) Mt. Ag'ung	Indonesia
(d) Mt. Lascor	Equador

50. How many types of emergency can be declared by the President of India?
(a) 1 (b) 2
(c) 3 (d) 4

PAPER–II

1. Major fields of Home Science are
(a) 3 (b) 2
(c) 6 (d) 5

2. The heart's primary function is to pump blood to which two main areas?
(a) Lungs and heart
(b) Lungs and rest of body
(c) Main arteries and the aorta
(d) Capillaries and lungs

3. Which sentence is false?
(a) Changes in eating habits and medications are effective treatment for some hernias
(b) It is very uncommon for women to have hernias
(c) Hernias that cause severe pain require immediate attention
(d) Some hernias in babies will disappear on their own before the child turns into an adult

4. How can health improvements be quantified and measured?
(a) We cannot
(b) Using quality and length of life
(c) Comparing health status to the state of complete physical, mental and social well-being
(d) Using only monetary terms

5. What characterizes the interactionist approach to language acquisition?
(a) Language is an interaction between speaker and listener
(b) Language is the link between what you think and what you do
(c) There is a link between the environmental and biological factors in the process of acquiring language
(d) There is a link among different languages

6. Which one of the following is most distinctively a trait?
(a) Ecstasy (b) Trustfulness
(c) Anger (d) Happiness

7. The ability to successfully cope with one's own emotions and those others is known as
(a) Theory of mind
(b) Internal working model
(c) Emotional competence
(d) Strange situation

8. Encouraging or enforcing independence in our babies and young children promotes
(a) Emotional maturity
(b) Independence
(c) Instills a fundamental belief that their needs will not be met
(d) All of the above

9. "Science goes with the method, not with the subject-matter" said by
(a) Newton (b) Stuart Chase
(c) H.E. Bliss (d) Bradford

10. What is the best way to prevent back injury?
(a) Exercise to strengthen your back and reduce stress
(b) Lose excess weight

(c) Maintain good posture
(d) All of the above

11. Isotonic exercise is an exercise where
(a) A muscle changes in length but the tone remains the same
(b) The length of the muscle does not change but there is a change in the tone
(c) The tone of the muscle is constant
(d) The muscle becomes longer and thicker as the origin and insertion move away from each other

12. Which of these would be the healthiest choice for a snack?
(a) Cookies (b) Chips
(c) Peanuts (d) None

13. Which of the following is not the way to make sure you meet the highest standards of personal hygiene?
(a) Limit the jewellery that you wear
(b) Long hair must be tied back
(c) Clean your teeth regularly
(d) Wash your hands regularly

14. How many calories does water contain?
(a) 50 (b) 100
(c) 200 (d) None of these

15. Where is your liver?
(a) On top of the stomach
(b) Below the gall bladder
(c) Near the rectum
(d) Below the large intestines

16. Why do we dream?
(a) To stimulate our brain during sleep
(b) To fulfill wishes and desires
(c) To maintain our memory function
(d) No one knows for sure

17. How often should your toothbrush be replaced?
(a) Every eight to 10 weeks
(b) Every three or four months
(c) Every other month
(d) Every month

18. **Assertion (A):** Both vitamin A and fat are required for vision in the dark.
Reason (R): Fat helps in absorption of vitamin A in the gut.
Codes:
(a) (A) is true but (R) is false
(b) (A) is false but (R) is true
(c) Both (A) and (R) are true
(d) Both (A) and (R) are false

19. **Assertion (A):** Night blindness in children is caused by the deficiency of vitamin A in the diet.
Reason (R): Beta-carotene is a precursor of vitamin A, so foods rich in carotene pigments should be fed to children.
Codes:
(a) (A) is true but (R) is false
(b) (A) is false but (R) is true
(c) Both (A) and (R) are true
(d) Both (A) and (R) are false

20. Match the food items with their cooking properties:

List I	List II
A. Egg white	(i) Flavouring
B. Corn Starch	(ii) Smoking point
C. Vanilla	(iii) Foaming
D. Oil	(iv) Thickening

Codes:	**A**	**B**	**C**	**D**
(a)	(iii)	(iv)	(i)	(ii)
(b)	(ii)	(i)	(iv)	(iii)
(c)	(iv)	(i)	(iii)	(ii)
(d)	(iii)	(i)	(ii)	(iv)

21. Match the colour of fruit and vegetable in List I with the pigment in List II:

List I	List II
A. Green	(i) Carotenoids
B. Deep yellow	(ii) Chlorophyll
C. White	(iii) Anthocyanin
D. Purple	(iv) Flavones

Codes:	**A**	**B**	**C**	**D**
(a)	(i)	(iv)	(iii)	(ii)
(b)	(ii)	(i)	(iv)	(iii)

(c)	(iv)	(i)	(iii)	(ii)
(d)	(iii)	(i)	(ii)	(iv)

22. Match the items in List I with List II:

List I	**List II**
A. Geyser	(i) Condenser
B. Refrigerator	(ii) Choke
C. Cooking range	(iii) Gas Cylinder
D. Tube light	(iv) Thermostat

Codes:	**A**	**B**	**C**	**D**
(a)	(i)	(iv)	(iii)	(ii)
(b)	(ii)	(i)	(iv)	(iii)
(c)	(iv)	(i)	(iii)	(ii)
(d)	(iii)	(i)	(ii)	(iv)

23. **Assertion (A):** Before sundrying the vegetable should be blanched.
    Reason (R): High temperature used in blanching kills certain micro-organisms but does not inactivate the enzymes.
    Codes:
    (a) (A) is true but (R) is false
    (b) (A) is false but (R) is true
    (c) Both (A) and (R) are true
    (d) Both (A) and (R) are false

24. Arrange the following Vitamin A deficiency symptoms according to its manifestation in the disease.
    (i) Bitot's spot (ii) Night blindness
    (iii) Xeropthalmia (iv) Keratomalacia
    Codes:
    (a) (i), (ii), (iii), (iv) (b) (ii), (iii), (iv), (i)
    (c) (ii), (i), (iii), (iv) (d) (ii), (iii), (i), (iv)

25. **Assertion (A):** Consumption of lythrus stivus causes lathyrism, a crippling disease.
    Reason (R): Lythrus stivus contains a water soluble toxic alkaloid called BOAA.
    Codes:
    (a) (A) is true but (R) is false
    (b) (A) is false but (R) is true
    (c) Both (A) and (R) are true
    (d) Both (A) and (R) are false

26. How can food poisoning occur?
    (a) Eating hamburger that's pink in the centre
    (b) Eating unrefrigerated hard cooked eggs from an Easter egg hunt the day before
    (c) Eating reheated leftovers from a week ago
    (d) All of the above

27. What lifestyle factor aids in the treatment of eczema?
    (a) Increase essential fatty acids in your diet
    (b) Take Vitamin K
    (c) Do more exercise
    (d) None of these

28. **Assertion (A):** Egg yolk is used for making mayonnaise.
    Reason (R): Egg yolk serves as an emulsifying agent in preparation of mayonnaise.
    Codes:
    (a) (A) is true but (R) is false
    (b) (A) is false but (R) is true
    (c) Both (A) and (R) are true
    (d) Both (A) and (R) are false

29. For a successful outcome of the nutrition programme for the community, state the sequential order of steps to be taken:
    (i) Implementation
    (ii) Mobilising resources
    (iii) Monitoring and evaluation
    (iv) Priorities problem
    (v) Identify target
    (vi) Setting objectives
    Codes:
    (a) (v), (iv), (vi), (ii), (i), (iii)
    (b) (ii), (i), (iv), (iii), (v), (vi)
    (c) (iii), (iv), (i), (ii), (vi), (v)
    (d) (i), (iii), (ii), (iv), (v), (vi)

30. **Assertion (A):** Time is the human resource.
    Reason (R): Time is the easiest to be measured but one of the most difficult to understand.

Codes:
(a) (A) is true but (R) is false
(b) (A) is false but (R) is true
(c) Both (A) and (R) are true
(d) Both (A) and (R) are false

31. Match the following authors with the concepts they have introduced:
List I
A. Vygotsky B. Piaget
C. Spearman D. Montessori
List II
(i) PWRE
(ii) Zone of proximal development
(iii) General factor
(iv) Auto education

Codes:	A	B	C	D
(a)	(i)	(iv)	(iii)	(ii)
(b)	(ii)	(i)	(iii)	(iv)
(c)	(i)	(ii)	(iv)	(iii)
(d)	(iii)	(i)	(ii)	(iv)

32. Match the items in List I with List II:

List I	**List II**
A. Shabnam	(i) Gujarat Embroidery
B. Laddu Jalebi	(ii) Jamdani
C. Taipchi	(iii) Chikankari
D. Pachhi Patti	(iv) Bandhni

Codes:	A	B	C	D
(a)	(ii)	(iv)	(iii)	(i)
(b)	(ii)	(i)	(iv)	(iii)
(c)	(iii)	(i)	(iv)	(ii)
(d)	(iii)	(ii)	(i)	(iv)

33. **Assertion (A):** Same pattern can be used for knitted and women fabrics.
Reason (R): Knitted and women fabrics have same properties.
Codes:
(a) (A) is true but (R) is false
(b) (A) is false but (R) is true
(c) Both (A) and (R) are true
(d) Both (A) and (R) are false

34. Arrange the following processes in the correct order. Use the code given below:
(i) Bundling (ii) Spreading
(iii) Marker making (iv) Cutting
Codes:
(a) (i), (ii), (iii), (iv) (b) (ii), (iii), (iv), (i)
(c) (ii), (i), (iii), (iv) (d) (ii), (iii), (i), (iv)

35. **Assertion (A):** Rayon garments undergo progressive shrinkage.
Reason (R): Hence care has to be taken while drying and ironing.
Codes:
(a) (A) is true but (R) is false
(b) (A) is false but (R) is true
(c) Both (A) and (R) are true
(d) Both (A) and (R) are false

36. **Assertion (A):** In a seam slits are given in onward curve.
Reason (R): Smaller area falls over bigger area.
Codes:
(a) (A) is true but (R) is false
(b) (A) is false but (R) is true
(c) Both (A) and (R) are true
(d) Both (A) and (R) are false

37. Match the following items:
List I
A. Bias binding B. Under-stitching
C. Notches D. Stay-stitching
List II
(i) Turning the seam easily
(ii) Finishing the raw edge
(iii) Removing extra fullness from the seam
(iv) To retain shape

Codes:	A	B	C	D
(a)	(i)	(iv)	(iii)	(ii)
(b)	(ii)	(i)	(iii)	(iv)
(c)	(iv)	(i)	(iii)	(ii)
(d)	(iii)	(i)	(ii)	(iv)

38. Match the fiber given in List I to the appearance given in List II:

List I	**List II**
A. Wool	(i) Glass rod structure
B. Linen	(ii) Scales

C. Silk (iii) Convolutions
D. Cotton (iv) Nodes

Codes:	A	B	C	D
(a)	(i)	(iv)	(iii)	(ii)
(b)	(i)	(ii)	(iii)	(iv)
(c)	(iv)	(i)	(iii)	(ii)
(d)	(iii)	(i)	(ii)	(iv)

39. **Assertion (A):** In pattern making basic control dart can be shifted to any location without changing the fit of the garment.
Reason (R): Angle of the dart changes accordingly.
Codes:
(a) (A) is true but (R) is false
(b) (A) is false but (R) is true
(c) Both (A) and (R) are true
(d) Both (A) and (R) are false

40. Match the items in List I with List II:
List I
A. Lycra
B. Balucharies
C. Cupra ammonium rayon
D. Fashion adoption theory
List II
(i) Dubraj Das (ii) J.P. Benberg
(iii) Dupont (iv)

Codes:	A	B	C	D
(a)	(i)	(iv)	(iii)	(ii)
(b)	(ii)	(i)	(iv)	(iii)
(c)	(i)	(ii)	(iv)	(iii)
(d)	(iii)	(i)	(ii)	(iv)

41. The main step of Scientific Method is:
1. Selection and analysis of problem
2. Formulation of Hypothesis
3. Data Collection
4. Preparation of report
Codes:
(a) 1, 3, 4 (b) 2, 3, 4
(c) 1, 2, 3 (d) All the above

42. **Assertion (A):** The existence of a correlation between two variables can be shown to exist only when there is variability.
Reason (R): If one of the variables is a constant, with no variability, then the correlation coefficient is not even defined.
Codes:
(a) (A) is true but (R) is false
(b) (A) is false but (R) is true
(c) Both (A) and (R) are true and (R) is the correct explanation
(d) Both (A) and (R) are false

43. **Assertion (A):** Pre-testing of a tool of research is essential to carry out sound research.
Reason (R): Vague and unclear/difficult questions can be modified or replaced.
Codes:
(a) Both (A) and (R) are true
(b) (A) is true but (R) is false
(c) (A) is false but (R) is true
(d) Both (A) and (R) are false

44. Arrange the following steps in research in the correct sequence:
(i) Sample Selection
(ii) Research Question
(iii) Data Collection
(iv) Research Design
(v) Objectives
Codes:
(a) (ii), (i), (iii), (iv), (v)
(b) (iv), (i), (iii), (ii), (v)
(c) (ii), (v), (i), (iv), (iii)
(d) (ii), (iii), (i), (iv), (v)

45. **Assertion (A):** Home Management is not an all encompassing concept compared to decision-making or problem-solving.
Reason (R): Home Management does not consider the totality of managerial functioning.
Codes:
(a) (A) is true but (R) is false
(b) (A) is false but (R) is true
(c) Both (A) and (R) are true
(d) Both (A) and (R) are false

Read the following passage and answer the questions 46 to 50:

India is dedicated to free institutions and principles of democracy. We are striving to give everyone an opportunity and raise the standard of living for all. A democracy is one where people have the right to live their own lives and develop themselves in their own way under the guidance of their chosen representatives. If our political democracy is to succeed, it is essential that it be buttressed by steps towards economic equality or what has been referred to as the 'socialistic pattern of society'. Poverty and unemployment hold the biggest threat to the successful working of our democratic system.

46. One may infer from the paragraph that in a socialistic pattern of society
    (a) to provide employment to all is the greatest problem
    (b) the socialist party dominates
    (c) all the inhabitants are treated equal
    (d) None of these
47. The successful working of Indian democratic system is under a threat of
    (a) economic inequality
    (b) poverty
    (c) unemployment
    (d) All the above
48. In a democratic system
    (a) commodities are freely bought and sold
    (b) government serves the people
    (c) the government is run by the people themselves
    (d) people do not have political freedom
49. The word buttressed in the paragraph means
    (a) Supported (b) Dictating
    (c) Declared (d) Guided
50. Democracy can fail if there is
    (a) opportunity for development
    (b) a weak government
    (c) economic inequality
    (d) unemployment

PAPER–III

1. BCG inoculation is done for
   (a) Measles (b) Cholera
   (c) T.B. (d) Pneumonia
2. Intake of iron and iodine gives protection against
   (a) Beri-Beri and goiter
   (b) Osteoporosis and Beri-Beri
   (c) Anemia and goiter
   (d) Anemic and rickets
3. This study determines frequency with which something occurs with something else.
   (a) Descriptive (b) Practical
   (c) Diagnostic (d) Experimental
4. Suggestion is conveyed through
   (a) Similar medium (b) Pictures
   (c) Language (d) All of these
5. In the rural sector the responsibility of primary education lies with
   (a) Gram Panchayata
   (b) District Council
   (c) Co-operative Societies
   (d) Both (a) and (b)
6. The properties which make wool a popular fibre?
   (i) Warmth
   (ii) Resiliency
   (iii) Felting
   (iv) Easily damaged by moths and alkalies
   Codes:
   (a) (i), (iii) (b) (i), (ii)
   (c) (i), (ii), (iii), (iv) (d) (i), (ii), (iii)
7. Who stated "If science is poorly taught and badly learnt, it is little more than burdening the mind with dead information, and it could degenerate even into a new superstition"?
   (a) Froeble
   (b) Montessori

(c) Rousseau
(d) Kothari Commission Report

8. The main advantage of partnership is
(a) Limited liability
(b) Easy getting into business
(c) Flexibility
(d) Tax saving

9. Felting is a term applied to the progressive shrink age of wool. Felting occurs when fibre is subjected to
(a) Friction (b) Moisture
(c) Heat (d) All of these

10. This study aim at gaining familiarity with a phenomena or which aim at achieving insights into the phenomena or studies which deal with formulation of a more precise research problem or developing a hypothesis
(a) Exploratory (b) Fractal
(c) Experimental (d) Descriptive

11. Included in the agencies of socialism are:
(i) Family (ii) Peers, school
(iii) Organizations (iv) Media
Codes:
(a) (i), (ii) (b) (i), (ii)
(c) (i), (ii), (iii), (iv) (d) (i), (ii), (iii)

12. The Scientific Management was criticised on the grounds that:
1. It did not put forward a fully developed theory.
2. The Social and Psychological factors were emphasised by it.
3. It oversimplified the worker motivation.
4. It viewed efficiency in mechanistic term only.
5. It emphasised only physiological variables of production.
Select the correct code:
Codes:
(a) 1, 2, 3 and 4 (b) 1, 2, 3 and 5
(c) 1, 3, 4 and 5 (d) 1, 2, 4 and 5

13. Stain of adhesive tape can be removed by
(a) Neutralize with vinegar
(b) Harden with ice cube and rub off with fingers, then perchlorate ethylene or other solvent
(c) Neutralizing with ammonia
(d) None of above

14. In audio-visual aid teaching students can
(a) Comment (b) Question
(c) Discuss (d) All of these

15. Education according to nature means
(a) Return to the nature
(b) Study of natural laws and their application to process of education
(c) To educate according to the law nature of human development
(d) All of the above

16. 'Body building food' are rich in
(a) Fats (b) Minerals
(c) Carbohydrates (d) Protein

17. Common method to develop and play with darts is
(a) Close & cup
(b) Slash & spread
(c) Pivot method
(d) All of these

18. State which is/are true?
(i) Asbestos occurs as veins or strips in rocks.
(ii) Asbestos fibres are 3/8″ to 3/4″ in length.
(iii) Asbestos is used for padding for laundry presses belting for conveying hot materials, brake-lining and in clothes such as gloves aprons, etc.
(iv) The physical structure of asbestos makes it very difficult to open into yarns because it is lacking in length and cohesiveness.
Codes:
(a) (i), (iii) (b) (i), (iv)
(c) (i), (ii), (iii), (iv) (d) (i), (ii), (iii)

19. Taylor's theory of Scientific Management was criticised as the mechanistic theory because
(a) It viewed men as adjuncts of the machine or industrial robots
(b) It over-simplified the worker motivation
(c) It stressed on the physiological aspects of the organisation
(d) It under-emphasised the Sociological and Psychological dimensions of the organisation

20. Who stated "A purposive selection denotes the method of selecting a number of groups of units in such a way that selected groups together yields as nearly as possible the same averages or proportion as the totality with respect of thsoe characteristics which are already a matter of statistical knowledge"?
(a) P.V. Young
(b) Dr. Shyam Anand
(c) Adolph Jenson
(d) Smith and Whyte

21. Match the following:
List I
A. The cocoons of wild silk worm
B. Doupion silk yarn
C. Waste silk
D. Cross-section of silk fibre
E. Rod-like almost circular fibres
List II
(i) Triangle with rounded corners
(ii) Responsible for the luster of silk
(iii) Pierced so the fibre are shorter than reeled silk
(iv) Yarn is uneven irregular and larger in diameter
(v) Comprised of tangled man of silk on the outside of cocoon

Codes:	A	B	C	D	E
(a)	(i)	(ii)	(v)	(iv)	(iii)
(b)	(iii)	(v)	(iv)	(ii)	(i)
(c)	(iii)	(iv)	(v)	(i)	(ii)
(d)	(iv)	(iii)	(ii)	(i)	(v)

22. Flow and movement which creates interest in design
(a) Repetition (b) Radiation
(c) Gradation (d) Rhythm

23. The chart or the diagram should be
(a) Properly exhibited
(b) Given sufficient time
(c) Explained
(d) All of these

24. The child with approach response towards the mother will show
(a) Outgoing
(b) Friendly
(c) Favourable social attitude
(d) All of these

25. The difference between a university and a deemed university is that the former
(a) is much bigger in size
(b) is established by the act of legislature
(c) is established by the central government
(d) looks after only affiliated colleges

26. **Assertion (A):** Special rules and procedures are followed in the import and export trade.
Reason (R): The need for import and export trade is explained by the principles of 'Comparative Cost Theory'.
Codes:
(a) Both A and R are true and R is the correct explanation of A
(b) Both A and R are true but R is not a correct explanation of A
(c) A is true but R is false
(d) A is false but R is true

27. State which is/are true?
(a) According to the quota sampling universe is first divided into different Strata than the number to be selected from different stratum is decided

(b) Stratified sampling is a combination of both random sampling and purposive selection
(c) Purposive selection is at time very cheap
(d) All of these

28. The hook at the end of the rod of the Takli is for
(a) Winding (b) Binding
(c) Show (d) Pulling fibre

29. Which of the following is/are true?
(a) The Puranas tell us that Spinning and Weaving were important handicrafts
(b) The work of weaving during Arth shastra was done only by women and their ages depended upon the fineness of the yarn which they spun
(c) Worsted fabric came from Worsted in England
(d) All of these

30. pH value varies from 1 to 14 where 7 is
(a) Neutral (b) Alkaline
(c) Acidic (d) None of these

31. State which is/are true?
(a) If and when laggard adopt an innovation it usually occurs after one or more innovations have replaced the earlier innovation
(b) Laggards have virtually no contact with the mass media
(c) Laggards have the lowest social status and income of all adopter groups
(d) All of these

32. For most people activities pile up on each other at certain times of the day, the week, the month, or the season. These packed period are called
(a) time load (b) peak loads
(c) work curves (d) None of these

33. According to Ayurvedic Science orange juice is always good for health because
(a) Source of Vitamin C
(b) Not very expensive
(c) Its sweet
(d) It's a liquid diet

34. The process from fibres to textile in the right sequence is
(i) Textile (ii) Yarn
(iii) Fibres (iv) Fabric
Codes:
(a) (i), (ii) (b) (i), (iv)
(c) (i), (ii), (iii), (iv) (d) (iii), (ii), (iv), (i)

35. The phrase "equal educational opportunity" means
(a) Equal opportunity to have the type of education for which one is suited
(b) Provision of the same type of education
(c) Providing opportunity for all to get education at any level
(d) Ensuring admission to all for the desired stream of education

36. Kinds of stratified sampling are
(i) Proportional stratified sample
(ii) Disproportion stratified sample
(iii) Stratified weighted sample
(iv) Stratified unweighted sample
Codes:
(a) (i), (ii) (b) (i), (iv)
(c) (i), (ii), (iii), (iv) (d) (i), (ii), (iii)

37. .... is a simple running stitch, used to fill the straight curved lines in the floral designs.
(a) Khatawa (b) Phanda
(c) Taipchi (d) Mussi

38. State which is/are false?
(a) Rice contains less protein than wheat does but the protein of rice is of better quality.
(b) The outer layers of cereals are richer in protein than the inner starchy kernel.
(c) Defatted oilseed cakes which are very rich sources of protein are considered only for cattle feed and manures.
(d) All of these.

39. Disadvantages of stratified sampling are
    (a) Undue weight make the sample unrepresentative
    (b) Proportion difficult in equal strata
    (c) Bias in sample
    (d) All of these

40. Ways to reduce dissonance include
    (a) Eliminate or alter some elements
    (b) Rationalize the situation
    (c) Seek additional information
    (d) Any one

41. Kalamkari uses
    (a) Acid dyes (b) Basic dyes
    (c) Indigo vat dyes (d) Reactive dyes

42. Symptoms like irritability, headache, nausea, forceful vomiting are result of
    (a) intake of large amounts of Vit. A over prolonged period
    (b) fasting
    (c) hot climate
    (d) None of the above

43. Education as an investment aims at
    (a) Enhancing productivity
    (b) Cultural development
    (c) Development of democratic outlook
    (d) Satisfaction of learners

44. In Mahabharata the wife has been called the root of
    (i) Dharma (ii) Prosperity
    (iii) Enjoyment (iv) Conflict

    Codes:
    (a) (i), (ii) (b) (i), (iv)
    (c) (i), (ii), (iii), (iv) (d) (i), (ii), (iii)

45. Which of the following is true of vegetables fibre?
    (a) Cotton has 91% cellulose linen has 70%
    (b) Its chemical composition is carbon dioxide, hydrogen and oxygen
    (c) Vegetable fibre made of cellulose
    (d) All of these

46. A heavy cause fabric with apronounced rub effect
    (a) Rep (b) Shanting
    (c) Bengaline (d) None of these

47. PERT stands for
    (a) Program Entry Review Transition
    (b) Program Evaluation for Retail Transaction
    (c) Program Evaluation and Review Feed
    (d) None of above

48. The number of families residing in a particular village or the number of studens studying in a college or number of females and males serving in an office is an example of
    (i) Indifenite Universe
    (ii) Definite Universe

    Codes:
    (a) (i) only (b) (ii) only
    (c) Both (i) and (ii) (d) None of these

49. Key problems of Textile Industry include
    (a) Quality (b) Handlooms
    (c) Prices (d) All of above

50. Criterian for choosing conventional and non-conventional standards could be
    (a) Effect on concerned
    (b) Quality and social acceptability of standard
    (c) Cost
    (d) All of the above

ANSWER SHEET

PAPER—I

1. (d)	2. (d)	3. (c)	4. (d)	5. (d)
6. (a)	7. (b)	8. (d)	9. (d)	10. (d)
11. (d)	12. (c)	13. (c)	14. (b)	15. (a)
16. (d)	17. (d)	18. (b)	19. (c)	20. (b)
21. (a)	22. (b)	23. (c)	24. (c)	25. (c)
26. (b)	27. (b)	28. (c)	29. (b)	30. (b)

31. (a)	32. (b)	33. (c)	34. (a)	35. (b)
36. (d)	37. (b)	38. (d)	39. (c)	40. (a)
41. (a)	42. (b)	43. (a)	44. (a)	45. (b)
46. (c)	47. (c)	48. (c)	49. (d)	50. (c)

PAPER—II

1. (d)	2. (b)	3. (c)	4. (c)	5. (a)
6. (b)	7. (c)	8. (d)	9. (b)	10. (d)
11. (b)	12. (b)	13. (a)	14. (c)	15. (b)
16. (d)	17. (b)	18. (b)	19. (c)	20. (a)
21. (b)	22. (c)	23. (c)	24. (c)	25. (c)
26. (d)	27. (c)	28. (d)	29. (a)	30. (c)
31. (b)	32. (a)	33. (d)	34. (b)	35. (c)
36. (a)	37. (b)	38. (b)	39. (a)	40. (d)
41. (d)	42. (b)	43. (c)	44. (c)	45. (d)
46. (c)	47. (d)	48. (b)	49. (a)	50. (c)

PAPER—III

1. (b)	2. (c)	3. (c)	4. (d)	5. (d)
6. (b)	7. (d)	8. (b)	9. (d)	10. (a)
11. (c)	12. (c)	13. (c)	14. (d)	15. (d)
16. (d)	17. (a)	18. (c)	19. (a)	20. (c)
21. (c)	22. (c)	23. (d)	24. (d)	25. (d)
26. (b)	27. (d)	28. (d)	29. (d)	30. (c)
31. (d)	32. (b)	33. (a)	34. (d)	35. (a)
36. (d)	37. (c)	38. (d)	39. (d)	40. (d)
41. (a)	42. (a)	43. (a)	44. (d)	45. (b)
46. (a)	47. (c)	48. (b)	49. (a)	50. (d)

MOCK TEST–3
PAPER–I

1. Which among the following gives more freedom to the learner to interact?
   (a) Small group discussion
   (b) Lectures by experts
   (c) Use of film
   (d) Viewing country-wide classroom program on TV

2. While designing communication strategy feed-forward studies are conducted by
   (a) Media (b) Audience
   (c) Communicator (d) Satellite

3. A theory is correct because
   (a) its derivations match with most observations
   (b) its advocate has written a big volume to establish it
   (c) it is supported by a large number of scholars
   (d) it has a large number of followers

4. Which of the following are true about the concepts?
   I. Concepts have different meanings in different contents.
   II. Concepts are the blocks from which theories are built.
   III. Concepts are ideas, abstractions, that do not have meaning in themselves.

   Codes:
   (a) II only (b) I and III
   (c) I and II (d) All of these

5. The most sensible idea about teaching and research is that
   (a) they interfere with each other
   (b) they are two entirely different kinds of activities
   (c) they cannot go together
   (d) they are two sides of the same coin

6. Which of the following is quality of a teacher?
   (a) He should know the child psychology
   (b) He should evoke curiosity of the pupils by presenting the subject matter in an effective manner with clear explaining leading to better understanding of the matter
   (c) He should be trained in various teaching methodologies
   (d) All of these

7. Which of the following is/are true about research?
   (i) Gives emphasis to the development of theories, principles and generalisation, which are very helpful in accurate prediction regarding the variable understudy.
   (ii) It is always directed towards the solution of a problem.
   (iii) It is always based upon empirical or observable evidences.

   Codes:
   (a) Both (i) and (ii)
   (b) Both (i) and (iii)
   (c) Both (ii) and (iii)
   (d) All of the above

8. Which of the following methods of teaching encourages the use of maximum senses?
   (a) Team teaching method
   (b) Problem-solving method
   (c) Laboratory method
   (d) Self-study method

9. A non-fictional literary composition that forms an independent part of a publication, as a newspaper or magazine is known as
   (a) Symposium (b) Paper
   (c) Article (d) None of these

10. Photo bleeding means
    (a) Photo placement
    (b) Photo cropping
    (c) Photo colour adjustment
    (d) Photo cutting

11. Attitudes, concepts, skills and knowledge are products of
    (a) Explanation (b) Learning
    (c) Research (d) Heredity

12. To study the relationship of family size with income a researcher classifies his population into different income slabs and then takes a random sample from each slab. Which technique of sampling does he adopt?
    (a) Systematic Sampling
    (b) Random Sampling
    (c) Stratified Random Sampling
    (d) Cluster Sampling

13. In business communication, the major obstacles arise because of the
    (a) psychological barriers
    (b) physical barriers
    (c) organisational barriers
    (d) mechanical barriers

14. The most important question that a researcher is interested to use statistical techniques in his problem then he has to see
    (a) whether worthwhile inferences could be drawn
    (b) whether the data could be quantified
    (c) whether appropriate statistical techniques are available
    (d) whether analysis of data would be possible

15. How can the objectivity of the research be enhanced?
    (a) Through its validity
    (b) Through its impartiality
    (c) Through its reliability
    (d) All of these

16. Which one of the following is not correct? A belief becomes a scientific truth when it
    (a) can be replicated
    (b) is established experimentally
    (c) is arrived by logically
    (d) is accepted by many people

17. **Statement:** All cars are ducks. All ducks are birds.

    Conclusions:
    (i) All birds are cars.
    (ii) All cars are birds.

    Choose the correct one.
    (a) Only conclusion (i) follows
    (b) Only conclusion (ii) follows

(c) Both (i) and (ii) follow
(d) Neither (i) nor (ii) follows

18. Research can be conducted by a person who
(a) is a hard worker
(b) has studied research methodology
(c) holds a postgraduate degree
(d) possesses thinking and reasoning ability

19. Action-research is
(a) A longitudinal research
(b) An applied research
(c) A research carried out to solve immediate problems
(d) All of the above

Read the following passage and answer the questions 20 to 24:

The genesis of service tax emanates from the ongoing structural transformation of the Indian economy, whereby presently more than one-half of GDP originates from the services sector. Despite the growing presence of the services sector in the Indian economy it remained out of the tax net prior to 1994-95, leading to a steady deterioration in tax-GDP ratio. The service tax was introduced in 1994-95 on a select category of services at a low rate of five percent. While the service tax rate and the coverage of services being taxed have increased ever since, the combined tax-GDP ratio of the Centre and States, nevertheless, deteriorated from 16.4 percent in 1985-86 to 14.1 percent in 1999-2000. It may be noted that between 1990-91 and 1998-99, the share of industrial sector in GDP dropped by 6.4 percentage points whereas almost 64 percent of the tax revenue was generated by indirect taxes for which industrial sector continues to be the principal tax base. On the other hand, during the same period, the share of services sector in GDP has increased by 10 percentage points and this sector has still remained poorly taxed.

The rationale for service tax, therefore, lies not only in arresting the falling tax-GDP ratio but also in *ipso facto* improving allocative efficiency in the economy as well as promoting equity. Against this backdrop, the service tax needs to be designed taking into account the fact that (i) the share of services in GDP is expanding; (ii) failure to tax services distorts consumer choices and encourages spending on services at the expense of goods; (iii) untaxed service traders are unable to claim Value Added Tax (VAT) on service inputs, which encourages businesses to develop in-house services, creating further distortions; and (iv) most services that are likely to become taxable are positively correlated with expenditure of high-income households and, therefore, service tax improves equity.

In the Indian context, taxation of services assumes importance in the wake of the need for improving the revenue system, ensuring a measure of neutrality in taxation between goods and services and eventually helping to evolve an efficient system of domestic trade taxes, both at the Central and the State levels.

20. What, according to the passage, was the impact of exclusion of service tax till the first half of the last decade of the past century?
(a) Service sector used to flourish exorbitantly
(b) There was no impact as there was no service tax
(c) There was a steady deterioration in the GDP
(d) Tax-GDP ratio had steadily and gradually aggravated

21. Levying service tax is most likely to achieve which of the following?
(i) Promoting equity.
(ii) Check on reducing tax-GDP ratio.
(iii) Enhancement in allocative efficiency.

Codes:
(a) Both (ii) and (iii)
(b) Both (i) and (iii)
(c) Both (i) and (ii)
(d) All the three

22. The origin of service tax is attributed to
(a) metamorphosis of our country's economy
(b) increase in Gross Domestic Product (GDP)
(c) existence of service sector
(d) tax of the future

23. Which of the following factors helps service tax to improve fairness across different economic strata of society?
(a) It improves revenue system
(b) Taxable services are mostly those that are utilised by the rich
(c) Untaxed service traders are prevented from claiming value added tax
(d) Encouragement to in-house services is effected

24. Which of the following is most likely to provide neutrality to various economic activities?
(a) Consistency in tax structure and revenue buoyancy
(b) Increase in revenue buoyancy
(c) fairness in tax administration
(d) Equity and efficiency in various activities

25. Which of the following is classified in the category of the developmental research?
(a) Descriptive research
(b) Philosophical research
(c) Action research
(d) All the above

26. The education aims at the fullest realisation of all the potentialities of children. It implies that
I. it is necessary that their attitudes are helpful, encouraging and sympathetic.
II. teacher and parents must know what children are capable of and what potentialities they possess.
III. they should provide suitable opportunities and favourable environmental facilities which are conducive to the maximum growth of children.

Choose the correct one.
Codes:
(a) II and III (b) I and III
(c) I and II (d) All of them

27. How many times has the preamble of Indian Constitution been amended so far?
(a) Once (b) Twice
(c) Thrice (d) Never

28. The relationship between earth, mountains and forests can be represented as

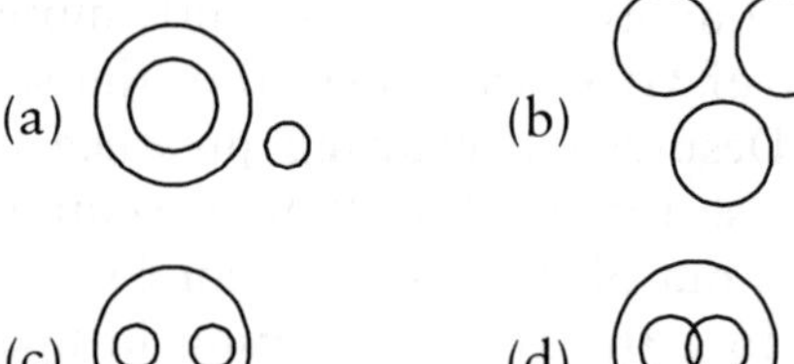

29. Central Fuel Research Institute is situated in
(a) Pune (b) Jadugoda
(c) Lucknow (d) Kolkata

30. The letters in the first set have certain relationship. On the basis of this relationship what is the right choice for the second set?
AST : BRU :: NQV : ?
(a) OPW (b) ORW
(c) MPU (d) MRW

31. The number of students in four classes A, B, C, D and their respective mean marks obtained by each of the class are given below:

	Class A	Class B	Class C	Class D
Number of students	10	40	30	20
Arithmetic mean	20	30	50	15

The combined mean of the marks of four classes together will be
(a) 15 (b) 32
(c) 50 (d) 20

32. Communication with oneself is known as
(a) Organisational communication
(b) Interpersonal communication
(c) Intrapersonal communication
(d) Grapevine communication

33. The number system which is not a positional notation system is
(a) Binary (b) Octal
(c) Roman (d) Decimal

34. Which of the following options will complete the series?
AZ, GT, MN, ?, YB.
(a) TS (b) KF
(c) RX (d) SH

35. If '367' means 'I am happy'; '748' means 'You are sad' and '469' means 'Happy and sad' in a given code, then which of the following represents 'and' in that code?
(a) 4 (b) 6
(c) 3 (d) 9

36. What is the excess 3 code?
(a) self-algebraic code
(b) cyclic complimenting code
(c) cyclic algebraic code
(d) self-complimenting code

37. Which of the following is not created by the Act of Parliament?
(a) Railway Board
(b) Atomic Energy Commission
(c) Backward Class Commission
(d) University Grants Commission

38. Which of the following is radioactive pollutant?
(a) Nickel (b) Iron
(c) Chlorine (d) Thorium

39. The first Indian experimental geostationary communication satellite was
(a) Skylab (b) Apple
(c) INSAT-1A (d) INSAT-1B

40. Which one of the following is a research tool?
(a) Diagram (b) Questionnaire
(c) Graph (d) Illustration

41. Which article of the constitution provides safeguards to Naga Customary and their social practices against any act of Parliament?
(a) Article 371B (b) Article 371A
(c) Article 263 (d) Article 371C

42. **Statement:** Although the city was under kneedeep water for a week in this monsoon, there is no outbreak of any water borne disease.
Assumptions:
(i) Waterborne disease usually spreads in monsoon.
(ii) Water concentration at a place leads to waterborne disease.
Choose the correct option.
(a) Only assumption (i) is implicit
(b) Only assumption (ii) is implicit
(c) Both (i) and (ii) are implicit
(d) Neither (i) nor (ii) is implicit

43. Books and records are the primary sources of data in
(a) laboratory research
(b) historical research
(c) participatory research
(d) clinical research

44. The Kothari Commission's report was entitled on
(a) Learning to be adventure
(b) Education and National Development
(c) Education and socialisation in democracy
(d) Diversification of Education

45. What is the term used for a half byte?
(a) Word (b) Bit
(c) Nibble (d) Bug

46. C-band transponder in satellites uses the frequency range
(a) 12 GHz to 14 GHz
(b) 4 GHz to 6 GHz
(c) 2 GHz to 4 GHz
(d) None of these.

47. Which of the following water pollutants is the cause of sterility in human beings?
(a) Manganese (b) Mercury
(c) Arsenic (d) None of these

48. Match List I with List II and select the correct answer using the codes given below.

List I (Institutes)
A. Central Arid Zone Institute
B. Space Application Centre
C. Indian Institute of Public Administration
D. Headquarters of Indian Science Congress

List II (Cities)
(1) Kolkata (2) New Delhi
(3) Ahmedabad (4) Jodhpur

Codes:	A	B	C	D
(a)	4	3	2	1
(b)	4	2	1	3
(c)	3	1	2	4
(d)	1	2	4	3

The total CO_2 emissions from various sectors are 5 mmt. In the Pie Chart given below, the percentage contribution to CO_2 emissions from various sectors is indicated.

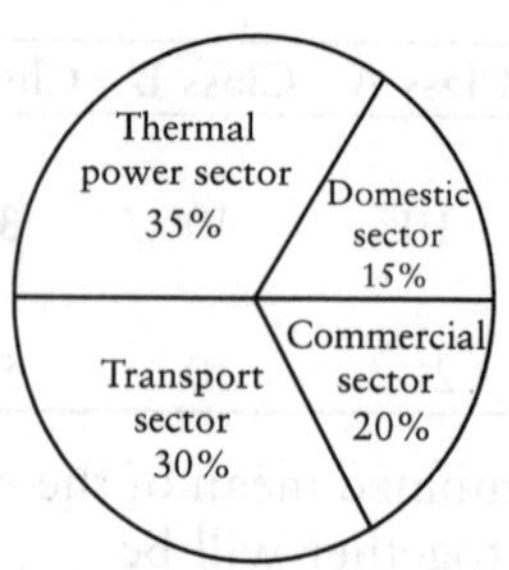

49. What is the absolute CO_2 emission from domestic sector?
(a) 1.75 mmt (b) 0.75 mmt
(c) 1.5 mmt (d) 2.5 mmt

50. What is the absolute CO_2 emission for combined thermal power and transport sectors?
(a) 1.5 mmt (b) 3.25 mmt
(c) 4 mmt (d) 2.5 mmt

PAPER–II

1. What causes warts?
(a) Bacteria (b) Virus
(c) Poor hygiene (d) Toads

2. In modern times there is increase in
(a) Nuclear family (b) Joint family
(c) Both (a) and (b) (d) None of these

3. Which of these would be the healthiest choice for a snack?
(a) Cookies (b) Chips
(c) Peanuts (d) None

4. How many servings of fruits and vegetables should you have every day?
(a) 1-3 (b) 2-6
(c) 5-9 (d) 10-12

5. What is a blood clot?
(a) A blockage in a blood vessel
(b) Blood that has thickened into a soft clump
(c) An impurity in blood
(d) A scab

6. How much calcium do we need to be healthy?
   (a) 100 mg per day
   (b) 400 mg per day
   (c) 700 mg per day
   (d) No fixed amount
7. Next to bacterially caused gum disease the most common cause of gum disease is
   (a) accidents such as football injuries, car crashes, falls
   (b) self-inflicted brushing trauma
   (c) eating hot and spicy foods
   (d) smoking cigarettes and chewing tobacco
8. Who are most susceptible to shingles?
   (a) Newborn infants
   (b) People who've received the chickenpox vaccine
   (c) People who've had chickenpox and are undergoing treatment for cancer or AIDS
   (d) Elderly people who've never had chickenpox
9. What is a symptom of hereditary patterned baldness?
   (a) Rapid hair loss
   (b) One or more patches of hair loss
   (c) Thinning hair
   (d) Breaking of hair shafts
10. UNICEF organization works for the welfare of
   (a) Children (b) Old people
   (c) Patients (d) Pregnant women
11. What is a symptom of a blood clot?
   (a) Muscle pain
   (b) Lack of pulse in the affected extremity
   (c) Bluish skin tone
   (d) All of the above
12. Smoking increases your susceptibility to which of the following?
   (a) Flu, pneumonia, tuberculosis
   (b) Arthritis, lupus
   (c) Infertility, menstrual cramps, and irregular periods
   (d) All of the above
13. How does one get a chronic disease?
   (a) From smoking
   (b) From eating too much
   (c) You catch it from your parents
   (d) All of the above
14. You should exercise at least
   (a) Two days/week
   (b) Three days/week
   (c) Four days/week
   (d) Five days/week
15. Arrange the following teaching learning methods in order of learner's ability:
   (i) A video show
   (ii) Laboratory method
   (iii) Demonstration
   (iv) Radio talk
   Codes:
   (a) (ii), (i), (iii), (iv) (b) (iv), (i), (iii), (ii)
   (c) (i), (ii), (iii), (iv) (d) (ii), (iii), (i), (iv)
16. Arrange the following foods in decreasing order of carotene content:
   (i) Jaggery (ii) Maize
   (iii) Curry leaves (iv) Pumpkin
   Codes:
   (a) (iv), (i), (ii), (iii) (b) (iv), (iii), (ii), (i)
   (c) (iii), (ii), (i), (iv) (d) (iii), (iv), (ii), (i)
17. The correct sequence for determination of proteins by kjeldahl method is:
   (i) Drying and weighing the sample
   (ii) Distillation
   (iii) Digestion with H_2SO_4
   (iv) Titration
   Codes:
   (a) (i), (iv), (iii), (ii)
   (b) (ii), (i), (iv), (iii)
   (c) (iv), (ii), (i), (iii)
   (d) (iii), (i), (ii), (iv)

18. Match the following:

List I

A. Spectrophotometer
B. Soxlet Apparatus
C. HPLC
D. Muffle furnace

List II

(i) Retinol
(ii) Iron
(iii) Total inorganic content
(iv) Oil

Codes:	**A**	**B**	**C**	**D**
(a)	(iii)	(iv)	(i)	(ii)
(b)	(ii)	(i)	(iv)	(iii)
(c)	(iv)	(i)	(iii)	(ii)
(d)	(iii)	(i)	(ii)	(iv)

19. **Assertion (A):** Hyperlipidaemia is generally related to an increase in the lipids of blood.

Reason (R): The use of safflower (Kardi) oil, corn-oil, or sesame oil are not preferred for hyperlipidaemic patient.

Codes:

(a) (A) is true but (R) is false
(b) (A) is false but (R) is true
(c) Both (A) and (R) are true
(d) Both (A) and (R) are false

20. **Assertion (A):** Cloudiness occurs in clod tea.

Reason (R): It is due to the reaction of tannins and caffeine with acid.

Codes:

(a) A is true but R is false
(b) Both A and R are true
(c) A is false and R is true
(d) Both A and R are false

21. Give the correct sequence of foods in decreasing order of iron content:

(i) Liver (ii) Apple
(iii) Dates (iv) Wheat flour
(v) Lotus stem

Codes:

(a) (i), (ii), (iii), (iv), (v)
(b) (iv), (i), (v), (ii), (iii)
(c) (ii), (i), (iii), (iv), (v)
(d) (ii), (iii), (i), (iv), (v)

22. Arrange in sequence the phases of fat absorption:

(i) Emulsification
(ii) Esterification
(iii) Mucosal uptake
(iv) Chylomicron formation

Codes:

(a) (i), (ii), (iii), (iv) (b) (ii), (iii), (iv), (i)
(c) (i), (iii), (ii), (iv) (d) (ii), (iii), (i), (iv)

23. Arrange the steps of cotton spinning system in the correct sequence:

(i) Drawing (ii) Carding
(iii) Combing (iv) Roving

Codes:

(a) (ii), (i), (iii), (iv) (b) (i), (iii), (ii), (iv)
(c) (i), (ii), (iii), (iv) (d) (ii), (iii), (i), (iv)

Read the following passage and answer the questions 24 to 27:

Political education may be defined as the preparation of a citizen to take well informed, responsible and sustained action for participation in the national struggle for the realization of the socio-economic objectives of the country. The over-riding socio-economic objectives in India are the abolition of poverty and the creation of a modern democratic, secular and socialist society in place of the present traditional, feudal, hierarchical and inegalitarian one.

Under the British rule, the Congress leaders argued that political education was an important part of education and refused to accept the official view that education and politics should not be mixed with one another. But when they came to power in 1947 they almost adopted the British policy and began to talk of education being defiled by politics. 'Hands off education' was the call to political parties. But in spite of it, political infiltration into the educational system has greatly increased in the sense that different political parties vie with each other to capture the minds of teachers and students. The wise academicians wanted political support, without political interference. What we have actually received is infinite political interference with little genuine political support. This interference with the educational system by political parties for their own ulterior motives is no political education at all; and with the all-round growth of elitism, it is hardly a matter for surprise that real political education within the school system (which really means the creation of a commitment to social transformation) has been even weaker than in the pre-independence period.

At the same time, the freedom struggle came to an end and the major non-formal agency of political education disappeared. The press could and did provide some political education. But it did not utilize the opportunity to the full and the stronghold of vested interests continued to dominate it. The same can be said of political parties as well as of other institutions and agencies outside the school system which can be expected to provide political education.

24. According to the passage political education in the real sense should prepare
    (a) citizens for social change.
    (b) well-informed politicians.
    (c) responsible students of political science.
    (d) devoted social workers.

25. The theme of the passage could be
    (a) British rule in India and Education.
    (b) Education and Politics.
    (c) Education for Freedom.
    (d) Leadership and Education.

26. The author emphasizes in the passage that
    (a) non-formal agencies of political education do not exist in India.
    (b) vested interests dominate politics.
    (c) real political education is lacking in India.
    (d) the Britishers were opposed to real political education.

27. The author condemns the
    (a) role of the Britishers in organizing education in India.
    (b) role of the Congress in politics after independence.
    (c) political interference in education in India.
    (d) role of the Press in political education.

28. Symptoms of shock include
    (a) Rapid, weak pulse
    (b) Confusion
    (c) Pale, cold clammy skin
    (d) Breathless and nausea

29. What are the advantages of having a baby without medication?
    (a) Babies born without drugs are more active and alert
    (b) Right after birth the mother can comfort, stroke and gaze at her baby
    (c) Breast feeding is more easily established
    (d) All of the above

30. What is efficiency in health care?
    (a) The allocation of resources between individuals and social groups
    (b) The allocation of resources to maximize health benefits
    (c) The allocation of resources to achieve the expected result
    (d) The allocation of resources to reduce cost

31. Extension learner learn the ideas and practices by
    (i) Doing (ii) Reading
    (iii) Watching (iv) Neighbour

    Codes:
    (a) (i), (ii) and (iii) are correct
    (b) (i), (iii) and (iv) are correct

(c) (i) and (ii) are correct
(d) (i) and (iii) are correct

32. Smokers are how much more likely than non-smokers to develop the scaly, red, chronic skin condition called psoriasis?
(a) 25% (b) 50%
(c) Twice (d) 400 times

33. **Assertion (A):** Community Development Programme was started after Independence.
Reason (R): Community Development Programme aims at self-reliant and rural development.
Codes:
(a) (A) is true but (R) is false
(b) (A) is false but (R) is true
(c) Both (A) and (R) are true
(d) Both (A) and (R) are false

34. Match the List I with List II:
List I
A. Folder B. Journals
C. Leaflet D. Bulletin
List II
(i) Single sheet of small size paper
(ii) Single printed sheet of big size paper
(iii) Containing research information
(iv) Printed bound booklet

Codes:	A	B	C	D
(a)	(ii)	(iii)	(i)	(iv)
(b)	(ii)	(i)	(iv)	(iii)
(c)	(iv)	(i)	(iii)	(ii)
(d)	(iii)	(i)	(ii)	(iv)

35. Arrange the elements of communication to form a model:
(i) Message (ii) Audience
(iii) Source (iv) Channel
Codes:
(a) (i), (iv), (iii), (ii) (b) (i), (iii), (ii), (iv)
(c) (ii), (i), (iii), (iv) (d) (iii), (i), (iv), (ii)

36. **Assertion (A):** Celiac disease is an autoimmune inflammatory disease of small intestine.
Reason (R): It is precipitated by the ingestion of gluten.
Codes:
(a) (A) is true but (R) is false
(b) (A) is false but (R) is true
(c) Both (A) and (R) are true
(d) Both (A) and (R) are false

37. **Assertion (A):** A kwashiorkor child shows oedema of the lower limbs.
Reason (R): The kidneys are not able to excrete sodium thus causing water retention.
Codes:
(a) (A) is true but (R) is false
(b) (A) is false but (R) is true
(c) Both (A) and (R) are true
(d) Both (A) and (R) are false

38. Sleeves most appropriate for infants garment are:
I. Leg of Mutton II. Saddler
III. Kimono IV. Raglan
Find the right combination according to code:
Codes:
(a) II and III are correct
(b) III and IV are correct
(c) I and II are correct
(d) II and IV are correct

39. Match the following:

List I	List II
A. Kratomalacia	(i) Symmetrical Dermatitis
B. Rickets	(ii) Moon Face
C. Pellagra	(iii) Pale skin
D. Kwashiorkor	(iv) Blindness
	(v) Pigeon Chest

Codes:	A	B	C	D
(a)	(iv)	(v)	(i)	(ii)
(b)	(ii)	(i)	(iv)	(iii)
(c)	(iv)	(i)	(iii)	(ii)
(d)	(iii)	(i)	(v)	(iv)

40. Match the following in List I with List II:

List I

A. Resources
B. Human Resources
C. Economic Resources
D. Non-Human Resources

List II

(i) Ability skill
(ii) Materials and human abilities
(iii) Tangible resources
(iv) Knowledge, time, community resources
(v) Resources and in production and distribution

Codes:	A	B	C	D
(a)	(iii)	(iv)	(i)	(ii)
(b)	(iv)	(iii)	(v)	(ii)
(c)	(iv)	(i)	(iii)	(ii)
(d)	(ii)	(i)	(v)	(iii)

41. Goals of the elderly include:
(i) Family relations
(ii) Good health
(iii) Education
(iv) Vocational pursuits

Codes:
(a) (i) and (iii) (b) (i) and (ii)
(c) (ii) and (iii) (d) (iv) only

42. **Assertion (A):** The quality of decision determine the quality of management.
Reason (R): Decision-making occurs when there is a problem to solve or some choice to make.

Codes:
(a) (A) is true but (R) is false
(b) (A) is false but (R) is true
(c) Both (A) and (R) are true
(d) Both (A) and (R) are false

43. **Assertion (A):** Need assessment is carried out to identify the gap between the present and the desired situation.
Reason (R): Objectives of programme planning are based on need assessment.

Codes:
(a) (A) is true but (R) is false
(b) (A) is false but (R) is true
(c) Both (A) and (R) are true
(d) Both (A) and (R) are false

44. Match the following:

List I

A. Wechsler scale
B. The perspective of the social group is considered
C. Think of one aspect of a relationship at a time
D. Defects which are results of alcohol consumption

List II

(i) Intelligence
(ii) Centring
(iii) Social conventional role thinking
(iv) Fetal alcohol syndrome (FAS) during pregnancy

Codes:	A	B	C	D
(a)	(iii)	(iv)	(i)	(ii)
(b)	(ii)	(i)	(iv)	(iii)
(c)	(ii)	(iii)	(i)	(iv)
(d)	(iii)	(i)	(ii)	(iv)

45. Panchayati Raj Institution in the hierarchy of governance from grassroots upwards is:
(i) Gram Sabha
(ii) Block Panchayat
(iii) District Panchayat
(iv) Gram Panchayat

Codes:
(a) (i), (ii), (iii), (iv) (b) (ii), (i), (iv), (iii)
(c) (i), (iv), (ii), (iii) (d) (i), (iii), (ii), (iv)

46. Sequence the scales of measurement from the lowest to the highest:
(i) Interval scale (ii) Ordinal scale
(iii) Nominal scale (iv) Ratio scale

Codes:
(a) (iv), (i), (ii), (iii) (b) (iv), (iii), (ii), (i)
(c) (iii), (ii), (i), (iv) (d) (iii), (iv), (ii), (i)

47. Match the List I with List II:

List I
A. Change in knowledge
B. Change in attitude
C. Change in confidence
D. Change in skill

List II
(i) Self-reliance
(ii) Doing things
(iii) What people know
(iv) Reaction towards certain things

Codes:	**A**	**B**	**C**	**D**
(a)	(ii)	(iv)	(i)	(iii)
(b)	(ii)	(i)	(iv)	(iii)
(c)	(iii)	(iv)	(i)	(ii)
(d)	(iii)	(i)	(ii)	(iv)

48. Give the correct sequence in writing a Research Proposal:
(i) Review of literature
(ii) Introduction
(iii) Bibliography
(iv) Objectives
(v) Methodology
(vi) Analysis of data

Codes:
(a) (i), (iv), (iii), (ii), (v), (vi)
(b) (ii), (i), (iv), (iii), (vi), (v)
(c) (iv), (i), (ii), (iii), (v), (vi)
(d) (iv), (ii), (i), (v), (vi), (iii)

49. **Assertion (A):** Retention of learning is more when variety of learning experiences are provided by the teacher.
Reason (R): Retention is facilitated when two or more senses are used at a time of learning.

Codes:
(a) Both (A) and (R) are true
(b) (A) is true but (R) is false
(c) (A) is false but (R) is true
(d) Both (A) and (R) are false

50. Match the communication medium from List I to category in List II:

List I	**List II**
A. Puppets	(i) Graphic aid
B. Charts	(ii) Electronic
C. Computer	(iii) Traditional media
D. Print	(iv) Mass media

Codes:	**A**	**B**	**C**	**D**
(a)	(i)	(iv)	(iii)	(ii)
(b)	(ii)	(i)	(iv)	(iii)
(c)	(iii)	(i)	(ii)	(iv)
(d)	(iii)	(ii)	(i)	(iv)

PAPER–III

1. The Scientific Management is based upon which of the following assumptions?
   1. Application of the scientific methods to organisational problems leads to efficiency.
   2. The good worker is one who accepts orders, but does not initiate actions.
   3. Worker is more important than the work.
   4. Each worker is interested in maximizing his monetary rewards.

   Select the correct rewards:

   Codes:
   (a) 1, 2 and 3 (b) 1, 2 and 4
   (c) 2, 3 and 4 (d) 1, 2, 3, and 4

2. Charts using is an advantage in
   (i) Information in gist
   (ii) Facts and figures clear
   (iii) Information interesting
   (iv) Logical combination

   Codes:
   (a) (i), (ii) (b) (i), (iv)
   (c) (i), (ii), (iii), (iv) (d) (i), (ii), (iii)

3. The old marketing concept offers key guidelines for
   (a) Integration (b) Organising
   (c) Planning (d) All of these

4. The purpose of the report
   (a) Widest use in public
   (b) Broadcasting of generalization
   (c) Dissipation of knowledge
   (d) All of these

5. The status of women was lowered even further during the .... period(s).
   (i) Buddhist (ii) Musi
   (iii) British (iv) Modern
   Codes:
   (a) (i), (ii) (b) (i), (iv)
   (c) (i), (ii), (iii), (iv) (d) (i), (ii)

6. The main problem for determining educational policy in India is that
   (a) people having higher technical education do not have employment opportunities at all
   (b) people of higher technical education have unemployment
   (c) people with higher technical education do not find enough opportunity in India
   (d) All of the above

7. Match the following:
   List I
   A. Thiamine sparing action in terms of fat means.
   B. Yeast outer layer of rice wheat and other cereal.
   C. Thiamine requirement is expressed
   D. Riboflavin.
   E. Scrotal dermatitis.
   List II
   (i) high thiamine content.
   (ii) in terms of calorie intake and it is about 0.5 mg of vitamin per 1000 calories.
   (iii) presence of fat in the diet reduces the need for the thiamin.
   (iv) is concerned with several oxidization processes inside the cell.
   (v) reboflavin deficiency.

Codes:	A	B	C	D	E
(a)	(iv)	(iii)	(ii)	(i)	(v)
(b)	(v)	(iv)	(iii)	(ii)	(i)
(c)	(iii)	(i)	(ii)	(iv)	(v)
(d)	(v)	(iv)	(i)	(ii)	(iii)

8. The report should also mention
   (a) Criteria for selection
   (b) Size of sample
   (c) Sampling method
   (d) All of these

9. The process followed by crochet and shuttle is
   (a) Looping (b) Twisting
   (c) Knotting (d) All of these

10. Resiliency is the ability of a fibre to return to shape after
    (i) Compression
    (ii) Bending
    (iii) Creasing
    (iv) Similar deformation
    Codes:
    (a) (i), (ii) (b) (i), (iv)
    (c) (i), (ii), (iii), (iv) (d) (i), (ii), (iii)

11. A plain red chaddar worn for daily wear in house. It has formal booties far apart from the house
    (a) Thirma (b) Tilpatra
    (c) Suber (d) Saloo

12. The oldest method in psychology is
    (a) introspection (b) observation
    (c) case study (d) clinical method

13. In Aitereya Upanishad, the wife has been termed as
    (a) Queen (b) Ardhangini
    (c) Companion (d) Servant

14. Who stated this on satellite and its impact on distance education? "In some cases hermes (the satellite) brought people together in a way that was every bit as emotionally moving as it was intellectually stimulating. In other cases

students became bored technical problems made effective interaction impossible information seemed colourless and static".

(a) Geoff Potter
(b) Dr. Shyam Anand
(c) Rajiv Gandhi
(d) Sam Pitroda

15. Objective standards are the earnest standards to identify that influence much of one's life as they are rigid standards.
(a) Object Standards
(b) Qualitative Standards
(c) Quantitative standards
(d) None of these

16. Experimental method starts with some problems which have
(a) no solution for a brief time span
(b) no adequate solution
(c) an immediate solution
(d) None of the above

17. Which of the following are the principles of Scientific Management?
1. Development of a science of work
2. Different Piece Rate Plan
3. Standardisation of tools and equipments
4. Scientific selection of workman.
5. Co-operation between Managers and workers.

Select the correct code:

Codes:

(a) 1, 3, 4 and 5 (b) 1, 4 and 5
(c) 1, 2, 3 and 4 (d) 1, 2, 3, 4 and 5

18. The disadvantage of cross sectional research is the differences between persons of different ages stemming from the fact that they have experienced contrasting social or cultural conditions. This factor is termed as
(a) Side-effect (b) Self-experience
(c) Life experience (d) Whort effect

19. Which of the following is/are true?
(a) Low orientation produces low strength and high elongation. In this molecules lie in random arrangement
(b) Vedic Indians were fond of Suvasas or beautiful garments
(c) Molecules within fibres parallel to each other are highly oriented associated with good fibre strength and low elongation
(d) All of these

20. Interval Scales have
(a) Equal appearing units
(b) No equal appearing units
(c) No statistical value
(d) No mathematical Design

21. Factors considered while selecting kitchen utensils—
(i) Size of the family
(ii) Method of cooking
(iii) Durability of utensil
(iv) Safety, weight and price

Codes:

(a) (i), (ii) (b) (i), (iv)
(c) (i), (ii), (iii), (iv) (d) (i), (ii), (iii)

22. The various programmes which supervisor might to take up in the capacity of consultant and advisor involves?
(a) Study groups
(b) Faculty meetings
(c) Organisation of workshops
(d) All of these

23. Karnataka accounts for ..... % of country's total production of silk.
(a) 40 (b) 50
(c) 60 (d) 70

24. Akbar wore two shawls at a time. This was termed as
(a) Ruffle (b) Gamacha
(c) Stool (d) Doshala

25. Mixed cotton and silk fabrics. It means permitted and refers to the prohibition of the use of pure silk by Muslim men

(a) Amru (b) Bafts
(c) Mashru (d) Himru

26. The first rating scale was developed by
(a) Starch (1910)
(b) Diggory(1953)
(c) Ebbinghaus(1885)
(d) J.B.Watson (1913)

27. Values play major role in determining
(a) Attitudes (b) Standards
(c) Goals (d) All of these

28. Textile fabrics originally took their names from the place. Where they first acquired excellence and retained them long after the local manufacture had been transferred elsewhere. These are
(i) Damask from Damascus
(ii) Satin from Zay-town in China
(iii) Sindon, Sandalin from Sindh
(iv) Calico from Calicut
Codes:
(a) (i), (ii) (b) (i), (iv)
(c) (i), (ii), (iii), (iv) (d) (i), (ii), (iii)

29. State which is/are true?
The broad lines on which diets for groups of persons can be improved are
(a) increased use of green leafy vegetables.
(b) introduction of cheap flesh foods two or three times a week.
(c) increased intake of pulses wherever possible.
(d) All of these.

30. Radio experiments in the use of radio for promoting literacy and education was conducted as early as
(a) 1930s (b) 1940s
(c) 1900s (d) 1920s

31. The prevailing system of education has the following defects. Give one appropriate defect.
(a) No trace of information that the student has understood
(b) More emphasis on the written examination of long hours
(c) No proper assessment of answer books
(d) Emphasis merely on the best of knowledge and information of the student but how far his thoughts, logic, ideas are developed cannot be understood

32. Guides for judging quality can include—
i. Handle ii. Fibre yarn
iii. Weave iv. Finish
Codes:
(a) i, ii (b) i, iv
(c) i, ii, iii, iv (d) i, ii, iii

33. The rubber tube of the gas cylinder show bubbles on application of soapy solution, it means
(a) Soap does not stay on tube
(b) There is a leak
(c) It dissolves in soapy water
(d) None of these

34. Arrange the stages of psycho-sexual development in correct sequence:
I. Phallic stage II. Genital stage
III. Oral stage IV. Latency stage
V. Anal stage
Codes:
(a) II, IV, I, V, III (b) I, II, III, V, IV
(c) III, V, I, IV, II (d) V, IV, III, II, I

35. Which of the following were introduced by Mughal empire?
(i) Tooshi yarn (ii) Shah tush
(iii) silk (iv) wool
Codes:
(a) (i),(ii) (b) (iii), (iv)
(c) (i), (ii), (iii), (iv) (d) (i), (ii), (iii)

36. 70% of it is present in teeth and bones aid provides strength to it.
(a) Sodium (b) Fluorine
(c) Iodine (d) Magnesium

37. The method of 'paired comparison' was introduced

(a) Watson (b) Galton
(c) Cohn (d) Weber

38. For reducing expenditure on technical education
(a) Technical educational institutions should start taking donations
(b) It is necessary to reduce expenses on instruments and equipments of technical education
(c) It is necessary to provide apprenticeship training through companies
(d) It is necessary to reduce the number of technical educational institutions

39. Which of the following steps are involved in the James Mursell (1951) or WED approach in problem solving?
(i) Comprehensive picture as a whole
(ii) Identifying the essential elements and ordering them in terms of relevance
(iii) Gathering and ordering the necessary details
(iv) Preoccupation carry and conflict identified

Codes:
(a) (i), (ii) (b) (i), (iv)
(c) (i), (ii), (iii), (iv) (d) (i), (ii), (iii)

40. Learning through satellite is basically learning by
(a) Seeing (b) Imagination
(c) Guidance (d) Unitation

41. The Central Advisory Board of Education was established in
(a) 1921 (b) 1930
(c) 1911 (d) 1915

42. Which of the following is/are true?
(i) In making observation of naturally occurring behaviour anecdotes may be substituted for genuine observation or interpretation for description.
(ii) Observation methods have also been brought into the laboratory.
(iii) Case histories are important sources of data for studying individuals.
(iv) Case histories may also be based on a longitudinal study.

Codes:
(a) (i), (ii) (b) (i), (iv)
(c) (i), (ii), (iii), (iv) (d) (i), (ii), (iii)

43. Language is supposed to be
(a) a nomenclature for cataloging experience
(b) a medium of self-development
(c) a medium for social communication
(d) a system of symbols for problem solving effectively

44. India made nylon filament in the year
(a) 1974 (b) 1986
(c) 1980 (d) 1962

45. A proposition which can be put to determine its validity is called
(a) Variable (b) Error
(c) Problem (d) None of these

46. Match the following

List I
A. Embroidery shawls now produced
B. Woollen shawls are named
C. Kurtas firans caps rugs
D. Shekargarh designs on shawls
E. Influence on Kashmir

List II
(i) Ranjit Singh of Punjab encouragement
(ii) of Persia
(iii) Kanikar or Tillikar
(iv) Made by earlier Rafugars
(v) Called Amblikar or Ambli work

Codes:	A	B	C	D	E
(a)	(v)	(iii)	(iv)	(i)	(ii)
(b)	(iii)	(ii)	(v)	(iv)	(i)
(c)	(i)	(iii)	(ii)	(v)	(iv)
(d)	(v)	(iv)	(i)	(ii)	(iii)

47. State which is/are true?
(a) The factors cause the pressure as individual feels to conform to groups he

is a member include; (i) information and trust; (ii) deviancy; (iii) Characteristics of the group; (iv) Charactersics of the situation; and (v) characteristics of the individual
(b) People respond differently to various levels of "newness" of an idea, practice or product
(c) Since perception is largely determined by cultured people of different cultures often perceive the same phenomenon in different fashions
(d) All of these

48. A pregnant woman should avoid
(a) stale food
(b) deep fried food and sweets
(c) spicy food
(d) All of the above

49. The higher education is still dominated by
(a) Mother-tongue (b) English
(c) Hindi (d) All of these

50. .... has said about interview that "In other words it is a purposive conservation whose purpose may vary widely to include for example, a meeting undertaking to collect information".
(a) Vivien (b) Richards
(c) John Madge (d) Fred N. Kerlinger

ANSWER SHEET

PAPER—I

1. (a)	2. (c)	3. (a)	4. (d)	5. (d)
6. (d)	7. (d)	8. (c)	9. (b)	10. (c)
11. (b)	12. (c)	13. (c)	14. (b)	15. (d)
16. (b)	17. (a)	18. (d)	19. (c)	20. (d)
21. (d)	22. (a)	23. (b)	24. (a)	25. (d)
26. (d)	27. (a)	28. (d)	29. (b)	30. (a)
31. (b)	32. (c)	33. (c)	34. (d)	35. (d)
36. (d)	37. (a)	38. (d)	39. (b)	40. (b)
41. (b)	42. (c)	43. (b)	44. (b)	45. (c)
46. (b)	47. (a)	48. (a)	49. (b)	50. (b)

PAPER—II

1. (b)	2. (a)	3. (a)	4. (a)	5. (b)
6. (d)	7. (d)	8. (c)	9. (c)	10. (a)
11. (d)	12. (b)	13. (d)	14. (b)	15. (b)
16. (c)	17. (c)	18. (a)	19. (a)	20. (b)
21. (c)	22. (c)	23. (a)	24. (a)	25. (b)
26. (c)	27. (c)	28. (c)	29. (d)	30. (c)
31. (c)	32. (d)	33. (b)	34. (a)	35. (d)
36. (b)	37. (c)	38. (b)	39. (a)	40. (d)
41. (b)	42. (a)	43. (c)	44. (c)	45. (c)
46. (c)	47. (c)	48. (d)	49. (a)	50. (c)

PAPER—III

1. (b)	2. (c)	3. (c)	4. (d)	5. (a)
6. (c)	7. (c)	8. (d)	9. (d)	10. (c)
11. (d)	12. (a)	13. (c)	14. (a)	15. (c)
16. (b)	17. (b)	18. (d)	19. (d)	20. (a)
21. (c)	22. (d)	23. (d)	24. (d)	25. (d)
26. (d)	27. (a)	28. (c)	29. (d)	30. (a)
31. (b)	32. (c)	33. (b)	34. (c)	35. (d)
36. (d)	37. (c)	38. (c)	39. (d)	40. (c)
41. (a)	42. (c)	43. (a)	44. (d)	45. (c)
46. (c)	47. (d)	48. (d)	49. (b)	50. (c)

MOCK TEST–4
PAPER–I

1. Chlorophyll is related to chloroplast in the same way as vulture is related to
(a) Air (b) Flesh
(c) Birds (d) Wings

2. In which language the newspapers have highest circulation?
(a) Hindi (b) English
(c) Malyalam (d) Bengali

3. Factorial Analysis is used
(a) to test the hypothesis
(b) to know the difference between two variables
(c) to know the difference among the many variables
(d) to know the relationship between two variables

4. Which of the following statements is correct?
(a) Variability is the source of problem
(b) Objectives of research are stated in first chapter of the thesis
(c) Researcher must possess analytical ability
(d) All of the above

5. The best way for a teacher to introduce a new subject is by
(a) relating it to previously studied subject or course material
(b) giving a broad outline of the subject
(c) relating it to daily life situation
(d) Any of these

6. The most important function of education is
(a) Human resource development
(b) Political development
(c) Industrial development
(d) Economic development

7. Which one of the following Telephonic Conferencing with a radio link is very popular throughout the world?
(a) Telepresence
(b) TPS
(c) Video teletext
(d) Video conference

8. If a researcher does not get a satisfactory explanation to certain occurrences
(a) he would not be at rest until he gets an appropriate explanation
(b) he should give a damn to it perhaps it is not worth knowing
(c) he would wait until he comes across a right person who may explain it to him
(d) he would visit a nearby research institute to find out whether an answer could be obtained

9. Which of the following is characteristic of a hypothesis?
(a) It can be tested
(b) It must be clear in concept
(c) It must consists of known fact
(d) All of these

10. The main objective of FM station in radio is
(a) Tourism, Interaction and Entertainment
(b) Entertainment only
(c) Entertainment, Information and Interaction
(d) Information, Entertainment and Tourism

11. Inductive logic studies the way in which a premise may
(a) not support but entail a conclusion
(b) support and entail a conclusion
(c) support a conclusion without entailing it
(d) neither support nor entail a conclusion

12. The Prime Minister is the chairman of
(a) Minorities Commission
(b) Planning Commission
(c) Finance Commission
(d) None of these

13. One of the following is not a quality of researcher.
(a) His assertion to outstrip the evidence
(b) Unison with that of which he is in search

(c) He must be of alert mind
(d) Keenness in enquiry

14. Which of the following pollutants is not emitted from the transport sector?
(a) Carbon monoxide
(b) Oxides of nitrogen
(c) Chlorofluorocarbons
(d) Poly aromatic hydrocarbons

15. Ozone layer is present in the
(a) Troposphere (b) Ionosphere
(c) Mesosphere (d) Stratosphere

16. A journalist need to be ___ while covering an event.
(a) impartial (b) partial
(c) meticulous (d) None of these

17. How many types of political units existed in India at the time of independence?
(a) 1 (b) 2
(c) 3 (d) 4

18. Ecological footprint represents
(a) CO_2 emissions per person
(b) forest cover
(c) energy consumption
(d) area of productive land and water to meet the resources requirement

19. The aim of value education to include in students is
(a) the social values
(b) the political values
(c) the moral values
(d) the economic values

Read the following passage and answer the questions 20 to 24:

At one time it would have been impossible to imagine the integration of different religious thoughts, ideas and ideals. That is because of the closed society, the lack of any communication or interdependence on other nations. People were happy and content amongst themselves; they did not need any more. The physical distance and cultural barriers prevented any exchange of thoughts and beliefs. But such is not the case today. Today, the world has become a much smaller place, thanks to the adventures and miracles of science. Foreign nations have become our next-door neighbours. Mingling of population is bringing about an interchange of thought. We are slowly realising that the world is a single cooperative group. Other religions have become forces with which we have to reckon and we are seeking for ways and means by which we can live together in peace and harmony. We cannot have religious unity and peace so long as we assert that we are in possession of the light and all others are groping in the darkness. That very assertion is a challenge to a fight. The political ideal of the world is not so much a single empire with a homogeneous civilisation and single communal group as a brotherhood of free nations differing profoundly in life and mind, habits and institutions, existing side by side in peace and order, harmony and cooperation and each contributing to the world its own unique and specific best, which is irreducible to the terms of the others.

The cosmopolitanism of the eighteenth century and the nationalism of the nineteenth are combined in our ideal of a world commonwealth, which allows every branch of the human family to find freedom, security and self-realisation in the larger life of mankind. I see no hope for the religious future of the world, if this ideal is not extended to the religious sphere also. When two or three different systems claim that they contain the revelation of the very core and centre of truth and the acceptance of it is the exclusive pathway to heaven, conflicts are inevitable. In such conflicts, one religion will not allow others to steal a march over it and no one can gain ascendancy until the world is reduced to dust and ashes. To obliterate every other religion than one's own is a sort of Bolshevism in religion which we must try to prevent. We can do so only if we accept something like the Indian solution, which seeks the unity of religion not in a common creed but in a common quest. Let us believe in the unity of spirit and not of organisation, a unity which secures ample liberty not only for every individual but for every type of organised life which has proved itself effective.

20. According to the passage, the political ideal of the contemporary world is to
    (a) create a world commonwealth preserving religious diversity of all the nations
    (b) create a single empire with a homogeneous civilisation
    (c) foster the unity of all the religions of the world
    (d) None of these
21. According to the passage, religious unity and peace can be obtained if
    (a) we believe that truth does matter and will prevail
    (b) we believe that the world is a single co-operative group
    (c) we do not assert that we alone are in possession of the real knowledge
    (d) we believe in a unity of spirit and not of organisation
22. Which of the following is most opposite in meaning of the word "profoundly" as used in the passage?
    (a) Marginally (b) Meagerly
    (c) Hardly (d) Scarcely
23. Which of the following, according to the passage, is the 'Indian solution'? Unity of religions in a common
    (a) Creed (b) Belief
    (c) Organisation (d) Search
24. According to the passage, what is Bolshevism in religion?
    (a) To make changes in a religion so that it becomes more acceptable
    (b) To ridicule the views sincerely held by others
    (c) To accept others' religious beliefs and doctrines to be as authentic as ours
    (d) To adhere to rigid dogmatism in religion
25. Which is not 24 hours news channel?
    (a) Aajtak
    (b) Zee News
    (c) Lok Sabha Channel
    (d) NDTV 24×7
26. Which of the following is not a source of pollution in soil?
    (a) Hydropower plants
    (b) Transport sector
    (c) Agriculture sector
    (d) Thermal power plants
27. Which institution brought co-ordination and co-operation between Union and States in the field of education?
    (a) CCCE (Council for Co-ordination and Cooperation on Education)
    (b) NCERT (National Council for Educational Research and Training)
    (c) CABE (Central Advisory Board of Education)
    (d) None of these
28. In this question four words are given, out of which three are alike and fourth one is different. Choose the odd one out.
    (a) Spectacle (b) Pageant
    (c) View (d) Display
29. Which of the following is not a natural hazard?
    (a) Tsunami
    (b) Flash floods
    (c) Nuclear accident
    (d) Earthquake
30. **Statement:** Should all electronic goods be exempted from the custom duty?
    Arguments:
    I. No, it will reduce the income of the government and development activities will be adversely affected.

II. No, local manufacturers will be unable to compete with technology of foreign manufacturers.
(a) Only I is strong
(b) Only II is strong
(c) Both are strong
(d) None of them is strong

31. The Minimata disease of Japan in 1953 was caused by eating fish contaminated by
(a) Nickel (b) Cadmium
(c) Lead (d) Mercury

32. Kishanganga power project has now become the new sour point in Indo-Pak relations. This project is situated on which of the following rivers?
(a) Indus (b) Chenab
(c) Bias (d) Jhelum

33. In a certain code, ROUNDS is written as RONUDS. How will PLEASE will be written in the same code?
(a) PLASEE (b) LPAESE
(c) PLAESE (d) LPAEES

34. **Statement:** Most labourers are poor.
Conclusions:
(i) Some labourers are poor.
(ii) All labourers are not poor.
Which of the following is implied?
(a) Only (i) is implied
(b) Only (ii) is implied
(c) Both (i) and (ii) are implied
(d) Neither (i) nor (ii) is implied

35. One-rupee currency note in India bears the signature of
(a) Finance Minister of India
(b) Finance Secretary of Government of India
(c) The President of India
(d) Governor, Reserve Bank of India

36. Name the kind of pen used to draw directly on the digitizing tablet.
(a) Computer Pen (b) Puck/stylus
(c) Light Pen (d) None of these

37. FERA was changed to FEMA in 1998, FEMA stands for
(a) Foreign Exchange Monitoring Act
(b) Foreign Exchange Management Administration
(c) Foreign Exchange Management Act
(d) Foreign Exchange Maintenance Act

38. The Lok Sabha can be dissolved before the expiry of its normal five-year term by
(a) The Speaker of Lok Sabha
(b) The Prime Minister
(c) The President on the recommendation of the Prime Minister
(d) None of the above

39. Match the List I with the List II and select the correct answer from the codes given below:
List I (Commissions and Committees)
A. First Administrative Reforms Commission.
B. Paul H. Appleby Committee I.
C. K. Santhanam Committee.
D. Second Administrative Reforms Commission.
List II (Years)
(1) 2005 (2) 1962
(3) 1966 (4) 1953

Codes:	A	B	C	D
(a)	1	3	2	4
(b)	3	4	2	1
(c)	4	2	3	1
(d)	2	1	4	3

40. Internet is
(a) a commercial information service run by Zift Davis Co. in United States of America.
(b) a network owned and run by US Government.

(c) a network for education, news and entertainment run by United Nations and owned by the people of world.
(d) a network not owned by any body but used by all including governments agencies, universities, United Nations, etc. all round the globe.

41. Which of the following was created for the co-ordination and maintenance of standards in higher education?
(a) SCERT
(b) UGC
(c) NCERT
(d) Higher Education Information System Project

42. In communication chatting in Internet is
(a) Non-verbal communication
(b) Verbal communication
(c) Parallel communication
(d) Grapevine communication

43. The unit kIPS (thousand instruction per second) is used to measure the speed of
(a) Tape drive (b) Processor
(c) Disk drive (d) Printer

44. Data (information) is stored in computers as
(a) Matter (b) Files
(c) Directories (d) Floppies

45. Laser Scanners are capable of scanning bar codes upto a distance of
(a) 35 cm (b) 8 cm
(c) 25 cm (d) 45 cm

46. The coldest place on earth is
(a) Siachin (b) Halifex
(c) Verkhoyansk (d) Chicago

47. Memory unit is one part of
(a) Central Processing Unit
(b) Input device
(c) Control unit
(d) Output device

Study the following graph carefully and answer questions 48 to 50.

Export of Engineering Goods

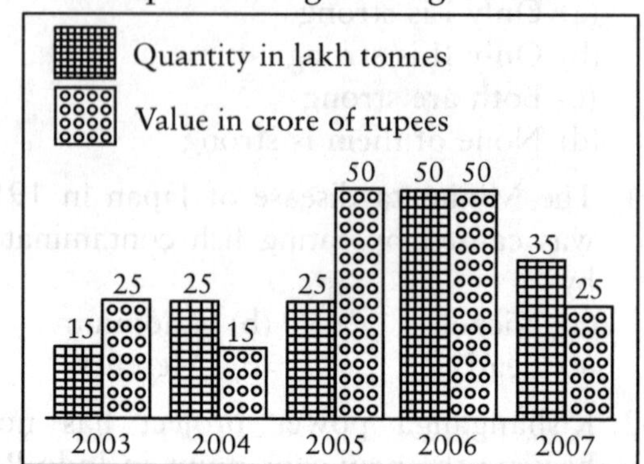

48. In which year the quantity of engineering goods' exports was maximum?
(a) 2006 (b) 2005
(c) 2007 (d) 2003

49. In which year the quantity of exports was 100 percent higher than the quantity of previous year?
(a) 2003 (b) 2007
(c) 2006 (d) 2005

50. In which year the value of engineering goods decreased by 50 percent compared to the previous year?
(a) 2006 (b) 2004
(c) 2007 (d) 2005

PAPER–II

1. Subsidized pricing is followed in
(a) Fast food establishment
(b) Air catering
(c) Industrial cafeteria
(d) Restaurant

2. Absorption of carotene requires the following nutrients in the diet
(a) Fat (b) Protein
(c) Carbohydrate (d) Vitamin D

3. The carbohydrates should not be totally restricted for IDDM patients diet because
(a) It will cause constipation
(b) It will cause ketosis
(c) It will not give satiety value
(d) It will not provide adequate energy

4. Recommended dietary allowances for 0-6 months old infant for protein is
(a) 1 g/kg body weight
(b) 1.5 g/kg body weight
(c) 1.65 g/kg body weight
(d) 2.05 g/kg body weight

5. A chemical finish exclusively given to cotton to increase lustre, strength and dyeability is
(a) Fulling (b) Crabbing
(c) Bleaching (d) Mercerization

6. Bitot spot is an indicator of
(a) Ascorbic acid deficiency
(b) IDD
(c) VAD
(d) IDA

7. Diagonal ridges are characteristic feature of
(a) Twill weave (b) Dobby weave
(c) Swivel weave (d) Jacquard weave

8. Addition of selected nutrients, not normally present in a particular food is called
(a) Fortification (b) Enrichment
(c) Supplementation (d) Restoration

9. Dart size for a dress for a person with a heavy bust would be
(a) longer and narrower
(b) longer and wider
(c) shorter and narrower
(d) shorter and wider

10. The important factor that governs the selection of needle is
(a) Type of fabric
(b) Type of thread
(c) Stitch length
(d) Tension of thread

11. A small room can be made look larger by using
(a) warm colours on opposite walls
(b) cool colours on all walls
(c) neutral colours on all walls
(d) light shade on two walls and dark shade on the another two walls

12. The growth dimension that is most affected by Intra-Uterine-Growth Retardation (IUGR) is
(a) Height (b) Weight
(c) Motor skills (d) Mental Skills

13. Location of window is important for
(a) Ventilation and lighting
(b) Ventilation and appearance
(c) Ventilation and aeration
(d) Light and appearance

14. Important landmark for determining the desirable height of the work place is
(a) Home maker's height
(b) Equipment to be used
(c) Home maker's elbow height
(d) Home maker's eye level

15. The term that is fast replacing the use of the term "welfare" in the development work is
(a) Enablement (b) Upliftment
(c) Empowerment (d) Development

16. The theory that views the child as developing within a dynamic system of relationship at several levels of the surrounding system is
(a) The ethological theory
(b) The ecological system theory
(c) Information processing theory
(d) Piaget's cognitive theory

17. The process of systematic and unbiased collection of data and their scientific appraisal is
(a) Informal Evaluation
(b) Formal evaluation
(c) Summative Evaluation
(d) Terminal Evaluation

18. The person who adopt a new idea much ahead of other members in a community are
    (a) Innovators (b) Early adopters
    (c) Early majority (d) Laggards

19. An in-depth comprehensive study of a person, a social group, a community or a programme is referred as
    (a) Exploratory study
    (b) Descriptive study
    (c) Analytical study
    (d) Case study

20. F-test is used
    (a) when there are more than two groups
    (b) to check accuracy of data
    (c) to check design of experiment
    (d) when analysis of variance is needed

21. **Assertion (A):** Obesity and heart disease is a result of excessive energy intake and reduced physical activity.
    Reason (R): Sedentary lifestyle and availability of high energy density foods leads to degenerative disease.
    Codes:
    (a) (A) is false and (R) is true
    (b) (A) is true and (R) is false
    (c) Both (A) and (R) is true but (R) alone is not the correct explanation
    (d) Both (A) and (R) are false

22. **Assertion (A):** The success of a food service operation depends heavily on the menu planning of the establishment.
    Reason (R): Menu serves many functions and forms the core of all activities in a food service establishment.
    Codes:
    (a) (A) is true and (R) is false
    (b) (A) is false but (R) is true
    (c) Both (A) and (R) are false
    (d) Both (A) and (R) are true

23. **Assertion (A):** Iron absorption is hindered by the presence of phytates in the food.
    Reason (R): Phytates bind the iron and make it unavailable for absorption.
    Codes:
    (a) Both (A) and (R) are true
    (b) (A) is true and (R) is false
    (c) (A) is false but (R) is true
    (d) Both (A) and (R) are true but (R) is not the complete explanation

24. **Assertion (A):** Class I change of work simplification relates to change in hand and body motions.
    Reason (R): Using two minutes noodles is an example of the same.
    Codes:
    (a) (A) and (R) are true
    (b) (A) is true but (R) is partially correct
    (c) (A) is true but (R) is false
    (d) (A) is false and (R) is true

25. **Assertion (A):** There is more shrinkage towards the length of the fabric.
    Reason (R): Warp yarns are stretched while on the loom.
    Codes:
    (a) (A) is true and (R) is false
    (b) (A) is false but (R) is true
    (c) Both (A) and (R) are true
    (d) Both (A) and (R) are false

26. **Assertion (A):** Permissive style of parenting is the best style.
    Reason (R): The parents do not interfere in any matter of the children.
    Codes:
    (a) (A) is not true and (R) is true
    (b) (A) and (R) both are false
    (c) Both (A) and (R) are true
    (d) (A) is false and (R) is partially true

27. **Assertion (A):** All research studies must begin with formulation of hypothesis.
    Reason (R): Hypothesis will help the researcher to make generalisation about the population.

Codes:
(a) Both (A) and (R) are true
(b) (A) is true but (R) is false
(c) (A) is false but (R) is true
(d) Both (A) and (R) are true but (R) is not the correct explanation

28. **Assertion (A):** Extensive education is a two way process of education.
Reason (R): The target groups get required information and scientists get the feed back.
Codes:
(a) Both (A) and (R) are true but (R) is not a correct explanation
(b) (A) is false and (R) is also false
(c) (A) is true and (R) is false
(d) (A) is true and (R) is also true and (R) is a correct explanation

29. **Assertion (A):** Effective planning requires built in method of monitoring and evaluation.
Reason (R): Monitoring enables to bring out the needed changes then and there to reach the desired goal within the stipulated period.
Codes:
(a) (A) is true but (R) is false
(b) Both (A) and (R) are true
(c) (A) is false but (R) is true
(d) Both (A) and (R) are true but (R) is not the correct explanation

30. Correct layouts of unidirectional fabrics for garment cutting are
(i) Crosswise fold (ii) Lengthwise fold
(iii) Double fold (iv) Open
Codes:
(a) (i), (ii) and (iii) are correct.
(b) (ii), (iii) and (iv) are correct.
(c) (i), (iii) and (iv) are correct.
(d) (i), (ii) and (iv) are correct.

31. The correct sequence for the preparation of tomato sauce is
(i) Blanching and pealing
(ii) Selecting good quality tomatoes
(iii) Cooking and adding preservatives
(iv) Bottling
Codes:
(a) ii, i, iii, iv (b) i, iii, ii, iv
(c) iv, i, iii, ii (d) iii, ii, iv, i

32. Identify the statement giving the correct sequence of foods in decreasing order of vitamin A content
(a) milk, liver, maize, tomato
(b) liver, milk, tomato, maize
(c) tomato, milk, liver, maize
(d) milk, tomato, maize, liver

33. Staff selection involves eight distinct steps. Write the correct order in which these are followed
(i) Screening applications
(ii) Testing skills
(iii) Preparation of job requirements
(iv) Holding interviews
(v) Appraisal
(vi) Assessment of candidates
(vii) Medical examination
(viii) Contractual agreement
Codes:
(a) iv, v, i, ii, iii, vii, vi, viii
(b) iii, i, iv, v, vii, ii, vi, viii
(c) i, iv, vi, ii, iii, v, vii, viii
(d) ii, i, iii, iv, v, vii, vi, viii

34. Arrange constituent processes of observational learning in correct sequence:
(i) Production (ii) Motivation
(iii) Retention (iv) Attention
Codes:
(a) (iii), (iv), (i) and (ii)
(b) (iv), (iii), (i) and (ii)
(c) (ii), (i), (iii) and (iv)
(d) (i), (ii), (iii) and (iv)

35. Implementation is second step in the management process and the sequence is
(i) Put plan into aaction
(ii) Make the adjustment

(iii) Check the progress
(iv) Modify the plan

Codes:

(a) i, iii, ii, iv (b) i, ii, iii, iv
(c) i, ii, iv, iii (d) iv, iii, ii, i

36. Match the method of research tools from List I to List II:

List I

A. A planned methodical watching the subject or situation
B. The opinion of subjects in group are observed and noted by researcher.
C. A document that contains a set of questions.
D. A set of structured questions in which responses are recorded by researcher.

List II

(i) Focus Group Discussion
(ii) Interview
(iii) Observation
(iv) Questionnaire

Codes:	A	B	C	D
(a)	(i)	(iv)	(ii)	(iii)
(b)	(i)	(iii)	(iv)	(ii)
(c)	(iii)	(i)	(iv)	(ii)
(d)	(ii)	(i)	(iv)	(iii)

37. Match the items in List I with the items in List II

List I

A. Throat plate B. Feed dog
C. Pressure foot D. Stop motion

List II

i. Holds the fabric in place
ii. provides smooth surface for stitching
iii. Stops the sewing mechanisms
iv. Moves the fabric ahead

Codes:	A	B	C	D
(a)	i	iii	ii	iv
(b)	ii	iv	i	iii
(c)	iii	ii	iv	i
(d)	iv	i	iii	ii

38. Match the following items in List I with List II

List I

A. Specimen B. Model
C. Diorama D. Mockups

List II

i. Enlarged version of original
ii. Miniature replica of an object in working condition
iii. Miniature replica of an object
iv. Scenic representation of the original
v. Sample which represents the whole

Codes:	A	B	C	D
(a)	v	ii	iv	i
(b)	iv	v	i	ii
(c)	iii	iv	ii	i
(d)	v	iii	iv	ii

39. Match the glands with their respective hormones:

A. α cells pancreas i. Adrenal corticoid steroid
B. Adrenal cortex ii. Insulin
C. β cells pancrease iii. Prolactin
D. Pituitary iv. Glucagon

Codes:	A	B	C	D
(a)	iv	i	ii	iii
(b)	i	ii	iii	iv
(c)	iv	iii	i	ii
(d)	ii	i	iii	iv

40. Match the symbols in List I with words in List II.

List I	List II
A. md	i. Chi-square
B. Σ	ii. mean
C. χ^2	iii. Sum of confidence
D. X	iv. Median

Codes:	A	B	C	D
(a)	ii	i	iii	iv
(b)	iv	iii	i	ii
(c)	i	ii	iv	iii
(d)	iv	iii	ii	i

41. Match the fashion terms given in List I with their meanings given in List II.

List I	List II
A. Classic	i. exclusive custom fitted clothing
B. Fad	ii. ready to wear
C. Haute-couture	iii. last through ages
D. Pret-a-porter	iv. short lived craze

Codes:	A	B	C	D
(a)	i	ii	iii	iv
(b)	iii	iv	i	ii
(c)	ii	iii	iv	i
(d)	iv	i	ii	iii

42. Aspects of a Good Lesson Plan
(i) Objectives
(ii) Teacher's Activities
(iii) Learning Experiences
(iv) Teaching aids
(v) Appraisal
Codes:
(a) (i), (iii), (iv) and (v) are correct.
(b) (ii), (iii), (iv) and (v) are correct.
(c) (i), (iv) and (v) are correct.
(d) All of the above.

43. **Assertion (A):** Pasteurization in milk is done to destroy the microbes.
Reason (R): It is tested for the presence of lactic acid in milk.
Codes:
(a) Both (A) and (R) are false.
(b) Both (A) and (R) are true.
(c) (A) is true but (R) is false.
(d) (A) is false but (R) is true.

44. **Assertion (A):** Standing in a static posture is fatiguing.
Reason (R): Blood circulation is affected in the extremities while standing for work.
Codes:
(a) (A) is false but (R) is true.
(b) (A) is true and (R) is false.
(c) Both (A) and (R) are true, but (R) is not the complete explanation.
(d) Both (A) and (R) are false.

45. Match the Nutritional Assessment Methods in List I with Tools used for measurement in List II:

List I (Nutrient)
A. Dietary Survey B. Anthropometry
C. Biochemical D. Clinical
List II (Foods)
(i) Hb
(ii) Bitot spot
(iii) FFQ
(iv) Bomb Calorimeter
(v) MUAC
(vi) HPLC

Codes:	A	B	C	D
(a)	(iii)	(vi)	(iv)	(i)
(b)	(iv)	(iii)	(i)	(vi)
(c)	(vi)	(iv)	(v)	(ii)
(d)	(iii)	(v)	(i)	(ii)

46. Arrange the following in the proper sequence of communication:
I. Message II. Source
III. Decoder IV. Encoder
V. Destination
Codes:
(a) (I), (II), (III), (IV), (V)
(b) (II), (I), (IV), (III), (V)
(c) (II), (I), (III), (IV), (V)
(d) (II), (I), (III), (V), (IV)

47. The correct sequence of steps involved in behaviour change communication are
(i) Action (ii) Interest
(iii) Attention (iv) Satisfaction
(v) Conviction (vi) Desire
Codes:
(a) (ii), (vi), (iv), (iii), (i), (v)
(b) (iii), (ii), (vi), (v), (i), (iv)
(c) (i), (ii), (iii), (iv), (v), (vi)
(d) (vi), (v), (iv), (iii), (ii), (i)

48. Which of the following packages are examples of aseptic packaging?
(A) Tetra pack boxes (B) Paper bag
(C) Milk bottle (D) Plastic bag
(E) Aluminium foil
Codes:
(a) (C) & (E) (b) (A) & (E)
(c) (C) & (D) (d) (A) & (C)

49. **Assertion (A):** Lock stitch is appropriate for stitching stretch fabrics.
Reason (R): Lock stitch stretches with fabric stretch.
Codes:
(a) (A) is right, but (R) is wrong.
(b) (A) is wrong, but (R) is right.
(c) Both (A) and (R) are right.
(d) Both (A) and (R) are wrong.

50. **Assertion (A):** Summative evaluation tries to measure end results of a programme.
Reason (R): This will help to decide whether to continue or discontinue the programme.
Codes:
(a) Both (A) and (R) are correct, (R) is the correct explanation.
(b) Both (A) and (R) are correct, (R) is not the correct explanation.
(c) (A) is true, but (R) is false.
(d) (A) is false, but (R) is true.

PAPER–III

1. Out of some generalisations some conclusions sare drawn—
(i) Deductive method
(ii) Inductive method
Codes:
(a) (i) only (b) (ii) only
(c) Both (i) and (ii) (d) None of these

2. Who has written "Five techniques tested to study family decision in household processes"?
(a) Jean M. Stekle (b) Hurley
(c) K. Lewin (d) A.J. Marrow

3. Ministry of textile was created in November
(a) 1977 (b) 1989
(c) 1959 (d) 1970

4. Which of the following is/are the characteristics of Kanjiwaram saris?
(i) Korvai i.e. solid contrast border
(ii) Pelni i.e. palla in contrast warp yarn
(iii) Motives inspired by temples
(iv) Only in green colour
Codes:
(a) (i), (ii) (b) (i), (iv)
(c) (i), (ii), (iii), (iv) (d) (i), (ii), (iii)

5. A running account of the behaviour of a particular child for a stated period of time. It is
(a) Self-reports
(b) Mail records
(c) Diary records
(d) Anecdotal records

6. The challenge of meal-planning includes
(a) Availability
(b) Resources-time energy stall aptitude, etc.
(c) Likes of members
(d) All of the above

7. A type of consequence to be accepted in decision making but not always recognized is the existence of dissonance. Where dissonance exists there is invest and some efforts to reduce it. This is the statement of
(a) H. Knight (b) Arun Jaitely
(c) Leon Festinger (d) G.O. Johnson

8. Which of the following is/are applicable to mass communication?
(i) Indirect
(ii) Impersonal
(iii) Lack means of immediate feedback
(iv) One-way
Codes:
(a) (i), (ii) (b) (i), (iv)
(c) (i), (ii), (iii), (iv) (d) (i), (ii), (iii)

9. Each data enter in Z^2 test is known as
(a) Cell (b) Line
(c) Row (d) Column

10. For raising the educational standards of the university

(a) students opting for higher education should be selected on the basis of intellectual tests
(b) occupational and industrial development is essential with higher education
(c) state policy should be effective
(d) Both (a) and (b)

11. Match the following:

List I
A. Brand name
B. Quality marks
C. Registered Trade Marks
D. Factors important in washing or dry cleaning
E. The provision of washing symbols

List II
(i) usually indicated by a superscript R in a circle
(ii) temperature, time, washing medium and mechanical action
(iii) optional
(iv) used by manufactures to advise the consumer or dry cleaning of special high quality products
(v) product which may be supplied by different symbols manufacturers conform to certain written qualities standards

Codes:	A	B	C	D	E
(a)	(iv)	(v)	(i)	(ii)	(iii)
(b)	(v)	(i)	(iv)	(iii)	(ii)
(c)	(i)	(iii)	(ii)	(v)	(iv)
(d)	(v)	(iv)	(iii)	(i)	(ii)

12. In Navodaya Vidyalayas, which level of students can study?
(a) I to XII (b) VI to XII
(c) VI toX (d) None of these

13. Primary socialization takes place in—
(i) Infancy (ii) Childhood
(iii) Late childhood (iv) Adolesence
Codes:
(a) (i), (ii) (b) (i), (iv)
(c) (i), (ii), (iii), (iv) (d) (i), (ii), (iii)

14. In which year was the University Grants Commission established?
(a) 1952 (b) 1954
(c) 1953 (d) 1963

15. State which is/are true?
(a) The more the homemaker knows about the time required to do each task connected with food buying and preparation the better will be the management of this resources
(b) The material resources money determines the types of food selected markets visited, method of buying by the home-maker
(c) A homemaker requires knowledge ability the energy to coordinate the flow of adequate supplies and their preparation into meals
(d) All of these

16. Strawberry on preservation sometimes becomes rusty brown. It is due to
(a) Presence of oxygen
(b) High content of phenolic compounds
(c) Reducing sugars
(d) All of the above

17. Why it is so important to quote people in order to understand what someone means?
(a) Contextual meaning
(b) Structural meaning
(c) Denotative meaning
(d) Connotative meaning

18. School Administration in practice includes—
(i) The Principal (ii) The Teacher
(iii) The People (iv) The Office Staff
Codes:
(a) (i), (ii) (b) (i), (iv)
(c) (i), (ii), (iii), (iv) (d) (i), (ii), (iii)

19. Nutritional care means
(a) execution of knowledge to suit individualised needs and background
(b) meals which are accepted and attractive

(c) use of nutritional knowledge in lanning meals
(d) All of the above

20. Who started the New Education Policy?
(a) Rajiv Gandhi
(b) Atal Bihari Vajpayee
(c) Morarji Desai
(d) Indira Gandhi

21. Psychological factors contributing to ADHD include—
(i) Parental intrusiveness
(ii) Overestimation
(iii) Rejection
(iv) Pampering
Codes:
(a) (i), (ii) (b) (i), (iv)
(c) (i), (ii), (iii), (iv) (d) (i), (ii), (iii)

22. If citric acid is used to curdle milk then it is used for making
(a) Panner (b) Sandesh
(c) Jalebi (d) None of these

23. State which is/are true?
(a) Although we use signs to share thought or meaning with other the two terms i.e. signs and meaning are not synonomous
(b) Good communicator are people who select words that they feel will elicit the intended meaning
(c) Non-verbal signs communicate feelings preference and liking and either to support or to contracted verbal communication
(d) All of these

24. The energy content of a food is measured in terms of its
(a) fuel value (b) fat
(c) diet balance (d) None of these

25. According to 2011 census the total percentage from among the illeterates is 36.17 that means 2/3rd of the total population is uneducated. What implication this data has in terms of resources utilization?
(i) Both factors are not inter-related
(ii) In absence of education and knowledge resources used will be limited
(iii) Data is applicable to villages
(iv) None of these
Codes:
(a) (i), (ii) (b) (iii) only
(c) (i), (ii), (iii), (iv) (d) (i), (ii), (iii)

26. The preparation of curd quality depends on—
(i) Expertise in adding curd
(ii) Milk quality and condition
(iii) Time given for setting
(iv) How much curdling required
Codes:
(a) (i), (ii) (b) (i) only
(c) (i), (ii), (iii), (iv) (d) (i), (ii), (iii)

27. Democratic control does not imply regimentation of dictatorship. It is sufficiently flexible based not on the rules of the rod but on—
(i) Rule of law
(ii) Professional and personal ethics
(iii) Demand of social properties
(iv) Need of objectives
Codes:
(a) (i), (ii) (b) (i), (iv)
(c) (i), (ii), (iii), (iv) (d) (i), (ii), (iii)

28. Which of these would be the healthiest choice for a snack?
(a) Cookies (b) Chips
(c) Peanuts (d) None

29. By pick glass
(a) No. of yarns per inch seen
(b) Twist no. in yarns counted
(c) A fixed portion of cloth is viewed
(d) All of these

30. Educational Psychology is branch of Psychology. Psychology is a science. Who is the father of experimental Psychology?

(a) Boring (b) Hull
(c) Wundt (d) Tolman

31. "Income management may be defined as planning, controlling and evaluating the use of all types of income". Who said it?
(a) Elizabeth E. Hoyt
(b) F.D. Roosevalt
(c) Nickell and Dorsey
(d) Gross and Crandall

32. Daniel Lorner terms them 'mobility multiplies and Wilbur Schramm considers them to be' mobility multipliers.
(a) Individual communication
(b) Group discussion
(c) Mass media
(d) Group communication

33. The two characteristics in which a behaviour can be termed as normal or problem are its—
(i) frequency
(ii) intensity
(iii) distraction
(iv) counter productiveness
Codes:
(a) (i), (ii) (b) (i), (iv)
(c) (i), (ii), (iii), (iv) (d) (i), (ii), (iii)

34. State which is/are true?
(a) After the composition of food is known, to calculate the fuel value the use of water factor is done
(b) The word vitamin was invented in 1911 by a Polish Chemist Casmir Funk who was trying to extract from rice hulls a chemical substance that would cure Beri-Beri
(c) Functions of food are physiological, psychological and social
(d) All of these

35. A rudimentary literate achieves a standard which a child reaches after
(a) 5 or 6 years (b) 6 or 7 years
(c) 3 or 4 years (d) 4 or 5 years

36. Egg fat is easily digestable because
(a) Phospholipids (b) Cooked
(c) Emulsified (d) None of these

37. Pioneering work in the field of separation of protein from leaf and grass was done in 1961 by
(a) Pirie
(b) Agriculture college
(c) Home-science college
(d) None of these

38. These groups communicate among and within themselves in terms of their status and the nature of their relationships.
(a) Gossip groups (b) Local groups
(c) Macro groups (d) Micro groups

39. Approaches to understand women's participation in development have gone through the following phases:
(a) Welfare, Women in Development, Gender and Development
(b) Welfare, Gender and Development, Women in Development
(c) Women in Development, Welfare, Gender and Development
(d) Gender and Development, Women in Development, Welfare

40. If a business woman orders a market survey to be conducted for her product the report submitted must be
(a) Elaborate (b) Simple
(c) Non-technical (d) Technical

41. Who among the following proposed that cognitive development passes through discrete stages and that these are discontinuous?
(a) Montessori (b) Erickson
(c) Praget (d) Frobel

42. Which of the following is primary concern to educational psychologist?
(a) The formulation of hypothesis
(b) The discovery of practical solutions to educational problems

(c) The development of professional insights into the principles underlying the teaching art
(d) The discovery of teaching procedures of maximum effectiveness

43. Match the following:

List I

A. Well-balanced diets
B. Child should consume
C. If funds do not permit
D. Milled rice eaters
E. Growth of the fetus placenta and maternal tissues

List II

(i) give butter skimmed milk reconstituted from skimmed milk powder to children. It is cheaper
(ii) save high metabolic activity
(iii) need protective foods like pulses, milk, green vegetable, fruit etc.
(iv) at least 250 mL of milk
(v) are in general more expensive than de ficient ones

Codes:	A	B	C	D	E
(a)	(v)	(iv)	(i)	(iii)	(ii)
(b)	(iv)	(v)	(ii)	(i)	(iii)
(c)	(iii)	(ii)	(iv)	(v)	(i)
(d)	(ii)	(i)	(iii)	(iv)	(v)

44. The transmission symbols may be either
(a) Visual (b) Numbers
(c) Words (d) Action

45. Maturation refers to .... changes from conception to death,
(i) neurophysiological changes
(ii) bio-chemical changes—

Codes:
(a) (i) only (b) (ii) only
(c) Both (i) and (ii) (d) None of these

46. Which of the following are long-term goals?
(i) Economic stability
(ii) Good health
(iii) Discharging social responsibilities
(iv) House

Codes:
(a) (i), (ii) (b) (i), (iv)
(c) (i), (ii), (iii), (iv) (d) (i), (ii), (iii)

47. "Extension is a communication intervention to use resources strategically to manipulate seemingly casual factors in a social process as considered desirable by the intervening party." It is stated by
(a) J.A.C. Brown
(b) K. Kautilya
(c) Rolling
(d) Dr. G. Shivarudrappa

48. The main criteria in judging the coffee quality—
(i) Strength (ii) Flavour
(iii) Aroma (iv) Acidity

Codes:
(a) (i), (ii) (b) (i), (iv)
(c) (i), (ii), (iii), (iv) (d) (i), (ii), (iii)

49. O.J. Harris had suggested some point to be considered by the sender. Which of the following is/are his suggestions?
(i) The sender should attempt to remove biases and tensions that may cloud his own mind
(ii) It is desirable to learn as much about the receiver as possible before communicating with him/her
(iii) Repetitions of message may be helpful in conveying the intended thoughts
(iv) Message should be timed so that they are received when they are needed and are not misconducted

Codes:
(a) (i), (ii) (b) (i), (iv)
(c) (i), (ii), (iii), (iv) (d) (i), (ii), (iii)

50. Carotene in the body changes into Vita A in the
(a) Gall Bladder (b) Intestine
(c) Liver (d) Pancreas

ANSWER SHEET

PAPER —I

1. (c)	2. (b)	3. (c)	4. (d)	5. (d)
6. (a)	7. (a)	8. (a)	9. (d)	10. (c)
11. (c)	12. (b)	13. (a)	14. (c)	15. (d)
16. (b)	17. (b)	18. (d)	19. (c)	20. (d)
21. (c)	22. (a)	23. (d)	24. (b)	25. (c)
26. (a)	27. (c)	28. (c)	29. (c)	30. (a)
31. (d)	32. (a)	33. (c)	34. (c)	35. (b)
36. (b)	37. (b)	38. (c)	39. (b)	40. (d)
41. (b)	42. (a)	43. (b)	44. (b)	45. (c)
46. (c)	47. (a)	48. (a)	49. (c)	50. (c)

PAPER—II

1. (c)	2. (a)	3. (b)	4. (c)	5. (d)
6. (c)	7. (a)	8. (a)	9. (c)	10. (a)
11. (b)	12. (b)	13. (a)	14. (c)	15. (b)
16. (b)	17. (b)	18. (a)	19. (d)	20. (a)
21. (c)	22. (d)	23. (a)	24. (c)	25. (a)
26. (a)	27. (b)	28. (b)	29. (a)	30. (b)
31. (a)	32. (b)	33. (c)	34. (b)	35. (a)
36. (c)	37. (b)	38. (d)	39. (a)	40. (b)
41. (b)	42. (d)	43. (c)	44. (c)	45. (d)
46. (b)	47. (b)	48. (d)	49. (d)	50. (a)

PAPER—III

1. (a)	2. (a)	3. (b)	4. (c)	5. (c)
6. (d)	7. (c)	8. (c)	9. (a)	10. (d)
11. (c)	12. (b)	13. (c)	14. (c)	15. (d)
16. (b)	17. (a)	18. (c)	19. (d)	20. (a)
21. (a)	22. (b)	23. (d)	24. (a)	25. (b)
26. (c)	27. (c)	28. (d)	29. (d)	30. (c)
31. (c)	32. (c)	33. (a)	34. (d)	35. (c)
36. (c)	37. (a)	38. (d)	39. (a)	40. (c)
41. (c)	42. (d)	43. (a)	44. (c)	45. (c)
46. (c)	47. (c)	48. (c)	49. (c)	50. (c)

MOCK TEST–5
PAPER–I

1. Dewry defines education as a
   (a) theoretical need
   (b) social need
   (c) personal need
   (d) psychological need
2. All of the following statements about a teacher are correct except the one.
   (a) A teacher changes his/her attitudes and behaviour according to the need of the society
   (b) A teacher is a friend, guide and philosopher
   (c) A teacher distinguishes between students
   (d) A teacher is the leader in the class
3. A person cannot be an effective teacher if he
   (a) teaches moral values
   (b) is a strict disciplinarian
   (c) knows his subject well
   (d) has no interest in teaching
4. The most important single factor in underlying the success of a teacher is
   (a) organisational ability
   (b) scholarship
   (c) communicative ability
   (d) personality and his ability to relate to the class and to the pupils
5. If you are irritated and show rashness because of the inadequate behaviour of another teacher, what do you think about your own behaviour?

(a) Your behaviour is also a sign of maladjustment and so try to control yourself when you are maltreated
(b) It is justified because behaviours are echoice
(c) Your behaviour is not good because elders have the right to behave you in this way
(d) All of the above

6. The term 'SITE' stands for
(a) Satellite Instructional Teachers Education
(b) Satellite International Television Experiment
(c) Satellite Instructional Television Experiment
(d) Satellite Indian Television Experiment

7. Team teaching has the potential to develop
(a) highlighting the gaps in each other's teaching
(b) competitive spirit
(c) cooperation
(d) the habit of supplementing the teaching of each other

8. In any research one should
(a) not try out anything blindly but wait until a sudden flash appears in his mind
(b) know everything in the area without bothering to learn the details of any
(c) know more and more about less and less in certain specific sub area
(d) None of these

9. Determine the nature of the following definition:
'Poor' means having an annual income of ₹ 10,000.
(a) Lexical (b) Persuasive
(c) Precising (d) Stipulative

10. Which of the following methods implies the collection of information by way of investigators own examination without interviewing the respondents?
(a) Random probability sampling
(b) Observation
(c) Posting questionnaire
(d) Schedule method

11. Why do teachers use teaching aid?
(a) For students' attention
(b) To make teaching fun-filled
(c) To make students attentive
(d) To teach within understanding level of students

12. On which of the following statements there is consensus among educators?
(a) Disciplinary cases should be totally neglected in the class
(b) Disciplinary cases should be sent to the principal only when other means have failed
(c) Disciplinary cases should never be sent to principal's office
(d) None of these

13. Good evaluation of written material should not be based on
(a) Logical presentation
(b) Comprehension of subject
(c) Linguistic expression
(d) Ability to reproduce whatever is read

14. A good researcher lays his hands on
(a) any area as long as manpower and fundings are available in plenty
(b) a specific area and tries to understand in minute details
(c) several areas and tries to understand them at fundamental level
(d) None of these

15. The basis on which assumptions are formulated
(a) Universities
(b) Cultural background of the country
(c) Specific characteristics of the castes
(d) All of these

Read the following passage and answer the questions 16 to 20:

India is dedicated to free institutions and principles of democracy. We are striving to give everyone an opportunity and raise the standard of living for all. A democracy is one where people have the right to live their own lives and develop themselves in their own way under the guidance of their chosen representatives. If our political democracy is to succeed, it is essential that it be buttressed by steps towards economic equality or what has been referred to as the 'socialistic pattern of society'. Poverty and unemployment hold the biggest threat to the successful working of our democratic system.

16. One may infer from the paragraph that in a socialistic pattern of society
    (a) to provide employment to all is the greatest problem
    (b) the socialist party dominates
    (c) all the inhabitants are treated equal
    (d) None of these
17. The successful working of Indian democratic system is under a threat of
    (a) economic inequality
    (b) poverty
    (c) unemployment
    (d) All the above
18. In a democratic system
    (a) commodities are freely bought and sold
    (b) government serves the people
    (c) the government is run by the people themselves
    (d) people do not have political freedom
19. The word buttressed in the paragraph means
    (a) Supported (b) Dictating
    (c) Declared (d) Guided
20. Democracy can fail if there is
    (a) opportunity for development
    (b) a weak government
    (c) economic inequality
    (d) unemployment
21. Aspect ratio of TV screen is
    (a) 4:3 (b) 3:4
    (c) 2:3 (d) 2:4
22. Which of the following is not a product of learning?
    (a) Knowledge (b) Attitudes
    (c) Maturation (d) Concepts
23. The first paper for the human beings was developed by
    (a) The Aryans
    (b) The Babilonians
    (c) The Chinese
    (d) The Sumerians
24. Which sequence in turn will lead one to face the west direction from which one starts turning?
    (a) Right, right, left, right, left right
    (b) Left, right, left, left, right, right
    (c) Right, right left, left, right, right
    (d) Left, left, right, left, right, left
25. Fill in the blank with the most appropriate choice. _____ is the supreme medium to express yesterday, today and tomorrow with its own unique language.
    (a) Television (b) Cinema
    (c) Radio (d) Newspaper
26. In which language the newspapers have highest circulation?
    (a) Tamil (b) English
    (c) Bengali (d) Hindi
27. Amit is the son of Rahul. Sarika, Rahul's sister has a son Sonu and a daughter Rita. Raja is the maternal uncle of Sonu. How is Rita related to Raja.
    (a) Aunt (b) Sister
    (c) Daughter (d) Niece
28. **Statement:** A man must be wise to be a good wrangler. Good wrangler's are all talkative and boring.

Conclusions:

I. All the wise persons are boring.

II. All the wise persons are good wranglers.

Choose the correct option.

(a) Only conclusion I follows
(b) Only conclusion II follows
(c) Both I and II follow
(d) None of these

29. What is the number that comes next in the sequence?

2, 5, 9, 19, 37, ...

(a) 74 (b) 75
(c) 76 (d) 78

30. Match List I with List II and select the correct answer using the codes given below:

List I	List II
A. Pandit Jasraj	1. Hindustani vocalist
B. Kishan Maharaj	2. Sitar
C. Ravi Shankar	3. Tabla
D. Udai Shankar	4. Dance

Codes:	A	B	C	D
(a)	1	2	3	4
(b)	1	3	4	2
(c)	1	3	2	4
(d)	3	2	1	4

31. Who developed the ability to speak?

(a) Aryans (b) Neanderthal
(c) Cro-Magnon (d) Dravidians

32. In what way does communication in small group differ from that in the large group?

(a) Large group communication provides better feedback
(b) Small group provides far more interaction among the participants
(c) Interaction in small group is more restrictive
(d) Small group takes less time to convey the message

33. What is the main aim and objective of provision for feedback in communication system?

(a) Understand more about the content
(b) To make communication better by adjusting at both ends of Encoder and Decoder
(c) Identify the defect of communication
(d) Make necessary modification in communication system

34. Communications bandwidth that has the highest capacity and is used by microwave, cable and fibre optics lines is known as

(a) Carrier wave (b) Hyper-link
(c) Broadband (d) Bus width

35. In a certain code, CLOCK is written as KCOLC. How would STEPS be written in that code?

(a) SPETS (b) SPEST
(c) SPSET (d) SEPTS

36. Which one of the following is not an argument?

(a) Ram is not at home, so he must have gone to town
(b) Ram insulted me so I punched him in the nose
(c) If today is Tuesday, tomorrow will be Wednesday
(d) Since today is Tuesday, tomorrow will be Wednesday

Direction: (37-41) Study the following pie chart and answer the questions based on it. Following pie chart represents the investment done by Timas Finance Ltd. in the various sectors. (All investments are in ₹ crores)

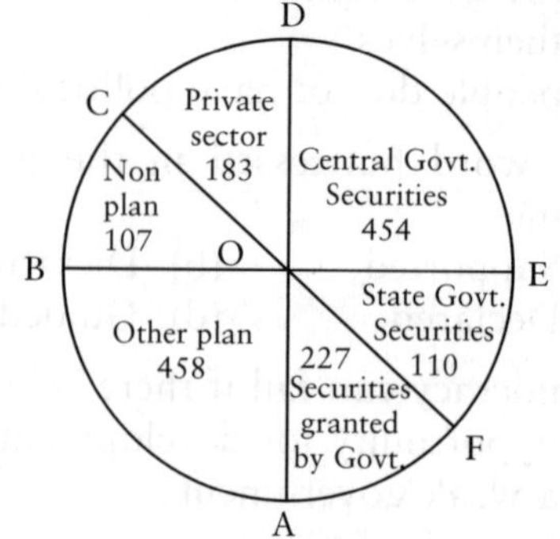

37. The percentage or gross investment in state government securities is nearly
(a) 7.1% (b) 9.2%
(c) 8.6% (d) 7.8%

38. The investment in plan and non-plan sector together is more or less than the investment in government securities (Central and State) by
(a) less, 106 crores (b) more, 4 crores
(c) more, 1 crores (d) more, 111 crores

39. The magnitude of ∠AOC is nearly
(a) 132° (b) 123°
(c) 126° (d) 115°

40. The ratio of area of the circle above ∠COF to the area of the circle below it is about
(a) 1 (b) 0.92
(c) 0.94 (d) 0.96

41. The investment in private sector is nearly what percent higher than the investment in State Government Security?
(a) 44% (b) 66%
(c) 54% (d) 46%

42. How many numbers between 100 and 300 begin or end with 2?
(a) 120 (b) 110
(c) 100 (d) 180

43. Which of the following operating system is used on mobile phones?
(a) Windows XP
(b) Windows Vista
(c) Android
(d) All of the above

44. Structure of logical argument is based on
(a) Linguistic expression
(b) Material truth
(c) Formal validity
(d) Aptness of examples

45. HTML is used to create
(a) machine language program
(b) high level program
(c) web page
(d) web server

46. Which of the following pollutants affects the respiratory tract in humans?
(a) Aerosols
(b) Sulphur dioxide
(c) Nitric oxide
(d) Carbon monoxide

47. Which of the following sources of energy has the maximum potential in India?
(a) Wind energy
(b) Solar energy
(c) Ocean thermal energy
(d) Tidal energy

48. In a deductive argument conclusion is
(a) Additional to the premises
(b) Entailed by the premises
(c) Summing up of the premises
(d) Not necessarily based on premises

49. What is the range of the numbers which can be stored in an eight bit register?
(a) – 127 to + 128 (b) – 127 to + 127
(c) – 128 to + 128 (d) – 128 to + 127

50. Universal Product Code (UPC), a pattern of bars printed on merchandise can be read by
(a) Product Code Reader
(b) Bar Code Reader
(c) Code Reader
(d) Card Reader

PAPER–II

1. What is Threonine?
(a) A mineral (b) Amino Acid
(c) Vitamin C (d) None of these

2. The only way to stop the spread of HIV infection is through
(a) regular treatment of infected persons
(b) isolation of infected persons
(c) prevention
(d) voiding direct contact with infected person

3. What causes vertigo?
   (a) Insufficient rest
   (b) An inner-ear problem
   (c) Poor diet
   (d) Excessive weight
4. One of the dimensions of colour is
   (a) Proportion
   (b) Shade
   (c) Combination of colour
   (d) Hue
5. Following is not a direct system of yarn numbering.
   (a) Cotton count (b) Denier
   (c) Metric count (d) Tex
6. An example of cross-sectional study is
   (a) Comparing individuals of various ages at the same time
   (b) Continued observations of the same individuals
   (c) Careful description by the researcher
   (d) One that requires no manipulation
7. A researcher wishing to graphically represent the Infant Mortality Rate in different States of India would do it by
   (a) Histogram (b) Bar Diagramme
   (c) Pie Chart (d) Frequency Curve
8. Which of these foods contains no protein?
   (a) Butter (b) Rice
   (c) Peanut butter (d) Kale
9. What are the four components of physical fitness?
   (a) Mental acuity, muscular strength, physical dexterity and energy efficiency
   (b) Aerobic endurance, cardiovascular strength, muscle density, mental outlook
   (c) Cardio respiratory endurance, muscular strength, muscular endurance and flexibility
   (d) Low body fat, agility, muscular appearance and cardio capacity
10. In a shoulder yoke grain line is marked
   (a) Parallel to Centre front
   (b) Parallel to Centre back
   (c) Perpendicular to centre front
   (d) Perpendicular to centre back
11. Which of the following is an essential fatty acid?
   (a) Palmitic acid (b) Stearic acid
   (c) Linoleric acid (d) Oleic acid
12. What is derived demand?
   (a) The demand for health
   (b) The demand for health care
   (c) The demand expressed by a health professional
   (d) The demand motivated by a health professional
13. The importance of drinking water immediately after a reflexology treatment is to
   (a) calm the client
   (b) flush out the toxins
   (c) stop micturition
   (d) induce perspiration
14. In hepatic coma the diet given is
   (a) High protein
   (b) Low protein
   (c) High carbohydrate
   (d) High protein, high calorie
15. The year of establishment of 'Asiatic Society of Calcutta' is
   (a) 1684 (b) 1912
   (c) 1884 (d) 1784
16. "Historical research is the application of the scientific method of inquiry to historical problems" said by
   (a) A.J. Wood (b) J.B. Best
   (c) Mouley (d) W.H. George
17. The book *Classification of Sciences* was written by
   (a) Charles Darwin (b) Bacon
   (c) Herbert Spencer (d) Ranganathan

18. Who defined that "Design is the process of making decision before the situation arises in which the decision is to be carried out."?
(a) Hegel (b) A.L. Edward
(c) Ackaff (d) S.R. Ranganathan

19. What is a photic sneezer?
(a) Someone who sneezes at will
(b) Someone who sneezes when being photographed
(c) Someone who sneezes when exposed to bright light
(d) Someone who sneezes when pinched

20. Colon cancer occurs more commonly in
(a) Men
(b) Women
(c) Both men and women
(d) None of these

21. In countries where the spread of HIV/AIDS is slowing or declining, it is primarily because
(a) Young men and women are being given the knowledge to adopt safe behaviour
(b) Young men and women are being given the tools and services to adopt safe behaviour
(c) Young men and women are provided with protective environment to develop the skills necessary to avoid infection
(d) All of these

22. The most appropriate fluid to give to a conscious patient suffering from hypothermia is
(a) Cool freshwater
(b) Sweet carbonated drinks
(c) A small amount of alcohol
(d) Warm, sweet drinks

23. Women over 50 should consume
(a) 1,500 milligrams of calcium/day
(b) Six glasses of non-fat milk/day
(c) Three Tums/Oscal tablets/day
(d) Any of the above

24. Where in the body is the labyrinth?
(a) Ear (b) Throat
(c) Eye (d) Leg

25. Give the correct sequence in writing a Research Proposal:
(i) Review of literature
(ii) Introduction
(iii) Bibliography
(iv) Objectives
(v) Methodology
(vi) Analysis of data

Codes:
(a) (i), (iv), (iii), (ii), (v), (vi)
(b) (ii), (i), (iv), (iii), (vi), (v)
(c) (iv), (i), (ii), (iii), (v), (vi)
(d) (iv), (ii), (i), (v), (vi), (iii)

26. **Assertion (A):** Retention of learning is more when variety of learning experiences are provided by the teacher.
Reason (R): Retention is facilitated when two or more senses are used at a time of learning.

Codes:
(a) Both (A) and (R) are true
(b) (A) is true but (R) is false
(c) (A) is false but (R) is true
(d) Both (A) and (R) are false

27. **Assertion (A):** Solar energy is termed as non-renewable energy.
Reason (R): It is an energy that can be conserved by using black coloured apparatus.

Codes:
(a) (A) is true but (R) is false
(b) (A) is false but (R) is true
(c) Both (A) and (R) are true
(d) Both (A) and (R) are false

28. Give the correct threading sequence pattern of a sewing machine:
(i) Needle
(ii) Spool
(iii) Thread take up lever
(iv) Tension discs

Codes:
(a) (iv), (i), (ii), (iii) (b) (iv), (iii), (ii), (i)
(c) (iii), (ii), (i), (iv) (d) (ii), (iv), (iii), (i)

29. Give the correct sequence of attaching a facing on the neckline:
(i) Neatening the seam allowance
(ii) Stitching the facing on neckline
(iii) Slitting the seam allowance
(iv) Edge stitching the facing
Codes:
(a) (i), (iv), (iii), (ii) (b) (ii), (i), (iii), (iv)
(c) (iii), (i), (ii), (iv) (d) (ii), (iii), (i), (iv)

30. **Assertion (A):** Bulimia nervosa is defined by little eating or reduced intake of food over a long period of time.
Reason (R): Little eating is used to describe the consumption of food that is much smaller than most people would eat during a similar period of time.
Codes:
(a) (A) is true but (R) is false
(b) (A) is false but (R) is true
(c) Both (A) and (R) are true
(d) Both (A) and (R) are false

31. **Assertion (A):** Hyperlipidaemia is generally related to an increase in the lipids of blood.
Reason (R): The use of safflower (Kardi) oil, corn-oil, or sesame oil are not preferred for hyperlipidaemic patient.
Codes:
(a) (A) is true but (R) is false
(b) (A) is false but (R) is true
(c) Both (A) and (R) are true
(d) Both (A) and (R) are false

32. While washing fabrics of protein fibers bleeding can be prevented by:
(i) Vinegar (ii) Common salt
(iii) Washing soda (iv) Acetic acid
Codes:
(a) (i) and (iv) are correct
(b) (ii) and (iii) are correct
(c) (iii) and (iv) are correct
(d) (i) and (ii) are correct

33. Give the correct sequence of foods in decreasing order of iron content:
(i) Liver (ii) Apple
(iii) Dates (iv) Wheat flour
(v) Lotus stem
Codes:
(a) (i), (ii), (iii), (iv), (v)
(b) (iv), (i), (v), (ii), (iii)
(c) (ii), (i), (iii), (iv), (v)
(d) (ii), (iii), (i), (iv), (v)

34. Arrange in sequence the phases of fat absorption:
(i) Emulsification
(ii) Esterification
(iii) Mucosal uptake
(iv) Chylomicron formation
Codes:
(a) (i), (ii), (iii), (iv) (b) (ii), (iii), (iv), (i)
(c) (i), (iii), (ii), (iv) (d) (ii), (iii), (i), (iv)

35. **Assertion (A):** Egg yolk is used for making mayonnaise.
Reason (R): Egg yolk is added to give bright yellow colour to mayonnaise.
Codes:
(a) (A) is true but (R) is false
(b) (A) is false but (R) is true
(c) Both (A) and (R) are true
(d) Both (A) and (R) are false

36. **Assertion (A):** Three persons sitting at different places can have a common talk through audio/video conferencing.
Reason (R): Internet and electronic media facilitate the contact amongst different persons at a time.
Codes:
(a) (A) is true but (R) is false
(b) (A) is false but (R) is true
(c) Both (A) and (R) are true
(d) Both (A) and (R) are false

37. **Assertion (A):** A management is an end in itself.
Reason (R): Home management is a means to achieve family goals.
Codes:
(a) (A) is correct but (R) is false
(b) (A) is false but (R) is correct
(c) Both (A) and (R) are correct
(d) Both (A) and (R) are false

38. Write the sequence of programmes of rural development by the years of commencement
(i) National Rural Employment Programme
(ii) Food for Work Programme
(iii) Development of Women and Children in Rural Areas
(iv) Jawahar Gram Samridhi Yojana
Codes:
(a) (i), (ii), (iii), (iv) (b) (i), (iii), (ii), (iv)
(c) (ii), (i), (iii), (iv) (d) (ii), (iii), (i), (iv)

39. **Assertion (A):** Proper work posture reduces energy requirement.
Reason (R): Proper posture means keeping parts in alignment, therefore reduces energy cost.
Codes:
(a) (A) is true but (R) is false
(b) (A) is false but (R) is true
(c) Both (A) and (R) are true
(d) Both (A) and (R) are false

40. **Assertion (A):** Self-concept is an image of a person. It is the way one perceives oneself, one's abilities and limitations.
Reason (R): Self-concept is the understanding of the self, in comparison to the past self, without social comparison.
Codes:
(a) (A) is true but (R) is false
(b) (A) is false but (R) is true
(c) Both (A) and (R) are true
(d) Both (A) and (R) are false

41. Match List I with List II:
List I
A. Socialisation socially
B. Heteronomous taking Morality personality
C. Animism
D. Identification non-living
List II
(i) Rules are socially agreed principles
(ii) Unconsciously on the style and of another person
(iii) Learning social rules and norms
(iv) Belief that objects are living

Codes:	**A**	**B**	**C**	**D**
(a)	(iii)	(i)	(ii)	(iv)
(b)	(ii)	(i)	(iv)	(iii)
(c)	(iv)	(i)	(iii)	(ii)
(d)	(iii)	(iv)	(ii)	(i)

42. Match the following list of standardization marks from List I with products in List II:

List I	**List II**
A. Agmark	(i) Squash
B. FPO	(ii) Shawl
B. ISI	(iii) Honey
D. Wool mark	(iv) Biscuits

Codes:	**A**	**B**	**C**	**D**
(a)	(i)	(iv)	(iii)	(ii)
(b)	(ii)	(i)	(iv)	(iii)
(c)	(iv)	(i)	(iii)	(ii)
(d)	(iii)	(i)	(iv)	(ii)

43. Match the List I with List II:
List I
A. Folder B. Journals
C. Leaflet D. Bulletin
List II
(i) Single sheet of small size paper
(ii) Single printed sheet of big size paper
(iii) Containing research information
(iv) Printed bound booklet

Codes:	**A**	**B**	**C**	**D**
(a)	(ii)	(iii)	(i)	(iv)
(b)	(ii)	(i)	(iv)	(iii)

(c)	(iv)	(i)	(iii)	(ii)
(d)	(iii)	(i)	(ii)	(iv)

44. Match the List I with List II:

List I

A. *Textbook of Mass Communication and Media*
B. *Extension Education and Communication*
C. *Participatory Rural Approval*
D. *Education and Communication for Development*

List II

(i) Neela Mukherjee
(ii) O.P. Dharma and O.P. Bhatnagar
(iii) Uma Joshi
(iv) V.K. Dubey and Indira Bishnoi

Codes:	**A**	**B**	**C**	**D**
(a)	(iv)	(iii)	(i)	(ii)
(b)	(iii)	(iv)	(i)	(ii)
(c)	(iv)	(i)	(iii)	(ii)
(d)	(iii)	(i)	(ii)	(iv)

45. Match the following Equipment in List I with food items which use them in List II:

List I	**List II**
A. Bainmaric	(i) Mutton curry
B. Salamander	(ii) Chapati
C. Steam cooker	(iii) Pizza
D. Food processor	(iv) Rice
E. Griddles	(v) Vegetable
	(vi) Ice cream

Codes:	**A**	**B**	**C**	**D**	**E**
(a)	(i)	(iii)	(iv)	(v)	(ii)
(b)	(ii)	(i)	(iv)	(iii)	(v)
(c)	(iv)	(i)	(iii)	(v)	(ii)
(d)	(iii)	(i)	(ii)	(iv)	(v)

46. This consists of two lists of statements regarding educational aids. Match the List I with List II:

List I

A. Flannel Board B. Illustration
C. Lettering D. Colours

List II

(i) Big, bold and simple
(ii) Plywood, hardwood or cardboard
(iii) Large, bold and printed
(iv) Few and pleasing

Codes:	**A**	**B**	**C**	**D**
(a)	(iii)	(iv)	(i)	(ii)
(b)	(ii)	(i)	(iv)	(iii)
(c)	(iv)	(i)	(iii)	(ii)
(d)	(i)	(ii)	(iv)	(iii)

Read the following passage and answer the Question Nos. 47 to 50:

The decisive shift in British Policy really came about under mass pressure in the autumn and winter of 1945 to 46—the months which Penderel Moon while editing Wavell's Journal has perceptively described as 'The Edge of a Volcano'. Very foolishly, the British initially decided to hold public trials of several hundreds of the 20,000 I.N.A. prisoners (as well as dismissing from service and detaining without trial no less than 7,000). They compounded the folly by holding the first trial in the Red Fort, Delhi in November 1945, and putting on the dock together a Hindu, a Muslim and a Sikh (P.K. Sehgal, Shah Nawaz, Gurbaksh Singh Dhillon). Bhulabhai Desai, Tejbahadur Sapru and Nehru appeared for the defence (the latter putting on his barrister's gown after 25 years), and the Muslim League also joined the countrywide protest. On 20 November, an Intelligence Bureau note admitted that "there has seldom been a matter which has attracted so much Indian public interest and, it is safe to say, sympathy...this particular brand of sympathy cuts across communal barriers". A journalist (B. Shiva Rao) visiting the Red Fort prisoners on the same day reported that 'There is not the slightest feeling among them of Hindu and Muslim.... A majority of the men now awaiting trial in the Red Fort is Muslim. Some of these men are bitter that Mr. Jinnah is keeping alive a controversy about Pakistan. The British became extremely nervous about the I.N.A. spirit spreading to the Indian Army, and in January the Punjab Governor reported that a Lahore reception for released I.N.A. prisoners had been attended by Indian soldiers in uniform.

47. Which heading is more appropriate to assign to the above passage?
    (a) Wavell's Journal
    (b) Role of Muslim League
    (c) I.N.A. Trials
    (d) Red Fort Prisoners
48. The trial of P.K. Sehgal, Shah Nawaz and Gurbaksh Singh Dhillon symbolises
    (a) communal harmony
    (b) threat to all religious persons
    (c) threat to persons fighting for the freedom
    (d) British reaction against the natives
49. I.N.A. stands for
    (a) Indian National Assembly
    (b) Indian National Association
    (c) Inter-national Association
    (d) Indian National Army
50. The majority of people waiting for trial outside the Red Fort and criticising Jinnah were the
    (a) Hindus
    (b) Muslims
    (c) Sikhs
    (d) Hindus and Muslims both

PAPER–III

1. Which of the following was discovered in 1935?
   (a) Vit. K (b) Vit. B_{12}
   (c) Vit. D (d) Vit. E
2. It combines with iron to produce hemoglobin in the body.
   (a) Sulphur (b) Sodium
   (c) Copper (d) Zinc
3. Which of the following are characteristic of goals?
   (i) Goals keep changing
   (ii) Society effect goals
   (iii) All goals are not of equal importance
   (iv) Goal formation is a continous process
   Codes:
   (a) (i), (ii) (b) (i), (iv)
   (c) (i), (ii), (iii), (iv) (d) (i), (ii), (iii)
4. Components of motor skills.
   (a) Impulsion (b) Precision
   (c) Flexibility (d) All of these
5. Which of the following cereal is rich in Vit. A?
   (a) Bajra (b) Rice
   (c) Yellow maize (d) Wheat
6. Who defines rapport during interview "personal relationship of mutual trust and respect based on a feeling of confidence and security in other person"?
   (a) Symonds (b) Ruth Strang
   (c) Hilgard (d) Mussen
7. The development of a characteristic pleasant flavour in ripened fruit involves
   (a) Production of volatile substance and essential oil
   (b) Increase in sugar
   (c) Decrease in acidity
   (d) All of the above
8. Rabri comprises
   (a) Clotted cream (b) Whole milk
   (c) Skimmed milk (d) None of these
9. Egg has all the nutrients for body growth except—
   (i) Calcium (ii) Vit. C
   (iii) Vit. E (iv) Niacin
   Codes:
   (a) (i), (ii) (b) (i), (iv)
   (c) (i), (ii), (iii), (iv) (d) (i), (ii), (iii)

10. It is the receiver who receives the message and tries to
(a) Understand (b) Act
(c) Interpret (d) Perceive

11. The conditions which are controlled during storage of fruits is/are
(a) Atmospheric help
(b) Humidity
(c) Temperature
(d) All of the above

12. Flavonoid pigments are
(a) of two types
(b) Found in cell sap
(c) Water-soluble
(d) All of the above

13. Whose viewpoint is this "Checking evaluating and defining values periodically is crucial for effective managment"?
(a) Cross and Grandall
(b) Dr. K. Kautilya
(c) Goodyear and Klohr
(d) P. Eberman

14. Carotenoids like chlorophyll are—in water.
(a) Natural (b) Soluble
(c) Insoluble (d) None of these

15. When phonemes are combined and put together to form words are called Morphemes where phonemes are
(a) babbling
(b) lallation
(c) sounds which make language
(d) cooing

16. Communication is a primary tool for effective.
(a) Impact
(b) Reading
(c) Speaking
(d) Behaviour change

17. Children grow and function best in the clearly structured environment one which is orderly and consistent. Key element of structure involve
(a) Established method of handling
(b) Adequately defined roles
(c) Clearly defined standards and limits
(d) All of these

18. It can be said that the design tells us
(a) How to make observation
(b) How to analyse the quantitative representation of the observation
(c) What observation to make
(d) All of these

19. **Assertion (A):** High capital gearing leads to greater speculation.
Reason (R): Proportion of equity share capital in relation to the total capital comprising the other securities is small leading to capitalisation being highly geared.
Codes:
(a) Both (A) and (R) are true and (R) is the correct explanation of (A)
(b) Both (A) and (R) are true but (R) is not a correct explanation of (A)
(c) (A) is true but (R) is false
(d) (A) is false but (R) is true

20. Example of aggregate fruits that develop from flowers that have a number of pistils.
(a) Raspberries (b) Strawberry
(c) Blackberry (d) All of the above

21. "Colour planning should where feasible, be in terms of a whole unit-house apartment, factory and so on." Who said it?
(a) Abul Kalam (b) M.J. Akbar
(c) Rutt (d) M.J. Alexander

22. A child who goes to a nursery school before joining the primary school adjusts himself much better and fares well in primary classes because
(a) he had group experiences
(b) he has gained better emotional control

(c) he has developed proper habits and attitudes
(d) All of the above

23. State which is/are true?
(a) Communication is something one does with another person, not something one does to another person.
(b) The technology-oriented media has come to influence every form of communication.
(c) The sender in communication is an active member in the relationship and the receiver as passive.
(d) Human receivers are bombarded with stimuli from many sources simultaneously. A human selects the one source he will be tuned to at any moment of time.

24. The pattern and organization of the curriculum will primarily, determine—
(i) Efficacy of instruction
(ii) Objectives
(iii) Social cultural relevance
(iv) Needs of community
Codes:
(a) (i), (ii) (b) (i), (iv)
(c) (i), (ii), (iii), (iv) (d) (i), (ii), (iii)

25. Match the following:
List I
A. Design will give an idea
B. Once the data through different techniques collected
C. Each research will have a design
D. Different designs will help
E. Each design is bound i.e., have limitations
List II
(i) Of its choice favouring his own methodological theoretical and personal orientation
(ii) Testing different hypothesis
(iii) Of time, money, personal budget availability of data and native of respondents
(iv) To what techniques will be used
(v) How will that be analysed

Codes:	A	B	C	D	E
(a)	i	iii	iv	v	ii
(b)	v	iv	iii	ii	i
(c)	iv	v	i	ii	iii
(d)	v	iv	iii	i	ii

26. A good teacher should know or anticipate the occurrence of a plateau.
(a) Yes
(b) No
(c) It is professional
(d) Challenge and remedy it

27. Of the following organisations, the easiest to wind up is the
(a) Public Limited Company
(b) Multinational Corporation
(c) Private Limited Company
(d) Partnership Firm

28. Insight may be defined as
(a) a form of inspiration—a flash of light
(b) a form of intuition
(c) a sudden reorganisation of experience
(d) None of these

29. **Assertion (A):** Home Management is not an all encompassing concept compared to decision-making or problem-solving.
Reason (R): Home Management does not consider the totality of managerial functioning.
Codes:
(a) (A) is true but (R) is false
(b) (A) is false but (R) is true
(c) Both (A) and (R) are true
(d) Both (A) and (R) are false

30. Which of the following are visual aids?
(i) Black Board
(ii) Posters
(iii) Public address system
(iv) Flash cards
Codes:
(a) (i) and (iii) are correct
(b) (i), (ii) and (iv) are correct

(c) (i), (ii) and (iii) are correct
(d) (ii), (iii) and (iv) are correct

31. **Assertion (A):** With increase in family income the proportionate expenditure on food will increase.
Reason (R): As family income increases the family will be spending more money on food.
Codes:
(a) (A) is true but (R) is false
(b) (A) is false but (R) is true
(c) Both (A) and (R) are true
(d) Both (A) and (R) are false

32. **Assertion (A):** The ego is rational, controlling component of the personality.
Reason (R): Ego operates on the basis of the pleasure principle and control personality.
Codes:
(a) Both (A) and (R) are true
(b) (A) is true but (R) is false
(c) (A) is false but (R) is true
(d) Both (A) and (R) are false

33. Rh incompatibility occurs, when blood of:
(a) Mother is Rh +ve and fetus is Rh –ve
(b) Mother is Rh –ve and fetus is Rh +ve
(c) Mother is Rh –ve and fetus is Rh –ve
(d) Mother is Rh +ve and fetus is Rh +ve

34. **Assertion (A):** Hypertension is a risk factor for CHD.
Reason (R): High blood pressure leads to raised cholesterol levels.
Codes:
(a) (A) is true but (R) is false
(b) (A) is false but (R) is true
(c) Both (A) and (R) are true
(d) Both (A) and (R) are false

35. Sequence the scales of measurement from the lowest to the highest:
(i) Interval scale (ii) Ordinal scale
(iii) Nominal scale (iv) Ratio scale
Codes:
(a) (iv), (i), (ii), (iii) (b) (iv), (iii), (ii), (i)
(c) (iii), (ii), (i), (iv) (d) (iii), (iv), (ii), (i)

36. The component of controlling in which actions and outputs are examined in compliance with standard is
(a) Adjusting (b) Changing
(c) Checking (d) Assessing

37. Contingency approach of Management holds
(a) that job should be segmented
(b) that organization should be seen as whole
(c) that activities to be adjusted to suit situations
(d) that productivity is increased by opportunity

38. **Assertion (A):** A prospects is a formal summary of proposed work.
Reason (R): It is an evaluation tool used by professional for assessment.
Codes:
(a) (A) is true but (R) is false
(b) (A) is false but (R) is true
(c) Both (A) and (R) are true
(d) Both (A) and (R) are false

39. Evaluation of any development programme is done against
(a) Desires (b) Cost
(c) Resources (d) Objectives

40. Which one of the following pairs is not correctly matched?
(a) An indepth study of a person is referred to as analytical study.
(b) In questionnaire in a logical sequence from easy to move difficult questions.
(c) Rorschach test consists of ten cards having prints of ink blots.
(d) Quizzes and tests are used to assess the memorising and analytical ability of respondents.

41. A portion of output reentered as input to affect succeeding output is
(a) Feedback (b) Deferred resource
(c) Throughput (d) Black box

42. The variance is:
(i) Directly proportional to the average squared difference between all pairs of observations
(ii) Smallest when calculated from the mean
(iii) Denoted by symbol
(iv) Described as the dispersion of the distribution
Codes:
(a) (i) and (iii) are correct
(b) (ii) and (iii) are correct
(c) (i), (ii and (iii) are correct
(d) (i), (ii and (iv) are correct

43. A researcher wishing to graphically represent the Infant Mortality Rate in different States of India would do it by
(a) Histogram (b) Bar Diagramme
(c) Pie Chart (d) Frequency Curve

44. Which of the following dart is drawn till the pivot point?
(a) French dart (b) Fish dart
(c) Designers dart (d) Dressmakers dart

45. **Assertion (A):** To identify the polyester fibre it is important to negate the presence of nylon and acrylic by dissolving in hot phenol and concentrated nitric acid.
Reason (R): Polyester is insoluble in both hot phenol and concentrated nitric acid.
Codes:
(a) (A) is true but (R) is false
(b) (A) is false but (R) is true
(c) Both (A) and (R) are true
(d) Both (A) and (R) are false

46. Which among the following are advertised under 'classified category'?
I. Job vacancy II. Matrimonial
III. Coffee powder IV. Bicycles
Codes:
(a) I and II are correct
(b) II and IV are correct
(c) III and IV are correct
(d) I and III are correct

47. A drop in testosterone as men age can cause
(a) decreased energy and strength
(b) sexual dysfunction
(c) depression
(d) all of the above

48. Arrange the right sequence in decreasing order of protein content in food:
(i) Bread (ii) Cheese
(iii) Butter (iv) Boiled egg
Codes:
(a) (iv), (i), (ii), (iii)
(b) (iv), (iii), (ii), (i)
(c) (iii), (ii), (i), (iv)
(d) (iv), (ii), (i), (iii)

49. The enzyme responsible for digestibility of fats in human body is
(a) Lipase (b) Amylase
(c) Renin (d) Protease

50. Identify statement giving the correct sequence of foods in decreasing order of calcium content.
(a) Rice, Milk, Spinach, Ragi
(b) Spinach, Ragi, Milk, Rice
(c) Milk, Ragi, Spinach, Rice
(d) Milk, Spinach, Rice, Ragi

ANSWER SHEET

PAPER—I

1. (b)	2. (c)	3. (d)	4. (d)	5. (a)
6. (c)	7. (d)	8. (c)	9. (c)	10. (b)
11. (b)	12. (b)	13. (a)	14. (b)	15. (b)
16. (c)	17. (d)	18. (b)	19. (a)	20. (c)
21. (a)	22. (c)	23. (c)	24. (b)	25. (b)
26. (b)	27. (d)	28. (d)	29. (b)	30. (c)

31. (c) 32. (b) 33. (b) 34. (c) 35. (a)
36. (b) 37. (a) 38. (c) 39. (a) 40. (c)
41. (b) 42. (b) 43. (c) 44. (b) 45. (c)
46. (c) 47. (b) 48. (b) 49. (d) 50. (b)

PAPER—II

1. (b) 2. (c) 3. (b) 4. (d) 5. (a)
6. (a) 7. (a) 8. (d) 9. (d) 10. (d)
11. (c) 12. (d) 13. (b) 14. (b) 15. (c)
16. (d) 17. (c) 18. (c) 19. (c) 20. (c)
21. (d) 22. (d) 23. (d) 24. (a) 25. (d)
26. (a) 27. (a) 28. (d) 29. (b) 30. (b)
31. (a) 32. (d) 33. (c) 34. (c) 35. (a)
36. (b) 37. (c) 38. (c) 39. (c) 40. (a)
41. (a) 42. (d) 43. (a) 44. (b) 45. (a)
46. (d) 47. (c) 48. (a) 49. (d) 50. (b)

PAPER—III

1. (a) 2. (c) 3. (c) 4. (d) 5. (c)
6. (a) 7. (d) 8. (a) 9. (b) 10. (c)
11. (b) 12. (c) 13. (b) 14. (c) 15. (c)
16. (d) 17. (d) 18. (d) 19. (d) 20. (d)
21. (d) 22. (d) 23. (c) 24. (c) 25. (c)
26. (a) 27. (d) 28. (c) 29. (d) 30. (b)
31. (c) 32. (b) 33. (b) 34. (b) 35. (c)
36. (a) 37. (d) 38. (a) 39. (d) 40. (a)
41. (a) 42. (d) 43. (a) 44. (b) 45. (c)
46. (a) 47. (d) 48. (d) 49. (a) 50. (c)